A DIGEST OF THE KRASNYI ARKHIV—RED ARCHIVES

VOLUMES 31–106

a DIGEST of the KRASNYI ARKHIV—RED ARCHIVES
Volumes 31-106

Compiled and annotated by
LEONA W. EISELE
under the direction of
Andrei A. Lobanov-Rostovsky

ANN ARBOR · THE UNIVERSITY OF MICHIGAN PRESS
1955

COPYRIGHT 1955 BY THE UNIVERSITY OF MICHIGAN

Library of Congress Catalog Card Number: 48–3251

Paperback ISBN: 978-0-472-75125-9

PREFACE

THE *Krasnyi Arkhiv,* or *Red Archives,* is one of the most important publications of the Central Archive Department of the Union of Soviet Socialist Republics. Between 1922 and 1941 the Department issued 106 volumes of this historical journal, containing documents of the greatest significance for students of Russian civilization. This material—some of it available to the public for the first time—was published as it was found in the archives of the tsarist and Soviet governments and in various private depositories. It illuminates the social, scientific, political, economic, and cultural development of Russia from the seventeenth century to the present time.

Each group of documents is ordinarily preceded by an introduction written by a Soviet historian, who presents the background and indicates the significance of the data. There are, as well, short documents and occasional articles based on archival notes. These appear in each volume under the heading "From an Archivist's Notebook."

Much of the journal deals with the rise of the revolutionary movement in Russia and with the establishment of the Soviet regime. The international relations of tsarist Russia receive extensive treatment, as does the history of minority nationality groups living in the USSR. There is, in addition, information on the history of Russian economy, philosophy, science, and literature.

The documents take the form, for the most part, of personal diaries and correspondence, reports of government ministries and officials, exchanges of diplomatic communiqués, and instructions to civil and military authorities.

The *Digest of the Krasnyi Arkhiv* is intended to serve as a guide to this collection of source materials. The first part of the *Digest,* covering Volumes 1-30 of the *Krasnyi Arkhiv,* was published by the Cleveland Public Library—with Leonid S. Rubinchek as the compiler—in 1947. Work on the remaining volumes was in progress until the winter of 1950, when the project was discontinued. Subsequently, with the gracious coöperation of the Cleveland Library, arrangements were made for its resumption under the sponsorship of the University of Michigan. The present study, which takes the *Krasnyi Arkhiv* through Volume 106, was assisted by a grant from the Horace H. Rackham School of Graduate Studies of the University.

The methods employed in compiling this section of the *Digest* differ somewhat from those of Part I, and the format has been revised in various ways to make the material more accessible. Since it was thought desirable to place this guide to research materials in the hands of scholars as soon as possible, no attempt was made to provide exhaustive references to additional sources of information. For the same reason, although the earlier volume of the *Digest* contains translated excerpts from the original, this volume does not. The value of a complete translation of the *Krasnyi Arkhiv* is as obvious as is the inadequacy of fragmentary quotations out of context. But it is hoped that the *Digest* will interest students to the extent that they will translate for publication those documents that are of particular significance.

The Library of Congress system of transliteration has been adopted, with a few modifications. In endings of proper nouns the Library of Congress use of *ii* for the Russian ий has been changed to *y*. In adjective endings, the Library of Congress system is unaltered. Where a word begins with the Russian я it has been transliterated *ya*, rather than *ia*. Similarly, where a word begins with ю it has been transliterated *yu*, rather than *iu*.

Russian given names have been Anglicized throughout, except where the spelling of a Russian name has been popularly accepted in English usage. The most literal form of transliteration has been used for patronymics.

Dates previous to February 1, 1918, are given in the old Russian reckoning according to the Julian calendar, which was, depending on the century, from ten to thirteen days behind the Western, Gregorian, calendar. Official government documents and papers written abroad are very often double-dated, with the Julian and Gregorian dates—e.g., January 2/15, 1917. If no double-dating appears, the date is according to the Julian reckoning. After February 1, 1918, all dates are according to the Gregorian calendar.

Persons and places have been identified wherever possible. Information of this nature not indicated in the *Krasnyi Arkhiv* but obtained from other sources has been put in brackets. When doubt exists as to the complete accuracy of such information, it has been put in brackets with a question mark.

Part I of the *Digest* has neither a table of contents nor an index. Since it is hoped that a revised edition of Part I will be undertaken, in order to make it available once more and to supply supplementary aids, it did not seem practical—nor was it possible for other reasons—to include references to Part I in the Index to the present volume. A list of the titles of the articles in Volumes 1–30 is, however, given in the Appendix.

Numerous cross references to articles in the *Krasnyi Arkhiv* occur in the pages that follow. Where no other journal is cited, *"Krasnyi Arkhiv"* is to be understood throughout. For complete coverage in regard to particular persons and events mentioned in the *Digest* for Volumes 31–106, such citations should, of course, be supplemented by reference to the Index.

CONTENTS

	PAGE
PREFACE	v

Digest

(Listed below are the titles of the articles described in this volume; the page numbers refer to the present work. Volume and pages in the Russian original are indicated for each article under the description given in the *Digest*.)

Diary of the Ministry of Foreign Affairs 1915–1916	1
The Disintegration of Kolchak's Campaign (From the Diary of V. N. Pepeliaev)	2
S. Y. Witte's Struggle with the Agrarian Revolution	3
P. L. Antonov in the Petropavlovsk Fortress	3
The Constitutional Projects of the Early 1880's	4
The Moscow Address to Alexander II in 1870 (From the Correspondence of K. P. Pobedonostsev with I. S. Aksakov) . . .	5
New Manuscripts and Materials on Pushkin. By M. Tsiavlovsky .	5
A. S. Pushkin's Poem "The Monk"	6
Autographs of the Members of the Ufa Conference	6
Life in Ecclesiastical Circles before the Revolution (From the Letters of Archbishop Antony of Volhynia to Metropolitan Flavian of Kiev)	6
Materials Relating to the History of the Release of N. G. Chernyshevsky	7
The Escape of Sergius Degaev. By S. Valk	8
Materials Relating to the History of the Struggle with the Socialist Movement in Tsarist Russia. By N. Beliavsky	8
An Unpublished Letter of A. I. Herzen	8

Contents

	PAGE
Diary of the Ministry of Foreign Affairs 1915–1916 (Conclusion)	9
The February Revolution in the Baltic Fleet (From the Diary of I. I. Rengarten)	9
Materials Relating to the History of the Foreign Policy of Wrangel's Government (Economic Relations with France)	10
Mobilization of Reaction in 1906	11
A. S. Pushkin's Poem "The Monk"	12
I. S. Turgenev's Letters to P. V. Annenkov	12
P. A. Stolypin and the French Press in 1911	12
Russian Metal Industry and International Trusts. By V. Semennikov	13
Materials Relating to the History of the Struggle with the Revolution of 1905. By G. Vereshchagin	13
Parodies on the Tsarist Manifestoes of 1856 and 1857	14
The Czechoslovakian Question and Tsarist Diplomacy 1914–1917. By A. Popov	14
The April Days of 1917 in Petrograd	14
Kolchak and Finland	14
The Conference of Governors in 1916	15
The Diary of A. A. Polovtsov (1877–1878)	15
The *Socialist*, Organ of the Southwestern Group of the Will of the People Party	16
S. G. Nechaev's Proclamation to Students	16
The Ishutinites in Prison and Exile. By M. Klevensky	17
New Material concerning Pushkin's Duel and Death (From the Correspondence of A. Y. Bulgakov and Prince P. A. Viazemsky)	17
The Czechoslovakian Question and Tsarist Diplomacy 1914–1917 (Conclusion). By A. Popov	18
The Uprising in Central Asia in 1916	18
The Struggle with Strikes on the Eve of the World War	19
Materials Relating to the History of Intervention in Siberia	19
Materials Relating to the History of the Rise of the World War (Triple Entente and Germany after Agadir)	20

Contents xi

PAGE

The Struggle with the Revolutionary Movement in the Caucasus in the Stolypin Era (From the Correspondence of P. A. Stolypin with Count I. I. Vorontsov-Dashkov) 20

Alexander III concerning "Socialist Contamination" 21

Conditions in the Rear of "The Armed Forces of South Russia" . . 21

A Parody in Verse on the Accusatory Speech of Zhelikhovsky at the Trial of the 193 21

Prince P. V. Dolgorukov and M. K. Elpidin 22

Karakozov's Attempt on Alexander II (From the Diary of a Contemporary) 22

V. M. Friche 22

The Baltic Fleet on the Eve of October (From the Diary of I. I. Rengarten) 23

The Provisional Government of Autonomous Siberia 23

Materials Relating to the History of the Tsarist National Minority Policy 24

The Struggle with the Revolutionary Movement in the Caucasus in the Stolypin Era (From the Correspondence of P. A. Stolypin with Count I. I. Vorontsov-Dashkov) (Conclusion) 24

"The Alliance of October 17" in 1906 25

The Uprising in Bezdna 25

Nicholas Romanov concerning the Assassination of P. A. Stolypin . 26

The Tactics of the High Command in the February Revolution . . 26

L. N. Tolstoy under the Blows of the Censor. By N. Apostolov . . 26

From the Correspondence of V. A. Maklakov with the National Center in 1919 27

The Provisional Government of Autonomous Siberia (Conclusion) . 27

Materials Relating to the History of the Tsarist National Minority Policy (Conclusion) 28

"The Alliance of October 17" in 1906 (Conclusion) 28

Materials Relating to the History of the Trial of the Twenty-one (Letters and Testimony of P. F. Yakubovich) 29

The Bezdna Uprising of 1861 29

The Petersburg Clergy and the Ninth of January 29

Contents

	PAGE
New Materials concerning L. N. Tolstoy. By N. Belchikov	30
Materials Relating to the History of the Peasant Uprising against Liberation in 1861	30
The Echoes of the Decembrist Uprising	31
Tsarist Russia and Mongolia 1913–1914	31
Foreign Policy of the Counterrevolutionary Governments at the Beginning of 1919 (From the Documents of the Paris Legation)	31
Materials Relating to the History of the Trial of the Twenty-one (Letters and Testimony of P. F. Yakubovich) (Continued)	32
Count A. K. Benckendorff concerning Russia 1827–1830 (Yearly Reports of the Third Department and the Gendarmerie)	32
From the Archives of A. P. Chekhov (Unpublished Letters and Documents)	33
Order Number Two	33
Second Issue of the Workers' Leaflet *Zerno*	34
Materials Relating to the Biography of A. A. Krasovsky	34
A. S. Pushkin under the Surveillance of the Police	34
January 9 in St. Petersburg	34
Twenty-five Years Ago (From the Diary of Leo Tikhomirov)	35
Materials Relating to the History of the Trial of the Twenty-one (Conclusion) (Letters and Testimony of P. F. Yakubovich)	35
Count A. K. Benckendorff concerning Russia 1827–1830 (Conclusion)	36
Russia and the United States at the Time of the Civil War [in the United States]	36
The Naval Punitive Battalions in the Baltic Region	37
An Unpublished Letter of N. P. Ogarev. By B. Kozmin	37
A. S. Pushkin and Count M. S. Vorontsov. By P. Shchegolev	38
A New Account of the Execution of the Decembrists	38
Wrangeliana (From Materials of the Provisional Government's Paris "Embassy")	38
Twenty-five Years Ago (From the Diary of Leo Tikhomirov) (Continued)	39
Materials Relating to the History of the Struggle with the Agrarian Movement 1905–1906	39

Contents

	PAGE
"Princes of the Church" (From the Diary of A. N. Lvov)	40
Materials Relating to the Trial of Adrian Mikhailov, Veimar, and Others	40
"Bloody Sunday" in St. Petersburg (From the Police Department's Censorship of Letters concerning January 9, 1905)	41
Materials Relating to the History of the "Peaceful Penetration" of Europeans into Ethiopia. By B. Veber	41
Wrangeliana (Conclusion)	42
Materials Relating to the History of the Struggle with the Agrarian Movement 1905–1906 (Conclusion)	42
Twenty-five Years Ago (From the Diary of Leo Tikhomirov) (Continued)	43
"Princes of the Church" (From the Diary of A. N. Lvov) (Conclusion)	43
Reports of Adjutant General A. R. Drenteln to Alexander II (April–November, 1879)	43
March 1, 1881	44
S. G. Nechaev and the Tula Arms Workers	44
Materials Relating to the History of the Escape of Yaroslav Dombrovsky. By A. Chernov	45
Russia and the Algeciras Conference	45
The February Revolution in Petrograd (February 28—March 1, 1917)	46
Twenty-five Years Ago (From the Diary of Leo Tikhomirov) (Conclusion)	46
With the Staff of Admiral E. I. Alexeiev (From the Diary of E. A. Planson)	46
Protest of Russian Political Exiles in 1888	47
"Red Guards" in Riga in 1906	47
[Comments of] Nicholas Romanov concerning the Revolutionary Movement in the Army in 1905–1906	47
The Turkish Revolution 1908–1909	48
Dispersal of the Second State Duma	48
From the Diary of Grand Duke Constantine Romanov	49
Materials Relating to the History of the Nechaev Trial	49
The Execution of the Participants in the Kronstadt Rebellion of 1906	50

Contents

	PAGE
Materials Relating to the History of the Revolutionary Movement in the Army on the Eve of 1905	50
N. N. Romanov and the American Concession for a Siberian-Alaskan Railroad in 1905. By G. Vereshchagin	50
The Turkish Revolution 1908–1909 (Continuation)	51
The Kerch Quarries in 1919	51
The Beilis Trial as Appraised by the Police Department	52
From the Diary of Grand Duke Constantine Romanov	52
Russian Soldiers on the Western Front in World War I	52
New Documents concerning the Algeciras Conference and the Loan of 1906	53
Materials Relating to the History of the "Ideological" Struggle of the Autocracy with the Revolutionary Movement in the Army	53
A Letter of the Worker P. A. Alexeiev	53
The Paris Commune of 1871 (Okunev's Communiqués to [Prince A. M.] Gorchakov, May 1–25, 1871)	54
The Turkish Revolution 1908–1909 (Conclusion)	54
Materials Relating to the History of French Intervention in Odessa	55
An Article of M. Gorky Forbidden by the Censor	55
Notes of A. F. Rediger concerning 1905	56
From the Diary of Grand Duke Constantine Romanov (Conclusion)	56
F. M. Dostoevsky's Testimony on the Petrashevsky Affair	56
After March 1, 1881	57
Materials Relating to the History of the Trial of Lieutenant P. P. Shmidt	57
V. V. Vereshchagin's Letters to Emperor Nicholas Romanov in 1904	57
Materials Relating to the History of Liberal Public Opinion in the 1860's	58
The Diary of V. N. Lamsdorff	58
The Cadets in 1905–1906 (Materials of the Central Committee of the Popular Freedom or Cadet Party)	59
The Baltic Fleet in the July Days of 1917	59
The Diary of A. A. Polovtsov (1895–1900)	59

Contents

	PAGE
Count A. K. Benckendorff concerning Russia in 1831–1832	60
F. M. Dostoevsky's Testimony on the Petrashevsky Affair (Conclusion)	60
A. I. Nelidov's Note in 1882 concerning Occupation of the Straits	61
An Unknown Satirist of the 1860's. By N. Belchikov	61
Nicholas I and European Reaction 1848–1849	62
The Project for Seizure of the Bosporus in 1896	62
M. N. Muraviëv's Journey Abroad in 1897	63
Poland and South Russian Counterrevolution (Economic Relations of Poland with [General A. I.] Denikin and [Baron P. N.] Wrangel)	63
The Cadets in 1905–1906 (Conclusion)	63
N. M. Romanov's Notes	64
Autocracy and the Vatican on the Eve of the Imperialistic War	64
Spanish Revolution of 1873–1874	65
Materials Relating to the History of the Destruction of Kolchak's Armed Forces	65
N. M. Romanov's Notes (Conclusion)	65
Reports of Lieutenant General Seliverstov and Adjutant General Drenteln to Alexander II (August–December, 1878)	66
P. A. Stolypin and the Sveaborg Uprising. By S. L. Ivanov	66
Materials Relating to the History of Emigration in the 1860's. By B. Kozmin	66
Materials Relating to the Sino-Japanese War 1894–1895	67
Materials Relating to the History of the First Hague Conference, 1899	67
Intervention and Northern Counterrevolution	68
The Progressive Bloc 1915–1917	69
From the Correspondence of Tsar Nicholas and Marie Romanov (1907–1910)	69
From Officers' Letters from the Front in 1917	69
The Purge of the Commanding Staff of the Tsarist Army in 1906	70
Contents of the Previous Volumes of the Journal *Krasnyi Arkhiv*	70
On the Death of Michael Nikolaevich Pokrovsky (1868–1932). By the editors of *Krasnyi Arkhiv*	70

Contents

	PAGE
A Few Documents from the Tsarist Archives concerning M. N. Pokrovsky	71
First Steps of Russian Imperialism in the Far East (1888–1903)	71
The United States of America and Tsarist Russia in the 1890's	71
The Progressive Bloc 1915–1917 (Continuation)	72
A. P. Mohrenheim's Letter concerning French Politics in the Near East (1896)	72
Materials Relating to the History of the Intelligentsia of the 1860's	73
Tsarist Russia and Persia in the Epoch of the Russo-Japanese War	73
Materials Relating to the History of the October Days in Petrograd (From Materials of the Petrograd Military-Revolutionary Committee)	73
The Fleet after the October Victory	74
The Church and the Buriat-Mongol Russification in Tsarist Russia	74
Adrian Mikhailov and Count M. T. Loris-Melikov	74
From the Correspondence of S. M. and N. M. Romanov in 1917	75
Foreign Diplomats concerning the Revolution of 1905	75
Materials Relating to the History of the Labor Movement in Karaganda	75
The Peking Spiritual Mission and Russo-Chinese Trade 1830–1850. By G. L.	76
P. N. Miliukov's Diary	76
New Materials concerning the Hague Peace Conference of 1899	76
Materials Relating to the History of the Moscow Military-Revolutionary Committee (November 1/14—November 10/23, 1917)	77
The Tsarist Government and the Beilis Trial	77
Karl Marx and Tsarist Censorship	77
Anglo-Russian Rivalry in Persia 1890–1906	78
Anglo-German Rapprochement in 1898	78
The Progressive Bloc 1915–1917	78
The Last Hours of the Provisional Government in 1917	79
The Workers' Strike at Bromlei Factory in 1903	79
The Romanovs and Railroad Concessions in the 1870's	79
May 1 Postage Stamps of the Latvian Bolsheviks in 1917	79

Contents xvii

	PAGE
Rumanian Sigurantsa	80
Materials Relating to the History of "Workers' Groups" under the Central War Industrial Committee	80
First State Duma in Vyborg	80
Materials Relating to the History of the Polish Insurrection of 1863 (The Hitherto Unknown Manuscript of Oscar Aveide: "Short Sketch of Recent Events in Poland, 1861–1864")	81
July Days of 1917	81
The Counterfeit Manifesto of 1861. By B. Kozmin	81
The Russian "Parliamentary" Delegation Abroad in 1916 (P. N. Miliukov's Report to the Military-Naval Commission of the [Fourth] State Duma, June 19, 1916)	82
General A. M. Zaionchkovsky's Note concerning the Dobrudja Operation of 1916	82
Materials Relating to the History of the Potsdam Agreement of 1911	82
M. N. Katkov and Alexander III in 1886–1887	83
Bolshevization of the Front before the July Days of 1917	83
Moscow Students and Professors on the Eve of the February Revolution	83
The Press in the Kerensky Era	84
The Labor Movement in the Koenig Factory in 1917. By G. Linko	84
From F. A. Golovin's Notes	84
William II concerning the Seizure of Port Arthur by Russia	84
Materials Relating to the History of the Convocation of the Second Congress of the Russian Social Democratic Labor Party	85
A Few Documents about M. S. Olminsky from the Gendarmerie Archives	85
P. A. Shuvalov concerning the Congress of Berlin 1878	85
The Cadets in the Days of the Galician Devastation of 1915	86
P. B. Struve's Letters to S. D. Sazonov in 1915	86
Anglo-Spanish Conflict 1898–1899	86
Dzhizak Uprising of 1916	87
From the Memoirs of A. F. Rediger	87
Tsarist Censorship and Gendarmerie concerning Clara Zetkin	87

Contents

	PAGE
Memoirs of A. I. Kozmin	88
Peasant [Resolutions] concerning the Brest Peace in 1918	88
O. Bismarck's Letters to A. M. Gorchakov	88
The Stavka and the Moscow Committee of Public Safety in 1917	89
Ufa Conference and the Provisional Siberian Government	89
From Leo Tikhomirov's Diary (1907)	89
From Correspondence of Tsarist Officials on the Eve of War and Revolution	90
Tsarist Government concerning the Straits Problem 1898–1911	90
Along Lenin's Path (On the Tenth Anniversary of Lenin's Death). By Y. Berzin and V. Maksakov	90
Ten Years Ago	90
Archival Documents on the Biography of V. I. Lenin (1887–1914)	91
On the Eve of the Russo-Japanese War (December, 1900—January, 1902)	92
Boris Nikolsky's Diary (1905–1907)	92
A Few Dates in the Life and Work of J. M. Sverdlov (From Documents of the Archive of the Revolution, 1885–1915)	92
A Survey of Archival Materials on the History of the Factory Krasnyi Perekop (1722–1929)	93
Nicholas Romanov concerning the Anglo-Boer War	93
Materials Relating to L. N. Tolstoy's Biography (1901–1902)	93
Nicholas Romanov's Marginal Notes. By G. Nikolskaia	94
Materials Relating to the History of the Autocracy's Struggle with the Revolutionary Movement in the Army in the 1880's. By M. Akhun and D. Zinevich	94
Contents of the Previous Volumes of the Journal *Krasnyi Arkhiv*	94
Tsarist Russia's International Financial Position at the Time of the World War (A. I. Shingarev's Report to the Military-Naval Commission of the [Fourth] State Duma, June 20, 1916)	94
Arrest of the Duma "Quintet" in 1914	95
Materials Relating to the History of the Labor Movement on the Eve of the World War	95

Contents

	PAGE
The Soldiers' Frame of Mind on the Eve of the World War	95
Materials Relating to the Question of Preparedness for World War (From Documents of the Russian Military and Political Intelligence, 1913–1914)	96
Nicholas Romanov in the First Days of the World War	96
The Struggle for a Labor Press on the Eve of the World War	96
An Unpublished Letter of V. M. Garshin	97
The First Days of the World War	97
The Devastation of Serbia in 1915 and the "Help" of the Allies	97
Anglo-Russian Relations in Persia at the Time of the World War	98
Soldiers' Letters during the World-War Years (1915–1917)	98
The Moscow Military-Revolutionary Committee	98
Materials Relating to the History of the Revolution of 1905 in Sormovo Factory (The Diary of a Nizhni Novgorod Factory Inspector for 1905)	99
After Tsushima (From the Diary of Lieutenant A. S. Zarin)	99
Sergius M. Kirov, 1886–1934	99
Materials Relating to the History of the Labor Movement at the Time of the World War (Strikes in the Kostroma Area)	100
Materials Relating to the History of Gvozdevshchinism (Bulletins of the Labor Group of the Central War Industrial Committee)	100
German Intervention and the Don Government in 1918	100
Materials Relating to the History of the Semënovites in 1919	101
Anatole France and Tsarist Censorship	101
The Diary of A. A. Polovtsov	101
Nicholas II, "Doctor of Russian History"	102
Before Tsushima	102
V. V. Kuibyshev (1888–1935)	102
Strengthen Revolutionary Vigilance!	102
Materials Relating to the History of the Struggle for the Third Party Congress (December, 1903—March, 1905)	103
Materials Relating to the History of "Bloody Sunday" in Petersburg (Reports of the Procurator of the St. Petersburg Chamber of Justice, E. I. Vuich, to the Minister of Justice)	103

Contents

	PAGE
A. N. Kuropatkin's Diary (March 31—November 21[sic], 1904)	103
The Execution of the Ivanovo Voznesensk Workers in 1915	104
A Few Dates in the Life and Work of V. V. Kuibyshev (According to Documents of the Central Archive of the Revolution 1888–1916). By V. Dalago	104
Intervention in the Caucasus and Counterrevolution among the Mountain Tribes	104
Materials Relating to the History of the Autocracy's Struggle with the Labor Movement	105
Boris Nikolsky and Gregory Rasputin	105
The Interrogation of Pugachev's Ataman A. Khlopusha	105
From the Editors	106
Materials Relating to the History of the Anglo-Russian Agreement of 1907	106
"A Satrap's Circuit" (The Notes of A. A. Tatishchev on Dubasov's Punitive Expedition in the Chernigov Province)	106
The Battleship *Prince Potemkin Tavrichesky* at Odessa	107
A. N. Kuropatkin's Diary (March 31—November 20, 1904)	107
Materials Relating to the Thirtieth Anniversary of the Ivanovo Voznesensk General Strike (May 12/25 to July 1/14, 1905)	107
Materials Relating to the History of the Struggle for Worker Control	108
E. Pugachev's Interrogation in Moscow 1774–1775	108
Materials Relating to the History of the Counterrevolution of 1905	108
Nicholas II, "Emperor of Kaffirs"	108
Tsarist Censorship concerning the Works of F. Engels	109
Peasants' Agitation in Kherson Province in 1905	109
Materials Relating to the History of the Revolutionary Movement in the Army in 1905–1906 (Uprising of the Seventh Reserve Cavalry Regiment in Tambov)	109
Moscow Military-Revolutionary Committee	110
Potash Factories in the Smolensk District in the Seventeenth Century	110
Materials Relating to the History of the Mastery of the Northern Sea Route (Bering's Expedition 1732–1743)	110
The Police and A. P. Chekhov's Funeral	111

Contents

	PAGE
Church Fraud Disclosed at the Opening of the Relics of Pitirim Tambovsky. By B. Kandidov	111
The Collapse of Wrangel	111
Ten Years Since the Day of M. V. Frunze's Death	112
Boulangism and Tsarist Diplomacy	112
The Strike of the Ivanovo Voznesensk Factory Weavers in 1895	112
From Leo Tikhomirov's Diary (The Stolypin Era)	113
Materials Relating to the History of the Mastery of the Northern Sea Route	113
The Church and the Reforms of 1861	113
Denikinites concerning Conditions in the Rear of Their Army	114
A. A. Sergeev	114
Police Surveillance of Anna Ilinichna Ulianova-Elizarova (A Few Dates in the Life and Activities of Anna Ilinichna Ulianova-Elizarova)	114
The Collapse of Wrangel	114
Materials Relating to M. V. Frunze's Revolutionary Activity (1905–1912)	115
December Days in the Donets Basin in 1905	115
The Peasant Movement in the Central Part of Russia in 1905 (From Materials of the Kursk, Orlov, Voronezh, and Chernigov Provinces)	115
From Leo Tikhomirov's Diary (The Stolypin Era, 1908)	116
Materials Relating to the History of the Mastery of the Northern Sea Route	116
Presnia in December 1905	116
Moscow Students and L. N. Tolstoy's Death	117
N. A. Dobroliubov	117
Seventy-five Years Ago	117
Tsarism in the Struggle with the Labor Movement in the Years of Its Ascent	118
Materials Relating to the History of the Ural Factories (According to a Gendarmerie Survey)	118
The Agrarian Movement in Smolensk Province 1905–1906	118

Contents

	PAGE
Materials Relating to the History of the Mastery of the Northern Sea Route	119
From Leo Tikhomirov's Diary (The Stolypin Era, 1909)	119
Bismarck concerning the Situation in Europe in 1868	119
Moscow University in the October Days of 1905	120
N. G. Chernyshevsky in Viliuisk	120
A Journey from Petersburg to Moscow—A. N. Radishchev and Tsarist Censorship	120
On the Front of Historical Science—In the Sovnarkom of the USSR and the Central Committee of the All-Union (Bolshevik) Communist Party	120
Decree of the Central Committee of the All-Union (Bolshevik) Communist Party and the Council of People's Commissars of the USSR	121
Remarks in Connection with the Synopsis of the Textbook *History of the USSR*	121
Remarks concerning the Synopsis of the Textbook *Modern History*	121
Materials concerning the Organization of the Competition for the Best Textbook for Beginning Schools on the Elementary Course in the History of the USSR with a Short Instruction in General History	121
Materials Relating to the History of the Peace of Paris 1856	121
The Reform of 1861 and the Peasant Movement	122
Student Movement in 1901	122
The Search for Precious Metals in the North in the Seventeenth and Eighteenth Centuries	122
New Documents concerning N. A. Dobroliubov	123
From Leo Tikhomirov's Diary	123
The Toiling Cossacks of the Don Region concerning the Brest Peace and Defense of the Soviet Land	124
A Governor in the Role of Propagator of the Koran	124
From the History of the Shostka Gun-Powder Works	124
Agitation in Kharkov Province in the Years of the Imperialistic War	125
The Revolutionary Cossacks of the Don in the Struggle with Counter-revolution	125

Contents

	PAGE
Documents concerning the Khodynka Catastrophe of 1896	125
Workers' Movement in the Petersburg Factories in May, 1901	125
Materials Relating to the History of the "Yakut Union"	126
First Railroads in Russia	126
Materials Relating to the History of the Buriats in the Seventeenth Century	126
The Search for Precious Metals in the North in the Seventeenth and Eighteenth Centuries (Conclusion)	126
N. G. Chernyshevsky's [Shorthand] Code. By N. Alexeiev	127
The Suppression by Tsarism of the Honoring of T. Shevchenko's Memory	127
Materials Relating to the Biography of P. G. Zaichnevsky	127
Portrait of Gorky	127
The Constitution of the USSR	128
Workers' Letters to *Zvezda* and *Pravda*	128
Illegal Work of the Bolshevik Faction of the Fourth State Duma (According to Documents of the Police Department)	128
The Kronstadt Rebellion of 1906	128
The Serf Peasantry of the Village of Barashev-Usad in the First Half of the Nineteenth Century	129
Agitations of the Serf Peasants of the Village of Krasnyi Kut	129
Construction of a Dnieper Dockyard in the Eighteenth Century	129
Unpublished Letters of A. S. Pushkin	129
The Proletarian Red Cross in Petrograd (October, 1917—June, 1918)	130
Alexander Nevsky Monastery on the Eve of the Overthrow of the Autocracy	130
Materials Relating to the Question of the Property Status of the Decembrist, Prince S. G. Volkonsky	130
To Comrade Gregory Konstantinovich Ordzhonikidze	130
Materials Relating to the Activities of G. K. Ordzhonikidze in the Years of the Civil War (From Documents of the Central Archive of the October Revolution and the Central Archive of the Red Army)	131

Contents

	PAGE
A Few Dates in the Underground Party Work of G. K. Ordzhonikidze 1903–1912	131
Chronology of Gorky's Life and Works	131
Struggle for Land in 1917 (Kazan Province)	131
The Agrarian Movement in Chernigov Province 1905–1906	132
Materials Relating to the History of the Autocracy's Struggle with the Agrarian Movement in 1905–1907	132
Tsarist Russia and the Hawaiian Islands	133
Materials Relating to the History of Relations of the Kazakhs with Tsarist Russia in the Eighteenth Century	133
N. P. Balabin's Memoirs	134
V. I. Lenin's Address to the Tula Workers	134
A. M. Gorky and the Publishing Business	134
Materials Relating to the History of N. G. Chernyshevsky's Exile	134
Farmsteads at the Beginning of the Nineteenth Century	135
Decision of the Extraordinary Eighth Congress of Soviets of the USSR concerning the Confirmation of the Constitution (Basic Law) of the Union of Soviet Socialist Republics	135
The Constitution (Basic Law) of the USSR	135
Autocracy and Suffrage in the Minority Regions of Tsarist Russia	135
Autocracy and Woman Suffrage	136
The Strike in Tver in 1885	136
The Kazan Clothiers in 1836	136
Agitation of the Workers at the Merchant Nosov's Factory at Shuisk in 1822–1824	136
Agrarian Relations in Prerevolutionary Dagestan	136
Agitation of Peasants of Belgorod and Mitropol Villages in 1682	137
Lyceum Letters of A. M. Gorchakov 1814–1818	137
An Unpublished Autograph of A. S. Pushkin	137
Government Bulletin on the Death of Gregory K. Ordzhonikidze	137
Alexander Sergeevich Pushkin. By E. Cherniavsky	138
Unpublished Autographs of A. S. Pushkin	138

Contents XXV

	PAGE
Lyceum Letters (From A. M. Gorchakov's Notes)	138
Pushkin's Youth (An Unpublished Article by V. Briusov)	139
Pushkin's Works and Tsarist Censorship (From Archive Materials)	139
Effect on Tsarist Troops of A. S. Pushkin's Ode "Freedom"	139
P. A. Viazemsky and the Death of A. S. Pushkin. By N. Belchikov	139
Portrait of J. V. Stalin	140
Concerning the Shortcomings of the Party Work and Measures for Liquidating the Trotskyites and Other Double-Dealers	140
Concluding Remarks of Comrade Stalin at the Plenum of the Central Committee of the All-Union (Bolshevik) Communist Party, March 5, 1937	140
Zvezda and *Pravda* and Tsarist Censorship	140
In the Tsarist Army on the Eve of the February Bourgeois-Democratic Revolution (Agitation in the Two Hundred Twenty-third Odoevsky Regiment of the Thirty-fourth Army Corps)	141
The People's Demand for Nicholas Romanov's Imprisonment in a Fortress	141
The Provisions Situation in Moscow, March–June 1917	141
From Documents on the Organization of the Red Army	141
The Lena Military Execution of 1912	142
Tsarism in the Struggle with A. I. Herzen	142
Working Women of Southern Ossetia in the Struggle for Soviets	142
Comrade Stalin's Letter to Compilers of the History of the All-Union (Bolshevik) Communist Party	143
Instructions to the Delegates of the Second All-Russian Congress of Soviets	143
The All-Russian Communist Subbotnik of May 1, 1920	143
The Partisan Movement in the Maritime Province	144
Materials concerning the Occupation of Northern Sakhalin by Japanese Troops, 1920–1925	144
Materials Relating to the History of the Civil War in Yakutsk in 1922	145
The Rise of the Labor Movement before the First Imperialistic War	145
May 1 in Tsarist Russia (1892–1903)	145

xxvi *Contents*

	PAGE
A Decree of the Central Executive Committee of the USSR at the Fourth Session of Its Seventh Convocation	146
Regulations concerning Elections to the Supreme Soviet of the USSR	146
Assistance to the Red Army from Communist Subbotniks during the Civil War	146
Concerning the Lena Execution (The Inquiry of the Social Democratic Faction in the Fourth State Duma)	146
Working Conditions during Construction of the Petersburg-Moscow Railroad (1843–1851)	147
A Russian Volunteer in the Ranks of the Spanish Insurgents in 1830	147
Moscow in 1812 (From Memoirs of Adam Glushkovsky)	147
M. E. Saltykov-Shchedrin as Inspector General	148
Attempts at Mastery of the Natural Resources of Ossetia in the Eighteenth Century	148
Decree of the Members of the Government Commission on the Competition for the Best Textbook for Third and Fourth Classes of Secondary Schools on the History of the USSR	148
Tsarist Ministers concerning Universal Suffrage	149
Personal Expenses of Manufacturer M. A. Morozov	149
[Decree Setting] the Date of Elections to the Supreme Soviet of the USSR	149
Concerning the Announcement of the Composition of the Central Election Commission for Elections to the Supreme Soviet of the USSR	149
An Appeal of the Central Committee of the All-Union (Bolshevik) Communist Party	150
Second All-Russian Congress of Soviets (Questionnaire Filled Out by Bolshevik Delegates to the Second Congress of Soviets)	150
Preparation by the Army and Its Leadership of the Great October Socialist Revolution	150
Orders and Decrees of the Petrograd Military-Revolutionary Committee on Questions of the Press in the Days of the October Revolution	150
Materials Relating to the Prerevolutionary Past of Moscow	151
Comrade J. V. Stalin's Speech	151
Materials Relating to the Twentieth Anniversary of the Third All-Russian Congress of Soviets	151

Contents

	PAGE
Delegates of the Petrograd Garrison at the Front	152
Materials Relating to the History of the Revolutionary Struggle of the Kolomna Workers in 1917	152
The First Steps in Building Soviet Power in the Village (From Resolutions of Meetings of Peasants and Informative Résumés of the People's Commissariat of Agriculture, December, 1917—February, 1918)	152
Taseev Partisan District in 1919	153
Eighteenth-Century Project for Connecting the Moscow River with the Volga	153
Attempts at Mastery of the Natural Resources of Ossetia in the Eighteenth Century (Continuation)	153
Comrade Ivanov's Letter and Comrade Stalin's Answer	154
Materials [to Be Used in Commemorating] the Twentieth Anniversary of the Workers' and Peasants' Red Army and Navy (Topics for Propagandists)	154
Three Telegrams of V. I. Lenin	154
J. Stalin concerning Three Characteristics of the Red Army	154
Comrade Voroshilov's Address at the Jubilee Session of the Plenum of the Moscow Soviet, Dedicated to the Tenth Anniversary of the Red Army, February 25, 1928	155
Materials Relating to the Twentieth Anniversary of the Workers' and Peasants' Red Army (From Documents on the History of the Organization of the Red Army)	155
The Working Class and Trade Unions in the Creation of the Red Army	155
Agitational Trips of M. I. Kalinin in the Civil War Years	156
Materials Relating to the Revolutionary Activities of G. K. Ordzhonikidze	156
The *Communist Manifesto* and Russian Censorship	156
Materials Relating to the History of the Celebration of International Women's Day in Russia	157
Germany's Seizure of Kiaochow in 1897	157
Italy's Aggressive Plans in Connection with Negotiations concerning the Renewal of the Triple Alliance	157
Agitation of the Chuvash Peasantry in 1842	158

Contents

	PAGE
Materials Relating to the History of Kazakhstan in the Eighteenth Century	158
Materials Relating to the Fiftieth Anniversary of V. M. Garshin's Death (From Materials of the Censorship Committee)	158
The Struggle of Tsarist Censorship with A. S. Serafimovich's Works	159
Byron in Greece (On the One-Hundred-and-Fiftieth Anniversary of His Birth)	159
Comrade Stalin's Speech at the Kremlin Reception for Workers in Higher Schools, May 17, 1938	159
Concerning Schools of Higher Education (Comrade V. M. Molotov's Speech at the First All-Union Conference of Workers in Higher Schools, May 15, 1938)	159
The Tsarist Government and G. Y. Sedov's Polar Expedition	160
Materials Relating to the History of the General Strike in South Russia in 1903	160
Andizhan Uprising of 1898	160
Materials Relating to the History of the Franco-Russian Agreement of 1859	161
Attempts at Mastery of the Natural Resources of Ossetia in the Eighteenth Century (Conclusion)	161
Powerful Weapon of Bolshevism	162
In Memory of Twenty-six Baku Commissars	162
Materials Relating to the History of the Carrying into Effect of Lenin's Decree concerning Land	162
Materials Relating to the History of the Struggle of Supply Detachments of Workers for Bread and the Strengthening of Soviet Power (1918–1920)	163
Austrian Revolution of 1848 and Nicholas I	163
Peasant Movement at the End of the Nineteenth Century (1881–1894)	164
Student Agitation 1901–1902	164
Materials Relating to the History of the Development of Steam Navigation on the Volga (P. P. Melnikov's Note "Voyage on the Volga")	164
Concerning the Formulation of Party Propaganda in Connection with the Publication of *A Short Course in the History of the All-Union (Bolshevik) Communist Party*	165

Contents xxix

	PAGE
Suchan Valley in the Years of the Civil War	165
German Occupation of Polesie (Byelorussia)	165
Franco-German Crisis of 1875	166
Materials Relating to the History of the Labor Movement in the 1880's and 1890's	166
Agitation at the Glushkovsky Clothing Factory (1797–1798)	167
Materials Relating to the History of the Kara-Kalpaks of the Eighteenth Century	167
The Struggle of the Tsarist Government and Censorship with T. G. Shevchenko's "Kobzar" (On the One-Hundred-and-Twenty-Fifth Anniversary of His Birth)	167
New Data concerning Lado Ketskhoveli's Murder	168
New Materials concerning N. G. Chernyshevsky's Dissertation	168
Subject Index of *Krasnyi Arkhiv* for 1938	168
Comrade Stalin's Report at the Eighteenth Party Congress concerning the Work of the Central Committee of the All-Union (Bolshevik) Communist Party	168
V. I. Lenin in the Years of the Imperialistic War	169
Commemoration of the Twentieth Anniversary of J. M. Sverdlov's Death	169
Kandeevka Uprising in 1861	169
Materials Relating to the History of Factory Legislation in 1861	170
Materials Relating to the History of the Nenets People in the 1830's and 1840's (The Movement of the Vauli Piettomin)	170
Materials Relating to the History of the Kara-Kalpaks of the Eighteenth Century (Conclusion)	170
Materials Relating to the History of the Pan-Germanic Union	171
Materials Relating to P. A. Moiseenko's Exile in Archangel	171
[The Role of] M. V. Frunze in the Organization of the Victory over [A. V.] Kolchak	171
Russia and Prussia in the Schleswig-Holstein Question	172
Materials Relating to the History of the Labor Movement at the End of the 1890's and "The Union for the Emancipation of the Working Class"	172

	PAGE
The Strike in Kharkov on May 1, 1900	173
Materials Relating to the History of Russia's Relations with the Turkmen in the Eighteenth Century	173
From Correspondence of N. I. Kostomarov with [S. N.] Shubinsky, Editor of *Istoricheskii Vestnik*	173
Petrograd Workers in the Struggle with Yudenich	173
The Railroad Workers' Strike in the Tiflis Workshops (1900)	174
Concerning the Pedagogical Activity of Ilia Nikolaevich Ulianov	174
Russo-American Relations at the Time of the Civil War in the United States	174
Elections in Paris to the Estates General in 1789 (From the Letters of a Contemporary)	175
Description of the History of the Kalmuck People	175
Great Fear in Auvergne	175
Materials Relating to the History of the Electrification of the Russian Soviet Federated Socialist Republic	176
Materials Relating to the History of the Civil War in the Ukraine in 1918	176
Materials Relating to International Relations in the First Years of the French Revolution (1789–1790)	177
July Strikes and Demonstrations of 1914	177
Materials Relating to the History of Events in the Ukraine in 1708 (On the Two-Hundred-and-Thirtieth Anniversary of the Battle of Poltava)	177
Materials Relating to the Centennial of the Pulkovo Astronomical Observatory	178
Socialistic Forms of Agriculture 1918–1919	178
Materials Relating to the History of the Electrification of the Russian Soviet Federated Socialist Republic (Continuation)	179
Unions in the Struggle for a Rise in the Productivity of Labor in the Civil War Years	179
Episodes from the War Activity of Russian Aircraft 1914–1917	179
Materials Relating to the Question of Patents for Inventions in Russia in the 1830's	180

Contents xxxi

	PAGE
Note of N. G. Chernyshevsky concerning Liberation of the Peasants	180
Tsarist Censorship concerning "Popular" Publications of M. Y. Lermontov's Works	180
Description of the History of the Kalmuck People (Continuation)	181
Materials Relating to L. N. Tolstoy's Biography	181
Letters of the Artist V. G. Schwartz	181
Leader of the People. By E. Yaroslavsky	181
Struggle for Bread in 1918–1919	182
Materials for S. M. Kirov's Biography	182
Materials Relating to the History of the Prague Conference	182
Comrade Kirov's Activity in the Organization of Tomsk Social Democrats	182
V. I. Chapaev's Military Career	183
A. P. Chekhov—Manuscripts, Letters, Materials	183
Contents of the Issues of the Journal *Krasnyi Arkhiv* for 1939	183
Lenin's Legacy Embodied in Life [A Eulogy of Lenin]	183
Responses to V. I. Lenin's Death	184
White Finns in the Service of Anglo-French Interventionists in 1919	184
Chapaev's Military Career	184
Materials Relating to the History of Intervention in the North	184
Life of Soldiers in the Tsarist Army	185
Position of Peasants in Western Byelorussia in the Nineteenth Century	185
I. N. Ulianov's Struggle for Elementary Schools	185
Herzen and Tsarist Censorship (On the Seventieth Anniversary of His Death)	185
Tsarist Censorship concerning the Ukrainian Writer I. Franko	186
To the Faithful Companion in Arms of Lenin and Stalin—Viacheslav Mikhailovich Molotov	186
To the Faithful Companion in Arms of Lenin and Stalin, the Head of the Soviet Government—V. M. Molotov	186
Viacheslav Mikhailovich Molotov (Short Biography). By G. A. Tikhomirov	187

Contents

	PAGE
The Civil War in Finland (1918)	187
Russian Soldiers' Uprising in France in 1917	187
Armed Struggle of Novorossisk Workers in December, 1905	187
The Peasant Movement in Western Transcaucasia 1902–1905	187
Beginning of Railroad Construction in Russia	188
The Current Problems of the Journal *Krasnyi Arkhiv*. By E. Yaroslavsky	188
A Short Review of Documents Published in *Krasnyi Arkhiv* (On the Publication of the One-Hundredth Issue of the Journal *Krasnyi Arkhiv*)	188
M. V. Frunze on the Turkestan Front	189
Agricultural Exposition of 1923	190
Materials Relating to the Biography of P. F. Lesgaft	190
New Materials concerning M. V. Lomonosov	190
I. S. Turgenev in Spasskoe-Lutovino (Reminiscences of S. G. Shchepkina)	190
From the Diary of V. P. Gaevsky (1883–1887)	191
From P. I. Tchaikovsky's Correspondence	191
Military-Revolutionary Committee of Estonia in 1917 and the Beginning of 1918 (From the Protocols of the Military-Revolutionary Committee)	191
Rumanian Arbitrariness in Bessarabia (1918)	192
Suppression of the Left Socialist Revolutionaries' Revolt in Moscow in 1918	192
Materials Relating to the History of the Rise of Agricultural Communes and Artels in the USSR (1918)	192
The Polish War of 1794 in Reports and Accounts of A. V. Suvorov	193
Materials Relating to the History of Moscow (Description of Moscow after the Fire of April 10, 1629)	193
Materials Relating to the Sojourn of Russian Troops in France in 1917	194
Materials Relating to the History of the Struggle of the Lithuanian People for Soviet Power in 1918–1919	194
Materials Relating to the History of the Struggle of the Karelian People for Soviet Power	194

Contents

	PAGE
Materials Relating to the History of the Labor Movement in the Ukraine in 1905	195
Revolutionary Events in the Baltic Provinces in 1905	195
Materials Relating to the History of the Revolution of 1905–1907 in Byelorussia	195
Anglo-Russian Incident with the Schooner *Vixen* (1836–1837)	195
Materials Relating to the Fortieth Anniversary of *Iskra*	196
Legislative Enactments of the Soviet Government of Latvia (1918–1919)	196
Armed Rebellion in Motovilikha in December, 1905	197
Materials on the History of Labor's Control over Production (1917–1918)	197
A Russian Military Agent's Dispatches on the Anglo-Boer War	197
Larga and Kagul (Material concerning the Military Activities of [Count P. A.] Rumiantsev-Zadunaisky)	198
D. I. Pisarev and Tsarist Censorship	198
Ancient Russian Charter of 1368	198
To Comrade Kliment Efremovich Voroshilov	198
The Circulation of the Works of V. I. Lenin in Prerevolutionary Russia (1894–1905)	199
Materials Relating to the Military Activities of Comrade Timoshenko during the Civil War in the USSR	199
The Revolutionary Activity of Comrade V. V. Kuibyshev in Samara (1916–1918)	199
Student Conditions in Trade Schools in Prerevolutionary Tver	200
Use by the Interventionists of the Northern Sea Route (1918–1919)	200
Materials Relating to the Belgian Revolution of 1830	200
First Russian Submarine Project	201
Contents of the Issues of the Journal *Krasnyi Arkhiv* for 1940	201
Archival Materials on the Revolutionary Activities of J. V. Stalin 1908–1913	201
The Persian Revolution 1905–1911 and Bolsheviks of Transcaucasia	201
Materials Relating to the History of the Right-Bank Ukrainian Peasantry's Struggle against the Central Council (Ukrainian Popular Assembly) and the Provisional Government in 1917	202

Contents

	PAGE
At a Great Grave (Revolutionary Feelings among the Ukrainian Peasantry in Connection with T. G. Shevchenko's Death)	202
Materials Relating to the Biography of Shamil	202
Tsarism's Struggle with the Revolutionary Press in 1905	203
New Materials on M. E. Saltykov-Shchedrin	203
Materials Relating to the History of the Moscow Bolshevik Labor Press in the Years of Revolutionary Upheaval (1913–1914)	204
Materials Relating to the Thirty-fifth Anniversary of the Fourth (Unifying) Congress of the RSDLP	204
Agitation of Peasants on the Estates in Georgia Belonging to the Imperial Family 1905–1906	204
Peasant Agitation in Kharkov Province (1861–1862)	205
Materials on the History of Sericulture in Russia	205
England in the Face of Napoleon I's Invasion (1801–1805)	205
New Materials on Gleb Uspensky	206
Materials Relating to the Biography of Kosta Khetagurov	206
Letters of A. V. Suvorov	206
The Offensive on the Southwestern Front in May and June, 1916	207
A Valuable Contribution to the History and Theory of Soviet Military Science	207
APPENDIX—Titles of Articles in *Krasnyi Arkhiv*, Volumes 1–30	209
INDEX	223

A DIGEST OF THE KRASNYI ARKHIV
Volumes 31–106

VOLUME 31, 1928

31 (1928): 3–50

DIARY OF THE MINISTRY OF FOREIGN AFFAIRS 1915–1916. Introduction by the editors of *Krasnyi Arkhiv*.

Daily notes made in the Russian Ministry of Foreign Affairs during July, 1914, appeared in "The Beginning of the War of 1914," 4 (1923): 5–62. Notes have not been found for the period between July 19, 1914, and April 9, 1915.

The editors state that although the diary published here is typewritten and unsigned there is reason to believe that it was kept by Baron M. F. Schilling, chief of the office of the Ministry of Foreign Affairs. It consists of fragmentary entries dated from April 9, 1915, through December 28, 1915.

The diary describes the satisfaction of Italian Ambassador Marquis A. Carlotti and Russian Minister of Foreign Affairs S. D. Sazonov upon Italy's entry into the war, and gives a detailed account of Italian, French, Belgian, and British attempts to bring Rumania in on the side of the Allies, and of Germany's overtures to Rumania.

It contains, in addition, matter relevant to the following subjects: talk of a separate Russian peace with Hungary and, later, with Germany; reasons for the inactivity of the Serbian army; Belgian consternation over rumors that France would annex Luxembourg at the war's end; the British proposal of an offensive through the Dardanelles or through Greece and Serbia into Hungary; the Russian proposal to entice Bulgaria into the war on the side of the Allies by promising it territory in Macedonia; rumors that Ivan Goremykin would replace Sazonov; British concern over Russian internal affairs; the advisability of an immediate occupation of Tehran by Russia; French attempts to get Russian troops to the western front; the Salonika expedition; and the beginnings of Russo-Japanese *rapprochement*.

Publication of the diary is concluded in 32 (1929): 3–87.

31 (1928): 51–80

THE DISINTEGRATION OF KOLCHAK'S CAMPAIGN (From the Diary of V. N. Pepeliaev). Introduction by the editors of *Krasnyi Arkhiv*.

The introduction is a brief biography of Victor Nikolaevich Pepeliaev, minister of internal affairs and later premier in Admiral A. V. Kolchak's government. Pepeliaev was active in overthrowing the Ufa Directorate and in establishing Kolchak's regime. He and Kolchak were arrested in Nizhneudinsk, imprisoned in Irkutsk, and shot there on the night of February 7, 1920.

Pepeliaev traces the fortunes of Kolchak's forces from July through October, 1919, and comments on the evacuation of Perm, the Finns' demand for independence as a price for their march on Petrograd, relations with Japan, the influence of Arthur Balfour and Winston Churchill in securing British aid for Kolchak, and the necessity for the reorganization of Kolchak's army. He mentions conferences with Roland Sletor Morris, American ambassador in Tokyo, as well as with representatives of Japan, England, Finland, and Estonia. Included, also, are comments on the following matters: reports submitted by Kolchak's generals; the meetings of the ministers of Kolchak's government; the "West Russian Government" established in Berlin in October, 1919; the appearance of the first impostor Tsarevitch Alexis; the question of establishing normal relations with Germany; and the arrest of members of the Cadet National Center in Moscow.

For additional material in *Krasnyi Arkhiv* on Kolchak's campaign, see: "The Events in Omsk and Kolchak," 7 (1924): 201–246; "The Omsk Events and Kolchak," 8 (1925): 176–192; "French Intervention in South Russia," 19 (1926): 3–38; "From the History of Kolchak's Campaign," 28 (1928): 225–228; "Materials Relating to the History of the Destruction of Kolchak's Armed Forces," 49 (1931): 55–91; "[The Role of] M. V. Frunze in the Organization of the Victory over Kolchak," 93 (1939): 3–50; "White Finns in the Service of Anglo-French Interventionists in 1919," 98 (1940): 31–67.

For additional material in *Krasnyi Arkhiv* on events in Siberia during this period, see: "The Provisional Government of Autonomous Siberia," 29 (1928): 86–138, 35 (1929): 37–106, and 36 (1929): 31–60; "The French Military Mission in Siberia and the Specially Commissioned Cossack Regiments," 29 (1928): 206–209; "Autographs of the Members of the Ufa Conference," 31 (1928): 202–204; "Materials Relating to the History of Intervention in Siberia," 34 (1929): 126–165; "Ufa Conference and the Provisional Siberian Government," 61 (1933): 58–81; "The Partisan Movement in the Maritime Province," 82 (1937): 40–89; "Materials concerning the Occupation of Northern Sakhalin by Japanese Troops, 1920–1925," 82 (1937): 90–118; "Suchan Valley in the Years of the Civil War," 91 (1938): 16–88.

31 (1928): 81–102

S. Y. WITTE'S STRUGGLE WITH THE AGRARIAN REVOLUTION. Introduction by I. Tatarov.

The documents published here are minutes of two meetings of a "special council" called by Nicholas II to consider measures for suppressing agrarian unrest in 1906. Those present at the conference on January 28, 1906, were Count S. Y. Witte, premier; Grand Duke Nicholas Nikolaevich, chairman of the Council of State Defense; P. N. Durnovo, minister of internal affairs; Colonel S. S. Savich of the Gendarmerie; Lieutenant General A. F. Rediger, minister of war; Lieutenant General I. Palitsyn, chief of the General Staff; and Major General A. A. Polivanov of the General Staff. At this meeting the committee considered the possibility of redeploying troops from the Far East to put down the unrest. At its meeting on March 1, 1906, the council devised a plan for coöperation between military and civilian authorities in the event of the use of armed force for this purpose.

For additional material in *Krasnyi Arkhiv* on agrarian unrest, see Volumes 11–12 (1925), devoted exclusively to documents on the history of the Revolution of 1905. See also: "Peasant Unrest during 1905," 9 (1925): 66–93; "The Agrarian Measures of 1906," 15 (1926): 214–216; "On the History of Stolypin's Agrarian Reforms," 17 (1926): 81–90; "Materials Relating to the History of the Struggle with the Agrarian Movement 1905–1906," 39 (1930): 76–107 and 40 (1930): 41–58; "Peasants' Agitation in Kherson Province in 1905," 71 (1935): 17–38; "The Peasant Movement in the Central Part of Russia in 1905," 73 (1935): 126–169; "The Agrarian Movement in Smolensk Province 1905–1906," 74 (1936): 92–141; "The Agrarian Movement in Chernigov Province 1905–1906," 78 (1936): 98–127; "Materials Relating to the History of the Autocracy's Struggle with the Agrarian Movement in 1905–1907," 78 (1936): 128–160; "The Peasant Movement in Western Transcaucasia 1902–1905," 99 (1940): 90–126; "Agitation of Peasants on the Estates in Georgia Belonging to the Imperial Family 1905–1906," 106 (1941): 40–57.

31 (1928): 103–117

P. L. ANTONOV IN THE PETROPAVLOVSK FORTRESS. Introduction by S. Valk.

Valk briefly describes Antonov's career from the time when he joined the Will of the People party in 1880 up to and including his arrest and imprisonment in Petropavlovsk fortress on May 1, 1885. Police Chief P. N. Durnovo had attempted unsuccessfully to persuade Antonov to betray the leaders of his party. A note written by Antonov to a fellow prisoner was intercepted by the guards and given to Durnovo, who, pretending to be the prisoner Andrew Belousov, began corresponding with Antonov.

The notes published here are the Antonov-"Belousov" correspondence from August to October, 1885, in which Antonov, unaware of the deception, wrote of the activities and members of the Will of the People party.

For additional material in *Krasnyi Arkhiv* on the Will of the People party, see: "S. G. Nechaev at the Alexeev Ravelin," 5 (1924): 172–212; "The Unpublished 'Manifesto' of the Executive Committee of the 'Narodnaia Volia,'" 7 (1924): 247–249; "A Police Agent Writes of the Arrest of the Participants in the Attempted Assassination on March 1, 1887," 9 (1925): 297–300; "Gregory Goldenberg in the Peter and Paul Fortress," 10 (1925): 328–331; "An Autobiographic Statement by A. A. Kviatkovsky," 14 (1926): 159–175; "A Letter by Franz Yatsevich," 17 (1926): 185–186; "A. I. Zheliabov at Alexandrovsk," 18 (1926): 195–197; "N. I. Rysakov's Testimony," 19 (1926): 178–194; "From Documents of the People's Will Party," 20 (1927): 205–231; "The Student Union and the Execution of May 8, 1887," 21 (1927): 226–231; "The 'Confession' of Gregory Goldenberg," 30 (1928): 117–183; "The Escape of Sergius Degaev," 31 (1928): 219–222; "The *Socialist*, Organ of the Southwestern Group of the Will of the People Party," 33 (1929): 204–211; "Materials Relating to the History of the Trial of the Twenty-one," 36 (1929): 122–179, 37 (1929): 102–137, and 38 (1930): 70–108.

31 (1928): 118–143

THE CONSTITUTIONAL PROJECTS OF THE EARLY 1880's. Introduction by the editors of *Krasnyi Arkhiv*.

The first two of the three constitutional proposals published here were written by Count Paul P. Shuvalov. The first memorandum, drafted before the assassination of Alexander II on March 1, 1881, is divided into the following sections: (1) the inevitability of the establishment of a representative assembly; (2) the limiting of the rights of the people's representation; (3) the general character and organization of the people's representation; (4) the lower chamber; (5) the upper chamber; (6) the participation of zemstvos in a government assembly; (7) government activities.

A revised draft of Shuvalov's proposal was presented to Alexander III in May, 1882, divided into the following sections: (1) the temperament of society after the crime of March 1; (2) the moral ills of society; (3) measures for the elimination of these evils; (4) administrative measures; (5) the importance of preserving external peace; (6) the inadequacy of administrative measures only; (7) the necessity of moral influence on society; (8) the champions of sedition; (9) sedition sympathizers; (10) the sick condition of society; (11) the tenacity of native traditions; (12) the value of the people's representation; (13) the disadvantages of a temporary summons of deputies from the zemstvos; (14) the advantages of a perpetual representative institution; (15) the elective members of a government soviet; (16) the merits of this measure; (17) the anticipated result.

The third document is A. A. Bobrinsky's memorandum of March 11, 1881, calling for elected representatives to assist the new emperor, Alexander III.

For additional material in *Krasnyi Arkhiv*, see "On the History of Loris-Melikov's Constitution," 8 (1925): 132–152.

31 (1928): 144–154

THE MOSCOW ADDRESS TO ALEXANDER II IN 1870 (From the Correspondence of K. P. Pobedonostsev with I. S. Aksakov). Introduction by A. Presniakov.

Presniakov states that this address, written by Prince V. A. Cherkassky, edited by I. S. Aksakov, and adopted unanimously by the Moscow City Duma, pledged support to Alexander II in time of external stress in return for more civil rights. There are several excerpts from the address in the introduction, but the documents themselves are two letters concerning it. Aksakov's letter to K. P. Pobedonostsev, dated December 2, 1870, expresses his indignation over the fact that Alexander II had ignored the address. Pobedonostsev's reply of December 18, 1870, is firm in its opposition to granting freedom of the press, religion, and conscience.

31 (1928): 155–159

NEW MANUSCRIPTS AND MATERIALS ON PUSHKIN. By M. Tsiavlovsky.

Numerous manuscripts dated from 1796 to 1883 concerning the life and work of the Russian poet A. S. Pushkin were discovered in the family archives of Prince A. M. Gorchakov, who attended the Tsarskoe Selo Lyceum with Pushkin. Tsiavlovsky has listed all the Gorchakov documents, in the following groups: (1) Pushkin's autographs; (2) his literary works; (3) his correspondence; (4) material concerning Pushkin's duel and death; (5) albums.

For additional material in *Krasnyi Arkhiv* on Pushkin, see: "Dostoevsky on the Commemoration of Pushkin in the 1880's," 1 (1922): 367–405; "New Material on Pushkin," 28 (1928): 231–234 and 29 (1928): 218–223; "A. S. Pushkin's Poem 'The Monk,'" 31 (1928): 160–201 and 32 (1929): 183–190; "New Material concerning Pushkin's Duel and Death," 33 (1929): 222–235; "A. S. Pushkin under the Surveillance of the Police," 37 (1929): 237–245; "A. S. Pushkin and Count M. S. Vorontsov," 38 (1930): 173–185; "Unpublished Letters of A. S. Pushkin," 77 (1936): 181–190; "Lyceum Letters of A. M. Gorchakov, 1814–1818," 79 (1936): 175–206; "An Unpublished Autograph of A. S. Pushkin," 79 (1936): 207–209. Volume 80 (1937) is devoted, with one exception, to documents on Pushkin's life and work.

31 (1928): 160–201

A. S. Pushkin's Poem "The Monk." Introduction by P. Shchegolev.

Shchegolev discusses the history of the manuscript of "The Monk," which Prince A. M. Gorchakov said had been destroyed but which was actually preserved in the Gorchakov family archives and not made available to Pushkin scholars until some time after Gorchakov's death in 1883. Shchegolev also discusses Voltaire's influence on Pushkin's early works. A facsimile of the manuscript and the text of Part I of "The Monk" are published here.

The second and third parts of the poem appear in 32 (1929): 183–190. For references to additional material in *Krasnyi Arkhiv* on Pushkin, see the notes to "New Manuscripts and Materials on Pushkin," 31 (1928): 155–159.

FROM AN ARCHIVIST'S NOTEBOOK

31 (1928): 202–204

Autographs of the Members of the Ufa Conference

As a result of the Ufa Conference of September 8–23, 1918, the "All-Russian Provisional Government" was organized to coördinate counter-revolutionary activities in Russia. The Directorate of this government was composed of Nicholas D. Avksentev, N. I. Astrov, V. G. Boldyrev, P. V. Vologodsky, and N. V. Tchaikovsky. The material published here includes the names of forty members of the conference and brief statements by each.

For additional material in *Krasnyi Arkhiv*, see "Ufa Conference and the Provisional Siberian Government," 61 (1933): 58–81. For references to additional material on events in Siberia during this period, see the notes to "The Disintegration of Kolchak's Campaign," 31 (1928): 51–80.

31 (1928): 204–213

Life in Ecclesiastical Circles before the Revolution (From the Letters of Archbishop Antony of Volhynia to Metropolitan Flavian of Kiev)

One hundred and nineteen letters are published here, dated from May 31, 1905, to June 6, 1915. Archbishop Antony condemns the nihilistic movement in the church in 1905, is indignant at the appointment, in 1911, of Varnava Nakropin as bishop of Kargopol on Gregory Rasputin's recommendation, complains about the impossibility of religious reforms in 1913 and 1914 while Rasputin's influence is great, and speaks of his own attempts to reëstablish the patriarchate.

For additional material in *Krasnyi Arkhiv* on the Russian Orthodox Church, see: "The Struggle of the Synod against the Revolution," 25 (1927): 198–201; "The Petersburg Clergy and the Ninth of January," 36 (1929): 192–199; "Princes of the Church," 39 (1930): 108–148 and 40 (1930): 97–124; "Church Fraud Disclosed at the Opening of the Relics of Pitirim Tambovsky," 71 (1935): 172–176; "The Church and the Reforms of 1861," 72 (1935): 182–190.

31 (1928): 214–219

MATERIALS RELATING TO THE HISTORY OF THE RELEASE OF N. G. CHERNYSHEVSKY. Introduction by P. Sadikov.

The first of the three documents published here is a letter from Count Paul P. Shuvalov, head of the "Holy Guards" (a society organized to protect Alexander III from terrorists), to Nicholas Y. Nikoladze, a publicist who had assumed the position of mediator between the Holy Guards and the Will of the People party. Dated February 18, 1883, the letter speaks of a plea for mitigation of Chernyshevsky's punishment, to be presented at the coronation ceremonies. Nikoladze's reply, dated February 20, 1883, expresses the hope that the Will of the People party will not molest Alexander III before the coronation. The third document is an anonymous, undated draft of an appeal for Chernyshevsky's release.

For additional material in *Krasnyi Arkhiv* on Chernyshevsky, see: "A Contribution to the Biographies of N. G. and O. S. Chernyshevsky," 3 (1923): 298–299; "N. G. Chernyshevsky as Reported by the Agents of the Third Department (1861–1862)," 14 (1926): 84–127; "A. N. Pipin's Plea on Behalf of N. G. Chernyshevsky," 22 (1927): 210–235; "A Solved Problem," 25 (1927): 135–181; "On the Death of N. G. Chernyshevsky," 26 (1928): 151–168; "N. G. Chernyshevsky," 29 (1928): i–xvi; "Unpublished Memoirs of L. Tikhomirov," 29 (1928): 139–174; "N. G. Chernyshevsky and the Third Department," 29 (1928): 175–190; "N. G. Chernyshevsky in Viliuisk," 74 (1936): 204–209; "N. G. Chernyshevsky's [Shorthand] Code," 76 (1936): 221–225; "Materials Relating to the History of N. G. Chernyshevsky's Exile," 78 (1936): 252–254; "New Materials concerning N. G. Chernyshevsky's Dissertation," 91 (1938): 275–281; "Note of N. G. Chernyshevsky concerning Liberation of the Peasants," 96 (1939): 172–179.

31 (1928): 219–222

THE ESCAPE OF SERGIUS DEGAEV. By S. Valk.

Sergius P. Degaev, member of the Will of the People party, was arrested in December, 1882, for operating a secret printing press in Odessa. In exchange for his freedom, he agreed to betray the party leaders to Colonel G. P. Sudeikin, chief of the St. Petersburg Secret Police. Valk relates details of the escape arranged by Sudeikin when Degaev was being transferred from Kiev to Odessa in January, 1883.

Degaev's confession of his treachery may be found in "Unpublished Memoirs of L. Tikhomirov," 29 (1928): 139–174. For references to additional material in *Krasnyi Arkhiv* on the Will of the People party, see the notes to "P. L. Antonov in the Petropavlovsk Fortress," 31 (1928): 103–117.

31 (1928): 223–224

MATERIALS RELATING TO THE HISTORY OF THE STRUGGLE WITH THE SOCIALIST MOVEMENT IN TSARIST RUSSIA. By N. Beliavsky.

Beliavsky's article deals with the immigration of German Social Democrats to Russian territory in 1878 and the ensuing alarm in official Russian circles. Both Baron Freitag von Loringafen, Russian consul in Danzig, and Adjutant General Count [P. E.] Kotzebue, governor general of Warsaw, urged the Russian Ministry of Foreign Affairs to take steps to stem the socialist influx, which was motivated by German Chancellor Prince Otto von Bismarck's suppression of the socialists after the Reichstag elections of 1878 and after two attempts on the life of William I.

For additional material in *Krasnyi Arkhiv*, see "Alexander III concerning 'Socialist Contamination,'" 34 (1929): 222–224.

31 (1928): 224–226

AN UNPUBLISHED LETTER OF A. I. HERZEN. Introduction by B. Kozmin.

Herzen's letter, written in London on February 8, 1863, to A. A. Cherkesov in Heidelberg, contains his views on the Polish situation and requests acknowledgment of the money he had previously sent Cherkesov and A. A. Serno-Solovevich. Cherkesov, a Russian attorney, had met Herzen in London in 1862, and subsequently took an active part in the activities of the Land and Freedom party.

For additional material in *Krasnyi Arkhiv* on Herzen, see: "A. I. Herzen and the Censorship of the 1890's," 3 (1923): 223–228; "Korff's Polemics

A Digest of the Krasnyi Arkhiv 9

against Herzen," 10 (1925): 308-317; "Tsarism in the Struggle with A. I. Herzen," 81 (1937): 207-227; "Herzen and Tsarist Censorship," 98 (1940): 240-262.

VOLUME 32, 1929

32 (1929): 3-87

DIARY OF THE MINISTRY OF FOREIGN AFFAIRS 1915-1916 (Conclusion)

This diary, thought to have been kept by Baron M. F. Schilling, chief of the office of the Ministry of Foreign Affairs, begins in 31 (1928): 3-50.

The concluding entries are dated from January 12, 1916, to September 27, 1916. They contain references to the following subjects: the Russo-Japanese alliance, Russian internal affairs, Sweden's desire to remain neutral in World War I, the Franco-British proposals to establish an independent Arab kingdom and to divide Turkey's possessions, Rumania's entry into the war, the German plan for a separate peace with Japan and Russia, the appointment of B. V. Stürmer as Russian minister of foreign affairs, the negotiations for fortification of the Åland Islands, German activities in Poland, the conditions for Greece's entry into the war, and Italian relations with the Allies.

For notes kept in the Ministry of Foreign Affairs in July, 1914, see "The Beginning of the War of 1914," 4 (1923): 5-62.

32 (1929): 88-124

THE FEBRUARY REVOLUTION IN THE BALTIC FLEET (From the Diary of I. I. Rengarten). Introduction by A. Drezen.

Rengarten was a senior captain, the leader of a group of ranking officers in the Baltic fleet, at the time he kept this diary. In addition to the entries dated from January 2/15, 1917, to March 14/27, 1917, there are minutes of five meetings of officers of the Baltic fleet. The diary provides an insight into the morale of the officers and into their attitudes toward ministerial changes, Rasputin's murder and burial at Tsarskoe Selo, the Imperial Family, and the announcement of a German submarine blockade. There is a detailed account of the rebelliousness among the sailors manifested by the detention and murder of some of their officers. Speculation over America's entry into the war and the reaction of the officers to the abdication of Nicholas II and to the establishment of the Provisional Government are also recorded. The minutes of the officers' meetings reveal an interest in the military situation at the front, the Armenian question, the importance of the Dardanelles to Russia, the postwar demilitarization of the Åland Islands, and the contemporary political situation; they also contain suggestions for combating disturbances in the fleet.

For additional material in *Krasnyi Arkhiv* on unrest in the fleet, see: "The Disturbances in the Fleet in 1915," 9 (1925): 94–103; "The October Revolution in the Baltic Fleet," 25 (1927): 34–95; "The Baltic Fleet on the Eve of October," 35 (1929): 5–36; "The Baltic Fleet in the July Days of 1917," 46 (1931): 69–109; "The Fleet after the October Victory," 53 (1932): 63–99.

32 (1929): 125–157

MATERIALS RELATING TO THE HISTORY OF THE FOREIGN POLICY OF WRANGEL'S GOVERNMENT (Economic Relations with France). Introduction by A. Gukovsky.

Gukovsky states that these documents are some of the very few available on the economic policies of the counterrevolutionary governments. A footnote to the introduction lists the Russian commercial representatives in various countries, including P. A. Morozov, head of the Russian Trade Committee in the United States.

The documents reprinted here trace the development of Baron P. N. Wrangel's economic policies:

1. A copy of Wrangel's instructions to Vladimir Ivanovich Savitsky, Russian trade representative in Paris, is dated December 18, 1918.

2. Savitsky's communiqué of June 3, 1920, is a résumé of the progress made in attempting to establish sound economic relations abroad since his appointment on December 17, 1918.

3. Savitsky's lengthy memorandum from Paris on June 3, 1920, reports on the following topics: French military provisions; the sale of American provisions proposed by Senator [Henry F.] Hollis in December, 1919; railroads and railroad materials; the seizure of the Russian commercial fleet; agricultural machinery; the grain trade; the exploitation of forests and forest products; Crimean tobacco, wine, and wool.

4. An unsigned telegram dated April 28, 1920, to the French General [Charles ?] Mangin requests a trade and technical adviser in Sevastopol.

5. A letter, dated July 7, 1920, from Count Francis de Cheville, French financier, to M. V. Bernatsky, Wrangel's finance minister, states the necessity for immediate establishment by Wrangel's government of trade relations abroad in order to satisfy foreign friends and the people in territories occupied by Wrangel's army.

6. A letter apparently written by Cheville from Paris, dated May 11,

1920, to A. V. Krivoshein, premier of Wrangel's government, reiterates his views on economic policy.

7. A telegram, dated May 20, 1920, from G. de Curzon, director of the French Ministry of Trade, Industry, Post Office, and Telegraph, speaks of the difficulties in attempting to establish commercial relations with General A. I. Denikin and Wrangel.

8. Savitsky's communiqué of July 26, 1920, reviews his negotiations with Cheville, in which he emphasized the necessity for trade with Western Europe and for the Russian-French trading company (the "Russo-French Society of Trade, Industry, and Transport") organized in Paris. The company's rules of organization are also published here.

For additional material in *Krasnyi Arkhiv* on Wrangel, see: "The Beginning of General Wrangel's Campaign," 21 (1927): 174–181; "The Agrarian Policy of General Wrangel," 26 (1928): 51–96; "Conditions in the Rear of the Armed Forces of South Russia," 34 (1929): 224–228; "Wrangeliana," 39 (1930): 3–46 and 40 (1930): 3–40; "The Collapse of Wrangel," 72 (1935): 3–43 and 73 (1935): 19–73.

32 (1929): 158–182

MOBILIZATION OF REACTION IN 1906. Introduction by the editors of *Krasnyi Arkhiv*.

The introduction is an analysis of Russian internal affairs in 1905 and 1906, with special emphasis on the problems confronting P. A. Stolypin when he replaced Goremykin as premier.

The confidential document published here is the "Circular of Premier P. A. Stolypin to Governor Generals, Governors, and Town Authorities, September 15, 1906." In it Stolypin outlines measures for removing the economic causes of peasant unrest and for securing the coöperation of landowners and clergymen in solving the peasant problem. Stolypin proposes political measures for combating revolutionary propaganda in the army, and, in addition, discusses the organization and activities of political trade unions, the activities of terrorists, student disturbances, the judicial system, prisons, and censorship of the press.

For additional material in *Krasnyi Arkhiv* on the Stolypin era, see: "The Correspondence between Nicholas Romanov and P. A. Stolypin," 5 (1924): 102–128; "I. Balashev's Letter to P. A. Stolypin," 9 (1925): 291–294; "From [I. V.] Shcheglovitov's Archives," 15 (1926): 104–107; "On the History of Stolypin's Agrarian Reforms," 17 (1926): 81–90; "P. A. Stolypin and Capital Punishment during 1908," 19 (1926): 215–221; "P. A. Stolypin's Correspondence with Nicholas Romanov," 30 (1928): 80–88; "P. A. Stolypin and the

French Press in 1911," 32 (1929): 209–211; "The Struggle with the Revolutionary Movement in the Caucasus in the Stolypin Era," 34 (1929): 184–221 and 35 (1929): 128–150; "Nicholas Romanov concerning the Assassination of P. A. Stolypin," 35 (1929): 209–211; "P. A. Stolypin and the Sveaborg Uprising," 49 (1931): 144–148.

32 (1929): 183–190

A. S. PUSHKIN'S POEM "THE MONK"

Part I of Pushkin's original manuscript of "The Monk" appears in 31 (1928): 160–201. The second and third parts are published here.

For references to additional material in *Krasnyi Arkhiv* on Pushkin, see the notes to "New Manuscripts and Materials on Pushkin," 31 (1928): 155–159.

32 (1929): 191–208

I. S. TURGENEV'S LETTERS TO P. V. ANNENKOV. Introduction by N. Belchikov.

Belchikov states that these letters of Turgenev to P. V. Annenkov were thought to have been destroyed, but were discovered in Simbirsk in 1921. There are seventeen letters, dated from April 24/May 6, 1880, to December 29, 1882/January 10, 1883. The eighteenth letter was probably written in 1875. In this correspondence Turgenev discusses the state of his health; the Pushkin celebration in May, 1880; the dismissal of D. A. Tolstoy as minister of public education; the approaching marriage of Madame [Michelle (Pauline)], Viardot's youngest daughter; Turgenev's short story "Otchaiannyi" ("Desperate") and other literary works; and his association with V. M. Garshin and A. I. Herzen. The letters dated from October, 1880, were written from France.

For additional material in *Krasnyi Arkhiv* on Turgenev, see: "I. S. Turgenev in Spasskoe-Lutovino," 100 (1940): 195–228; "From the Diary of V. P. Gaevsky," 100 (1940): 229–243.

FROM AN ARCHIVIST'S NOTEBOOK

32 (1929): 209–211

P. A. STOLYPIN AND THE FRENCH PRESS IN 1911. Introduction by F. Drabkina.

Drabkina outlines the conflict between the [Third] State Duma and State Council, on the one hand, and P. A. Stolypin, on the other, over Stolypin's attempt to reintroduce the zemstvo regulations of June 12, 1890, in six western provinces of Russia. The ensuing internal crisis was covered by the foreign press.

The documents presented here include a telegram from A. P. Izvolsky, Russian ambassador in Paris, to Acting Minister of Foreign Affairs A. A. Neratov, on March 14/27, 1911, requesting a detailed explanation of the crisis for release to the French press. On March 15/28, Neratov forwarded the request to Stolypin with a note, which Stolypin answered the same day. The last document is a copy of Stolypin's telegram to Izvolsky.

For references to additional material in *Krasnyi Arkhiv* on Stolypin, see the notes to "Mobilization of Reaction in 1906," 32 (1929): 158–182.

32 (1929): 211–216

RUSSIAN METAL INDUSTRY AND INTERNATIONAL TRUSTS. By V. Semennikov.

Semennikov's article is a commentary on two letters to Premier P. A. Stolypin from a person identified only as "N. V." These letters, dated Brussels, March 6 and April 10, 1908, inform Stolypin of plans for an international steel trust in which Russia was to be the center of operations. In addition to publishing the letters, Semennikov comments on the political implications of syndicates and trusts.

32 (1929): 216–232

MATERIALS RELATING TO THE HISTORY OF THE STRUGGLE WITH THE REVOLUTION OF 1905. By G. Vereshchagin.

The source for Vereshchagin's article is the journal of "The Special Conference on the Revision of the Standing Government Orders and Exceptional Measures for the Okhrana" (the Ignatiev Commission), which functioned from May 5, 1905, to the beginning of June, 1905, after which work was suspended until January 17, 1906. Statistics on the revolutionary movement from 1894 to 1903 are taken from those compiled by Minister of Justice N. V. Muraviëv. Vereshchagin also quotes, in whole or in part, the following materials: (1) a letter of April 7, 1905, from Count Alexis Pavlovich Ignatiev to Nicholas Nikolaevich Sukhotin, governor general of Siberia, requesting information on internal security in Siberia; (2) Sukhotin's reply, with proposals for relieving agitation; (3) statistics compiled by Sukhotin on the growth of the revolutionary movement and of the revolutionary temperament in various strata of Russian society.

For references to additional material in *Krasnyi Arkhiv* on the Revolution of 1905, see the notes to "S. Y. Witte's Struggle with the Agrarian Revolution," 31 (1928): 81–102.

32 (1929): 232–238

Parodies on the Tsarist Manifestoes of 1856 and 1857. Introduction by B. Kozmin.

The first of the three documents presented here is a copy of a parody on the Manifesto of 1856 announcing the Peace of Paris. The second is a parody on the Manifesto of 1857 announcing the birth of Alexander II's son Sergius. The last document is P. V. Zavadsky's account of the organization, activities, and dissolution of a literary society in Kharkov responsible for the parodies.

VOLUME 33, 1929

33 (1929): 3–33

The Czechoslovakian Question and Tsarist Diplomacy 1914–1917. By A. Popov.

This article is based on documents in the Archive of the Revolution and Foreign Affairs in Moscow. Popov outlines Russo-Czechoslovakian relations at the time Czechoslovakia was endeavoring to secure its independence from Austria-Hungary. He reviews internal affairs in Czechoslovakia, the temperament of society, and the specific aims of each of the political parties. Tomáš Masaryk's role in these events is emphasized. Russian plans for the creation of a Czech state after the war and for the organization of the Czechoslovakian prisoners in Russia into a Czech corps are revealed. Publication of Popov's article is concluded in 34 (1929): 3–38.

33 (1929): 34–81

The April Days of 1917 in Petrograd. Introduction by V. Rakhmetov.

Prosecutor V. N. Sereda was ordered by the government to investigate the demonstrations in Petrograd in April, 1917. Sereda's summary of the case and the testimony of eight eyewitnesses of the demonstrations are published here.

33 (1929): 82–144

Kolchak and Finland. Introduction by N. Nelidov.

In 1918–1919 the Russian counterrevolutionary governments attempted to establish a base in Finland from which they could regain control of Petrograd. The documents presented here include the dispatches of P. V. Vologodsky, Admiral A. V. Kolchak's premier; I. I. Sukin, of the Ministry of Foreign Affairs; V. A. Maklakov, ambassador to France; Uget, Russian chargé d'affaires in Washington; and others. These documents deal with Finland's demand for recognition of its independence in return for aid to General N. N. Yudenich, with German influence in Finland, and with Kolchak's negotiations with General C. G. Mannerheim and the Allies.

For references to additional material in *Krasnyi Arkhiv* on Kolchak's campaign, see the notes to "The Disintegration of Kolchak's Campaign," 31 (1928): 51–80.

33 (1929): 145–169

THE CONFERENCE OF GOVERNORS IN 1916. Introduction by the editors of *Krasnyi Arkhiv*.

B. V. Stürmer's report to Nicholas II on May 8, 1916, published here, summarizes the work of the conference of governors of the central provinces. The minutes of the conference's five meetings are also printed, as is a list of participating ministers and governors.

Two questions were raised during the initial meeting of the conference: (1) Can the government expect the support of the nobility in each province? and (2) What is the zemstvos' role, and what are they doing? At the second meeting the conference examined the general attitude of factory workers toward the revolutionary movement, labor-management relations in specific plants, the growth of coöperatives, the press, the treatment of prisoners of war, measures for improving the police force, and war-commerce committees. The minutes of the third meeting include discussions on refugees, land ownership, sanitation problems and the scarcity of doctors, the necessity for better administrative personnel and for more trust and coöperation between civil and military authorities in the provinces. The urban population, peasants, and schools were on the agenda of the fourth meeting. The intricacies of the relationship between the provinces and the government ministries and elections to the Fourth State Duma were considered at the final meeting.

33 (1929): 170–203

THE DIARY OF A. A. POLOVTSOV (1877–1878)

These excerpts from the diary which Polovtsov, senator and president of the Imperial Russian Historical Society, kept during the Russo-Turkish War are dated from April 8, 1877, to November 22, 1878. Polovtsov records his opinions of the Russian high command, internal affairs, court life, international intrigue, and friction within the government ministries. He comments on the relationship of Alexander II and Princess Catherine Dolgorukova and analyzes the characters of Grand Duke Nicholas, Grand Duke Constantine, Prince A. M. Gorchakov, N. P. Ignatiev, Prince A. B. Lobanov-Rostovsky, General M. D. Skobelev, and others.

For other sections of Polovstov's diary published in *Krasnyi Arkhiv*, see: 3 (1923): 75–172; 4 (1923): 63–128; 46 (1931): 110–132; 59 (1933): 82–109; 67 (1934): 168–186.

FROM AN ARCHIVIST'S NOTEBOOK

33 (1929): 204–211

THE *Socialist*, ORGAN OF THE SOUTHWESTERN GROUP OF THE WILL OF THE PEOPLE PARTY. Introduction by S. Valk.

Valk briefly outlines the history of the press activities of the Will of the People party in Moscow, Odessa, Kharkov, and Kiev. The *Socialist*, the party paper, was published in Kiev in 1884, and was edited by Makar Nikolaevich Vasilev.

The first issue of the *Socialist*, dated February 19, 1884, is reprinted here. It states that the paper is to be a weapon in the revolutionary struggle against the Russian government, and it includes excerpts from foreign newspapers as well as reviews of revolutionary literature.

For references to additional material in *Krasnyi Arkhiv* on the Will of the People party, see the notes to "P. L. Antonov in the Petropavlovsk Fortress," 31 (1928): 103–117.

33 (1929): 211–213

S. G. NECHAEV'S PROCLAMATION TO STUDENTS. Introduction by B. Kozmin.

Kozmin notes that although Nechaev's first proclamation to students was widely publicized in 1869, the second, probably issued in January, 1870, had not been published before its appearance in this issue of *Krasnyi Arkhiv*. Written after Nechaev's second flight from Russia, the proclamation urges Russian students to take an active part in revolutionary agitation.

For additional material in *Krasnyi Arkhiv* on Nechaev, see: "The Ceremony at the Public Execution of S. G. Nechaev," 1 (1922): 280–281; "Nechaev at the Alexeev Ravelin," 4 (1923): 222–272, 5 (1924): 172–212, and 6 (1924): 77–123; "The Unsuccessful Provocation," 14 (1926): 148–158; "New Material on S. Nechaev," 15 (1926): 150–163; "On the History of the Nechaev Movement," 22 (1927): 241–245; "S. G. Nechaev and the Tula

Arms Workers," 40 (1930): 184–189; "Materials Relating to the History of the Nechaev Trial," 43 (1930): 116–165.

33 (1929): 213–221

THE ISHUTINITES IN PRISON AND EXILE. By M. Klevensky.

Klevensky bases this article on documents concerning three of the most active participants in the revolutionary movement of the 1860's, D. M. Karakozov, N. A. Ishutin, and I. I. Khudiakov. Each of them was arrested following Karakozov's attempt on the life of Alexander II in St. Petersburg on April 4, 1866. Klevensky's article contains excerpts from one letter which Karakozov wrote to Alexander II from prison, one which Ishutin wrote as he reflected on the prospects of an early death, and two which Khudiakov wrote from Verkhoiansk. Also reprinted here is an account of the interrogation of Khudiakov when it was apparent that he was losing his mind in exile.

For additional material in *Krasnyi Arkhiv* on Karakozov, see: "Karakozov's Trial," 3 (1923): 299–301; "Karakozov's Attempt of April 4, 1866," 17 (1926): 91–137; "Karakozov's Attempt on Alexander II," 34 (1929): 232–237.

33 (1929): 222–235

NEW MATERIAL CONCERNING PUSHKIN'S DUEL AND DEATH (From the Correspondence of A. Y. Bulgakov and Prince P. A. Viazemsky). Introduction by M. Tsiavlovsky.

In the letters published here Alexander Y. Bulgakov writes from Moscow on February 3, 1837, to his daughter Princess Olga Dolgorukova in Baden-Baden, describing in detail A. S. Pushkin's insulting note to Baron George Heckeren D'Anthès, Countess Marie Grigorevna Razumovskaia's ball, and the duel between D'Anthès and Pushkin. Bulgakov had secured his information from I. S. Turgenev. Information on Nicholas I's role in the affair, public reaction to Pushkin's death, and speculations on the fate of D'Anthès are contained in the second letter, dated February 10, 1837. Other letters from Bulgakov to his daughter and to Prince Viazemsky describe the sorrow of Pushkin's father. Viazemsky's correspondence with Bulgakov and Princess Dolgorukova reflects public opinion, which censured Pushkin very little.

For references to additional material in *Krasnyi Arkhiv* on Pushkin, see the notes to "New Manuscripts and Materials on Pushkin," 31 (1928): 155–159.

VOLUME 34, 1929

34 (1929): 3–38

THE CZECHOSLOVAKIAN QUESTION AND TSARIST DIPLOMACY 1914–1917 (Conclusion). By A. Popov.

This article, based on documents in the Archive of the Revolution and Foreign Affairs in Moscow, begins in 33 (1929): 3–33.

Popov discusses here the following materials and topics: a draft of [J.?] Dürich's proposal for the creation of a Czech state with the Russian tsar as king; details of the negotiations between Dürich and M. Stefanik at the general headquarters of the Russian army in 1916; data on Tomáš Masaryk's Western orientation and on Russian attempts to counteract it; friction among Czech leaders; the attitude of the Provisional Government toward the Czechoslovakian question; and the organization of the Czechoslovakian army in France.

34 (1929): 39–94

THE UPRISING IN CENTRAL ASIA IN 1916. Introduction by P. Galuzo.

A. N. Kuropatkin had been appointed governor general of Turkestan and commander of the armed forces in July, 1916, in an effort to quiet disturbances in that country. Galuzo states in the introduction to the documents printed here that Kuropatkin's diary and his reports to Nicholas II give the first historical account of the Central Asian uprising. Excerpts taken from the diary and a report by Kuropatkin to Nicholas II appear in these pages.

The entries in Kuropatkin's diary, dated from July 23 to December 22, 1916, are detailed observations which he made on his tour of inspection in Turkestan. The uprising began in protest against the drafting of men for manual labor at the front. Kuropatkin wrote a secret report to Nicholas II from Tashkent in February, 1917, in which he outlined the causes of the uprising; the initiation of emergency measures; and the military, political, and administrative steps which should be taken to improve conditions in Turkestan. Other entries in the diary show evidence of the discord Rasputin was causing in government circles.

For additional material in *Krasnyi Arkhiv* on the unrest in Central Asia in 1916, see: "The Uprising of the Kirghiz in 1916," 16 (1926): 53–75; "From the Diary of A. N. Kuropatkin," 20 (1927): 56–77; "Bokhara during 1917," 20 (1927): 78–122; "From the History of the Provisional Government's Policy toward National Minorities," 30 (1928): 46–79; "Dzhizak Uprising of 1916," 60 (1933): 60–91; "A Governor in the Role of Propagator of the Koran," 75 (1936): 188–191.

34 (1929): 95–125

THE STRUGGLE WITH STRIKES ON THE EVE OF THE WORLD WAR. Introduction by K. Sidorov.

Published here is the secret report of S. Timashev, minister of trade and industry, to the Council of Ministers, dated July 9, 1914. It summarizes the meetings of a special conference of interdepartmental representatives held on April 24 and May 1, 8, 22, and 29, 1914, to recommend methods of curbing strikes. The conference discussed the possibility of using more repressive measures against strikers, the revision of the 1886 law for hiring and firing laborers, and the establishment of mediation committees similar to those in England.

For additional material in *Krasnyi Arkhiv* on the labor movement, see: "A Summary of the Lessons of 1905 Drawn up by the Police Department," 18 (1926): 219–227; "Tsarism in the Struggle with the Labor Movement in the Years of Its Ascent," 74 (1936): 37–65; "The Rise of the Labor Movement before the First Imperialistic War," 82 (1937): 136–163; "July Strikes and Demonstrations of 1914," 95 (1939): 137–155.

34 (1929): 126–165

MATERIALS RELATING TO THE HISTORY OF INTERVENTION IN SIBERIA. Introduction by V. M.

These documents, dated from November 24/December 7, 1917, to January 27/February 9, 1918, throw light on the political struggle in Irkutsk and Tomsk. They are the reports of the following three French agents in Siberia: a certain Gendreau, a commercial agent; Henri Bourgeois, consul general; and Colonel [G.?] Pichon, military attaché. Their reports describe the civil war in Irkutsk, the Allies in Siberia, and the offensive of Ataman (Hetman) Gregory Semënov.

For references to additional material in *Krasnyi Arkhiv* on events in Siberia, see the notes to "The Disintegration of Kolchak's Campaign," 31 (1928): 51–80.

For additional material in *Krasnyi Arkhiv* on Semënov, see: "Wrangeliana," 40 (1930): 3–40; "Materials Relating to the History of the Semënovites in 1919," 67(1934): 131–146.

34 (1929): 166–183

MATERIALS RELATING TO THE HISTORY OF THE RISE OF THE WORLD WAR (Triple Entente and Germany after Agadir). Introduction by E. Adamov.

These documents consist of seven secret reports to the Russian General Staff from military attachés G. I. Nostits in France, N. S. Ermolov in England, and P. A. Bazarov in Germany. Nostits dispatched three reports to Y. G. Zhilinsky, chief of the Russian General Staff, on January 4/17, 1912, concerning the close coöperation between the French and Russian general staffs, the signing of protocols between the two countries, and the prospects of war with Germany.

In a dispatch from London, dated January 4/17, 1912, Ermolov informed Zhilinsky that the French anticipated an early war with Germany and that the declaration of an early war would be advantageous to Germany. On January 19/February 1, 1912, Nostits sent French General Joseph Joffre's analysis of the European situation and an outline of Russia's part in the early period of a war to Zhilinsky. Bazarov's report describes public opinion in Germany after the Agadir crisis. The last dispatch from Nostits, March 29/April 11, 1912, summarizes his conference with Joffre on Franco-German relations.

The first six documents appear in translation in the *Berliner Monatshefte*, VII (1929): 931–941.

34 (1929): 184–221

THE STRUGGLE WITH THE REVOLUTIONARY MOVEMENT IN THE CAUCASUS IN THE STOLYPIN ERA (From the Correspondence of P. A. Stolypin with Count I. I. Vorontsov-Dashkov). Introduction by S. Fuks.

Two documents are published here. The first is Premier P. A. Stolypin's letter of April 11, 1908, to Count I. I. Vorontsov-Dashkov, viceroy of the Caucasus, and the second is the viceroy's answer of July 23, 1908.

Both letters review in detail tsarist policies in the Caucasus. Stolypin outlines the extent of unrest in various regions of the Caucasus, quoting statistics on robbery and assault, and blames the widespread disturbances on the local authorities, who are not adhering to general government policies. In reply, Vorontsov-Dashkov refutes Stolypin's statistics, denies the accusations, surveys his activities as viceroy from 1905 to 1907, reports on the activities of the Armenian party, and recommends improvement of the police force in the Caucasus.

Publication of the viceroy's letter is concluded in 35 (1929): 128–150.

A Digest of the Krasnyi Arkhiv 21

For references to additional material in *Krasnyi Arkhiv* on Stolypin, see the notes to "Mobilization of Reaction in 1906," 32 (1929): 158–182.

FROM AN ARCHIVIST'S NOTEBOOK

34 (1929): 222–224

ALEXANDER III CONCERNING "SOCIALIST CONTAMINATION"

The rapid growth of the German Social Democratic party in the 1890's prompted Count Paul A. Shuvalov, Russian ambassador in Berlin, to send a special report to Minister of Foreign Affairs N. K. de Giers on November 18/30, 1893. The report, with Alexander III's marginal comments, is published in its entirety here. Alexander III wanted to "safeguard the village population from infection by socialist propaganda."

For additional material in *Krasnyi Arkhiv*, see "Materials Relating to the History of the Struggle with the Socialist Movement in Tsarist Russia," 31 (1928): 223–224.

34 (1929): 224–228

CONDITIONS IN THE REAR OF "THE ARMED FORCES OF SOUTH RUSSIA." Introduction by A. Gukovsky.

The document presented here provides information on the economic situation in the Crimea when it served as headquarters for General P. N. Wrangel's counterrevolutionary operations. L. A. Lipping, a person obviously in close contact with Wrangel's government, wrote a report on certain measures necessary for establishing order in the territory then occupied by the armed forces of South Russia. The report, dated Sevastopol, April 20, 1920, outlines a program for solving land, currency, trade, and production problems by expanding Crimean imports, reorganizing police and administrative offices, acquiring foreign capital, and dispatching a special mission to Germany.

For references to additional material in *Krasnyi Arkhiv* on Wrangel, see the notes to "Materials Relating to the History of the Foreign Policy of Wrangel's Government," 32 (1929): 125–157.

34 (1929): 228–230

A PARODY IN VERSE ON THE ACCUSATORY SPEECH OF ZHELIKHOVSKY AT THE TRIAL OF THE 193. Introduction by S. Valk.

One hundred and ninety-three members of the *Khozhdenie v Narod* ("To the People") movement were brought to trial in 1877 and 1878 for attempting to undermine the monarchy and establish a republic. This parody on Prosecutor Zhelikhovsky's speech was written in 1877 and distributed in pamphlet form by the Will of the People party in 1883.

For additional material in *Krasnyi Arkhiv* on the trial, see: "Letters Written by the Defendants in the Trial of the 193," 5 (1924): 129–163; "A Reverberation of the Trial of the 193," 27 (1928): 233–234; "The Finale of the Trial of the 193," 30 (1928): 184–199.

34 (1929): 231–232

PRINCE P. V. DOLGORUKOV AND M. K. ELPIDIN. Introduction by B. Kozmin.

Published here is a letter which Prince Peter V. Dolgorukov wrote his son Vladimir on November 4/16, 1866, in which he states that he had loaned money to M. K. Elpidin, a Russian emigrant in Geneva, who had used the loan to establish a secret printing press for revolutionary propaganda. Elpidin had escaped from Russia in 1865, after receiving a prison sentence for participation in peasant conspiracies in Kazan province two years earlier. Dolgorukov also informed his son that he had filed a complaint with Geneva authorities.

34 (1929): 232–237

KARAKOZOV'S ATTEMPT ON ALEXANDER II (From the Diary of a Contemporary)

These excerpts from the diary of G. Potulov, a resident of St. Petersburg, record the attitude of society toward D. M. Karakozov's attempt on Alexander II's life in the Summer Garden on April 4, 1866. Potulov writes of the investigation, the questioning of Karakozov, and the general surprise that a Russian, not a Pole, had attempted to assassinate the emperor.

For references to additional material in *Krasnyi Arkhiv* on Karakozov, see the notes to "The Ishutinites in Prison and Exile," 33 (1929): 213–221.

VOLUME 35, 1929

35 (1929): 3–4

V. M. FRICHE

A full-page picture of V. M. Friche (1870–1929) precedes the obituary of this author, teacher, and literary scholar, who served as an editor of *Krasnyi Arkhiv* from 1922 until his death.

35 (1929): 5–36

THE BALTIC FLEET ON THE EVE OF OCTOBER (From the Diary of I. I. Rengarten). Introduction by A. Drezen.

These excerpts from Captain Rengarten's diary are dated August 6 to September 26, 1917. Rengarten records the pessimistic attitude of the officers in his group, the receipt of inadequate information from the front, and the confusion over General L. G. Kornilov's offensive. There are also accounts of officers' meetings which were called in an attempt to unite the Baltic fleet.

For references to additional material in *Krasnyi Arkhiv* on unrest in the Baltic, see the notes to "The February Revolution in the Baltic Fleet," 32 (1929): 88–124.

35 (1929): 37–106

THE PROVISIONAL GOVERNMENT OF AUTONOMOUS SIBERIA. Introduction by V. Maksakov.

The documents presented here highlight the foreign relations of the Provisional Government of Autonomous Siberia. They include the following materials: letters and telegrams from the Provisional Government's representatives in Japan, China, and the United States concerning reactions abroad to events in Siberia; detailed accounts of the activities of foreigners in Russia, particularly after the Czechoslovakian occupation of Vladivostok on June 29, 1918; and minutes of cabinet meetings which reflect the foreign policy of the Provisional Government. There is also information on General D. Khorvat's attempt to overthrow the Provisional Government and an analysis of the political situation in Japan in the light of its effect upon the establishment of economic and commercial relations between Japan and Siberia.

The minutes of the Council on Foreign Affairs of the Provisional Government, which met on July 23, 27, and 29 and on August 4, 1918, record decisions regarding internal affairs, the desirability of acquiring American technical and financial assistance, and relations with Czechoslovakia and the Allies. The council's secretary, D. F. Orzheshko, reports on his conference with the American consul.

Publication of these documents is continued in 36 (1929): 31–60.

For references to additional material in *Krasnyi Arkhiv* on events in Siberia, see the notes to "The Disintegration of Kolchak's Campaign," 31 (1928): 51–80.

35 (1929): 107–127

MATERIALS RELATING TO THE HISTORY OF THE TSARIST NATIONAL MINORITY POLICY. Introduction by A. Arsharuni.

The introduction notes that in 1910 Premier P. A. Stolypin called a "special conference to work out measures for counteracting Tartar-Moslem influence in the Volga region." The first half of the proceedings of the conference, published here, traces the development of the Moslem movement, its spread to Russia, and its effect on the non-Russian population of European Russia, Siberia, the Steppes, and Central Asia. The conference decided that the activities of the Pan-Islamic and Pan-Turkish agitators must be curbed, for the outcome of a cultural struggle with more than 18 million Mohammedans would be difficult to predict.

Publication of these documents is concluded in 36 (1929): 61–83.

For additional material in *Krasnyi Arkhiv* on minority unrest, see: "The Uprising of the Kirghiz in 1916," 16 (1926): 53–75; "From Drafts of Notes by K. P. Pobedonostsev," 18 (1926): 203–207; "From the Diary of A. N. Kuropatkin," 20 (1927): 56–77; "From the History of the Provisional Government's Policy toward National Minorities," 30 (1928): 46–79; "The Uprising of 1916 in Central Asia," 34 (1929): 39–94; "The Church and the Buriat-Mongol Russification in Tsarist Russia," 53 (1932): 100–126; "Dzhizak Uprising of 1916," 60 (1933): 60–91; "A Governor in the Role of Propagator of the Koran," 75 (1936): 188–191.

35 (1929): 128–150

THE STRUGGLE WITH THE REVOLUTIONARY MOVEMENT IN THE CAUCASUS IN THE STOLYPIN ERA (From the Correspondence of P. A. Stolypin with Count I. I. Vorontsov-Dashkov) (Conclusion)

Publication of this correspondence between Premier P. A. Stolypin and Count I. I. Vorontsov-Dashkov, viceroy of the Caucasus, begins in 34 (1929): 184–221.

Count Vorontsov-Dashkov concludes his letter to Stolypin with a request for prison reforms in the Caucasus and for additional civil officials. Three Police Department memoranda of August, 1908, are also printed here; they report on the activities of the Armenian population in the Caucasus and on conditions in Daghestan.

For additional material in *Krasnyi Arkhiv* on Armenian nationalism and unrest in the Caucasus, see: "Letters by I. I. Vorontsov-Dashkov to Nicholas Romanov (1905–1915)," 26 (1928): 97–126; "New Data concerning Lado Ketskhoveli's Murder," 91 (1938): 271–275; "The Railroad Workers' Strike in the Tiflis Workshops (1900)," 94 (1939): 32–63; "The Peasant Movement in Western Transcaucasia 1902-1905," 99 (1940): 90-126; "Agitation of Peasants on the Estates in Georgia Belonging to the Imperial Family 1905-1906," 106 (1941): 40-57.

35 (1929): 151-175

"THE ALLIANCE OF OCTOBER 17" IN 1906. Introduction by V. Astrov.

The "Alliance of October 17" (the Octobrist party), represented commercial and industrial interests and the landowners. The documents given here are the proceedings of the Joint Conference of the St. Petersburg-Moscow central committees of the Octobrist party held in Moscow on January 8-9, 1906, under the chairmanship of D. N. Shipov. The principal point discussed was Premier S. Y. Witte's statement to the press that the Manifesto of October 17, 1905, had in no way altered the fundamental structure of the government, and that the emperor, therefore, remained the absolute ruler. The Octobrists had assumed that the manifesto instituted a constitutional monarchy. The conference, accordingly, considered the party's relationship to the government and to other parties having similar programs. An agenda for an Octobrist congress was planned.

Publication of these documents is concluded in 36 (1929): 84-121.

35 (1929): 176-208

THE UPRISING IN BEZDNA. Introduction by M. Nechkina.

The nineteen reports, telegrams, and letters published here concern the uprising in the village of Bezdna, Kazan province, on April 12, 1861. The peasant unrest was caused by Anton Petrov's misinterpretation of the Emancipation Manifesto. Major General Count A. S. Apraksin, sent to suppress the disturbances, gave an account to Alexander II on April 15 and 19, 1861, of the trial and execution of the young peasant Petrov. A copy of the military court's verdict in the case is also printed here. Additional reports, telegrams, and letters from government officials describe conditions in other sections of Kazan province. The final document is the report of a certain Untilov, state prosecutor in Kazan, on all peasant disturbances after the publication of the Emancipation Manifesto.

For additional material in *Krasnyi Arkhiv* on conditions at Bezdna, see: "The Funeral Oration of A. P. Shchapov over the Peasants Killed at Bezdna," 4 (1923): 407-410; "The Year 1861, from Notes of a Contemporary," 16 (1926): 118-164; "The Demonstration at the Funeral of the Peasants Killed at Bezdna, Kazan Province, in 1861," 17 (1926): 181-185; "A. P. Shchapov's Letter to Alexander II in 1861," 19 (1926): 150-165; "The Bezdna Uprising of 1861," 36 (1929): 180-191.

FROM AN ARCHIVIST'S NOTEBOOK

35 (1929): 209–211

NICHOLAS ROMANOV CONCERNING THE ASSASSINATION OF P. A. STOLYPIN. Introduction by A. Sergeev.

Stolypin was assassinated by Dmitry G. Bogrov on September 1/14, 1911, in a Kiev theater. In a letter to his mother, printed here, Nicholas II describes the assassination as he and his two daughters witnessed it. In a second letter, dated September 11/24, 1911, he discusses the considerations involved in selecting Stolypin's successor.

For references to additional material in *Krasnyi Arkhiv* on Stolypin, see the notes to "Mobilization of Reaction in 1906," 32 (1929): 158–182.

35 (1929): 212–215

THE TACTICS OF THE HIGH COMMAND IN THE FEBRUARY REVOLUTION. Introduction by S. Rabinovich.

In the letters given here General A. Lukomsky, quartermaster general, writes General A. M. Kaledin, commander of the Eighth Army, on March 20, 1917, explaining the necessity for the Provisional Government's decrees on soldiers' privileges. The decrees had been issued, over officers' protests, in an effort to win the confidence of the troops.

For additional material in *Krasnyi Arkhiv* on the Russian army, see: "General Alexeev and the Provisional Committee of the State Duma," 2 (1922): 284–286; "The Supreme Command during the First Days of the Revolution," 5 (1924): 213–240; "The Dismissal of N. N. Romanov as Commander-in-Chief," 10 (1925): 342–343; "The Revolution of February, 1917," 21 (1927): 3–78 and 22 (1927): 3–70.

35 (1929): 215–235

L. N. TOLSTOY UNDER THE BLOWS OF THE CENSOR. By N. Apostolov.

Apostolov briefly surveys the censorship imposed upon Tolstoy's works, beginning with *Childhood*, published in 1852.

For additional material in *Krasnyi Arkhiv* on Tolstoy, see: "L. N. Tolstoy and the Censorship," 1 (1922): 412–416; "Alexander III on Leo Tolstoy," 1 (1922): 417; "Documents Relating to L. N. Tolstoy," 4 (1923): 338–364; "Three Letters from L. N. Tolstoy to the Decembrist P. N. Svistunov," 6 (1924): 235–242; "L. N. Tolstoy and the Relief of Famine Victims," 6 (1924): 243–252; "Unpublished Letters of L. N. Tolstoy to V. A. and K. A. Islavin Rachinsky and Others," 7 (1924): 250–252; "The

A Digest of the Krasnyi Arkhiv 27

Attempt of Nicholas II to Censor Tolstoy's Works," 15 (1926): 230–234; "L. N. Tolstoy and N. M. Romanov," 21 (1927): 231–241; "The Research of L. N. Tolstoy at the Archives of the Ministry of Justice," 22 (1927): 245–250; "New Materials concerning L. N. Tolstoy," 36 (1929): 199–201; "Materials Relating to L. N. Tolstoy's Biography (1901–1902)," 63 (1934): 126–130; "Moscow Students and L. N. Tolstoy's Death," 73 (1935): 209–220; "Materials Relating to the Pre-Revolutionary Past of Moscow," 84 (1937): 199–260; "Materials Relating to L. N. Tolstoy's Biography," 96 (1939): 221–225; "A Short Review of Documents Published in Krasnyi Arkhiv," 100 (1940): 9–35.

VOLUME 36, 1929

36 (1929): 3–30

FROM THE CORRESPONDENCE OF V. A. MAKLAKOV WITH THE NATIONAL CENTER IN 1919. Introduction by M. Pokrovsky.

Presented here is a letter of April 19/May 2, 1919, from V. A. Maklakov, Provisional Government ambassador to Paris, to the Cadet (Constitutional Democratic party) National Center in Ekaterinodar, requesting information on affairs in Russia. In this letter Maklakov comments on the financial condition of the Allies, describes French, British, and American attitudes toward the civil war in Russia, and speculates on the postwar alignment of powers, particularly on Russo-German relations. He concludes with a dissertation on capitalism, socialism, and the future of Russia. On May 23/June 5, 1919, the Cadet National Center in Ekaterinodar sent Maklakov information, also given here, on the special emphasis in Ekaterinodar on Slav politics and data on French political aid and British material aid to the counterrevolutionary governments.

For additional material in Krasnyi Arkhiv, see: "Foreign Policy of the Counterrevolutionary Governments at the Beginning of 1919," 37 (1929): 69–101; "The Cadets in 1905–1906," 46 (1931): 38–68 and 47–48 (1931): 112–139; "The Cadets in the Days of the Galician Devastation of 1915," 59 (1933): 110–144; "Materials Relating to the History of Intervention in the North," 98 (1940): 125–144.

36 (1929): 31–60

THE PROVISIONAL GOVERNMENT OF AUTONOMOUS SIBERIA (Conclusion)

Publication of the documents dealing with the foreign relations of the Provisional Government of Autonomous Siberia begins in 35 (1929): 37–106. The reports of the Ministry of Foreign Affairs printed here are dated

August and September, 1918. V. A. Fëdorov, of the Ministry of Foreign Affairs, gives an account of his conferences with Dr. Girsa, of the Czechoslovakian National Council, on means of transmitting information to the United States, and with Japanese representatives on relations between Japan and the Provisional Government. Other reports provide information on the British expeditionary forces, on Ataman (Hetman) Kalmykov's plundering in the Maritime region, and on conferences with Sir Charles Eliot of Great Britian, Count de Martel of France, and [Tsuneo] Matsudaira of Japan.

For references to additional material in *Krasnyi Arkhiv*, see the notes to "The Disintegration of Kolchak's Campaign," 31 (1928): 51–80.

36 (1929): 61–83

MATERIALS RELATING TO THE HISTORY OF THE TSARIST NATIONAL MINORITY POLICY (Conclusion)

Publication of the proceedings of the "special conference to work out measures for counteracting Tartar-Moslem influence in the Volga region," called by Premier P. A. Stolypin in 1910, begins in 35 (1929): 107–127.

The conference considered cultural and educational methods of stemming the Islamic tide and turning non-Russian peoples toward Russian culture. In the second half of the proceedings, published here, the conference proposes the reorganization of Moslem schools, improvement in the quality of teachers, and stricter supervision in schools. It also urges local government officials to acquire a better understanding of the interests and needs of the foreign population. Administrative recommendations include the initiation of systematic government surveillance over all aspects of Moslem life and the coördination of the activities of the central and local government organs. The conference proceedings conclude with thirty-four specific recommendations.

36 (1929): 84–121

"THE ALLIANCE OF OCTOBER 17" IN 1906 (Conclusion)

Publication of the stenographic record of the meeting of the members of the St. Petersburg group of the Octobrist party on January 29, 1906, begins in 35 (1929): 151–175.

This record provides information on the following subjects: conditions in Russia; the party's insistence on the fulfillment of the terms of the Manifesto of October 17, 1905, as a means of preserving a unified Russia; the party's organizational problems; and criticisms of those of S. Y. Witte's policies which contradicted the manifesto.

36 (1929): 122–179

MATERIALS RELATING TO THE HISTORY OF THE TRIAL OF THE TWENTY-ONE (Letters and Testimony of P. F. Yakubovich). Introduction by S. Valk.

The introduction contains a history of the Will of the People party and a biography of P. F. Yakubovich, poet and revolutionary. Yakubovich's sixteen letters, dated from February to November, 1884, are given here; they are a source of firsthand information on the organization and policies of the Will of the People party. The letters were written to party members M. P. Ovchinnikov, M. P. Shebalin, M. N. Vasilev, N. M. Salova, L. A. Tikhomirov, and I. I. Popov.

Publication of these documents is continued in 37 (1929): 102–137 and 38 (1930): 70–108.

For additional material in *Krasnyi Arkhiv*, see "Two Letters of P. F. Yakubovich," 5 (1924): 258–262; "The *Socialist*, Organ of the Southwestern Group of the Will of the People Party," 33 (1929): 204–211.

36 (1929): 180–191

THE BEZDNA UPRISING OF 1861

This article, which gives the testimony of Bezdna peasants concerning Anton Petrov's interpretation of the Emancipation Manifesto, adds human-interest details to the documents published in 35 (1929): 176–208. Petrov's testimony is also published here.

For references to additional material in *Krasnyi Arkhiv* on the Bezdna uprising, see the notes to "'The Uprising in Bezdna," 35 (1929): 176–208.

FROM AN ARCHIVIST'S NOTEBOOK

36 (1929): 192–199

THE PETERSBURG CLERGY AND THE NINTH OF JANUARY. Introduction by A. Shilov.

On January 9, 1905, a group of workers marched to the tsar's palace to present a petition for civil rights. Many of them were killed when soldiers opened fire. The "Society for Diffusion of Religious and Moral Education in the Spirit of the Orthodox Church," composed of St. Petersburg clergymen, held four conferences after the "Bloody Sunday" tragedy of January 9, in which they discussed the events themselves and the background of Father Gapon, leader of the demonstration before the tsar's palace. The conference recommendations that are published here urge improvement of religious education among the working classes and the construction of churches in the larger industrial areas.

For references to additional material in *Krasnyi Arkhiv* on the church, see the notes to "Life in Ecclesiastical Circles before the Revolution," 31 (1928): 204–213.

For additional material in *Krasnyi Arkhiv* on the events of January 9, 1905, see: "The Notes of A. S. Ermolov," 8 (1925): 49–69; "Gapon's Letter," 9 (1925): 294–297; "January 9, 1905," 11–12 (1925): 1–26; "The Draft of a Manifesto concerning the Events of January 9, 1905," 11–12 (1925): 26–38; "Documents on the History of January 9, 1905," 11–12 (1925): 444–448; "January 9 in St. Petersburg," 38 (1930): 3–19; "Bloody Sunday in St. Petersburg," 39 (1930): 177–185; "From the Diary of Grand Duke Constantine Romanov," 43 (1930): 92–115; "Materials Relating to the History of Bloody Sunday in Petersburg," 68 (1935): 39–64.

36 (1929): 199–201

NEW MATERIALS CONCERNING L. N. TOLSTOY. By N. Belchikov.

Three letters of Tolstoy's are printed here. In one, to P. M. Daragan, governor of Tula province, dated April 23, 1864, Tolstoy complains of recent thefts of cattle and fruit trees from his estate. Two others to Alexander II pertain to Dmitry N. Tolstoy's debt to Major F. N. Dokhturov.

For references to additional material in *Krasnyi Arkhiv* on Tolstoy, see the notes to "L. N. Tolstoy under the Blows of the Censor," 35 (1929): 215–235.

36 (1929): 201–204

MATERIALS RELATING TO THE HISTORY OF THE PEASANT UPRISING AGAINST LIBERATION IN 1861. Introduction by M. Nechkina.

Nechkina points out that peasant reaction to the Emancipation Manifesto was strongest in Penza province, where the uprising in Kandeevka was similar to that in Bezdna. In a letter to the police inspector, reproduced here, the village priest of Polrovskoe describes the uprising in that village on April 5, 1861.

For references to additional material in *Krasnyi Arkhiv* on peasant unrest in 1861, see the notes to "The Uprising in Bezdna," 35 (1929): 176–208. See also: "The Church and the Reforms of 1861," 72 (1935): 182–190; "The Reform of 1861 and the Peasant Movement," 75 (1936): 62–82; "Kandeevka Uprising in 1861," 92 (1939): 91–132.

36 (1929): 204–218

THE ECHOES OF THE DECEMBRIST UPRISING. Introduction by B. Syroechekovsky.

These pages contain letters of relatives and friends of the Decembrists dated from January through March, 1826, and provide little-known biographical material on participants in the Decembrist Revolution of 1825.

Krasnyi Arkhiv, Volume 13 (1925), is devoted exclusively to the publication of new material on the Decembrists.

VOLUME 37, 1929

37 (1929): 3–68

TSARIST RUSSIA AND MONGOLIA 1913–1914. Introduction by A. Popov.

The documents presented here are from the files of the Russian Ministry of Foreign Affairs and trace Russia's relations with China and Mongolia in 1913 and 1914. They consist of telegrams, notes, and dispatches exchanged between the Ministry and Russian ambassadors abroad and between the Ministry and the Chinese government.

A complete English translation of this material appears in the *Chinese Social and Political Science Review*, Peiping, XVI, 4 (January, 1933): 652–688 and XVII, 1 (April, 1933): 170–205.

37 (1929): 69–101

FOREIGN POLICY OF THE COUNTERREVOLUTIONARY GOVERNMENTS AT THE BEGINNING OF 1919 (From the Documents of the Paris Legation). Introduction by I. Mints.

These documents are telegraphic dispatches received and sent by the Russian legation in Paris in January, February, and March, 1919. Paris was the receiving center for reports from all Civil War fronts and served as a connecting link between Omsk, Ekaterinodar, Archangel, and other counterrevolutionary posts. The documents deal, for the most part, with the following matters: the British policy toward national minorities in the Caucasus; the proposal for a conference of Allied, Soviet, and counterrevolutionary representatives on the Princes Islands, the speeches of David Lloyd George and Winston Churchill on the Russian Revolution of 1917; the Finnish demands for independence; the necessity for Allied troops in the Don area; the advisability of establishing credit in Paris and London and of opening accounts in the Shanghai banks; the withdrawal of Canadian forces from Siberia; Russia's role in the peace conference; the advisability of establishing one central authority to coördinate the activities of each of the counterrevolutionary centers; the Bessarabian rebellion against Rumania; Japanese and American plans for setting up international control of the Chinese-Eastern Railroad; British activities in Persia; relations of the Omsk government with Japan.

For additional material in *Krasnyi Arkhiv* on the foreign policy of the counterrevolutionary governments, see: "French Intervention in South Russia (December, 1918, to April, 1919)," 19 (1926): 3–38; "The British in the North (1918–1919)," 19 (1926): 39–52; "The Regional Government of the Crimea during 1918–1919," 22 (1927): 92–152; "The Crimea during 1918–1919," 28 (1928): 142–181 and 29 (1928): 55–85; "The Disintegration of Kolchak's Campaign," 31 (1928): 51–80; "Kolchak and Finland," 33 (1929): 82–144; "Materials Relating to the History of French Intervention in Odessa," 45 (1931): 53–80; "Intervention and Northern Counterrevolution," 50–51 (1932): 97–116; "White Finns in the Service of Anglo-French Interventionists in 1919," 98 (1940): 31–67; "Materials Relating to the History of Intervention in the North," 98 (1940): 125–144; "Use by the Interventionists of the Northern Sea Route (1918–1919)," 104 (1941): 151–198.

37 (1929): 102–137

MATERIALS RELATING TO THE HISTORY OF THE TRIAL OF THE TWENTY-ONE (Letters and Testimony of P. F. Yakubovich) (Continued)

Publication of these documents begins in 36 (1929): 122–179.

The letters and transcripts of testimony published here contain much biographical data and trace the activities of the Will of the People party from 1882 to 1884. Yakubovich testified on November 30 and on December 1, 3, and 4, 1884, in conjunction with the Trial of the Twenty-one.

These documents are continued in 38 (1930): 70–108.

For references to additional material in *Krasnyi Arkhiv*, see the notes to "Materials Relating to the History of the Trial of the Twenty-one," 36 (1929): 122–179.

37 (1929): 138–174

COUNT A. K. BENCKENDORFF CONCERNING RUSSIA 1827–1830 (Yearly Reports of the Third Department and the Gendarmerie). Introduction by A. Sergeev.

Benckendorff's reports to Nicholas I were based on information in the files of the Secret Police (Third Department). Of the three given here, "A Short Review of Public Opinion in 1827" records the state of public opinion in court circles, high society, the middle class, the army, the clergy, and among serfs and government officials. Benckendorff also reports on public opinion in the Baltic provinces, in Finland, and in Poland, and concludes that justice and commerce are the keys to improving conditions.

"A Short Review of Public Opinion in 1828" traces the effects of the Russo-Turkish War on the country's attitude toward Nicholas I and describes internal political intrigue and foreign espionage. There is also a survey of public opinion in the provinces and in each stratum of Russian society.

The third document is an account of the organization and activities of the Gendarmerie from its reorganization in 1827 to January 1, 1829, with special mention of outstanding gendarmes.

Publication of these documents is concluded in 38 (1930): 109–147.

37 (1929): 175–214

FROM THE ARCHIVES OF A. P. CHEKHOV (Unpublished Letters and Documents). Introduction by N. Lapin.

The materials printed here include one letter from Chekhov to his father, twenty-six letters to his mother (1897–1904), four letters and three telegrams to his brother M. P. Chekhov, two letters to M. P. Chekhov's wife, six letters to V. M. Lavrov, eleven to V. M. Sobolevsky, one to M. A. Sablin, four to A. S. Suvorin, one to V. A. Tikhonov, and two letters and one telegram to N. E. Efros. There are also two letters and nine telegrams from P. A. Sergeenko to Chekhov, and four telegrams from A. S. Suvorin. This correspondence provides information on the sale of Chekhov's works to A. F. Marx; a copy of the agreement with Marx is published here.

For additional material in *Krasnyi Arkhiv* on Chekhov, see: "A. P. Chekhov's Unpublished Story *Should I Speak or Keep Silent?*" 8 (1925): 237–239; "The Police and A. P. Chekhov's Funeral," 71 (1935): 170–172; "A. P. Chekhov—Manuscripts, Letters, Materials," 97 (1939): 177–182.

FROM AN ARCHIVIST'S NOTEBOOK

37 (1929): 215–219

ORDER NUMBER TWO. Introduction by F. Drabkina.

Drabkina writes that Order Number One of the Executive Committee of the Petrograd Soviet of Workers' and Soldiers' Deputies, issued March 1, 1917, was designed to transfer control of the army from the officers to soldiers' and sailors' committees in each military unit. On March 5, 1917, the Petrograd Soviet issued Order Number Two, a modification of Order Number One, which, however, was not widely distributed. It is printed here.

37 (1929): 219–230

SECOND ISSUE OF THE WORKERS' LEAFLET *Zerno*. Introduction by A. Shilov.

Zerno ("Grain"), a leaflet published in 1880–1881 by the "Black Partition Group" (*Chërnoperedeltsy*), appeared in six issues. Five issues were printed in the second volume of A. I. Nevsky's *Istoriko-Revoliutsionnyi Sbornik* ("Historical-Revolutionary Collection") in 1924. A mimeographed copy of the missing second issue was found later. Reprinted here, this issue explains "the new western socialist movement."

37 (1929): 230–237

MATERIALS RELATING TO THE BIOGRAPHY OF A. A. KRASOVSKY. Introduction by M. Klevensky.

The introduction is a biography of Lieutenant Colonel A. A. Krasovsky (*c.* 1822–1868), who was exiled to Siberia in 1862 for urging soldiers not to fire on the peasants in a Kiev province disturbance. Krasovsky committed suicide late in May, 1868, when he lost his way while attempting to escape from Siberia to China. The documents published here are Krasovsky's plea to Alexander II, written at Tobolsk, June 4, 1863; his last will and testament, written in Alexandrovsk, May 17, 1868; and excerpts from his notebook.

37 (1929): 237–245

A. S. PUSHKIN UNDER THE SURVEILLANCE OF THE POLICE. Introduction by G. Kostomarov.

These police reports from Moscow and St. Petersburg on Pushkin's activities from September, 1829, to October, 1832, record no instances of misconduct.

For references to additional material in *Krasnyi Arkhiv* on Pushkin, see the notes to "New Manuscripts and Materials on Pushkin," 31 (1928): 155–159.

VOLUME 38, 1930

38 (1930): 3–19

JANUARY 9 IN ST. PETERSBURG. Introduction by V. Nevsky.

"The Description of the Activities of Military Units on January 9, 1905," a report of the Ministry of War printed here, gives an account of the

A Digest of the Krasnyi Arkhiv 35

demonstrations in St. Petersburg and of the employment of military units in dispersing them. A supplement to this report lists the units stationed at specific points in each section of the city. Additional memoranda of the Ministry of War, with troop deployments appended, describe sporadic unrest on January 10, 11, and 12, 1905.

For references to additional material in *Krasnyi Arkhiv* on January 9, 1905, see the notes to "The Petersburg Clergy and the Ninth of January," 36 (1929): 192–199.

38 (1930): 20–69

TWENTY-FIVE YEARS AGO (From the Diary of Leo Tikhomirov). Introduction unsigned.

The editors have deleted the parts of Tikhomirov's diary concerned with his family affairs and many quotations from periodicals of these years. The entries, dated from January 3, 1904, to October 26, 1904, record Tikhomirov's opinions on the following topics: Far Eastern politics; finances and the stock exchange; the poor state of preparedness and rumors of war, culminating in the Japanese attack on Port Arthur; changes in public opinion as the war progressed; Minister of War A. N. Kuropatkin, Admiral E. I. Alexeiev, General M. D. Skobelev, and Minister of Internal Affairs V. K. von Plehve; Vice Admiral S. O. Makarov's death; destruction of the Russian fleet in the Far East; and unrest in St. Petersburg in October, 1904.

Publication of consecutive sections of the diary is continued in 39 (1930): 47–75, 40 (1930): 59–96, and 41–42 (1930): 103–147. Other sections appear in 61 (1933): 82–128; 72 (1935): 120–159; 73 (1935): 170–190; 74 (1936): 162–191; 75 (1936): 171–184.

For additional material in *Krasnyi Arkhiv* on Tikhomirov, see: "From the Archive of L. Tikhomirov," 6 (1924): 124–194; "Unpublished Memoirs of L. Tikhomirov," 29 (1928): 139–174.

38 (1930): 70–108

MATERIALS RELATING TO THE HISTORY OF THE TRIAL OF THE TWENTY-ONE (Conclusion) (Letters and Testimony of P. F. Yakubovich)

Publication of these documents begins in 36 (1929): 122–179 and 37 (1929): 102–137.

The documents given here are a continuation of P. F. Yakubovich's testimony at the Trial of the Twenty-one in March and May, 1885. His most active work as a member of the Will of the People party began in 1883, and is described here, as is Sergius Degaev's role in the organization, the murder of Colonel G. P. Sudeikin, chief of the St. Petersburg Secret

Police, and the publication of the tenth issue of the paper of the Will of the People party.

38 (1930): 109–147

COUNT A. K. BENCKENDORFF CONCERNING RUSSIA 1827–1830 (Conclusion)

Publication of Count Benckendorff's reports to Nicholas I begins in 37 (1929): 138–174.

Three reports are given here. The first, "A Picture of Public Opinion in 1829," contains an outline of the year's important events as reflected in public opinion, with particular emphasis on the Polish question and the Treaty of Adrianople. Benckendorff also describes public opinion on the activities and personnel of the Ministry of Finance, the Ministry of Internal Affairs, the Ministry of Justice, the Ministry of Education, the Ministry of Foreign Affairs, the Ministry of War, the Office of Water and Land Communications, the Maritime Department, the Post Office, the Gendarmerie, and the army.

"A Picture of Public Opinion in 1830" records public opinion on the following subjects: (1) the arrest of certain censors and journalists; (2) the Polish question and the opening of the Polish Sem by Nicholas I; (3) disorders in Sevastopol; (4) the cholera epidemic, particularly in Astrakhan province; (5) the administration of justice; (6) Nicholas I's trip to Finland; (7) the July (1830) Revolution in Paris; (8) the Polish uprising. Benckendorff concludes the report with a discussion of the spread of liberalism and the growing inclination toward innovation in young people's circles; he also lists the elements of society composing the revolutionary parties.

The third document is "An Account of the Activities of the Gendarmerie for 1830."

For additional reports in *Krasnyi Arkhiv* by Benckendorff, see "Count A. K. Benckendorff concerning Russia in 1831–1832," 46 (1931): 133–159.

38 (1930): 148–164

RUSSIA AND THE UNITED STATES AT THE TIME OF THE CIVIL WAR [IN THE UNITED STATES]. Introduction by E. A. Adamov.

The three documents published here are: (1) "Instructions to Rear Admiral [S. S.] Lesovsky, July 14/26, 1863, from Adjutant General N. Krabbe, executive secretary of the Ministry of Naval Affairs"; (2) "A Dispatch from Baron [Phillip] Brunnow, Russian ambassador in London, to

Prince [A. M.] Gorchakov, Russian minister of foreign affairs, October 5/17, 1863"; (3) "A Dispatch from Baron [E. A.] Stoeckl, Russian ambassador in Washington, to Baron Brunnow in London, September 11/23, 1863."

These documents appear in translation in the *Journal of Modern History*, II (1930): 586–611. The first is in English and the second and third are in French.

For additional material in *Krasnyi Arkhiv* on Russia and the American Civil War, see "Russo-American Relations at the Time of the Civil War in the United States," 94 (1939): 97–153.

FROM AN ARCHIVIST'S NOTEBOOK

38 (1930): 165–169

THE NAVAL PUNITIVE BATTALIONS IN THE BALTIC REGION. Introduction by A. Drezen.

Drezen points out that disturbances in the Baltic in 1905 forced the government to adopt stringent punitive measures, involving the use of military and naval forces under the direction of Governor General Sologub. Excerpts given here from reports of Captain Baron Ferzen and Captain Rikhter describe the suppression of unrest by their units in December, 1905.

For additional material in *Krasnyi Arkhiv* on agitation in the Baltic, see: "S. Y. Witte's Reports to Nicholas II," 11–12 (1925): 144–158; "The Baltic Region during 1905," 11–12 (1925): 263–288; "Revolutionary Events in the Baltic Provinces in 1905," 102 (1940): 114–156.

38 (1930): 169–173

AN UNPUBLISHED LETTER OF N. P. OGAREV. By B. Kozmin.

In the letter given here Ogarev writes I. P. Vorozhtsov, a merchant in Viatka province, on January 18, 1865, concerning his political philosophy after the Polish uprising and the liquidation of the Land and Freedom party. Vorozhtsov and Ogarev had met abroad in 1864 when Vorozhtsov was touring European phosphorus factories in preparation for establishing his own factory in Russia. Kozmin quotes from police interrogations of Vorozhtsov about his friendship with Ogarev.

For additional material in *Krasnyi Arkhiv* on Ogarev, see "Towards a Biography of N. O. [*sic*] Ogarev," 3 (1923): 207–217; "Materials Relating to the History of Emigration in the 1860's," 49 (1931): 148–154.

38 (1930): 173–185

A. S. Pushkin and Count M. S. Vorontsov. By P. Shchegolev.

Shchegolev's article traces the events, as reflected in the correspondence of Count M. S. Vorontsov, Count K. V. Nesselrode, A. S. Pushkin, and his friends, that resulted in Pushkin's move from Odessa to his father's estate in Pskov province. The move was instigated by Count Vorontsov, governor general of the Odessa region, under whose surveillance Pushkin lived in 1824.

For references to additional material in *Krasnyi Arkhiv* on Pushkin, see the notes to "New Manuscripts and Materials on Pushkin," 31 (1928): 155–159.

38 (1930): 185–188

A New Account of the Execution of the Decembrists. Introduction by M. Nechkina.

An excerpt from the memoirs of the Decembrist N. I. Lorer brings to print here for the first time this account of the execution in St. Petersburg of several Decembrists. The execution was supervised by Adjutant General Alexander Ivanovich Chernyshëv.

Volume 13 (1925) is devoted exclusively to publication of materials on the Decembrist Revolution of 1825.

VOLUME 39, 1930

39 (1930): 3–46

Wrangeliana (From Materials of the Provisional Government's Paris "Embassy"). Introduction by I. Mints.

The documents which appear here are an exchange of dispatches between officials of the Provisional Government stationed abroad and, for the most part, General P. N. Wrangel's government. Dated from June 7, 1920, to August 24, 1920, the dispatches were sent from Warsaw, Constantinople, Sevastopol, London, Bern, Bucharest, Tokyo, Rome, Brussels, Peking, Copenhagen, Sofia, Stockholm, Washington, Belgrade, Posen, and Christiana. The documents deal primarily with Allied assistance to General Wrangel, Red Cross relief work, the effect of the Soviet-Polish War on Wrangel's campaign, the difficulties of the Allies in sending aid to Poland, the Chinese-Eastern Railroad, the attitudes of Lloyd George and Churchill

A Digest of the Krasnyi Arkhiv 39

toward Russia, and agrarian reforms in the areas occupied by Wrangel's forces.

Publication of these documents is concluded in 40 (1930): 3–40.

For references to additional material in *Krasnyi Arkhiv* on Wrangel, see the notes to "Materials Relating to the History of the Foreign Policy of Wrangel's Government," 32 (1929): 125–157.

39 (1930): 47–75

TWENTY-FIVE YEARS AGO (From the Diary of Leo Tikhomirov) (Continued)
Publication of the diary begins in 38 (1930): 20–69.

This section of Tikhomirov's diary, dated from November 5, 1904, to August 29, 1905, records his opinions on the following topics: the November–December disorders in St. Petersburg; the rumors of reform and internal intrigue; the news of the Russo-Japanese War; the strikes in January, 1905; the demonstrations of January 9, 1905; the assassination and funeral of Grand Duke Sergius Aleksandrovich in February, 1905; the Imperial Family; and the Portsmouth Conference.

The diary is continued in 40 (1930): 59–96 and 41–42 (1930): 103–147.

For references to additional material in *Krasnyi Arkhiv* on Tikhomirov, see the notes to 38 (1930): 20–69.

39 (1930): 76–107

MATERIALS RELATING TO THE HISTORY OF THE STRUGGLE WITH THE AGRARIAN MOVEMENT 1905–1906. Introduction by S. Dubrovsky.

Dubrovsky states that the report of S. S. Khrulev, prosecutor of the Kharkov judicial district, the first of the two reports published here, is interesting as a reflection of the views of a tsarist official at a time when the revolutionary movement was spreading. The second report, that of Count I. A. Pototsky, the largest landowner in southwest Russia, discusses the agrarian movement in 1905 and 1906 from the viewpoint of the landowners.

Khrulev's report, written for the Ignatiev Commission in 1906, lists the reasons for the outbreak and the spread of peasant disorders, as well as the measures for preventing and suppressing them. He describes the unrest in 1902 and the disturbances in 1905, which spread throughout thirty provinces of central, northwest, and southwest Russia, the Vistula provinces, Bessarabia, the Baltic region, a few northern provinces, and the Caucasus. He discusses the peasants' attitude toward land during the era of serfdom and its repercussions in 1905–1906.

Publication of these documents is concluded in 40 (1930): 41–58.

For references to additional material in *Krasnyi Arkhiv* on the agrarian movement, see the notes to "S. Y. Witte's Struggle with the Agrarian Revolution," 31 (1928): 81–102.

39 (1930): 108–148

"PRINCES OF THE CHURCH" (From the Diary of A. N. Lvov). Introduction unsigned.

A. N. Lvov, according to the introduction, was a graduate of the St. Petersburg Theological Academy and a director of the Holy Synod's Archive and Library from 1889 to 1901. These excerpts from his diary, dated February 23, 1891, to May 5, 1893, present a curious picture of the life and the activities of Russian Orthodox clergymen.

Lvov writes of the frictions in clerical circles and analyzes the characters of the following men: V. K. Sabler, director of the Secretariat of the Holy Synod and, from 1892, assistant procurator; I. T. Butkevich, professor at Kharkov University; A. Khrapovitsky, rector of the Moscow Theological Academy; Metropolitan Platon of Kiev and his successor Metropolitan Ioannikii; Metropolitan Isidor of St. Petersburg and Novgorod, and his successor Palladii; and K. P. Pobedonostsev, procurator of the Holy Synod. Lvov also discusses the appointment of Nicholas Ziorov as archbishop of the Aleutian Islands in 1891. The entry for March 12, 1893, contains reminiscences of Pobedonostsev's objections to burying I. S. Turgenev in Russia.

Publication of Lvov's diary is continued in 40 (1930): 97–124.

For references to additional material in *Krasnyi Arkhiv* on the Russian Orthodox Church, see the notes to "Life in Ecclesiastical Circles before the Revolution," 31 (1928): 204–213.

39 (1930): 149–176

MATERIALS RELATING TO THE TRIAL OF ADRIAN MIKHAILOV, VEIMAR, AND OTHERS. Introduction by V. Nevsky.

The introduction is a biography of Adrian Fëdorovich Mikhailov (1853–1929), who was arrested for participating in the assassination of Adjutant General N. V. Mezentsov, chief of the Gendarmerie and head of the Third Department (Secret Police), on August 4, 1878. [O. E.] Veimar, a doctor by profession, was arrested as a suspected accomplice in the assassination and tried with Mikhailov. The documents printed here do not refer to him, however.

The memorandum of G. Kirillov, of the Third Department, given here, includes a report of Count M. T. Loris-Melikov's interview with Adrian Mikhailov in the Petropavlovsk fortress on May 15, 1880, the day after

A Digest of the Krasnyi Arkhiv 41

Mikhailov was sentenced to death for driving the carriage in which the assassins of Mezentsov, S. M. Kravchinsky (S. M. Stepnyak) and A. I. Barannikov, escaped. On May 16 the sentence was commuted to twenty years at hard labor. Kirillov's memorandum is dated May 19, 1880.

Other Third Department documents, also dated 1880, contain information on Barannikov, Alexander Dmitrievich Mikhailov, and their families and friends. Alexander Mikhailov, an active member of the Land and Freedom party, was one of the defendants in the Trial of the Twenty-one. He died in Petropavlovsk fortress on March 18, 1884. Adrian Mikhailov died in 1929, without leaving any memoirs.

For additional material in *Krasnyi Arkhiv* on Mezentsov's assassination, see: "From the Correspondence of S. M. Kravchinsky," 19 (1926): 195–202; "Reports of Lieutenant General Seliverstov and Adjutant General Drenteln to Alexander II," 49 (1931): 112–143; "Adrian Mikhailov and Count M. T. Loris-Melikov," 53 (1932): 127–138.

FROM AN ARCHIVIST'S NOTEBOOK

39 (1930): 177–185

"BLOODY SUNDAY" IN ST. PETERSBURG (From the Police Department's Censorship of Letters concerning January 9, 1905). Introduction by L. Brazhe.

Excerpts are printed here from ten letters which were written immediately after January 9 by persons of varied social status and which were intercepted by the Police Department. They indicate the repercussions of the events of January 9 in Moscow University and St. Petersburg and among economists, lawyers, and members of the laboring class.

For references to additional material in *Krasnyi Arkhiv* on January 9, see the notes to "The Petersburg Clergy and the Ninth of January," 36 (1929): 192–199.

39 (1930): 185–188

MATERIALS RELATING TO THE HISTORY OF THE "PEACEFUL PENETRATION" OF EUROPEANS INTO ETHIOPIA. By B. Veber.

Veber describes the negotiations between Karl Shwimmer, Austrian consul in Ethiopia, and the Ethiopian ruler Lej Yasu on providing Ethiopia with modern weapons of war. The source for this article is a dispatch, included here, from Chemerzin, Russian representative in Addis Ababa, dated June 2, 1914. Veber also records S. Y. Witte's description of

Leontiev's adventures in Ethiopia in 1897, when he was chief of the Russian legation there.

VOLUME 40, 1930

40 (1930): 3–40

WRANGELIANA (Conclusion)

Publication of these documents pertaining to Wrangel's government begins in 39 (1930): 3–46.

The documents given here are dated from August 23, 1920, to November 18, 1920. They contain information on the following subjects: difficulties involved in securing supplies from the United States for General P. N. Wrangel's forces; the problem of securing foreign recognition of the government of South Russia; attempts to obtain a loan from the United States; the necessity for air-force supplies; intrusions on Russian territory in the Far East; relations with Ataman (Hetman) Gregory Semënov; American Red Cross activities; anxiety over the Soviet-Polish peace; the situation in Siberia in the fall of 1920; the evacuation of the Crimea by General Wrangel's forces after the Soviet-Polish peace.

For references to additional material in *Krasnyi Arkhiv* on General Wrangel, see the notes to "Materials Relating to the History of the Foreign Policy of Wrangel's Government," 32 (1929): 125–157.

For additional material in *Krasnyi Arkhiv* on Semënov, see: "Materials Relating to the History of Intervention in Siberia," 34 (1929): 126–165; "Materials Relating to the History of the Semënovites in 1919," 67 (1934): 131–146.

40 (1930): 41–58

MATERIALS RELATING TO THE HISTORY OF THE STRUGGLE WITH THE AGRARIAN MOVEMENT 1905–1906 (Conclusion)

Publication of these reports by Prosecutor S. S. Khrulev of the Kharkov judicial district and Count I. A. Pototsky, the largest landowner in southwest Russia, begins in 39 (1930): 76–107.

Khrulev concludes his report to the Ignatiev Commission with recommendations for changes in the criminal code dealing with peasant disturbances. Count Pototsky in his memorandum to the minister of internal affairs records the exodus of landowners to urban areas and the peasants' prediction of a spring upheaval, which they hoped would result in agrarian reforms. He concludes with a review of the agrarian problem in the southwestern provinces, in which he notes the reasons for fewer disturbances in Volhynia, Podolia, and Kiev provinces.

For references to additional material in *Krasnyi Arkhiv* on the agrarian problem, see the notes to "S. Y. Witte's Struggle with the Agrarian Revolution," 31 (1928): 81–102.

40 (1930): 59–96

TWENTY-FIVE YEARS AGO (From the Diary of Leo Tikhomirov) (Continued)

Publication of Tikhomirov's diary begins in 38 (1930): 20–69 and is continued in 39 (1930): 47–75.

This section of the diary, dated from September 8, 1905, to November 5, 1905, describes the Revolution of 1905 in Moscow, student demonstrations at Moscow University, Count S. Y. Witte's position after the Portsmouth Conference, mass attacks on Moscow printing offices, general strikes, and the funeral of the revolutionary Nicholas E. Bauman.

This section of the diary is concluded in 41–42 (1930): 103–147.

40 (1930): 97–124

"PRINCES OF THE CHURCH" (From the Diary of A. N. Lvov) (Conclusion)

Publication of Lvov's diary begins in 39 (1930): 108–148.

Entries for 1893, 1894, 1895, 1896, and 1898, reproduced here, record moral degradation in theological academies, friction in church circles, and the Holy Synod's attempts to gain control over public education. Among the people Lvov characterizes are Metropolitan Sergius of Moscow and the wife of K. P. Pobedonostsev, procurator of the Holy Synod.

For references to additional material in *Krasnyi Arkhiv* on the Russian Orthodox Church, see the notes to "Life in Ecclesiastical Circles before the Revolution," 31 (1928): 204–213.

40 (1930): 125–175

REPORTS OF ADJUTANT GENERAL A. R. DRENTELN TO ALEXANDER II (April–November, 1879). Introduction unsigned.

Adjutant General N. V. Mezentsov, head of the Third Department (Secret Police) and chief of the Gendarmerie, was assassinated on August 4, 1878. A. R. Drenteln succeeded him on September 15, 1878.

Fifty-six reports to Alexander II, covering the period from April to mid-November, 1879, are published here; they deal with the following topics: disturbances in Rostov-on-Don in April, 1879; A. K. Soloviëv's attempt on

Alexander II's life, April 2, 1879; the arrest of the Stasov brothers; plans to counteract revolutionary activities; the investigation of Mezentsov's assassination; the assassination on February 9, 1879, of Major General Prince Dmitry Nikolaevich Kropotkin, military governor of Kharkov. In a letter to N. K. Shmidt, another Third Department official, Adjutant General Drenteln discusses the explosion on the Kursk Railroad, which was also an attempt on Alexander II's life. Footnotes to these documents contain Alexander II's opinions on the reports.

For references to additional material in *Krasnyi Arkhiv* on Mezentsov's assassination, see the notes to "Materials Relating to the Trial of Adrian Mikhailov, Veimar, and Others," 39 (1930): 149–176.

FROM AN ARCHIVIST'S NOTEBOOK

40 (1930): 176–184

MARCH 1, 1881. Introduction by S. Valk.

The documents printed here pertain to the assassination of Alexander II on March 1, 1881. Two reports (March 2 and 5) from Count M. T. Loris-Melikov, minister of internal affairs, to Alexander III suggest delay of the trial of the assassins until after the funeral. There is a copy of Alexander III's note of March 5 calling a ministerial meeting for the following day. A. A. Gerke's letter of June 28, 1881, to V. K. von Plehve describes his interview with his client Gesia Gelfman, one of the defendants. There is a copy of Miss Gelfman's note of June 23, 1881, to Alexander III, requesting commutation of her death sentence. I. P. Emelianov's testimony of April 22, 1881, is also published. He was one of the assassins, a member of the Will of the People party.

For additional material in *Krasnyi Arkhiv* on the assassination of Alexander II, see: "Moscow during the Events of March, 1881," 14 (1926): 252–257; "A. I. Zheliabov at Alexandrovsk," 18 (1926): 195–197; "N. I. Rysakov's Testimony," 19 (1926): 178–194; "After March 1, 1881," 45 (1931): 147–164.

40 (1930): 184–189

S. G. NECHAEV AND THE TULA ARMS WORKERS. Introduction by B. Kozmin.

Two unsigned reports from Moscow prosecutors to the minister of justice are given here. The first, dated February 8, 1870, reports on a secret society *Narodnaia Rasprava* ("The People's Retribution"), established in September, 1869, by Sergius Nechaev, which propagated revolutionary ideas and was active in Moscow, St. Petersburg, and especially among the workers at the Tula arms plant. The second report deals with the circulation of revolutionary propaganda in Tula.

For references to additional material in *Krasnyi Arkhiv* on Nechaev, see the notes to "S. G. Nechaev's Proclamation to Students," 33 (1929): 211–213.

40 (1930): 189–191

MATERIALS RELATING TO THE HISTORY OF THE ESCAPE OF YAROSLAV DOMBROVSKY. By A. Chernov.

Chernov's article provides further detail on Dombrovsky's escape from prison in December, 1864, after his confinement for participation in the Polish Insurrection of 1863. The article deals primarily with police surveillance over Dombrovsky's wife after his escape.

For additional material in *Krasnyi Arkhiv* on Dombrovsky, see: "The Escape of Yaroslav Dombrovsky," 22 (1927): 236–241; "Materials Relating to the History of the Polish Insurrection of 1863," 57 (1933): 100–139.

VOLUMES 41–42, 1930

41–42 (1930): 3–61

RUSSIA AND THE ALGECIRAS CONFERENCE. Introduction by A. Erusalimsky.

A draft of the "Secret Instructions to Count Cassini" dated Tsarskoe Selo, November 22, 1905, is given here. It traces the Moroccan question from the Anglo-French agreement of 1904, and instructs Count [A. P.] Cassini, Russia's senior representative at Algeciras, to act as mediator between Germany and France.

The remaining documents are dated from January through March, 1906. These include an exchange of telegrams between Cassini and Count V. N. Lamsdorff in which Cassini reports on conference proceedings and Lamsdorff sends supplementary comments and instructions. Other documents here show Russia's policy in regard to Morocco as reflected in the exchange of communiqués between Lamsdorff and Russian representatives in Paris, Berlin, London, and Bombay. There are also dispatches from Sir Cecil Spring-Rice, British chargé d'affaires in St. Petersburg, to Lamsdorff; from French Minister of Finance Raymond Poincaré to Russian Ambassador A. I. Nelidov; and from French Ambassador to Russia Louis Bompard to Lamsdorff. The final document is a draft of instructions to Spring-Rice from Sir Edward Grey, British secretary of state for foreign affairs.

For additional material in *Krasnyi Arkhiv*, see "New Documents concerning the Algeciras Conference and the Loan of 1906," 44 (1931): 161–165.

41–42 (1930): 62–102

THE FEBRUARY REVOLUTION IN PETROGRAD (February 28—March 1, 1917). Introduction by F. D.

The first set of documents of the three published here is composed of reports from observers of revolutionary activities to the Military Commission of the Provisional Committee of the State Duma. These reports are a minutely detailed account of the utter confusion in Petrograd on February 28, 1917. The second set of documents includes the personal notes of one of the members of the Military Commission; and the third set contains orders issued by the Military Commission for the occupation and seizure of government buildings, public utilities, streets, and train stations.

For references to additional material in *Krasnyi Arkhiv*, see: "The Supreme Command during the First Days of the Revolution," 5 (1924): 213–240; "Russia's Economic Status before the Revolution," 10 (1925): 67–94; "The Revolution of February, 1917," 21 (1927): 3–78 and 22 (1927): 3–70.

41–42 (1930): 103–147

TWENTY-FIVE YEARS AGO (From the Diary of Leo Tikhomirov) (Conclusion)

Publication of Tikhomirov's diary begins in 38 (1930): 20–69 and is continued in 39 (1930): 47–75 and 40 (1930): 59–96.

Dated from November 7, 1905, to April 28, 1906, these entries from the diary describe the unrest in Moscow in December, 1905, increased unemployment, Premier S. Y. Witte's retirement from the government, the calling of the First State Duma, and the restoration of Tikhomirov's civil rights by tsarist decree. Among the documents is a draft of the speech Tikhomirov was asked to write for the opening of the First State Duma by the tsar.

For references to other sections of the diary in *Krasnyi Arkhiv*, see the notes to 38 (1930): 20–69.

41–42 (1930): 148–204

WITH THE STAFF OF ADMIRAL E. I. ALEXEIEV (From the Diary of E. A. Planson). Introduction by A. Popov.

The introduction is a documented summary of the origins of the Russo-Japanese War. Planson was head of the diplomatic office attached to Admiral Alexeiev's staff and later a member of the Russian delegation at the Portsmouth Conference.

The entries in the Planson diary, dated from January 1 to November 2, 1904, were made at Port Arthur, Harbin, Mukden, and St. Petersburg.

Among the items recorded are the Japanese prewar demands regarding Manchuria and Korea, Planson's conferences with Admiral Alexeiev, and Alexeiev's attitude toward the Far Eastern question, the United States attitude toward the Russo-Japanese War, and Kuropatkin's arrival in the Far East. The diary emphasizes the diplomatic and personal aspects of the war, not the military.

For additional material in *Krasnyi Arkhiv* on the Portsmouth Treaty, see "Portsmouth Correspondence of S. Y. Witte and Others," 6 (1924): 3–47 and "Portsmouth," 7 (1924): 3–31.

For additional material in *Krasnyi Arkhiv* on the Russo-Japanese War, see "The Diary of A. N. Kuropatkin," 2 (1922): 5–117; 5 (1924): 82–101; "From the Diary of A. N. Kuropatkin," 7 (1924): 55–69 and 8 (1925): 70–100; "A. N. Kuropatkin's Diary," 68 (1935): 65–96 and 69–70 (1935): 101–126.

FROM AN ARCHIVIST'S NOTEBOOK

41–42 (1930): 205–213

PROTEST OF RUSSIAN POLITICAL EXILES IN 1888. Introduction by Felix Kon.

The letter presented here, drawn up by Siberian exiles and addressed to the emperor, contains a protest against the exile system and a request for specific reforms. A copy of the letter was confiscated on June 26, 1888, during a search of Vasily Barmin's home in Tobolsk.

41–42 (1930): 213–215

"RED GUARDS" IN RIGA IN 1906. Introduction by L. Brazhe.

The "Red Guards" was an armed group of revolutionaries organized in Riga in November, 1906. Published here is a report by Lieutenant Colonel Vasiley, head of the Riga Gendarmerie, on their activities. The table of organization of the Red Guards and one of their proclamations urging the residents of Riga to armed rebellion are also given.

For references to additional material in *Krasnyi Arkhiv* on the Baltic region during this period, see the notes to "The Naval Punitive Battalions in the Baltic Region," 38 (1930): 165–169.

41–42 (1930): 215–220

[COMMENTS OF] NICHOLAS ROMANOV CONCERNING THE REVOLUTIONARY MOVEMENT IN THE ARMY IN 1905–1906. Introduction by Kritsman.

Published here are officers' reports to Nicholas II on unrest in army units in Ekaterinodar, Minsk, Tver, Kiev, and Tula. There are also five reports from Lieutenant General A. F. Rediger, minister of war, with Nicholas' marginal comments.

For additional material in *Krasnyi Arkhiv* on unrest in the army in this period, see: "The Unrest in the Far Eastern Army," 11–12 (1925): 289–386; "A Soldier's Letter concerning the Events of January 9, 1905," 25 (1927): 188; "Materials Relating to the History of the Revolutionary Movement in the Army on the Eve of 1905," 43 (1930): 168–173; "Materials Relating to the History of the 'Ideological' Struggle of the Autocracy with the Revolutionary Movement in the Army," 44 (1931): 165–170; "The Purge of the Commanding Staff of the Tsarist Army in 1906," 50–51 (1932): 211–225; "Materials Relating to the History of the Revolutionary Movement in the Army in 1905–1906," 71 (1935): 39–59; "Life of Soldiers in the Tsarist Army," 98 (1940): 145–176.

VOLUME 43, 1930

43 (1930): 3–54

THE TURKISH REVOLUTION 1908–1909. Introduction by A. Popov.

The material presented here, dated from June 12/25, to July 31/August 13, 1908, was taken from a collection of documents entitled "The Turkish Constitution" in the Archive of Foreign Affairs. There are reports from Petriaev, in Macedonia, on the effect in the army and on the residents of Macedonia of Young Turk propaganda. There is also a Young Turk appeal to the Mohammedan people.

Dispatches from Kal in Bitolj (in Macedonia) and from Kokhmansky in Salonika describe local fighting. An exchange of telegrams between Russian Minister of Foreign Affairs A. P. Izvolsky and Count Alexander Konstantinovich Benckendorff, Russian ambassador in London, describes European concern over the Turkish Revolution. Minutes of the meetings of the Russian Ministry of Foreign Affairs are also published here, as are dispatches from Chargé d'Affairs Nelidov in Constantinople, Orlov in Üsküb, Korf in Rome, Evreinov in Belgrade, and Nekliudov in Paris.

Publication of these documents is continued in 44 (1931): 3–39 and 45 (1931): 27–52.

43 (1930): 55–91

DISPERSAL OF THE SECOND STATE DUMA. Introduction by I. Tatarov.

The Imperial Decree of June 3, 1907, dissolved the Second State Duma and called for new elections. The documents printed here provide information on its conferences during the preceding two days. Excerpts from the notes of F. A. Golovin, its chairman, deal with the Second State Duma's session of June 1, 1907, at which Kamyshansky, procurator of the St. Petersburg Chamber of Justice, and P. A. Stolypin demanded the expulsion of fifty-five Duma deputies accused of conspiring to overthrow the government. Golovin's notes on the Second State Duma meeting of June 2 record deliberations on the ultimatum. The journal of the meeting of Cadet party deputies on June 2 and the journal of the special Duma committee meeting for examination of the charges against the deputies are also published.

For references to additional material in *Krasnyi Arkhiv*, see: "The Correspondence between Nicholas II and P. A. Stolypin," 5 (1924): 102–128; "The Arrest and Trial of the Social Democratic Faction in the Second State Duma," 16 (1926): 76–117; "F. A. Golovin's Memoirs," 19 (1926): 110–149; "P. A. Stolypin's Correspondence with Nicholas Romanov," 30 (1928): 80–88; and "From F. A. Golovin's Notes," 58 (1933): 140–149.

43 (1930): 92–115

FROM THE DIARY OF GRAND DUKE CONSTANTINE ROMANOV. Introduction by N. Lapin.

Grand Duke Constantine (1858–1915) bequeathed his diary to the Academy of Science with the understanding that no one should have access to it until ninety years after his death. In 1929 the Soviets altered the policies of the Academy, and excerpts from the diary are published here. Dated from August 10, 1904, to February 9, 1905, the entries reflect the turbulence of the era of the Russo-Japanese War and the Revolution of 1905. They describe the concern of the Imperial Family over Russia's internal affairs, the struggle for parliamentary government, "Bloody Sunday" in St. Petersburg, and the assassination of Grand Duke Sergius.

Publication of the diary is continued in 44 (1931): 126–151 and 45 (1931): 112–129.

43 (1930): 116–165

MATERIALS RELATING TO THE HISTORY OF THE NECHAEV TRIAL. Introduction by B. Kozmin.

These are the reports and dispatches of N. D. Goremykin, Third Department (Secret Police) official, who was to coördinate the activities of the Moscow police and Gendarmerie. Dated from December 4, 1869, to February 12, 1870, the documents cover the period during which Ivan Ivanov's body was discovered and numerous members of the *Narodnaia Rasprava* ("The People's Retribution"), a secret society organized by S. G. Nechaev, were apprehended. Ivanov, one of the members, was murdered because he was believed to be a traitor to the organization. The dispatches trace the attempts to apprehend Nechaev, whose trial took place two years later.

For references to additional material in *Krasnyi Arkhiv* on Nechaev, see the notes to "S. G. Nechaev's Proclamation to Students," 33 (1929): 211–213.

FROM AN ARCHIVIST'S NOTEBOOK

43 (1930): 166–167

THE EXECUTION OF THE PARTICIPANTS IN THE KRONSTADT REBELLION OF 1906. Introduction by A. Drezen.

Colonel Valberg's report, printed here, is a detailed description of the execution of nineteen sailors who participated in the Kronstadt rebellion. The sailors were shot and dropped into the sea. Colonel Valberg was commanding officer of the infantry regiment responsible for the execution.

For additional material in *Krasnyi Arkhiv*, see: "P. A. Stolypin and the Sveaborg Uprising," 49 (1931): 144–148; "The Kronstadt Rebellion of 1906," 77 (1936): 91–116.

43 (1930): 168–173

MATERIALS RELATING TO THE HISTORY OF THE REVOLUTIONARY MOVEMENT IN THE ARMY ON THE EVE OF 1905. Introduction by M. Akhun and D. Zinevich.

Two letters are printed here. In a letter of September 23, 1903, to V. K. von Plehve, minister of internal affairs, General P. F. Luzanov outlined measures for combating political propaganda in the army. Plehve's letter of November 5, 1903, to Minister of War General A. N. Kuropatkin stated his opinions on the same problem.

For references to additional material in *Krasnyi Arkhiv* on unrest in the army, see the notes to "[Comments of] Nicholas Romanov concerning the Revolutionary Movement in the Army in 1905–1906," 41–42 (1930): 215–220. See also "Materials Relating to the History of the Autocracy's Struggle with the Revolutionary Movement in the Army in the 1880's," 63 (1934): 132–135.

43 (1930): 173–176

N. N. ROMANOV AND THE AMERICAN CONCESSION FOR A SIBERIAN–ALASKAN RAILROAD IN 1905. By G. Vereshchagin.

Vereshchagin's documented article describes a proposal to build a railroad through Siberia and Alaska, connecting Russia and Alaska by means of a tunnel under Bering Strait. Proposed by J. Jackson and Louis de Lobelle, the project was supported by Grand Duke Nicholas Nikolaevich. The Council of Ministers discussed the proposal on December 1, 1905, and referred it to a special commission for study. Published here is a summary of the meeting of the Council of Ministers.

VOLUME 44, 1931

44 (1931): 3-39

THE TURKISH REVOLUTION 1908-1909 (Continuation)

Publication of documents dealing with the Turkish Revolution begins in 43 (1930): 3-54.

The dispatches and reports printed here are dated from August 7/20, 1908, to March 14/27, 1909. There is a dispatch from V. Maikov, Russian embassy interpreter in Constantinople, on British support of the Young Turk movement. A dispatch from Chargé d'Affaires Nekliudov in Paris speaks of the origins of the Young Turk party and its activities in Paris. Urusov reports from Vienna on his conference with the foreign minister, Count A. L. von Aehrenthal, concerning the Balkans. From Berlin, Count N. D. Osten-Sacken gives an account of the German attitude toward the Turkish Revolution, and from Bulgaria, Colonel Leontiev describes the effects of the revolution on events in Bulgaria.

Interpreter Mandelshtam, Colonel Kholmsen, and Ambassador I. Zinoviev write of anarchy in Constantinople, public opinion there, the differences between the Turkish Constitution of 1876 and the new one, the relations between the sultan and his ministers, the fortification of the Bosporus, and an interview with the Young Turk leader Ahmed Riza Bey. There are also reports on the effects of the revolution in Smyrna and Salonika. Count Alexander Konstantinovich Benckendorff comments on public opinion in England, while Korf writes of conditions in Rome and of Italy's interest in a trans-Balkan railroad concession.

The documents are concluded in 45 (1931): 27-52.

44 (1931): 40-84

THE KERCH QUARRIES IN 1919. Introduction by A. Gukovsky.

The telegrams, letters, and stenographic reports of telephone conversations which are reproduced here sketch the role of the Kerch partisans in the struggle against General A. I. Denikin's forces in the spring of 1919. The documents trace the attempts of Denikin to drive the partisans from their base of operations in the Crimean stone quarries, the bombardment of the area by British vessels, and the final dispersal of the partisans in May, 1919.

44 (1931): 85–125

THE BEILIS TRIAL AS APPRAISED BY THE POLICE DEPARTMENT. Introduction by A. S. Tager.

The trial of Mendel Beilis, a Jewish worker accused of murdering a twelve-year-old boy for a religious ritual, was held in Kiev in the fall of 1913. The documents given here, dated from September 23 to November 21, 1913, are the dispatches of V. A. Diachenko and P. N. Liubimov to S. P. Beletsky, director of the Police Department. Reporting on the progress of the trial, they describe the tension in Kiev on the eve of the trial, the selection of a jury, and clerical testimony on Jewish rituals. The final document summarizes the testimony and the reaction in Kiev to Beilis' acquittal.

For additional material in *Krasnyi Arkhiv*, see "The Tsarist Government and the Beilis Trial," 54–55 (1932): 162–204.

44 (1931): 126–151

FROM THE DIARY OF GRAND DUKE CONSTANTINE ROMANOV

Publication of excerpts from the diary of Grand Duke Constantine Romanov begins in 43 (1930): 92–115.

The excerpts printed here are dated from February 11 to December 27, 1905. They describe the following people and events: the confined life of the Imperial Family; demonstrations of Moscow students in February, 1905; factory, school, and railroad strikes throughout the country; a memorandum signed by 342 university instructors advocating greater political freedom and a parliamentary form of government; N. A. Rimsky-Korsakov and agitation in the St. Petersburg Conservatory of Music; Theodore Roosevelt's offer to mediate between Japan and Russia; reactions of members of the Imperial Family to the Portsmouth Treaty; unrest in the Caucasus, Poland, and Finland; Maxim Gorky and the Academy of Science; the Manifesto of October 17, 1905; armed uprising in Moscow in December, 1905.

Publication of the diary is concluded in 45 (1931): 112–129.

FROM AN ARCHIVIST'S NOTEBOOK

44 (1931): 152–161

RUSSIAN SOLDIERS ON THE WESTERN FRONT IN WORLD WAR I. Introduction by A. Kovalev.

The thirteen communiqués given here, dated from December 5, 1915, to June 14/27, 1918, concern the transfer and the morale of Russian troops on the western front. The reports were issued from Athens, Paris, and Salonika.

For additional material in *Krasnyi Arkhiv*, see: "Russian Soldiers' Uprising in France in 1917," 99 (1940): 52–71; "Materials Relating to the Sojourn of Russian Troops in France in 1917," 101 (1940): 228–235.

44 (1931): 161–165

NEW DOCUMENTS CONCERNING THE ALGECIRAS CONFERENCE AND THE LOAN OF 1906. Introduction unsigned.

The letters presented here trace negotiations between French Minister of Finance Raymond Poincaré and Russian financial agent A. Rafalovich and Russian Ambassador A. I. Nelidov for a loan from France in March, 1906. Russia's financial situation is outlined, as is the influence of the Algeciras Conference on the negotiations.

For additional material in *Krasnyi Arkhiv*, see "Russia and the Algeciras Conference," 41–42 (1930): 3–61.

44 (1931): 165–170

MATERIALS RELATING TO THE HISTORY OF THE "IDEOLOGICAL" STRUGGLE OF THE AUTOCRACY WITH THE REVOLUTIONARY MOVEMENT IN THE ARMY. Introduction unsigned.

A list of proposals for "enlightening" the army, made by a military commission in 1905, is given here; it includes the introduction of political science and law courses into the curriculum of military academies. The courses are outlined and supplemented by a list of twenty-six persons qualified to present the lectures.

For references to additional material in *Krasnyi Arkhiv* on unrest in the army, see the notes to "[Comments of] Nicholas Romanov concerning the Revolutionary Movement in the Army in 1905–1906," 41–42 (1930): 215–220.

44 (1931): 170–173

A LETTER OF THE WORKER P. A. ALEXEIEV. Introduction by M. Klevensky.

Klevensky states that Peter Alekseevich Alexeiev was a worker engaged in revolutionary activities in the 1870's who was arrested for disseminating propaganda. Alexeiev's letter of April 7, 1881, published here, was written in the political prison in Mtsensk and is of psychological interest as an expression of the philosophy of a revolutionary during this era.

VOLUME 45, 1931

45 (1931): 3–26

THE PARIS COMMUNE OF 1871 (Okunev's Communiqués to [Prince A. M.] Gorchakov, May 1–25, 1871). Introduction by T. F.

The dispatches of [G. N.] Okunev, Russian ambassador in Paris, are presented here. Sent from Versailles, they provide information on the following subjects: the need for German aid in enforcing the blockade of Paris during the Commune; the victory of the republican parties in the French municipal elections of April 30; the siege of Fort Issy by the Versailles forces; the signing of the peace treaty between France and Germany; a review of the struggle for Paris; the meeting of the National Assembly. Also reprinted are the following materials attached to Okunev's dispatches: a copy of the Versailles government's proclamation promising to liberate Paris; an article entitled "Barricades in Paris" which appeared in a Paris newspaper; and a list of the names of forty-seven Poles who fought in the ranks of the Communards.

45 (1931): 27–52

THE TURKISH REVOLUTION 1908–1909 (Conclusion)

Publication of documents on the Turkish Revolution begins in 43 (1930): 3–54 and is continued in 44 (1931): 3–39.

The documents published in this volume are dated from March 31/April 13 to April 25/May 8, 1909. The dispatches of I. Zinoviev, Russian ambassador in Constantinople, deal mainly with the counterrevolution staged by the Constantinople garrison and with the role of the Macedonian army in routing the garrison. Dispatches from Sementovsky-Kurilo in Sofia describe the local reaction to counterrevolutionary activities and the possibility of coöperation between Serbia and Bulgaria. Obnorsky's dispatch from Belgrade also speaks of Serbo-Bulgarian relations. Colonel Leontiev writes from Bulgaria of possible Bulgarian mobilization, and M. Giers sends word from Bucharest of the Rumanian attitude toward Bulgarian independence.

Protopopov's dispatch from Adrianople notes the demands of soldiers in that area for the death or deposition of the sultan. Minister of Foreign Affairs A. P. Izvolsky's dispatches deal with Serbo-Bulgarian relations and the sending of two or three Russian cruisers from the Baltic fleet to the Mediterranean. A. I. Nelidov's communiqués from Paris concern the impending departure of French and British cruisers for Turkish waters. Bulatsel writes from Berlin of German plans to force England to diffuse its naval power. There are also three dispatches from Colonel Kholmsen on the situation in Constantinople.

45 (1931): 53-80

MATERIALS RELATING TO THE HISTORY OF FRENCH INTERVENTION IN ODESSA. Introduction by A. Gukovsky.

The history of French intervention in Odessa is described here in a report of Colonel Novikov of the General Staff of General A. I. Denikin's army. This report, "The Struggle with the Bolsheviks in the Novorossisk Region," discusses the following topics: the arrival of Allied military transport vessels in the Black Sea in December, 1918, when Simon Petliura had displaced General Paul Skoropadsky as master of the Ukraine; the arrival of French troops on December 17 and their coöperation with eight hundred volunteers under General Grishin-Almazov in driving Petliura from Odessa; the arrival of Greek troops and their occupation of Kherson and Nikolaev; Odessa as a political center thronged with refugees; Bolshevik propaganda in Odessa; the battle in the Voznesensk region between French and Bolshevik forces at the end of January, 1919; the loss of Kherson to the Soviets; the surrender of Nikolaev with its military supplies; French General D'Anselme's proclamation of martial law in the area of South Russia occupied by the Allies, February 27; the surrender of the town of Ochakov to the Bolsheviks, March 16/29; the evacuation of Odessa early in April, 1919. An appendix to Novikov's report contains eight military orders issued by General D'Anselme.

For additional material in *Krasnyi Arkhiv* on intervention in south Russia, see: "French Intervention in South Russia (December, 1918—April, 1919)," 19 (1926): 3-38; "The Regional Government of the Crimea during 1918-1919," 22 (1927): 92-152; "The Crimea during 1918-1919," 28 (1928): 142-181 and 29 (1928): 55-85.

45 (1931): 81-85

AN ARTICLE OF M. GORKY FORBIDDEN BY THE CENSOR. Introduction unsigned.

The *Krasnyi Arkhiv*, with Gorky's consent, published in this issue his article, "Inopportune," which had been suppressed by the censor in December, 1914. Gorky protests in this article against the writings of Fëdor Sologub, [M. P.] Artsybashev, [A. I.] Kuprin, and Leonid Andreev, who, he said, condemned the entire German people and thereby aided the press in spreading blind hatred of Germans.

For additional material in *Krasnyi Arkhiv* on Gorky, see: "Portrait of

Gorky," 77 (1936): 1; "Chronology of Gorky's Life and Works," 78 (1936): 23–84; "A. M. Gorky and the Publishing Business," 78 (1936): 250–252.

45 (1931): 86–111

NOTES OF A. F. REDIGER CONCERNING 1905. Introduction unsigned.

The introduction states that the memoirs of Lieutenant General A. F. Rediger, minister of war, written after the October Revolution, supplement the memoirs of Generals Rankh and A. N. Kuropatkin by illuminating the strategy and tactics employed in the suppression of the Revolution of 1905. The section of Rediger's memoirs presented here deals with events leading up to the Manifesto of October 17, ministerial changes, military suppression of agrarian unrest, and the naval and military reforms necessary in order to calm disturbances in the armed forces. Rediger evaluates the personalities and capabilities of Count S. Y. Witte and Generals Baron A. N. Meller-Zakomelsky, P. K. Rennenkampf, N. P. Linevich, V. I. Sollogub, A. A. Polivanov, and others.

For additional material in *Krasnyi Arkhiv*, see "From the Memoirs of A. F. Rediger," 60 (1933): 92–133.

45 (1931): 112–129

FROM THE DIARY OF GRAND DUKE CONSTANTINE ROMANOV (Conclusion).

Publication of excerpts from the diary of Grand Duke Constantine Romanov begins in 43 (1930): 92–115 and is continued in 44 (1931): 126–151.

Dated from January 9 to November 3, 1906, the entries given here discuss the following events: precautions taken to prevent disturbances on the first anniversary of "Bloody Sunday"; strikes on the Siberian railroad; the empress's reaction to the Manifesto of October 17, 1905; elections and the opening of the First State Duma; M. Gorky's trip to the United States in 1906; P. A. Stolypin's appointment as premier and the dissolution of the First State Duma; unrest in the Preobrazhensky regiment; the rebellions at Sveaborg and Kronstadt; the threat of a general strike in St. Petersburg; the attempt on Stolypin's life in August, 1906.

45 (1931): 130–146

F. M. DOSTOEVSKY'S TESTIMONY ON THE PETRASHEVSKY AFFAIR. Introduction by N. Belchikov.

Dostoevsky was arrested on April 23, 1849, for participating in discussions of current affairs organized by M. V. Butashevich-Petrashevsky. Dostoevsky's testimony, published here, contains much biographical material, a

A Digest of the Krasnyi Arkhiv 57

defense of his brother Michael, an account of his first meeting with Petrashevsky in the spring of 1846, and reports on the meetings which he attended.

Publication of the testimony is concluded in 46 (1931): 160–178.

FROM AN ARCHIVIST'S NOTEBOOK

45 (1931): 147–164

AFTER MARCH 1, 1881. Introduction by S. Valk.

Valk discusses in detail the reaction to the assassination of Alexander II in various social strata in Russia and in Western Europe. Two circulars, printed here, from Count M. T. Loris-Melikov, minister of internal affairs, and his successor Count A. P. Ignatiev (March and May, 1881) advise provincial governors on methods of pacifying local residents. There is also an exchange of communiqués between Baron V. B. Frederiks, governor of Tambov province, and Ignatiev on unrest in that province.

For references to additional material in *Krasnyi Arkhiv* on the assassination of Alexander II, see the notes to "March 1, 1881," 40 (1930): 176–184.

45 (1931): 164–166

MATERIALS RELATING TO THE HISTORY OF THE TRIAL OF LIEUTENANT P. P. SHMIDT. Introduction by E. Gorokhovskaia.

The discussion between two telegraph operators in Ochakov and Nikolaev is reproduced on these pages from their telegraphic tape. This exchange indicates that the soldiers of the Ochakov garrison, in conjunction with the sailors in Sevastopol, planned to rescue Lieutenant Shmidt from the prison in which he was confined for leading a mutiny on a Black Sea cruiser in November, 1905.

For additional material in *Krasnyi Arkhiv*, see: "The Correspondence of Lieutenant Shmidt," 1 (1922): 344–354; "The Execution of Shmidt, Chastnik, and Others," 5 (1924): 266–267; "The Execution of Afanasy Matushenko," 8 (1925): 250–254; "The Events of 1905 and Their Reflection Abroad," 9 (1925): 32–55; "S. Y. Witte's Reports to Nicholas II," 11–12 (1925): 144–158; "The Navy during 1905," 11–12 (1925): 193–262.

45 (1931): 167–171

V. V. VERESHCHAGIN'S LETTERS TO EMPEROR NICHOLAS ROMANOV IN 1904. Introduction by A. S.

Vereshchagin, noted Russian painter, served in the Russo-Turkish War of 1877–1878 and traveled in India, Turkestan, and the United States. Four of the five letters published here are dated from February 3 to March 23, 1904; the fifth is undated. Vereshchagin cautioned Nicholas II against Russian expansion into India and Afghanistan. His advice on Far Eastern affairs included a recommendation for the appointment of General A. N. Kuropatkin as commander-in-chief of the Far Eastern army. On the basis of more than a year's sojourn in the United States, Vereshchagin wrote of American antipathy toward Russia.

45 (1931): 171–176

MATERIALS RELATING TO THE HISTORY OF LIBERAL PUBLIC OPINION IN THE 1860's. Introduction by B. Kozmin.

The introduction gives the background for the arrest of P. V. Pavlov, professor at the University of St. Petersburg, for a speech on March 2, 1862, about internal conditions in Russia. The Secret Police agents' reports of March 3 and 4, reproduced here, describe the gathering at which Pavlov spoke and at which F. M. Dostoevsky, N. G. Chernyshevsky, and N. A. Nekrasov also appeared. In addition, there are two letters to Prince V. A. Dolgorukov, chief of the Gendarmerie, in which A. V. Golovin, minister of education, wrote of having admonished Pavlov.

VOLUME 46, 1931

46 (1931): 3–37

THE DIARY OF V. N. LAMSDORFF. Introduction by F. Rothstein.

V. N. Lamsdorff, for many years the closest adviser of Minister of Foreign Affairs N. K. de Giers, later became minister himself. His diary, dated from September 3, 1894, to February 17, 1895, is presented here. It deals with the following subjects: the immediate effects of the death of Alexander III, October 20, 1894; Nicholas II's inexperience and lack of political information; the influence of the empress on Nicholas II; the death of Giers, January 14, 1895; relations between Ferdinand of Bulgaria and Nicholas II; Giers's first audience with Nicholas II, November 4, 1894; the retirement of Count Paul A. Shuvalov, ambassador in Berlin, and the appointment of Prince A. B. Lobanov-Rostovsky in January, 1895, to succeed him; Shuvalov's letter of January 5/17, 1895, to Giers concerning his conference with William II on Russo-German relations; Lamsdorff's opinion of N. P. Shishkin, who replaced Giers temporarily; the choice of Lobanov to succeed Giers as minister of foreign affairs, February, 1895; Russo-Japanese relations and the Sino-Japanese War.

A Digest of the Krasnyi Arkhiv 59

46 (1931): 38-68

THE CADETS IN 1905-1906 (Materials of the Central Committee of the Popular Freedom or Cadet Party). Introduction by B. Grave.

In addition to a list of the members of the Cadet Central Committee, the minutes of Central Committee meetings held from October 21, 1905, to July 15, 1906, are published here. The principal matters discussed are party discipline, organizational questions, peasant representation at the party congress, peasant agitation, finances, the party's attitude toward the First State Duma, and preparations for a Cadet party congress.

Publication of these documents is continued in 47-48 (1931): 112-139.

46 (1931): 69-109

THE BALTIC FLEET IN THE JULY DAYS OF 1917. Introduction by A. Drezen.

The documents presented here cover the Provisional Government's investigation of Rear Admiral D. N. Verderevsky, commander of the Baltic fleet, who disregarded a government order to send four torpedo-boat destroyers from Helsingfors to quell the uprising in Petrograd on July 3-5, 1917. Upon reviewing the events in July, 1917, the government exonerated Verderevsky. Testimony of other high naval officials is also published here.

For references to additional material in *Krasnyi Arkhiv* on the Baltic fleet, see the notes to "The February Revolution in the Baltic Fleet," 32 (1929): 88-124.

46 (1931): 110-132

THE DIARY OF A. A. POLOVTSOV (1895-1900)

Polovtsov's entries in his diary for 1895 record his opinion of Ivan A. Vyshnegradsky, minister of finance from 1888 to 1892, and discuss a finance committee meeting of April 21, 1895. The entry for 1897 outlines the conclusions of the committee concerning gold coinage and monetary reform. The entries for 1899 deal with the peasant question, foreign capital in Russia, and opinions of government ministers and members of the Imperial Family. Other meetings of the finance committee are described in the entries for 1900, as are Russian international relations and the death of Grand Duchess Alexandra Petrovna, wife of Grand Duke Nicholas Nikolaevich.

For other sections of Polovtsov's diary published in *Krasnyi Arkhiv*, see 3 (1923): 75-172; 4 (1923): 63-128; 33 (1929): 170-203; 59 (1933): 82-109; 67 (1934): 168-186.

46 (1931): 133–159

COUNT A. K. BENCKENDORFF CONCERNING RUSSIA IN 1831–1832. Introduction by A. Sergeev.

The documents given here are an analysis of Russian internal affairs by Count Benckendorff, head of the Third Department (Secret Police), which was organized after the Decembrist Revolution in 1825. The first document, "Survey of Events and Public Opinion in 1831," deals with the following topics: public reaction to the Polish Insurrection of 1830–1831, and the role of the Gendarmerie in suppressing it; public sentiment concerning the cholera epidemic; disturbances in Novgorod province in July, 1831; a survey of the ministries of Justice, Internal Affairs, Finance, and Education, and of the General Staff of the army and the navy.

The second document, "Survey of Public Sentiment and of Various Parts of Government Administration in 1832," deals with public opinion, the administration of Poland, and the same four ministries mentioned in the report for 1831, as well as with the St. Petersburg police. In addition, there are reports which mention the achievements of specific people in the Third Department.

For additional material in *Krasnyi Arkhiv*, see "Count A. K. Benckendorff concerning Russia 1827–1830," 37 (1929): 138–174 and 38 (1930): 109–147.

46 (1931): 160–178

F. M. DOSTOEVSKY'S TESTIMONY ON THE PETRASHEVSKY AFFAIR (Conclusion)

Dostoevsky's testimony concerning his activities in the Petrashevsky groups begins in 45 (1931): 130–146.

Presented here in addition to the remainder of his testimony, given after his arrest in April, 1849, is a copy of the court's verdict sentencing Dostoevsky to death. Nicholas I finally commuted the sentence to four years at hard labor.

For additional material in *Krasnyi Arkhiv* on Dostoevsky, see "Unpublished Correspondence of N. A. Nekrasov," 1 (1922): 362–366; "Dostoevsky on the Commemoration of Pushkin in the 1880's," 1 (1922): 367–405; "F. M. Dostoevsky's Letter from the Fortress," 2 (1922): 234–239; "Dostoevsky and Pobedonostsev," 2 (1922): 240–255; "Reminiscences of A. G. Dostoevskaia," 3 (1923): 251–290; "The Fate of a Certain Parody by Dostoevsky," 3 (1923): 301–303; "Two Letters from F. M. Dostoevsky to M. N. Katkov," 4 (1923): 365–375; "F. M. Dostoevsky's Sojourn in the City of Tver," 4 (1923): 398–401; "D. I. Pisarev's Letters from the Fortress," 5 (1924): 248–

A Digest of the Krasnyi Arkhiv 61

257; *"Crime and Punishment,"* 7 (1924): 146–200; "M. V. Butashevich-Petrashevsky in Siberia," 10 (1925): 184–216; "A Project of F. M. Dostoevsky," 16 (1926): 224–228; "F. M. Dostoevsky as 'A Member of a Secret Society,'" 21 (1927): 241–244; "F. M. Dostoevsky's Letters," 27 (1928): 191–214.

FROM AN ARCHIVIST'S NOTEBOOK

46 (1931): 179–187

A. I. NELIDOV'S NOTE IN 1882 CONCERNING OCCUPATION OF THE STRAITS. Introduction by V. Khvostov.

Khvostov traces A. I. Nelidov's activities in Constantinople when Nelidov was Russian chargé d'affaires in 1877–1878, when he was on a special mission in 1882, and when he was ambassador, from May 15, 1883, to July 1, 1897. Nelidov's note to Alexander III, dated December 6/18, 1882, is published here; it outlines the reasons for Russia's occupation of the Straits, the various methods for such occupation, and the European entanglements involved. In addition, Nelidov discusses the disintegration of the Turkish empire.

For additional material in *Krasnyi Arkhiv* on the Straits, see: "Russo-German Relations," 1 (1922): 3–208; "Constantinople and the Straits," 6 (1924): 48–76 and 7 (1924): 32–54; "Tsarist Diplomacy on Russia's Tasks in the East in 1900," 18 (1926): 3–29; "The Project for Seizure of the Bosporus in 1896," 47–48 (1931): 50–70; "M. N. Muraviëv's Journey Abroad in 1897," 47–48 (1931): 71–89; "A. P. Mohrenheim's Letter concerning French Politics in the Near East (1896)," 52 (1932): 197–203.

46 (1931): 188–191

AN UNKNOWN SATIRIST OF THE 1860's. By N. Belchikov.

Belchikov discusses social satire in the 1850's and 1860's and outlines the career of E. P. Pertsov, a retired landlord and official in Kazan province, who had met the writer A. I. Herzen in London in 1858. Published here are three poems in which Pertsov satirizes Nicholas I and Alexander II. The poems were confiscated and Pertsov was arrested in 1861; he was sentenced to six months in prison and after his imprisonment was exiled to Viatka.

For additional material in *Krasnyi Arkhiv*, see "The Year 1861, from Notes of a Contemporary," 16 (1926): 118–164.

VOLUMES 47–48, 1931

47–48 (1931): 3–49

NICHOLAS I AND EUROPEAN REACTION 1848–1849. Introduction by R. Averbukh.

Averbukh discusses the reactionary movement in Europe, the proposed unification of Germany, the Polish problem, Constantinople and the Straits, and Anglo-Russian relations.

The documents published here outline Russian foreign policy in 1848–1849. There are ten dispatches from Baron Phillip I. Brunnow, Russian ambassador in London, to Count K. V. Nesselrode, minister of foreign affairs, dated from March 16/28, 1848, to May 25/June 6, 1849, and six dispatches from Count [P. I.] Medem, ambassador in Vienna, to Nesselrode, dated from August 25/September 5, 1848, to April 15/27, 1849. In a dispatch from Gitschin (in Bohemia), dated October 14/26, 1848, [F. P.?] Fonton reports to Nesselrode on his interview with Austrian Prince A. C. zu Windisch-Graetz. Nesselrode's dispatch of April 10, 1849, informs Medem of Russian military aid to Austria. The final document is Nesselrode's dispatch to Brunnow, July 20/August 1, 1849.

For additional material in *Krasnyi Arkhiv*, see "Austrian Revolution of 1848 and Nicholas I," 89–90 (1938): 155–207.

47–48 (1931): 50–70

THE PROJECT FOR SEIZURE OF THE BOSPORUS IN 1896. Introduction by V. Khvostov.

Of the two letters presented here, the letter from A. I. Nelidov, Russian ambassador in Constantinople, to N. P. Shishkin, Russian deputy minister of foreign affairs, on September 6/18, 1896, proposes Russian seizure of the Bosporus in the face of Balkan unrest, which came to a head in the Turkish massacre of Armenians in Constantinople. Nelidov's letter of November 18/30, 1896, proposes European settlement of the Armenian question and conversion of the Bosporus, by Russia, into a second Gibraltar.

Also reprinted are the conclusions of the ministerial conference, directed by the emperor on November 23, 1896, at which Nelidov was present and further plans were laid for seizure of the Bosporus. Count S. Y. Witte's objections to the plan are stated in a letter to Shishkin, dated November 24/December 6, 1896, which is published here together with an exchange of three communiqués between Nelidov and Shishkin in December, 1896, dealing with negotiations between Russia and France on the Turkish problem.

For references to additional material in *Krasnyi Arkhiv* on the Bosporus, see the notes to "A. I. Nelidov's Note in 1882 concerning Occupation of the Straits," 46 (1931): 179–187.

47–48 (1931): 71–89

M. N. Muraviëv's Journey Abroad in 1897. Introduction unsigned.

Two reports are published here from Minister of Foreign Affairs Count M. N. Muraviëv on the results of his visits to Paris and Berlin in January and February, 1897. The first report records his conferences with French Minister of Foreign Affairs Gabriel Hanotaux and President François Faure about the Far East, Europe, and Turkey, and the Russian desire for control of the Bosporus. French and Russian attitudes toward Germany, Austria, and England and French policies in Ethiopia and Egypt were also discussed.

The second report from Berlin records conversations with William II on the possibility of a division of Turkey, on German protection of Russia's European borders in the event that Russian interests compelled Russia to send all its troops to the Far East, and on apprehension over the possibility of an Anglo-American commercial alliance. Muraviëv also conferred with Prince [Chlodwig Karl Victor] Hohenlohe and Baron A. H. Marschall von Bieberstein.

47–48 (1931): 90–111

Poland and South Russian Counterrevolution (Economic Relations of Poland with [General A. I.] Denikin and [Baron P. N.] Wrangel). Introduction by A. Gukovsky.

Gukovsky states that the discovery of the documents published here proves the existence of an economic agreement between the Polish government and that of General A. I. Denikin. One of the documents is "A Temporary Trade Agreement between the Commander-in-Chief of the Forces of South Russia and the Government of the Polish Republic," apparently concluded on September 13, 1919. This agreement was the basis for later economic relations between Poland and Baron Wrangel's government. Other documents, dated from September 20, 1919, to May 25, 1920, describe subsequent negotiations and the actual exchange of goods.

47–48 (1931): 112–139

The Cadets in 1905–1906 (Conclusion)

Publication of documents dealing with the Cadet party in these years begins in 46 (1931): 38–68.

The minutes given here of the Cadet Central Committee meetings on August 2, 3, 27, 29, and 30, 1906, discuss the effectiveness of the Vyborg appeal, which was drafted by P. N. Miliukov and published in the name of two hundred deputies of the First State Duma. It appealed to the Russian people to make known their objection to the dispersal of the duma by refusing to pay taxes and to supply recruits for military service. Party policies, activities of other political parties, interparty relations, and the effect in agrarian areas of the dissolution of the First State Duma were also discussed.

For references to additional material in *Krasnyi Arkhiv* on the Cadets, see the notes to "From the Correspondence of V. A. Maklakov with the National Center in 1919," 36 (1929): 3–30. See also "Dispersal of the Second State Duma," 43 (1930): 55–91.

47–48 (1931): 140–183

N. M. ROMANOV's NOTES. Introduction unsigned.

These excerpts from the memoirs of Grand Duke Nicholas Mikhailovich, written from 1914 to 1916, describe his visit with Nicholas II and his family at the beginning of February, 1914. The legend that Alexander I had not died in Taganrog in 1825 but had actually made his way to Siberia, where he lived as the recluse Fëdor Kuzmich until 1863, was among the topics discussed by the Romanov family. The Grand Duke also criticizes in these notes the situation at the front during his tour of inspection from July 27 to October 17, 1914. He includes personal opinions of Generals [N. Y.] Ivanov, [M. V.] Alexeiev, [N. N.] Yanushkevich, [N. V.] Russky, and Danilov, Commander-in-Chief Grand Duke Nicholas Nikolaevich, and others.

Publication of these documents is continued in 49 (1931): 92–111.

For additional material in *Krasnyi Arkhiv*, see "L. N. Tolstoy and N. M. Romanov," 21 (1927): 231–241.

FROM AN ARCHIVIST'S NOTEBOOK

47–48 (1931): 184–188

AUTOCRACY AND THE VATICAN ON THE EVE OF THE IMPERIALISTIC WAR. Introduction by A. E.

The document printed here is a note which was drawn up in the Ministry of Foreign Affairs in January, 1914, and approved by the minister S. D. Sazonov, indicating that the government hoped to utilize Roman Catholic influence in Russia for the political interests of the tsarist regime.

A Digest of the Krasnyi Arkhiv 65

VOLUME 49, 1931

49 (1931): 3-54

SPANISH REVOLUTION OF 1873-1874. Introduction by E. Adamov.

Most of the dispatches published here, dated from July 11/23, 1873, to December 21, 1874/January 2, 1875, are from [Christian E.] Kudriavsky, Russian minister in Spain, to the Ministry of Foreign Affairs. They contain detailed information on the following matters: the effect of Spanish events on international relations; the actions of German and British naval commanders in Spanish waters; the demands of the Spanish General Contreras; conferences with foreign consuls in Spain; and the activities of General [D. E.] Sickles, United States minister to Spain, and of the American ship *Shenandoah*. There are also communiqués from Chancellor A. M. Gorchakov to Kudriavsky, instructing him to protect Russian trade in Spain but not to interfere in Spanish internal affairs.

49 (1931): 55-91

MATERIALS RELATING TO THE HISTORY OF THE DESTRUCTION OF KOLCHAK'S ARMED FORCES. Introduction by L. Andreev.

These Soviet historical documents are an account of the operations of the Twenty-seventh Rifle Division of the Red army from November, 1919, to January, 1920. They are reports on troop positions, military orders, and summaries of each operation. In addition, the amount of equipment and the number of personnel captured from Admiral A. V. Kolchak is listed. Histories of the Omsk, Novonikolaevsk, Taiga-Mari, and Akmolinsk operations are also given.

For references to additional material in *Krasnyi Arkhiv* on Kolchak, see the notes to "The Disintegration of Kolchak's Campaign," 31 (1928): 51-80.

49 (1931): 92-111

N. M. ROMANOV's NOTES (Conclusion)

Publication of excerpts from the memoirs of Grand Duke Nicholas Mikhailovich begins in 47-48 (1931): 140-183.

This section of the memoirs is divided into three parts. The "Dismissal of Minister of War Alexis Andreevich Polivanov, March 13, 1916," records the details of Polivanov's appointment and dismissal as well as the attitude of Nicholas II and Empress Alexandra Feodorovna toward him. "Details of Rasputin's Murder, December 16, 1916," is the account of the assassination of Rasputin as related by Felix Yusupov, one of the assassins. "How They All Betrayed Him," written April 26, 1917, discusses the complete abandonment of Nicholas II by many of the persons who had previously been close to him.

For additional material in *Krasnyi Arkhiv*, see "L. N. Tolstoy and N. M. Romanov," 21 (1927): 231–241.

49 (1931): 112–143

REPORTS OF LIEUTENANT GENERAL SELIVERSTOV AND ADJUTANT GENERAL DRENTELN TO ALEXANDER II (August–December, 1878). Introduction unsigned.

The fifteen reports presented here were written by Lieutenant General Seliverstov, for a short time head of the Third Department (Secret Police), in the period immediately after S. M. Kravchinsky assassinated Adjutant General N. V. Mezentsov. Adjutant General A. R. Drenteln, chief of the Gendarmerie, reported to Alexander II on the search for the assassin and on plans for curbing revolutionary activities.

For references to additional material in *Krasnyi Arkhiv* on Mezentsov's assassination, see the notes to "Materials Relating to the Trial of Adrian Mikhailov, Veimar, and Others," 39 (1930): 149–176.

FROM AN ARCHIVIST'S NOTEBOOK

49 (1931): 144–148

P. A. STOLYPIN AND THE SVEABORG UPRISING. By S. L. Ivanov.

In this article Ivanov outlines the measures employed by Premier P. A. Stolypin for ending the uprising of July 17–19, 1906, at the Sveaborg naval base and the sentences imposed on the participants.

For additional material in *Krasnyi Arkhiv*, see: "The Execution of the Participants in the Kronstadt Rebellion," 43 (1930): 166–167; "The Kronstadt Rebellion of 1906," 77 (1936): 91–116.

For references to additional material in *Krasnyi Arkhiv* on Stolypin, see the notes to "Mobilization of Reaction in 1906," 32 (1929): 158–182.

49 (1931): 148–154

MATERIALS RELATING TO THE HISTORY OF EMIGRATION IN THE 1860's. By B. Kozmin.

Kozmin's article deals with the lives of Russian political *émigrés*. In it he includes letters which were confiscated when Emily V. Evropeus was

A Digest of the Krasnyi Arkhiv 67

arrested on October 4, 1861, for smuggling books and letters into Russia. They provide information on Prince Peter V. Dolgorukov, A. I. Herzen, Natalia Ogarev (the wife of N. P. Ogarev), the composer Y. N. Golitsyn, and others.

For references to additional material in *Krasnyi Arkhiv* on Ogarev, see the notes to "An Unpublished Letter of N. P. Ogarev," 38 (1930): 169–173.

VOLUMES 50–51, 1932

50–51 (1932): 3–63

MATERIALS RELATING TO THE SINO-JAPANESE WAR 1894–1895. Introduction unsigned.

These documents include instructions from the Russian Ministry of Foreign Affairs to representatives abroad and dispatches from Russian diplomats in Japan, Korea, China, England, Germany, and France.

An English translation of these documents appears in the *Chinese Social and Political Science Review*, Peiping, XVII, 3 (October, 1933): 480–515 and XVII, 4 (January, 1934): 632–670.

For additional material in *Krasnyi Arkhiv*, see: "The Diary of V. N. Lamsdorff," 46 (1931): 3–37; "On the Eve of the Russo-Japanese War (December, 1900—January, 1902)," 63 (1934): 3–54.

50–51 (1932): 64–96

MATERIALS RELATING TO THE HISTORY OF THE FIRST HAGUE CONFERENCE, 1899. Introduction by L. Telesheva.

The letters, memoranda, and reports presented here trace the origin and development of the Hague Peace Conference as follows:

1. A secret letter from Minister of War A. N. Kuropatkin to Minister of Foreign Affairs Count M. N. Muraviëv, dated March 1/13, 1898, suggests a halt in the international armament race.

2. A memorandum of the Ministry of Foreign Affairs, dated March 24/April 5, 1898, makes a similar suggestion.

3. An undated letter from Grand Duke Alexis Aleksandrovich to Nicholas II favors the calling of a peace conference.

4. A report by Muraviëv to Nicholas II, August 9/21, 1898, states the reasons for the calling of a conference.

5. A letter from Urusov, Russian ambassador in Paris, to Muraviëv, dated August 27/September 8, 1898, outlines the French reaction to the proposed conference.

6. A report by Kuropatkin to Nicholas II, dated October 19/31, 1898, summarizes his trip abroad.

7. Undated comments by General Chanoine on Kuropatkin's memorandum show his reaction to them.

8. A report by Muraviëv to Nicholas II, November 11/23, 1898, suggests an international appeal for a conference.

9. An undated document presents a tentative draft of the proposed appeal to foreign powers.

10. A report by Muraviëv to Nicholas II, dated November 30/December 12, 1898, tells of William II's attitude toward the conference.

11. A draft of Muraviëv's memorandum to Nicholas II, December, 1898, deals with the procedures for calling the conference.

German translations of documents 1, 2, 4, 5, and 6 appear in *Berliner Monatshefte*, XI (June, 1933): 571–580 and XI (July, 1933): 679–692.

For additional material in *Krasnyi Arkhiv*, see "New Materials concerning the Hague Peace Conference of 1899," 54–55 (1932): 49–79.

50–51 (1932): 97–116

INTERVENTION AND NORTHERN COUNTERREVOLUTION. Introduction by I. Mints.

Dated from June 28 to October 7, 1919, the documents presented here are communiqués from the following: Lieutenant General Miller, commander of Russian counterrevolutionary forces on the northern front; Admiral A. V. Kolchak's government in Omsk; Major General Skobeltsyn, commander of Murmansk forces; and Russian representatives in Paris, London, and Stockholm. The material deals with the impending withdrawal of British troops from the northern front, the ensuing necessity for additional foreign aid, the proposed offensive to be launched from Finland, and details of the British withdrawal from the northern front in the fall of 1919.

For additional material in *Krasnyi Arkhiv* on intervention in North Russia, see: "The British in the North (1918–1919)," 19 (1926): 39–52; "The Disintegration of Kolchak's Campaign," 31 (1928): 51–80; "Kolchak and Finland," 33 (1929): 82–144; "Foreign Policy of the Counterrevolutionary Governments at the Beginning of 1919," 37 (1929): 69–101; "White Finns in the Service of Anglo-French Interventionists in 1919," 98 (1940): 31–67; "Materials Relating to the History of Intervention in the North," 98 (1940): 125–144; "Use by the Interventionists of the Northern Sea Route," 104 (1941): 151–198.

50–51 (1932): 117–160

THE PROGRESSIVE BLOC 1915–1917. Introduction by N. Lapin.

The documents given here are P. N. Miliukov's stenographic notes of the meetings of the presidium of the Progressive bloc of the Fourth State Duma, held from August 14, 1915, to September 3, 1915. They show the development of the attitude of the bloc on matters concerned with procedure, amnesty, the Jewish question, Finland, the Ukraine, and the Poles of the western region. A facsimile of a portion of the notes on the conference between representatives of the Progressive bloc and the Council of Ministers, August 27, 1915, is included, as is a list of the members comprising each of the factions of the bloc.

Publication of these documents is continued in 52 (1932): 143–196 and 56 (1933): 80–135.

50–51 (1932): 161–193

FROM THE CORRESPONDENCE OF TSAR NICHOLAS AND MARIE ROMANOV (1907–1910). Introduction by F. Notovich.

Nicholas II wrote these letters to his mother, the Dowager Empress Marie Feodorovna, while she was traveling abroad. Dated from March 1, 1907, to November 11, 1910, they contain much material on family affairs, Nicholas' opinions of various government officials, the dissolution of the Second State Duma, the Bosnian crisis, and Leo Tolstoy's death.

The letters of March 1, 22, and 29 and April 5, 1907, of October 9, 1908, of March 4, 18, and 19 and September 27, 1909, and of October 4 and November 11, 1910, appear in English translation in *The Secret Letters of the Last Tsar*, ed. Edward J. Bing (New York: Longmans, Green, 1938). This collection of confidential correspondence between Nicholas II and his mother does not contain translations of the letters of March 8 and 15 and July 13, 1907; of February 28, March 27, and October 8, 1908; and of March 5, 1909.

FROM AN ARCHIVIST'S NOTEBOOK

50–51 (1932): 194–210

FROM OFFICERS' LETTERS FROM THE FRONT IN 1917. Introduction by L. Andreev.

Dated from March 4 to July 3, 1917, these nine letters from officers at the front give an account of life there, the reaction to news from St. Petersburg, the gulf between officers and soldiers, and the meetings of officers in which current events were discussed.

For references to additional material in *Krasnyi Arkhiv* on conditions in the army, see the notes to "The Tactics of the High Command in the February Revolution," 35 (1929): 212–215 and to "[Comments of] Nicholas Romanov concerning the Revolutionary Movement in the Army in 1905–1906," 41–42 (1930): 215–220.

50–51 (1932): 211–225

THE PURGE OF THE COMMANDING STAFF OF THE TSARIST ARMY IN 1906. Introduction by T. Rakhmanova.

These pages present a résumé of the investigation by the commanding staff of those military units which participated in revolutionary activities in 1905, and include an anonymous letter written in December, 1905, to Minister of War General A. F. Rediger questioning the conformity of military commanders. There is an outline of the military units in which the greatest disorders had occurred, the district in which these units were stationed, the type of disorder, the names of the commanders and their commands at the time of the investigation, and reports on their competency.

For references to additional material in *Krasnyi Arkhiv* on unrest in the army, see the notes to "[Comments of] Nicholas Romanov concerning the Revolutionary Movement in the Army in 1905–1906," 41–42 (1930): 215–220. See also "Materials Relating to the History of the Autocracy's Struggle with the Revolutionary Movement in the Army in the 1860's," 63 (1934): 132–135.

50–51 (1932): 226–236

CONTENTS OF THE PREVIOUS VOLUMES OF THE JOURNAL *Krasnyi Arkhiv*

This is a list of the articles published in *Krasnyi Arkhiv*, Volumes 1–51.

VOLUME 52, 1932

52 (1932): 3

ON THE DEATH OF MICHAEL NIKOLAEVICH POKROVSKY (1868–1932). By the editors of *Krasnyi Arkhiv*.

The editors eulogize here the historian M. N. Pokrovsky, who died on April 10, 1932. His photograph, taken in 1924, is attached.

For additional material in *Krasnyi Arkhiv* on Pokrovsky, see "M. N. Pokrovsky," 30 (1928): 3–4; "A Few Documents from the Tsarist Archives concerning M. N. Pokrovsky," 52 (1932): 5–33.

52 (1932): 5-33

A FEW DOCUMENTS FROM THE TSARIST ARCHIVES CONCERNING M. N. POKROVSKY

These Secret Police documents, dated from June 1, 1907, to August 9, 1918, report on searches of M. N. Pokrovsky's living quarters, his activities as a member of the Social Democratic party, and the censorship of his writings, particularly of *Russkaia Istoriia s Drevneishikh Vremën* ("Russian History from Ancient Times"). Pokrovsky was a lecturer at Moscow University during this period.

For additional material in *Krasnyi Arkhiv* on Pokrovsky, see "M. N. Pokrovsky," 30 (1928): 3-4; "On the Death of Michael Nikolaevich Pokrovsky (1868-1932)," 52 (1932): 3.

52 (1932): 34-124

FIRST STEPS OF RUSSIAN IMPERIALISM IN THE FAR EAST (1888-1903). Introduction by A. Popov.

An English translation of the documents presented here—"Proceedings of the Special Committee on the Far East" for April 26/May 8, 1888, August 9/21, 1894, January 20/February 1, 1895, and March 30/April 11, 1895, and reports to the tsar from Minister of Foreign Affairs N. K. de Giers and Prince A. B. Lobanov-Rostovsky and from the governor general of the Amur, Dukhovsky—may be found in the *Chinese Social and Political Science Review*, Peiping, XVII, 2 (July, 1934): 236-281.

The following three documents are also published here, but are not translated in the *Chinese Social and Political Science Review:* (1) Minister of Finance Count S. Y. Witte's note of March 31/April 12, 1896, concerning Far Eastern policies, especially the construction of railroads as outlined in Dukhovsky's report; (2) the report of the minister of foreign affairs, dated November 11/23, 1897, and approved by Nicholas II, on the necessity for acquiring ports in the Far East; (3) the proposed agreement between the Russo-Chinese Bank and the Russian and Chinese governments, September 26/October 8, 1901.

52 (1932): 125-142

THE UNITED STATES OF AMERICA AND TSARIST RUSSIA IN THE 1890's. Introduction by F. Kelin.

The introduction to the three documents presented here is a history of Russo-American relations. The first document contains the instructions of Minister of Foreign Affairs Count M. N. Muraviëv to Count [A. P.] Cassini, Russian minister in Washington. The documents are dated February 10/January 29, 1898, and they review the following topics: Russo-American relations during the Civil War in the United States, American export of grain to Russia during the famine of 1891, the dispatch of a Russian squadron to the United States in 1893 at the time of the Columbian Exposition in Chicago, the sale of Alaska in 1867, the Monroe Doctrine, the acquisition by the United States of the Hawaiian Islands, the seal industry, and Canadian-American relations. The second document is a confidential letter from Count Cassini to Count V. N. Lamsdorff, assistant minister of foreign affairs. Dated Washington, June 11/23, 1898, the letter presents Cassini's first impressions of the policies of the United States, as well as his opinions on the annexation by the United States of the Philippine Islands and on the state of Anglo-American relations. The third document is a confidential dispatch from Cassini to Muraviëv, June 10/22, 1898, on the same matters.

52 (1932): 143–196

THE PROGRESSIVE BLOC 1915–1917 (Continuation). Introduction by N. Lapin.

Publication of these documents dealing with the Progressive bloc of the Fourth State Duma begins in 50–51 (1932): 117–160.

P. N. Miliukov's reports of eleven meetings of the Progressive bloc held at General [Baron A. N.] Meller-Zakomelsky's home between October 25, 1915, and February 2, 1916, are given here.

These documents are concluded in 56 (1933): 80–135.

FROM AN ARCHIVIST'S NOTEBOOK

52 (1932): 197–203

A. P. MOHRENHEIM'S LETTER CONCERNING FRENCH POLITICS IN THE NEAR EAST (1896). Introduction by V. Khvostov.

This letter, written in November, 1896, by A. P. Mohrenheim, Russian ambassador in Paris, to N. P. Shishkin, deputy minister of foreign affairs, briefly reviews French internal politics and reports on Mohrenheim's conference with French Minister of Foreign Affairs Gabriel Hanotaux on Russo-French policies in Turkey, Egypt, and the Dardanelles.

For additional material in *Krasnyi Arkhiv*, see: "A. I. Nelidov's Note in 1882 concerning Occupation of the Straits," 46 (1931): 179–187; "The Project for Seizure of the Bosporus in 1896," 47–48 (1931): 50–70.

A Digest of the Krasnyi Arkhiv

52 (1932): 203–206

MATERIALS RELATING TO THE HISTORY OF THE INTELLIGENTSIA OF THE 1860's. Introduction by B. Kozmin.

The letter published here was written in December, 1867, by V. A. Zaitsev, journalist, critic, and nihilist, to his sister in Geneva. It suggests the state of mind of Russian liberals in the 1860's.

VOLUME 53, 1932

53 (1932): 3–37

TSARIST RUSSIA AND PERSIA IN THE EPOCH OF THE RUSSO-JAPANESE WAR. Introduction by A. Popov.

The documents presented here are the secret instructions of Minister of Foreign Affairs Count V. N. Lamsdorff to the newly appointed minister in Tehran, Alexis Nikolaevich Speyer. Dispatched on September 30/October 13, 1904, they outline Russo-Persian relations, Russia's attitude toward the Persian economy, Persia's relations with its border nationalities, the possible role of Russia in Persian army reforms, expansion of telegraph lines in Persia, and political and strategic considerations in Anglo-Russian relations in Persia and in Asia in general.

For additional material in *Krasnyi Arkhiv*, see: "Anglo-Russian Rivalry in Persia 1890–1906," 56 (1933): 33–64; "Anglo-Russian Relations in Persia at the Time of the World War," 65–66 (1934): 86–117.

53 (1932): 38–62

MATERIALS RELATING TO THE HISTORY OF THE OCTOBER DAYS IN PETROGRAD (From Materials of the Petrograd Military-Revolutionary Committee). Introduction by V. Elagin.

Eighty-five communiqués, orders, and reports of the Petrograd Military-Revolutionary Committee on October 29, 1917, appear here. The journal of the committee's meeting on October 29 and the text of an appeal to Petrograd residents to support the revolution are also published.

For additional material in *Krasnyi Arkhiv*, see: "Second All-Russian Congress of Soviets," 84 (1937): 12–134; "Orders and Decrees of the Petrograd Military-Revolutionary Committee on Questions of the Press in the Days of the October Revolution," 84 (1937): 188–198.

53 (1932): 63–99

THE FLEET AFTER THE OCTOBER VICTORY. Introduction by A. Drezen.

The minutes of eight meetings of the First All-Russian Naval Congress, dated November 18–25, 1917, are printed here. The congress was held in Petrograd to consider naval reforms and reports from the Naval Revolutionary Committee.

The text of Lenin's address to the congress on November 22 is published in V. I. Lenin, *Sochinenia* ("Works"), (Leningrad, 1935–1937), XXII, 98–102.

53 (1932): 100–126

THE CHURCH AND THE BURIAT-MONGOL RUSSIFICATION IN TSARIST RUSSIA. Introduction by I. Shpitsberg.

A twenty-four-page report by Archbishop Serafin of Irkutsk to Assistant Procurator of the Synod P. S. Damansky appears here. Dated October 6, 1913, the report was written in answer to Damansky's request for reasons why so many Buriat-Mongols had forsaken Orthodoxy for Buddhism after 1905. The Archbishop discusses the effects of the manifestoes of April 17 and October 17, 1905, and reviews missionary activities among the Buriats in the nineteenth century. Two short reports also included deal with financial assistance granted by Admiral A. V. Kolchak's government in 1919 to Bandido Khambo-Lama, the Mongol religious leader in the Uriankhaisk region.

For references to additional material in *Krasnyi Arkhiv* on the national minority problem, see the notes to "Materials Relating to the History of the Tsarist National Minority Policy," 35 (1929): 107–127.

53 (1932): 127–138

ADRIAN MIKHAILOV AND COUNT M. T. LORIS-MELIKOV. Introduction by I. N.

The letters of Adrian Mikhailov and his sister to Alexander II and Count M. T. Loris-Melikov in May, 1880, which appear here are pleas for the commutation of Mikhailov's death sentence. Olga Natanson's plea for pardon is also published, as is Loris-Melikov's report of May 16, 1880, listing the sentences of the revolutionaries tried with Mikhailov.

For references to additional material in *Krasnyi Arkhiv* on Mikhailov, see the notes to "Materials Relating to the Trial of Adrian Mikhailov, Veimar, and Others," 39 (1930): 149–176.

A Digest of the Krasnyi Arkhiv

FROM AN ARCHIVIST'S NOTEBOOK

53 (1932): 139–150

FROM THE CORRESPONDENCE OF S. M. AND N. M. ROMANOV IN 1917. Introduction by A. S.

In this article are twelve letters from Grand Duke Sergius Mikhailovich, inspector general of artillery, to his brother Grand Duke Nicholas Mikhailovich, adjutant general, dated from March 9 to August 23, 1917. Among the events on which Grand Duke Sergius comments are Nicholas II's abdication, Sergius' personal concern for the safety of the ballerina Madame M. K. Kshesinskaia, conditions at staff headquarters at Mogilev, the dismissal of General M. V. Alexeiev and the trial of Minister of War General V. A. Sukhomlinov, the effectiveness of Leninist propaganda in the army, the transfer of the Imperial Family to Siberia, and revolutionary activities in Petrograd.

53 (1932): 151–158

FOREIGN DIPLOMATS CONCERNING THE REVOLUTION OF 1905. Introduction unsigned.

The materials presented here are in part excerpts from the dispatches of [Robert S.] McCormick, United States ambassador to Russia, to an American correspondent named Tomson, dated January 10/23, 1905, and to United States ambassador [George] Meyer in Rome, dated March 13/25, 1905. Thirteen other dispatches from British, Rumanian, Austrian, Bulgarian, Portuguese, and French representatives in Russia describe the Revolution of 1905 and venture personal predictions on the outcome of the struggle.

53 (1932): 158–162

MATERIALS RELATING TO THE HISTORY OF THE LABOR MOVEMENT IN KARAGANDA. Introduction by N. Bolotnikov.

An official government report, dated December 16, 1905, on unrest in the Karaganda area between December 7 and December 11, 1905, is printed here. It is supplemented by a petition signed by thirty-three workers in the Uspensky copper mine, belonging to a Frenchman, C. E. Carnot, in which the workers state that if their demands are not met in five days a general Russo-Kirghiz strike will result. Alimzhan Baichigirov was the ringleader, according to a police report.

53 (1932): 162–166

THE PEKING SPIRITUAL MISSION AND RUSSO-CHINESE TRADE 1830–1850.
By G. L.

The thesis of this article is that Russian missionaries in China in the mid-nineteenth century were there primarily as commercial agents. The article, written in 1932, is based on reports by the head of the mission in Peking.

VOLUMES 54–55, 1932

54–55 (1932): 3–48

P. N. MILIUKOV's DIARY. Introduction by Y. Berzin.

The main part of Miliukov's diary, which is printed here, is dated from April 16/29, to May 3/16, 1916. It was written while Miliukov was a member of the Russian parliamentary delegation abroad and is a record of conferences primarily concerned with the progress of World War I, the international aspects of the Polish question, Swedish-Russian and Swedish-Entente relations, and the Finnish question. The entries in the diary were made in Russia, Sweden, Norway, and England. Supplementing the diary are biographical notes on each of the members of the delegation and the itinerary for the journey.

For additional material in Krasnyi Arkhiv, see: "The Russian 'Parliamentary' Delegation Abroad in 1916," 58 (1933): 3–23; "Tsarist Russia's International Financial Situation at the Time of the World War," 64 (1934): 3–30.

54–55 (1932): 49–79

NEW MATERIALS CONCERNING THE HAGUE PEACE CONFERENCE OF 1899. Introduction by L. Telesheva.

Excerpts presented here from the diary of Minister of War General A. N. Kuropatkin, dated February 28, 1898, to January 12, 1899, reveal European reaction to the Russian proposal on disarmament and Kuropatkin's part in promoting the First Hague Peace Conference. Also printed here is a report of October 17/30, 1898, to Nicholas II, in which Minister of Foreign Affairs Count M. N. Muraviëv gives an account of his conferences with French President François Faure and his Minister of Foreign Affairs Théophile Delcassé and with Austria-Hungary's Emperor Franz Joseph and his minister Count [Agenor] Goluchowski. With Faure and Delcassé, Muraviëv discussed Far Eastern and Balkan affairs, Russo-French relations,

Crete, Fashoda, the Vatican, Anglo-French relations, and French internal affairs. With the emperor and Goluchowski, he discussed the Balkans and relations between Russia and Austria-Hungary.

54–55 (1932): 80–161

MATERIALS RELATING TO THE HISTORY OF THE MOSCOW MILITARY-REVOLUTIONARY COMMITTEE (November 1/14—November 10/23, 1917). Introduction by E. Rozhen.

The journal reprinted here itemizes 927 orders, resolutions, and permits of the Moscow Military-Revolutionary Committee, with extensive annotations. Rozhen states that this journal is of particular value since most of the documents cited have not been preserved; therefore, it is actually a chronological outline of many events in Moscow in November, 1917, about which no other data have been preserved.

54–55 (1932): 162–204

THE TSARIST GOVERNMENT AND THE BEILIS TRIAL. Introduction by A. S. Tager.

The forty-one documents presented here, dated from March 31, 1911, to April 15/23, 1914, deal with the trial, held in the fall of 1913, of Mendel Beilis, a Jewish worker accused of murdering a twelve-year-old boy for a religious ritual. They include the following materials: a report to the Holy Synod by Metropolitan Flavian of Kiev and Galicia on the murder of the boy; secret Police Department communiqués concerning the trial; an exchange of communiqués between the governor of the Kiev province, the Ministry of Foreign Affairs, the Ministry of Internal Affairs, and the Ministry of Justice on the political implications of the trial of Beilis; reports and letters sent between the Ministry of Foreign Affairs and its representatives in London, Washington, and the Vatican on international reaction to the trial.

For additional material in *Krasnyi Arkhiv*, see "The Beilis Trial as Appraised by the Police Department," 44 (1931): 85–125.

VOLUME 56, 1933

56 (1933): 5–32

KARL MARX AND TSARIST CENSORSHIP. Introduction unsigned.

The censors' reports given here on Karl Marx's works, dated from 1872 to 1916, deal with the following books: *Das Kapital, The Communist Man-*

ifesto, *Capitalism and Communism, Civil War in France (1870–1871), Wage-Labor and Capital, Class Struggle in France 1848–1850,* and *The Poverty of Philosophy.* These documents were published on the fiftieth anniversary of Marx's death. There is a picture of Marx, as well as excerpts from the writings of Friedrich Engels and Stalin on Marxism and Leninism.

56 (1933): 33–64

ANGLO-RUSSIAN RIVALRY IN PERSIA 1890–1906. Introduction unsigned.

The documents given here contain minutes of special conferences on Persian affairs. The meeting of February 4, 1890, was devoted to a discussion of means of securing a concession for a railroad connection between Russia and Persia and the possible reaction abroad, particularly in England. The conference of June 7, 1904, reviewed Russia's economic ventures in Persia and planned additional financial policies. The conference of August 12, 1905, was devoted to making plans for future loans to Persia and to discussing concessions to be gained from Persia, reorganization of the Persian army, and "foreign influence" in Persia. The conference of September 7, 1906, considered Anglo-Russian relations.

For additional material in *Krasnyi Arkhiv,* see: "Tsarist Russia and Persia in the Epoch of the Russo-Japanese War," 53 (1932): 3–37; "Anglo-Russian Relations in Persia at the Time of the World War," 65–66 (1934): 86–117.

56 (1933): 65–79

ANGLO-GERMAN RAPPROCHEMENT IN 1898. Introduction by L. Telesheva.

The correspondence published here between Russian Minister of Foreign Affairs Count M. Muraviëv, Count N. D. Osten-Sacken, and Baron Staal, is dated from June to December, 1898, and deals with the efforts of Osten-Sacken and Staal to secure information in Berlin and London on the terms of the Anglo-German agreement of August 18/30, 1898.

56 (1933): 80–135

THE PROGRESSIVE BLOC 1915–1917. Introduction by N. Lapin.

Publication of P. N. Miliukov's notes on the Progressive bloc of the Fourth State Duma begins in 50–51 (1932): 117–160 and is continued in 52 (1932): 143–196.

The material here is a continuation of Miliukov's notes on the fourteen meetings of the Progressive bloc held from October 3 to November 18, 1916, to discuss foreign and domestic policies.

FROM AN ARCHIVIST'S NOTEBOOK

56 (1933): 136–138

THE LAST HOURS OF THE PROVISIONAL GOVERNMENT IN 1917. Introduction by M. Levina.

P. I. Palchinsky, minister of trade and commerce in the Provisional Government, is the author of the description presented here of the last thirty-six hours of that government's existence, October 24–25, 1917. Palchinsky was, during the October days, assistant to the governor general of Petrograd.

56 (1933): 138–144

THE WORKERS' STRIKE AT BROMLEI FACTORY IN 1903. Introduction unsigned.

Police Department communications and Social Democratic proclamations given here deal with the five-day strike for shorter hours and higher pay at the Bromlei factory in Moscow in July, 1903.

56 (1933): 144–148

THE ROMANOVS AND RAILROAD CONCESSIONS IN THE 1870's. Introduction by K.

The entries given here from the diary of A. A. Polovtsov, senator and president of the Imperial Russian Historical Society, in June, 1871, and December, 1883, tell of the intrigue connected with the granting of concessions for Caucasian railroads, in which members of the Romanov family played a significant role. Other leading participants were Falkenhagen, Poliakov, and Efimovich.

Publication of other sections of Polovtsov's diary begins in 3 (1923): 75–172 and is continued in 4 (1923): 63–128; 33 (1929): 170–203; 46 (1931): 110–132; 59 (1933): 82–109; 67 (1934): 168–186.

VOLUME 57, 1933

57 (1933): 3–9

MAY 1 POSTAGE STAMPS OF THE LATVIAN BOLSHEVIKS IN 1917. Introduction by Y. B.

Latvian postage stamps picturing Karl Marx are reproduced here. The documents which also appear are the minutes of the Foreign Committee of the Latvian Social Democratic party, which were sent, together with two reports by A. A. Krasilnikov, of the Ministry of Internal Affairs, to the Police Department in April, 1914.

57 (1933): 10–42

RUMANIAN SIGURANTSA. Introduction by D. Zaslavsky.

The report of Colonel Palitsyn, Russian military attaché in Rumania, is published here. It is dated February 28, 1917, and describes the work and personnel of the Rumanian *Sigurantsa* ("Secret Police"). There are fifteen supplementary notes on espionage in Rumania, as well as notes on the personality of Panitesku, head of the Rumanian Secret Police.

57 (1933): 43–84

MATERIALS RELATING TO THE HISTORY OF "WORKERS' GROUPS" UNDER THE CENTRAL WAR INDUSTRIAL COMMITTEE. Introduction by I. Menitsky.

The Central War Industrial Committee was established in the summer of 1915. The first of the two reports presented in this article is dated February 15, 1917; it deals with the activities of the workers' group of the committee. The second document, "Some Considerations of the Contemporary Labor Movement and Measures Necessary for Its Regulation," was written by A. Konovalov, vice chairman of the committee, P. Kazakevich, assistant chairman, and one Omelchenko, assistant to the business manager.

For additional material in *Krasnyi Arkhiv*, see: "Materials Relating to the History of Gvozdevshchinism," 67 (1934): 28–92; "From the Editors," 68 (1935): 171–172.

57 (1933); 85–99

FIRST STATE DUMA IN VYBORG. Introduction unsigned.

The introduction states that the First State Duma was dispersed by the tsarist Manifesto of July 8, 1907, and that on July 9–10, some of the Duma deputies met in Vyborg. Published here are the minutes of these meetings, as well as a copy of Duma representative F. F. Kokoshkin's appeal to the Russian people to demand their political rights. There is also a statement by the Polish deputies.

For additional material in *Krasnyi Arkhiv* on the state dumas, see: "General Alexeev and the Provisional Committee of the State Duma," 2 (1922): 284–286; "Prince E. N. Trubetskoi's Letter to Nicholas II on the Dissolution of the First State Duma," 10 (1925): 300–304; "The Government's Frame of Mind during the Epoch of the First State Duma," 15 (1926): 214; "The Arrest and Trial of the Social Democratic Faction in the Second State Duma," 16 (1926): 76–117; "F. A. Golovin's Memoirs," 19 (1926): 110–149; "The 'Alliance of October 17' in 1906," 35 (1929): 151–175 and 36 (1929): 84–121; "Dispersal of the Second State Duma," 43 (1930): 55–91; "From F. A. Golovin's Notes," 58 (1933): 140–149; "Arrest of the Duma 'Quintet' in 1914," 64 (1934): 31–51; "Illegal Work of the Bolshevik Faction of the Fourth State Duma," 77 (1936): 61–90.

57 (1933): 100–139

MATERIALS RELATING TO THE HISTORY OF THE POLISH INSURRECTION OF 1863 (The Hitherto Unknown Manuscript of Oscar Aveide: "Short Sketch of Recent Events in Poland, 1861–1864"). Introduction by C. Yasinsky.

Yasinsky states that Oscar Aveide was a member of the Central National Committee of Poland and later a representative of the Polish Revolutionary Government in Lithuania. He was arrested on August 22, 1863. *Notes of Oscar Aveide on the Polish Uprising in 1863* was published in Warsaw in 1866. The "sketch" printed here is much shorter and was written in 1868, while Aveide was exiled in Viatka. This document, sent by the governor of Viatka to the minister of internal affairs, includes a brief survey of Polish history from the end of the Napoleonic Wars to 1861, a survey of Polish political groups and their leaders, and a discussion of the tsarist Manifesto of February 27, 1861. Part I of the notes concludes with an analysis of the Conscription Bill of 1863.

FROM AN ARCHIVIST'S NOTEBOOK

57 (1933): 140–142

JULY DAYS OF 1917. Introduction by V. Elagin.

The documents presented here are ten military reports on the activities of Lieutenant V. T. Stukantsev's second volunteer detachment in Petrograd, July 5–10, 1917.

57 (1933): 142–143

THE COUNTERFEIT MANIFESTO OF 1861. By B. Kozmin.

This is a copy of a parody on the Emancipation Manifesto of February 19, 1861, which the police accused N. G. Chernyshevsky of having written.

VOLUME 58, 1933

58 (1933): 3–23

THE RUSSIAN "PARLIAMENTARY" DELEGATION ABROAD IN 1916 (P. N. Miliukov's Report to the Military-Naval Commission of the [Fourth] State Duma, June 19, 1916). Introduction by N. Vanag.

P. N. Miliukov's report on the results of the visit of the Russian "parliamentary" delegation to England, France, Italy, and Sweden deals with the following subjects: the Straits problem; Alsace-Lorraine; the Polish question; the Balkans; the attitude of the United States toward World War I and the persecution of Jews in Russia; conditions in Rumania, Greece, and Bulgaria; conditions in the Scandinavian countries and Holland; the prospects for postwar alignments of powers; possible postwar territorial changes.

For additional material in *Krasnyi Arkhiv*, see "P. N. Miliukov's Diary," 54–55 (1932): 3–48.

58 (1933): 24–45

GENERAL A. M. ZAIONCHKOVSKY'S NOTE CONCERNING THE DOBRUDJA OPERATION OF 1916. Introduction by S. Budkevich.

Budkevich reviews the situation in Dobrudja from August to October, 1916, emphasizing the importance of the formation of a Russian corps to assist Rumanian forces in Dobrudja. General A. M. Zaionchkovsky was appointed commander of the Russian army corps sent to Dobrudja. His note of October 20, 1916, addressed to Nicholas II, is published here. It is divided into the following parts: (1) the condition of Rumanian troops and their officers; (2) measures for making a battleworthy Rumanian army; (3) the precariousness of the position of the Russian corps in the face of the predominance of Rumanian troops in the same theater of war; (4) the necessity of organizing the rear; (5) operational reports; (6) the harmful conduct of Russian military representatives in Rumania.

58 (1933): 46–57

MATERIALS RELATING TO THE HISTORY OF THE POTSDAM AGREEMENT OF 1911. Introduction by A. Erusalimsky.

Presented here are the minutes of a special ministerial conference on Russo-Persian relations held on October 15, 1910. Under the chairmanship of Premier P. A. Stolypin, the conference discussed Persian railroad construction as affected by the construction of the Baghdad railroad and Russo-German relations in Persia. It also considered Russia's general policies with regard to Persia in view of that country's unfriendly attitude toward Russia.

58 (1933): 58–85

M. N. KATKOV AND ALEXANDER III IN 1886–1887. Introduction by F. R.

Three notes from M. N. Katkov, publisher of the paper *Moskovskie Vedomosti* ("Moscow Journal"), to Alexander III in December, 1886, and January, 1887, are given here. They deal with affairs in Bulgaria and with Russo-German relations and their repercussions on Russia's over-all foreign policy. The comments of Minister of Foreign Affairs N. K. de Giers and Minister of Internal Affairs Count Dmitry Tolstoy on Katkov's reports also appear. Katkov opposed a Russo-German *rapprochement,* favoring instead a *rapprochement* with France.

58 (1933): 86–100

BOLSHEVIZATION OF THE FRONT BEFORE THE JULY DAYS OF 1917. Introduction by Vera Vladimirova.

The documents printed here indicate the political frame of mind of the soldiers in the army at various sectors of the front at the end of June and the beginning of July, 1917. They are communiqués from inspectors of the Provisional Government to the General Staff at Mogilev on the effectiveness of Bolshevik propaganda.

For references to additional material in *Krasnyi Arkhiv* on the army, see the notes to "The Tactics of the High Command in the February Revolution," 35 (1929): 212–215.

58 (1933): 101–130

MOSCOW STUDENTS AND PROFESSORS ON THE EVE OF THE FEBRUARY REVOLUTION. Introduction by I. Menitsky.

The government documents and university reports presented here trace student agitation in Moscow; they comprise the conclusions of the military procurator of the Moscow military district in the case of the Social Democratic student organization, "Marxist Group"; texts of Social Democratic leaflets found in Moscow University buildings in March, 1916; student resolutions protesting the military conscription of Jewish students; and leaflets distributed in October, 1916.

FROM AN ARCHIVIST'S NOTEBOOK

58 (1933): 131–133

THE PRESS IN THE KERENSKY ERA. Introduction by M. Levina.

Four Provisional Government documents concerning revolutionary agitation in the press in August and September, 1917, are printed here.

58 (1933): 133–140

THE LABOR MOVEMENT IN THE KOENIG FACTORY IN 1917. By G. Linko.

This article gives a history of the unrest in the Koenig spinning and thread factory in 1917, with a document listing the demands of the workers in each division of the factory and the factory superintendent's answers to each demand.

58 (1933): 140–149

FROM F. A. GOLOVIN'S NOTES. Introduction unsigned.

The notes printed here contain a biographical sketch of S. A. Muromtsev, professor at Moscow University and chairman of the First State Duma, written by F. A. Golovin, chairman of the Second State Duma. Golovin also briefly characterizes others of his contemporaries.

For additional material in *Krasnyi Arkhiv* on the First State Duma, see the notes above to "First State Duma in Vyborg," 57 (1933): 85–99.

58 (1933): 150–155

WILLIAM II CONCERNING THE SEIZURE OF PORT ARTHUR BY RUSSIA. Introduction by L. Telesheva.

Four letters are printed here from Count N. D. Osten-Sacken, Russian ambassador in Berlin, to Count M. N. Muraviëv, minister of foreign affairs. They record conferences with William II and Secretary of State for Foreign Affairs Bernhard von Bülow from December, 1897, to March, 1898, on Far Eastern affairs, including the occupation of Port Arthur by Russia and of Kiaochow by Germany. In these letters Osten-Sacken reports German assurances of support to Russia in the event of a Japanese or British menace to Russian activities in the Far East.

VOLUME 59, 1933

59 (1933): 3–67

MATERIALS RELATING TO THE HISTORY OF THE CONVOCATION OF THE SECOND CONGRESS OF THE RUSSIAN SOCIAL DEMOCRATIC LABOR PARTY. Introduction by V. Nevsky.

The documents published in this article cover the years 1902 and 1903 and include the following materials: copies of proclamations to the Russian people by the organizational committee of the Social Democratic party; correspondence of members of the organizational committee working in Russia with members working abroad, especially with Lenin's wife, N. K. Krupskaia; and communiqués of the Police Department with provincial Gendarmerie officials.

59 (1933): 68–81

A FEW DOCUMENTS ABOUT M. S. OLMINSKY FROM THE GENDARMERIE ARCHIVES. Introduction by P. Lepeshinsky.

The documents printed here trace the activities of Michael Stepanovich Olminsky (Aleksandrov) in the Social Democratic movement from 1894 to 1913.

59 (1933): 82–109

P. A. SHUVALOV CONCERNING THE CONGRESS OF BERLIN 1878. Introduction by V. Khvostov.

Notes on the Congress of Berlin, made by Count Peter A. Shuvalov, Russian ambassador in London and representative at the congress, are given here. They are prefaced by excerpts from the diary of Senator and President of the Imperial Russian Historical Society A. A. Polovtsov for July 3, 1881, in which Polovtsov recalls how Shuvalov came to write the notes.

The memoirs of Shuvalov appear in German translation in the *Berliner Monatshefte*, XVI (July–August, 1938): 603–632.

For other sections of Polovtsov's diary in *Krasnyi Arkhiv*, see: 3 (1923): 75–172; 4 (1923): 63–128; 33 (1929): 170–203; 46 (1931): 110–132; 67 (1934): 168–186.

59 (1933): 110–144

THE CADETS IN THE DAYS OF THE GALICIAN DEVASTATION OF 1915. Introduction by N. Lapin.

Excerpts from the minutes of the Constitutional Democratic party (Cadets) conference in Petrograd, June 6–8, 1915, appear here. Although matters of economics, finances, national minorities, and agrarian policy were discussed at the conference, which took place at the time of the military defeats in Galicia, only P. N. Miliukov's speech on the general political situation in Russia is published. Miliukov was one of the founders of the Cadets.

For references to additional material in *Krasnyi Arkhiv* on the Cadets, see the notes to "From the Correspondence of V. A. Maklakov with the National Center in 1919," 36 (1929): 3–30.

FROM AN ARCHIVIST'S NOTEBOOK

59 (1933): 145–148

P. B. STRUVE'S LETTERS TO S. D. SAZONOV IN 1915. Introduction by D. Zaslavsky.

Two letters of P. B. Struve, liberal political writer, to S. D. Sazonov, minister of foreign affairs, are published here. The first is dated June 10, 1915, and accuses General V. A. Sukhomlinov, minister of war, of gross incompetence. The second, dated July 3, 1915, outlines a nine-point economic program for Russia.

VOLUME 60, 1933

60 (1933): 3–59

ANGLO-SPANISH CONFLICT 1898–1899. Introduction unsigned.

The forty documents published here are dispatches to the Russian Ministry of Foreign Affairs from its representatives in Madrid, Tangier, Paris, Rome, and Berlin; they shed light on the Anglo-Spanish conflict, particularly on the issue of fortifying Gibraltar. The documents also provide information on the relations of Spain with Russia, Germany, France, and Italy, as well as on the Spanish-American War.

60 (1933): 60–91

DZHIZAK UPRISING OF 1916. Introduction by A. Shestakov.

The rebellion in Turkestan in 1916 caused by the draft of natives for military work in the rear is described in the documents given here, which record the government's investigation, the interrogation of participants and witnesses, and the findings of the court.

For references to additional material in *Krasnyi Arkhiv* on the uprising in Central Asia, see the notes to "The Uprising in Central Asia in 1916," 34 (1929): 39–94. For references to additional material on national minorities, see the notes to "Materials Relating to the History of the Tsarist Nationality Policy," 35 (1929): 107–127.

60 (1933): 92–133

FROM THE MEMOIRS OF A. F. REDIGER. Introduction by R. Zverev.

The notes for 1906 of Minister of War Lieutenant General A. F. Rediger that are given here are concerned with peasant unrest, the First State Duma, terrorist attempts on the lives of government officials, and the need for basic military reforms.

For references to additional material in *Krasnyi Arkhiv*, see the notes to "Notes of A. F. Rediger concerning 1905," 45 (1931): 86–111.

60 (1933): 134–141

TSARIST CENSORSHIP AND GENDARMERIE CONCERNING CLARA ZETKIN. Introduction unsigned.

Six censorship reports, dated from 1899 to 1914, are given here; they deal with the Social Democratic party's journal *Gleichheit* and the following works of its editor, Clara Zetkin: *Der Student und das Weib*, *Shkolnyi Vopros* ("The School Question"), and *Nachalo Zhenskogo Rabochego Dvizhenia v Germanii* ("The Origin of the Woman's Labor Movement in Germany"). There is also a report on a book by the German Socialist A. Hoffman, *Desiat Zapovedei i Imushchie Klassy* ("The Ten Commandments and the Propertied Classes"), which contains a letter from Zetkin to the author. It was through the efforts of the Gendarmerie that some of these works bearing on the activities of Clara Zetkin came to the attention of the censorship committee.

FROM AN ARCHIVIST'S NOTEBOOK

60 (1933): 142–156

MEMOIRS OF A. I. KOZMIN. Introduction by V. Maksakov.

Maksakov states that the document published here comprises only a portion of the memoirs of Kozmin, assistant commander of the Petrograd military district in the Kerensky government. The entries, dated from May to October, 1917, describe Kozmin's appointment by Kerensky, his work with the various military commands, and morale among the officers.

For additional material in *Krasnyi Arkhiv* on unrest in the army during World War I, see: "V. A. Sukhomlinov's Correspondence with N. N. Yanushkevich," 1 (1922): 209–272 and 2 (1922): 130–175; "The Revolutionary Movement in the Army during the World War," 4 (1923): 417–424; "The Stavka and the Ministry of Foreign Affairs," 26 (1928): 1–50; 27 (1928): 2–57; 28 (1928): 3–58; 29 (1928): 1–54; 30 (1928): 5–45; "The Soldiers' Frame of Mind on the Eve of the World War," 64 (1934): 73–84; "Life of Soldiers in the Tsarist Army," 98 (1940): 145–176.

60 (1933): 156–160

PEASANT [RESOLUTIONS] CONCERNING THE BREST PEACE IN 1918. Introduction unsigned.

Presented here are fifteen resolutions by peasant groups asking for acceptance of the terms of the Brest-Litovsk peace in February, 1918.

René Martel discusses these documents in "Nouveaux Documents d'histoire russe," *Le Monde slave* (June, 1934), p. 446.

VOLUME 61, 1933

61 (1933): 3–25

O. BISMARCK'S LETTERS TO A. M. GORCHAKOV. Introduction by A. Erusalimsky.

A Russian translation is given here of eighteen letters, originally in French and German, from Otto von Bismarck to Russian Minister of Foreign Affairs Prince A. M. Gorchakov. They are dated from August 22/September 3, 1860, to November 13, 1876. Among the political issues they discuss are the Polish Insurrection of 1863, Russo-Prussian relations, the Schleswig-Holstein and Luxembourg questions, and Russian internal affairs.

61 (1933): 26–57

THE STAVKA AND THE MOSCOW COMMITTEE OF PUBLIC SAFETY IN 1917. Introduction by E. Rozhen.

Forty-three communications exchanged between the Moscow Committee of Public Safety and the *Stavka* (the General Staff of the western front) from October 23 to November 1, 1917, are published in this article. The Bolshevik seizure of power in Moscow is traced step by step in these dispatches.

For additional material in *Krasnyi Arkhiv* on conditions in Moscow, see "The Moscow Military-Revolutionary Committee," 23 (1927): 64–148.

61 (1933): 58–81

UFA CONFERENCE AND THE PROVISIONAL SIBERIAN GOVERNMENT. Introduction by S. Piontkovsky.

The telegrams and letters printed here link the events in Siberia and the Far East with those in Ufa in 1918. They trace negotiations between the government at Ufa and the government at Omsk and the attempts to unite all the provisional governments into an all-Russian government during the Civil War.

For additional material in *Krasnyi Arkhiv*, see "Autographs of the Members of the Ufa Conference," 31 (1928): 202–204. For references to additional material on events in Siberia, see the notes to "The Disintegration of Kolchak's Campaign," 31 (1928): 51–80.

61 (1933): 82–128

FROM LEO TIKHOMIROV'S DIARY (1907). Introduction by V. Maksakov.

Entries in Tikhomirov's diary concerning family affairs and quotations from newspapers have been deleted from the notes which appear here, dated from December 31, 1906, to October 23, 1907. Tikhomirov reflects on the state of his "unhappy country," elections to the Second State Duma, the growth of socialism in Germany as evidenced in elections there, an attempt on Count S. Y. Witte's life in January, Moscow strikes, and the rise of the labor movement. He also appraises several government ministers.

For other sections of Tikhomirov's diary printed in *Krasnyi Arkhiv*, see 38 (1930): 20–69; 39 (1930): 47–75; 40 (1930): 59–96; 41–42 (1930): 103–147; 72 (1935): 120–159; 73 (1935): 170–190; 74 (1936): 162–191; 75 (1936): 171–184. For additional material on Tikhomirov, see: "From the Archive of L. Tikhomirov," 6 (1924): 124–194; "Unpublished Memoirs of L. Tikhomirov," 29 (1928): 139–174.

FROM AN ARCHIVIST'S NOTEBOOK

61 (1933): 129–135

FROM CORRESPONDENCE OF TSARIST OFFICIALS ON THE EVE OF WAR AND REVOLUTION. Introduction by D. Zaslavsky.

Count Vladimir Vladimirovich Musin-Pushkin, member of the Fourth State Duma, wrote in February, April, and December of 1914 to his father-in-law Count I. I. Vorontsov-Dashkov, viceroy of the Caucasus, on the political situation in Russia, the differences in opinion among the government ministers, and the effect of the war on the people. The three letters are published here.

61 (1933): 135–140

TSARIST GOVERNMENT CONCERNING THE STRAITS PROBLEM 1898–1911. Introduction by V. Khvostov.

Three notes from the files of the Ministry of Foreign Affairs are presented here. The first is a survey of the Straits problem in 1898; the second concerns the dispatch of the Black Sea fleet to the Far East in 1904; the third is a note of Russian jurist Baron M. de Taube on the Straits problem in 1905. Khvostov states that A. A. Giers, adviser in the Ministry of Foreign Affairs, gave A. A. Neratov, acting minister of foreign affairs, two of his personal notes on the Straits problem in 1911; attached to one of these notes were the documents published here, annotated by Giers.

VOLUME 62, 1934

62 (1934): 5–14

ALONG LENIN'S PATH (On the Tenth Anniversary of Lenin's Death). By Y. Berzin and V. Maksakov.

A full-page picture of Lenin is reproduced here, followed by Berzin's eulogy and exhortation to the Russian people to carry on in Lenin's footsteps. Maksakov describes the documents published in this volume, which is devoted exclusively to materials on Lenin's life and work.

62 (1934): 15–50

TEN YEARS AGO

On page 16 is a picture of Lenin lying in state. The following documents are published on pages 17–50:

1. [Pp. 17–18] "A bulletin of the Central Committee of the All-Union

A Digest of the Krasnyi Arkhiv 91

(Bolshevik) Communist party on the death of V. I. Lenin, Moscow, January 22, 1924."

2. [P. 19] "A government bulletin on Lenin's death, Kremlin, January 22, 1924."

3. [Pp. 19-21] "A bulletin concerning the history of the illness and death of V. I. Ulianov (Lenin), Moscow, January 23, 1924."

4. [Pp. 22-24] "An appeal of the Executive Committee of the Comintern and Profintern, January 23, 1924."

5. [Pp. 25-27] "To all workers of the USSR from the Eleventh Congress of Soviets of the Russian Soviet Federated Socialist Republic, Moscow, January 22, 1924."

6. [Pp. 28-29] "An appeal of the Second All-Union Congress of Soviets to toiling mankind, Moscow, January 26, 1924."

7. [Pp. 30-33] "The speech of Comrade Stalin at the meeting of the Second All-Union Congress of Soviets, January 26, 1924."

8. [Pp. 34-50] "Response of workers and peasants on the death of V. I. Lenin."

These documents, comprising forty letters and resolutions from individuals and from labor and peasant groups, are followed by a picture of Lenin and Stalin taken in 1922.

62 (1934): 53-248

ARCHIVAL DOCUMENTS ON THE BIOGRAPHY OF V. I. LENIN (1887-1914)

These biographical materials are divided according to the following periods and episodes in Lenin's life:

1. [Pp. 55-74] "Kazan and Samara (1887-1893)." Police Department communiqués concerning Lenin's student activities and the text of Lenin's diploma are reproduced here.

2. [Pp. 75-117] "Petersburg 'Union for the Emancipation of the Working Class' (1893-1896)." The Police Department reports given here deal with the activities of the Union and of Lenin as a member of the Union.

3. [Pp. 118-139] "Exile (1897-1900)." Among these documents are reports on Lenin's years in Siberia and on his marriage.

4. [Pp. 140-154] *"Iskra* Period (1901-1903)." These are police reports on Lenin's activities abroad when he was one of the editors of *Iskra* ("The Spark") and copies of letters written by his wife, N. K. Krupskaia.

5. [Pp. 155-172] "Second Congress and Party Split (1903-1904)." Additional letters written by Krupskaia and materials on the Kiev branch of the Russian Social Democratic Labor party are reprinted here.

6. [Pp. 173-214] "The Revolution of 1905-1907." Government records on the Revolution and letters written by Social Democrats and intercepted by police agents appear in this section.

7. [Pp. 215–222] "The Era of Reaction (1908–1910)." Reports of local government officials to the Police Department concerning the reactionary activities of Social Democrats in their areas are published here.

8. [Pp. 223–248] "The New Rise of the Labor Movement (1910–1914)." These documents are police reports and intercepted correspondence.

VOLUME 63, 1934

63 (1934): 3–54

ON THE EVE OF THE RUSSO-JAPANESE WAR (December, 1900—January, 1902). Introduction by I. Erukhimovich.

The documents published here include reports, telegrams, and letters exchanged by Minister of Foreign Affairs Count V. N. Lamsdorff with A. P. Izvolsky, minister in Tokyo, and with Giers, minister in Peking. Also included is the record of an interview between Japanese Minister Chang and Count Lamsdorff on March 12, 1901, on the state of Russo-Japanese relations at that time.

An English translation of these documents appears in the *Chinese Social and Political Science Review*, XVIII, 4 (January, 1935): 572–594; XIX, 1 (April, 1935): 125–139; and XIX, 2 (July, 1935): 234–267.

63 (1934): 55–97

BORIS NIKOLSKY'S DIARY (1905–1907). Introduction by D. Zaslavsky.

Boris Nikolsky was a leader of the monarchist organization *Russkoe Sobranie* ("Russian Society"). The sections of his diary published here sketch a vivid picture of Russian life in the ruling circles at the time of the Revolution of 1905. The only entry for 1907 is a survey of the origins of the monarchist organization *Soiuz Russkogo Naroda* ("Union of Russian People").

For additional material in *Krasnyi Arkhiv*, see "Boris Nikolsky and Gregory Rasputin," 68 (1935): 157–161.

63 (1934): 98–105

A FEW DATES IN THE LIFE AND WORK OF J. M. SVERDLOV (From Documents of the Archive of the Revolution, 1885–1915). Introduction by Y. B.

This list of archival documents pertaining to the period of Sverdlov's underground activities was published on the fifteenth anniversary of his death. In addition to the list of dated events, with indications of the documents pertaining to them, there are also pictures of Sverdlov from tsarist police files.

For additional material in *Krasnyi Arkhiv*, see "[Commemoration of] the Twentieth Anniversary of J. M. Sverdlov's Death," 92 (1939): 70-90.

63 (1934): 106-123

A SURVEY OF ARCHIVAL MATERIALS ON THE HISTORY OF THE FACTORY KRASNYI PEREKOP (1722-1929). Introduction unsigned.

This is a chronological list of documents on the history of the factory *Bolshaia Yaroslavskaia Manufaktura* ("Large Yaroslavl Factory") from its founding in 1722 to 1929. At the time of publication of these documents the factory, renamed *Krasnyi Perekop* ("Red Canal") after the October Revolution, was a huge textile plant.

FROM AN ARCHIVIST'S NOTEBOOK

63 (1934): 124-126

NICHOLAS ROMANOV CONCERNING THE ANGLO-BOER WAR. Introduction by Z.

Printed here is a letter from Nicholas II to his sister Xenia, from Jagdschloss Wolfsgarten, Post Egelsbach, on October 21, 1899, in which he speculates on the decisive role he could play in the outcome of the Anglo-Boer War if he were to order the mobilization of troops in Turkestan.

For additional material in *Krasnyi Arkhiv*, see "A Russian Military Agent's Dispatches on the Anglo-Boer War," 103 (1940): 130-159.

63 (1934): 126-130

MATERIALS RELATING TO L. N. TOLSTOY'S BIOGRAPHY (1901-1902). Introduction by V. Poliansky.

These twenty-six government reports and communiqués are dated from July 6, 1901, to June 25, 1902, when Tolstoy was critically ill in the Crimea. They concern measures for coping with or preventing popular demonstrations in the event of Tolstoy's death, and also arrangements for a special funeral train to carry his body from the Crimea to Yasnaia Poliana, his estate.

For references to additional material in *Krasnyi Arkhiv* on Tolstoy, see the notes to "L. N. Tolstoy under the Blows of the Censor," 35 (1925): 215-235.

63 (1934): 130–132

Nicholas Romanov's Marginal Notes. By G. Nikolskaia.

Nikolskaia's article is based on several documents concerning the Russian educational system; to these documents, which are given here, Nicholas II has added marginal comments on unrest in schools and universities from 1902 to 1906.

63 (1934): 132–135

Materials Relating to the History of the Autocracy's Struggle with the Revolutionary Movement in the Army in the 1880's. By M. Akhun and D. Zinevich.

Quoted in this article is a letter dated May 22, 1884, from General P. S. Vannovsky, minister of war, to A. K. Imeretinsky, head of the Central Military Court Department. The letter contains a demand for stricter military discipline and stresses the danger of revolutionary propaganda being disseminated in the army.

63 (1934): 136–146

Contents of the Previous Volumes of the Journal *Krasnyi Arkhiv*

This is a table of contents of *Krasnyi Arkhiv*, Volumes 1–63.

VOLUME 64, 1934

64 (1934): 3–30

Tsarist Russia's International Financial Position at the Time of the World War (A. I. Shingarev's Report to the Military-Naval Commission of the [Fourth] State Duma, June 20, 1916). Introduction by N. Vanag.

Shingarev was a member of the parliamentary delegation abroad in 1916. His report to the Fourth State Duma on June 20, which is printed here, reviews his contacts in England, France, Italy, Norway, and Sweden. In the course of the report and in the record of the debate which followed, there are numerous references to the unwillingness of the United States to extend credit to Russia.

Excerpts from these documents appear in French translation in René Martel's "Nouveaux Documents d'histoire russe," *Le Monde slave* (January, 1936), pp. 154–157.

A Digest of the Krasnyi Arkhiv 95

For additional material in *Krasnyi Arkhiv*, see: "P. L. Bark's Report to Nicholas II on the Budget for 1917," 17 (1926): 51–69; "The Financial Situation of Russia before the October Revolution," 25 (1927): 3–33; "P. N. Miliukov's Diary," 54–55 (1932): 3–48; "Russian 'Parliamentary' Delegation Abroad in 1916," 58 (1933): 3–23.

64 (1934): 31–51

ARREST OF THE DUMA "QUINTET" IN 1914. Introduction by A. Badaev.

Social Democratic deputies of the Fourth State Duma were arrested in November, 1914, for agitating against war with Germany. The documents presented here are reports from the Police Department, the court, and the Ministry of Justice on the arrest of deputies G. I. Petrovsky, A. E. Badaev, N. R. Shagov, M. K. Muranov, and F. N. Samoilov.

For additional material in *Krasnyi Arkhiv*, see "Illegal Work of the Bolshevik Faction of the Fourth State Duma," 77 (1936): 61–90. For references to additional material on the state dumas, see notes to "First State Duma in Vyborg," 57 (1933): 85–99.

64 (1934): 52–72

MATERIALS RELATING TO THE HISTORY OF THE LABOR MOVEMENT ON THE EVE OF THE WORLD WAR. Introduction by A. Spirova.

These Police Department documents deal with labor unrest among the textile workers in Kostroma province and with Social Democratic strength in that province in 1914.

For additional material in *Krasnyi Arkhiv* on labor unrest, see "Materials Relating to the History of the Labor Movement at the Time of the World War," 67 (1934): 5–27.

64 (1934): 73–84

THE SOLDIERS' FRAME OF MIND ON THE EVE OF THE WORLD WAR. Introduction by F. Notovich.

Dissatisfaction of Russian soldiers at the time of World War I is illustrated in four anonymous letters, published here, to General Dmitry Dubensky, editor of *Russkoe Chtenie* ("Russian Reading"), in December, 1913. Two of the editor's letters to the Ministry of War concerning the four anonymous letters are also published.

For references to additional material in *Krasnyi Arkhiv* on the army at the time of World War I, see the notes to "Memoirs of A. I. Kozmin," 60 (1933): 142–156.

64 (1934): 85–129

MATERIALS RELATING TO THE QUESTION OF PREPAREDNESS FOR WORLD WAR (From Documents of the Russian Military and Political Intelligence, 1913–1914). Introduction by E. Adamov.

The first set of documents of the two groups given here consists of reports from the chief of the Kiev military district to the chief of the General Staff. The second group is composed of reports from Russian military attachés to the quartermaster general of the General Staff in March, May, and June, 1914. The information in the first group is based on "anonymous" communications, while that in the second group is based on reports from official military agents who relayed intelligence concerning Austro-Hungarian and German preparations for war.

René Martel discusses these documents in "Nouveaux Documents d'histoire russe," *Le Monde slave* (January, 1936), p. 148.

FROM AN ARCHIVIST'S NOTEBOOK

64 (1934): 130–138

NICHOLAS ROMANOV IN THE FIRST DAYS OF THE WORLD WAR. Introduction by D. Zaslavsky.

The diary of Nicholas II for July, 1914, reproduced here, records his activities during the month, his reactions to the declaration of war, and French President Raymond Poincaré's visit to Russia.

For other sections of Nicholas' diary in *Krasnyi Arkhiv*, see: 20 (1927): 123–152; 21 (1927): 79–96; 22 (1927): 71–91; 27 (1928): 110–138.

Excerpts from the July entries may be found in French translation in René Martel's article "Nouveaux Documents d'histoire russe," *Le Monde slave* (January, 1936), pp. 152–153.

64 (1934): 139–143

THE STRUGGLE FOR A LABOR PRESS ON THE EVE OF THE WORLD WAR. Introduction by V. Dalago.

The journals *Pravda, Put Pravdy* ("The Way of Truth"), *Metallist* ("Metallurgist"), *Severnaia Rabochaia Gazeta* ("Northern Workers' Paper"), and *Mysl Truda* ("The Thought of Labor") are described in the reports of the Secret Police which are reprinted here and which also record the circulation and confiscation of these periodicals in 1914. A table indicating the daily circulation of *Pravda* from January 22 to March 8, 1914, appears. Among the documents are eleven letters that were written from

A Digest of the Krasnyi Arkhiv 97

various parts of Russia to the editorial offices of the labor papers, but that were intercepted by police agents before reaching their destinations.

For additional material in *Krasnyi Arkhiv*, see: "The Socialist Press during the Imperialist War," 2 (1922): 200–225; "Materials Relating to the History of the Moscow Bolshevik Labor Press in the Years of the Revolutionary Upheaval (1913–1914)," 105 (1941): 168–178.

64 (1934): 143–144

AN UNPUBLISHED LETTER OF V. M. GARSHIN. Introduction unsigned.

On February 25, 1880, the author V. M. Garshin wrote Count M. T. Loris-Melikov that he had never held membership in the Social Revolutionary party. The letter is printed here. Garshin had had an interview with Count Loris-Melikov on February 22.

For additional material in *Krasnyi Arkhiv*, see "Materials Relating to the Fiftieth Anniversary of V. M. Garshin's Death," 87 (1938): 174–182.

VOLUMES 65–66, 1934

65–66 (1934): 3–68

THE FIRST DAYS OF THE WORLD WAR. Introduction by A. Popov.

The ninety-nine documents published here, dated from July 23/August 5 to August 1/14, 1914, reveal the pressure exerted on the neutral countries to enter the war on the side of the Allies. The documents are the diplomatic communiqués of the Russian Ministry of Foreign Affairs and reports to Nicholas II. Dispatches were sent from representatives in Serbia, England, France, Turkey, Japan, Belgium, Denmark, Greece, Hungary, Bulgaria, Sweden, and Italy.

Excerpts from these documents appear in French translation in *Le Monde slave* (March, 1936), pp. 452–468.

65–66 (1934): 69–85

THE DEVASTATION OF SERBIA IN 1915 AND THE "HELP" OF THE ALLIES. Introduction by F. Notovich.

The documents printed here are two reports from the Russian military-naval attaché in Italy, Captain Behrens, to the chief of the General Staff of the navy, Admiral Rusin. They were written in December, 1915. Behrens reports on English, French, Russian, and Italian discussions of the difficulties involved in assisting Serbia.

65–66 (1934): 86–117

ANGLO-RUSSIAN RELATIONS IN PERSIA AT THE TIME OF THE WORLD WAR. Introduction by F. N.

Reproduced here is a note dated May 15/28, 1915, by I. Y. Korostovets, former Russian envoy in Persia, on the strengthening of Anglo-Russian relations in that country. The note discusses the following points: England's suspicion of Russian intentions in Persia and the influence of the Indian government; England's desire for influence in South Persia and Russia's activity in North Persia; the Persian revolution and internal affairs; instances of Anglo-Russian coöperation in Persia; the first and second cabinets of Mustoufi-al-Mamalik.

For additional material in *Krasnyi Arkhiv* on Persia, see: "Tsarist Russia and Persia in the Epoch of the Russo-Japanese War," 53 (1932): 3–37; "Anglo-Russian Rivalry in Persia 1890–1906," 56 (1933): 33–64.

65–66 (1934): 118–163

SOLDIERS' LETTERS DURING THE WORLD-WAR YEARS (1915–1917). Introduction by O. Chaadaeva.

Excerpts from 172 letters from Russian soldiers describing their life and the growth of revolutionary propaganda among troops at the front are published here. The excerpts are grouped under the following topics: (1) food and clothing rations at the front; (2) weapons at the front; (3) army regime and soldier-officer relations; (4) illness and hospitalization of soldiers; (5) failures on the front and the influence of defeats on the soldiers' morale; (6) surrender, desertion, and refusals to attack; (7) fraternization with the enemy; (8) interest in internal affairs and growth of revolutionary dissatisfaction at the front; (9) dissatisfaction with war and anticipation of peace; (10) soldiers and the land question.

For references to additional material in *Krasnyi Arkhiv* on the army at the time of World War I, see the notes to "Memoirs of A. I. Kozmin," 60 (1933): 142–156.

65–66 (1934): 164–192

THE MOSCOW MILITARY-REVOLUTIONARY COMMITTEE. Introduction by E. Rozhen.

The documents printed here are notes on the eight meetings of the Moscow Military-Revolutionary Committee held October 26–27, 1917. The editors of *Krasnyi Arkhiv* have included extensive annotations which throw additional light on the history of Moscow immediately after the Bolsheviks seized power.

For the minutes of other meetings of the committee in *Krasnyi Arkhiv*, see: 23 (1927): 64–148; 54–55 (1932): 80–161; 71 (1935): 60–115.

65–66 (1934): 193–247

MATERIALS RELATING TO THE HISTORY OF THE REVOLUTION OF 1905 IN SORMOVO FACTORY (The Diary of a Nizhni Novgorod Factory Inspector for 1905). Introduction by V. Zeltser.

The entries in factory inspector D. G. Dmitrash's diary, dated from January 4 to December 30, 1905, which are given here present an eyewitness account of the growing unrest in the Sormovo factory, which came to a climax in the December strike, when twenty-three were killed, fifty-one wounded, and one hundred arrested. The diary is a record of the inspector's work, as well as of his attitude toward the workers' demands.

FROM AN ARCHIVIST'S NOTEBOOK

65–66 (1934): 248–254

AFTER TSUSHIMA (From the Diary of Lieutenant A. S. Zarin). Introduction by F. A. Petrov.

Petrov states that Lieutenant A. S. Zarin was senior flag officer on the staff of Rear Admiral Enquist, commander of the squadron of cruisers which took part in the Battle of Tsushima, May 27, 1905, and which subsequently put in at Manila Bay for repairs and refueling. The section of Zarin's diary published here is dated from December 4 to December 30, 1905; it describes conditions after the ship left Manila, the sailors' frame of mind after the battle, and the effects of the news of the Revolution of 1905 on Russians far removed from the scene of events.

For additional material in *Krasnyi Arkhiv*, see "Before Tsushima," 67 (1934): 193–200.

VOLUME 67, 1934

67 (1934): 3–4

SERGIUS M. KIROV, 1886–1934

The two government statements published here concern Kirov's assassination in Leningrad, December 1, 1934; a photograph of Kirov also appears.

For additional material in *Krasnyi Arkhiv* on Kirov, see: "Strengthen Revolutionary Vigilance!" 68 (1935): 7–12; "Materials for S. M. Kirov's Biography," 97 (1939): 44–90; "Comrade Kirov's Activity in the Organization of Tomsk Social Democrats," 97 (1939): 124–140.

67 (1934): 5–27

MATERIALS RELATING TO THE HISTORY OF THE LABOR MOVEMENT AT THE TIME OF THE WORLD WAR (Strikes in the Kostroma Area). Introduction by M. Inozemtsev.

These communiqués of local and national government officials describe the labor movement in Kostroma in the summer and fall of 1915, with special emphasis on the strike in June, 1915.

For additional material in *Krasnyi Arkhiv*, see "Materials Relating to the History of the Labor Movement on the Eve of the World War," 64 (1934): 52–72.

67 (1934): 28–92

MATERIALS RELATING TO THE HISTORY OF GVOZDEVSHCHINISM (Bulletins of the Labor Group of the Central War Industrial Committee). Introduction by I. Menitsky.

K. A. Gvozdev was a member of the labor group of the Central War Industrial Committee. The five bulletins published here throw light on the group's activities during World War I. They describe labor's attitude toward the general labor problem, the relations of labor and the State Duma and of labor and management, the visit of French Minister of Armaments Albert Thomas to Russia, and the stabilization of currency.

For references to additional material in *Krasnyi Arkhiv* on the labor group, see the notes to "Materials Relating to the History of 'Workers' Groups' under the Central War Industrial Committee," 57 (1933): 43–84.

67 (1934): 93–130

GERMAN INTERVENTION AND THE DON GOVERNMENT IN 1918. Introduction by S. Piontkovsky.

The documents presented here, dated from June 12 to December 21, 1918, show the relations of the Don government with the Germans and remark on German interest in the wheat and coal of the Don area. They also indicate the desire of the Don government for German aid in fighting the Bolsheviks.

A Digest of the Krasnyi Arkhiv

For additional material in *Krasnyi Arkhiv*, see "German Occupation of Polesie (Byelorussia)," 91 (1938): 89–105.

67 (1934): 131–146

MATERIALS RELATING TO THE HISTORY OF THE SEMËNOVITES IN 1919. Introduction by V. Elagin.

These pages contain the testimony of Major General Ivan F. Shilnikov, one of Gregory Semënov's associates, who was arrested by the Soviets and interrogated in Irkutsk on February 25–27, 1919. Information is given on Ataman (Hetman) Semënov's struggle with the Bolsheviks in Siberia during the Civil War, as well as information on his relations with Japan and the Allies.

For references to additional material in *Krasnyi Arkhiv* on events in Siberia, see the notes to "The Disintegration of Kolchak's Campaign," 31 (1928): 51–80.

For references to additional material in *Krasnyi Arkhiv* on Semënov, see: "Materials Relating to the History of Intervention in Siberia," 34 (1929): 126–165; "Wrangeliana," 40 (1930): 3–40.

67 (1934): 147–167

ANATOLE FRANCE AND TSARIST CENSORSHIP. Introduction by L. Polianskaia.

Dated from April, 1893, to March, 1914, the censorship reports given here include material on the following works of Anatole France: *Opinions of Jerome Coignard, The White Stone, Penguin Island, The Gods Are Athirst,* and *The Revolt of the Angels.*

67 (1934): 168–186

THE DIARY OF A. A. POLOVTSOV. Introduction by D. Z.

These entries in Polovtsov's diary, dated from October 27 to December 29, 1894, when he was president of the Imperial Russian Historical Society and a member of the government council, describe the effect of Alexander III's death on the Russian people, life in Russian ruling circles, Nicholas II's first meeting with his Council of Ministers, and Polovtsov's impressions of Nicholas II in the early months of his reign.

For other sections of Polovtsov's diary published in *Krasnyi Arkhiv*, see: 3 (1923): 75–172; 4 (1923): 63–128; 33 (1929): 170–203; 46 (1931): 110–132; 59 (1933): 82–109.

FROM AN ARCHIVIST'S NOTEBOOK

67 (1934): 187–193

NICHOLAS II, "DOCTOR OF RUSSIAN HISTORY." Introduction by D. Zaslavsky.

The five letters published here, written in 1914 and 1915, reveal plans of the history professors at Moscow University to confer an honorary degree of Doctor of Russian History on Nicholas II.

67 (1934): 193–200

BEFORE TSUSHIMA. Introduction unsigned.

The introduction states that the letter by Lieutenant E. V. Sventorzhetsky printed here provides valuable information not found in Admiral [Z. P.] Rozhdestvensky's reports. Writing to Captain P. M. Vavilov of the Admiralty in late January, 1905, four months before the Battle of Tsushima, Sventorzhetsky describes in detail the transfer of the Baltic fleet to the Pacific. Sventorzhetsky, Admiral Rozhdestvensky's senior flag officer, lost his life at Tsushima.

For additional material in *Krasnyi Arkhiv*, see "After Tsushima," 65–66 (1934): 248–254.

VOLUME 68, 1935

68 (1935): 5–6

V. V. KUIBYSHEV (1888–1935)

Valerian Vladimirovich Kuibyshev, who died of a heart disease on January 25, 1935, was a member of the Politburo, vice chairman of the Council of People's Commissars of the USSR and of the Council of Labor and Defense, and president of the Commission of Soviet Control. The obituary published here is preceded by a portrait of Kuibyshev.

For additional material in *Krasnyi Arkhiv*, see: "A Few Dates in the Life and Work of V. V. Kuibyshev," 68 (1935): 119–124; "Revolutionary Activity of Comrade V. V. Kuibyshev in Samara (1916–1918)," 104 (1941): 103–142.

68 (1935): 7–12

STRENGTHEN REVOLUTIONARY VIGILANCE!

The editorial printed here discusses the assassination of S. M. Kirov and the opposition to the Soviet regime of the Zinoviev-Trotsky bloc.

A Digest of the Krasnyi Arkhiv 103

For references to additional material in *Krasnyi Arkhiv*, see the notes to "Sergius M. Kirov, 1886–1934," 67 (1934): 3–4.

68 (1935): 13–38

MATERIALS RELATING TO THE HISTORY OF THE STRUGGLE FOR THE THIRD PARTY CONGRESS (December, 1903—March, 1905). Introduction by Peter Miliukov.

The twenty-one letters published here were written by Social Democratic leaders to each other and were intercepted by the tsarist police. They are concerned with internal party struggles, particularly between the Mensheviks and the Bolsheviks. The letters were written by P. S. Zemliachka, M. M. Essen, L. E. Galperin, P. A. Krasikov, E. D. Stasova, V. A. Noskov, M. I. Ulianova, N. K. Krupskaia, and S. I. Gussev.

68 (1935): 39–64

MATERIALS RELATING TO THE HISTORY OF "BLOODY SUNDAY" IN PETERSBURG (Reports of the Procurator of the St. Petersburg Chamber of Justice, E. I. Vuich, to the Minister of Justice). Introduction by S. Piontkovsky.

Thirty reports written by Vuich between January 4 and February 24, 1905, appear here. They describe the strike of 12,000 workers at the Putilov factory on January 3 and Father Gapon's role in it; the wave of strikes throughout St. Petersburg in January, 1905; "Bloody Sunday," January 9, 1905, and the turmoil which followed it.

Volumes 11–12 (1925) of *Krasnyi Arkhiv* deal exclusively with documents on the history of the Revolution of 1905. For references to additional material on "Bloody Sunday," see the notes to "The Petersburg Clergy and the Ninth of January," 36 (1929): 192–199.

68 (1935): 65–96

A. N. KUROPATKIN'S DIARY (March 31—November 21 [*sic*], 1904). Introduction by S. Budkevich.

Dated from March 31 to July 31, 1904, the entries in General Kuropatkin's diary which are published here describe his relations with Viceroy of the Far East Admiral E. I. Alexeiev, naval action in the Russo-Japanese War, military strategy and battles, and Nicholas II's attitude toward the war. Kuropatkin was minister of war and chief of the Russian army in the Far East.

Publication of this section of Kuropatkin's diary is concluded in 69–70 (1935): 101–126.

For other sections of Kuropatkin's diary in *Krasnyi Arkhiv*, see: 2 (1922): 5–117; 5 (1924): 82–101; 7 (1924): 55–69; 8 (1925): 70–100; 20 (1927): 56–77; 34 (1929): 39–94; 54–55 (1932): 49–79.

68 (1935): 97–118

THE EXECUTION OF THE IVANOVO VOZNESENSK WORKERS IN 1915. Introduction by M. Inozemtsev.

Inozemtsev states that the shooting into the crowd of workers at Ivanovo Voznesensk in Vladimir province August 10, 1915, has received little attention in Russian historical literature, although protest strikes followed throughout Russia. The Police Department documents printed here deal with Social Democratic activities in Vladimir province, the strike at the Ivanovo Voznesensk factory, the shooting, and the subsequent investigation of the strike by the Fourth State Duma. Social Democratic proclamations are also given.

For additional material in *Krasnyi Arkhiv* on Ivanovo Voznesensk, see: "Materials Relating to the Thirtieth Anniversary of the Ivanovo Voznesensk General Strike," 69–70 (1935): 127–137; "The Strike of the Ivanovo Voznesensk Factory Weavers in 1895," 72 (1935): 110–119.

68 (1935): 119–124

A FEW DATES IN THE LIFE AND WORK OF V. V. KUIBYSHEV (According to Documents of the Central Archive of the Revolution 1888–1916). By V. Dalago.

This is a chronological list of Kuibyshev's revolutionary activities from 1905 to 1916, with an indication after each date of the depository in which the pertinent documents are preserved.

For additional material in *Krasnyi Arkhiv*, see: "V. V. Kuibyshev," 68 (1935): 5–6; "Revolutionary Activity of Comrade V. V. Kuibyshev in Samara (1916–1918)," 104 (1941): 103–142.

68 (1935): 125–153

INTERVENTION IN THE CAUCASUS AND COUNTERREVOLUTION AMONG THE MOUNTAIN TRIBES. Introduction by A. Ivanov.

The documents printed here throw light on the relations between the Russian counterrevolutionary movement in the mountain tribes of the

A Digest of the Krasnyi Arkhiv 105

Caucasus and British and German interventionists in the Caucasus in 1918 and 1919.

For additional material in *Krasnyi Arkhiv*, see: "The Democratic Government of Georgia and the English Command," 21 (1927): 122–173 and 25 (1927): 96–110; "In Memory of Twenty-six Baku Commissars," 89–90 (1938): 3–29.

FROM AN ARCHIVIST'S NOTEBOOK

68 (1935): 154–157

MATERIALS RELATING TO THE HISTORY OF THE AUTOCRACY'S STRUGGLE WITH THE LABOR MOVEMENT. Introduction by P. Z.

A report by N. M. Tseimern, governor of Vladimir province, on labor unrest in that province in 1898 and on the organization of special factory police to combat it is given here. The marginal comments of Nicholas II also appear.

68 (1935): 157–161

BORIS NIKOLSKY AND GREGORY RASPUTIN. Introduction by D. Z.

Nikolsky's entry in his diary for November 23, 1912, published here, records the details of his interview with Rasputin in which the intrigue connected with the temporary banishment of Rasputin to his native village in 1910 was discussed.

For additional material in *Krasnyi Arkhiv*, see "Boris Nikolsky's Diary (1905–1907)," 63 (1934): 55–97.

68 (1935): 162–171

THE INTERROGATION OF PUGACHEV'S ATAMAN A. KHLOPUSHA. Introduction by M. Zh.

The text of the interrogation of Ataman (Hetman) A. Khlopusha several months before his execution in Orenburg in 1774 provides valuable details on the organization of E. I. Pugachev's army, its weapons and ammunition, his relations with the inhabitants of the territories he occupied, and the role of the factory-attached peasants in the Pugachev Rebellion against Catherine II in 1773.

For additional material in *Krasnyi Arkhiv*, see: "The Ukases of E. I. Pugachev and His Staff," 8 (1925): 193–206; "E. Pugachev's Interrogation in Moscow 1774–1775," 69–70 (1935): 159–237.

68 (1935): 171–172

FROM THE EDITORS

This article is an editorial criticism of I. Menitsky's introductions to "Materials Relating to the History of 'Workers' Groups' under the Central War Industrial Committee," 57 (1933): 43–84 and to "Materials Relating to the History of Gvozdevshchinism," 67 (1934): 28–92.

VOLUMES 69–70, 1935

69–70 (1935): 3–39

MATERIALS RELATING TO THE HISTORY OF THE ANGLO-RUSSIAN AGREEMENT OF 1907. Introduction by S. Pashukanis.

A confidential note of I. A. Zinoviev, Russian ambassador in Constantinople, dated August 25, 1906, is published here; it discusses Russian and British policies in India, Afghanistan, Persia, and the Balkans. The journals of special ministerial conferences in the Russian Ministry of Foreign Affairs on February 1, April 14, and August 11, 1907, also appear. The first meeting considered an agreement with England on Persian affairs and the Baghdad railroad. The second meeting was concerned with the settlement of the Afghanistan question. The third meeting was devoted primarily to a discussion of the conclusion of the Anglo-Russian agreement on Afghanistan.

For additional material in *Krasnyi Arkhiv*, see "The Anglo-Russian Treaty of 1907 and the Partition of Afghanistan," 10 (1925): 54–66.

Excerpts from the journal of the meeting of February 1, 1907, may be found in English translation in Benno Aleksandrovich Siebert, *Entente Diplomacy and the World* (New York and London: The Knickerbocker Press, 1921), pp. 474–477.

69–70 (1935): 40–71

"A SATRAP'S CIRCUIT" (The Notes of A. A. Tatishchev on Dubasov's Punitive Expedition in the Chernigov Province). Introduction by I. Kuznetsov.

Kuznetsov states that General F. V. Dubasov was appointed governor general of Moscow after he had suppressed a peasant uprising in Chernigov province in 1905. Tatishchev was Dubasov's secretary on the punitive expedition. The documents printed here, which include a characterization of Dubasov, are Tatishchev's personal notes on the expedition. Excerpts from Dubasov's summary of the results of his expedition are also given.

For references to additional material in *Krasnyi Arkhiv* on agrarian unrest, see the notes to "S. Y. Witte's Struggle with the Agrarian Revolution," 31 (1928): 81–102.

A Digest of the Krasnyi Arkhiv 107

69–70 (1935): 72–100

THE BATTLESHIP *Prince Potemkin Tavrichesky* AT ODESSA. Introduction by M. Inozemtsev.

Three reports dealing with conditions in Odessa in 1905 and the revolt on the battleship *Potemkin* are given in this article. The report of Lieutenant General Bezradetsky to the Ministry of War presents a daily résumé of events in Odessa, June 13–28, 1905, and an account of the meeting on the *Potemkin* between representatives of rioting sailors and the army officers sent to quiet them. The report of Adjutant General Count A. P. Ignatiev to Nicholas II, July 18, 1905, analyzes the revolutionary movement as Ignatiev saw it on his mission to Odessa. A report, dated July 25, 1905, from A. A. Anatra, chairman of the Odessa Stock Exchange Committee, to Count Ignatiev describes the condition of trade and commerce in Odessa.

For additional material in *Krasnyi Arkhiv*, see: "The Execution of Afanasy Matushenko," 8 (1925): 250–254; "The Navy during 1905," 11–12 (1925): 193–262; "Materials Relating to the History of the Labor Movement in the Ukraine in 1905," 102 (1940): 75–113.

69–70 (1935): 101–126

A. N. KUROPATKIN'S DIARY (March 31—November 20, 1904)

Publication of this section of Kuropatkin's diary begins in 68 (1935): 65–96.

Entries published here are dated from August 3 to November 20, 1904. General A. N. Kuropatkin assumed command of Russian forces in the Far East on October 11, 1904. These entries in his diary deal primarily with the campaigns and strategy of the Russo-Japanese War.

For other sections of Kuropatkin's diary in *Krasnyi Arkhiv*, see: 2 (1922): 5–117; 5 (1924): 82–101; 7 (1924): 55–69; 8 (1925): 70–100; 20 (1927): 56–77; 34 (1929): 39–94; 54–55 (1932): 49–79. See also "With the Staff of Admiral E. I. Alexeiev," 41–42 (1930): 148–204.

69–70 (1935): 127–137

MATERIALS RELATING TO THE THIRTIETH ANNIVERSARY OF THE IVANOVO VOZNESENSK GENERAL STRIKE (May 12/25 to July 1/14, 1905). Introduction by S. Shesternin.

Published here are four letters which were written by workers to socialist publications abroad and which were intercepted by the police. There is also a workers' resolution of May 1, 1905, reaffirming the faith of the workers in the socialist revolution.

For additional material in *Krasnyi Arkhiv*, see: "The Execution of the

Ivanovo Voznesensk Workers in 1915," 68 (1935): 97–118; "The Strike of the Ivanovo Voznesensk Factory Weavers in 1895," 72 (1935): 110–119.

69–70 (1935): 138–158

MATERIALS RELATING TO THE HISTORY OF THE STRUGGLE FOR WORKER CONTROL. Introduction by G. Belkin.

The documents published here deal with the labor-management problem in Petrograd as reflected in the struggle from February to October, 1917, between V. I. Rykatkin, ammunitions-factory owner, and his employees.

69–70 (1935): 159–237

E. PUGACHEV'S INTERROGATION IN MOSCOW 1774–1775. Introduction by S. Piontkovsky.

In 1773 E. I. Pugachev led a rebellion against Catherine II, but he was defeated and captured in 1774. The text of his replies to the interrogation on November 4, 1774, is printed here. It provides extensive material on his family background and his activities until his arrival under armed guard in Moscow. It also provides source material for the study of the rebellion which bears his name. Piontkovsky states that this material has been little utilized by historians. He outlines briefly the events leading to Pugachev's execution in January, 1775.

For additional material in *Krasnyi Arkhiv*, see: "The Ukases of E. I. Pugachev and His Staff," 8 (1925): 193–206; "The Interrogation of Pugachev's Ataman A. Khlopusha," 68 (1935): 162–171.

FROM AN ARCHIVIST'S NOTEBOOK

69–70 (1935): 238–241

MATERIALS RELATING TO THE HISTORY OF THE COUNTERREVOLUTION OF 1905. Introduction by Z. I. Gurskaia.

N. A. Notovich was a landowner and, for a time, an editor of the journal *Finansovoe Obozrenie* ("Financial Review"). His report of November 7, 1905, to Count S. Y. Witte, which is published here, discusses the necessity for initiating practical measures to combat the spread of agrarian unrest in the villages.

69–70 (1935): 241–256

NICHOLAS II, "EMPEROR OF KAFFIRS." Introduction by D. Zaslavsky.

The documents in this article reveal the proposal of Boer General [P. J.] Joubert in February, 1905, that Russia organize an uprising in South Africa to aid the Boers in their struggle with the British. The correspondence between Minister of Foreign Affairs Count V. N. Lamsdorff and Ambassador A. I. Nelidov in Paris and Minister Koiander in Lisbon provides details of Nicholas II's interest in the proposal and Count Lamsdorff's disapproval of it.

VOLUME 71, 1935

71 (1935): 3–16

TSARIST CENSORSHIP CONCERNING THE WORKS OF F. ENGELS. Introduction by F. Konstantinov.

The fifteen reports of the Central Committee of Censorship of Foreign Literature presented here, dated 1871 to 1915, review the following of Engels' works: *The Condition of the Working Class in England, Ludwig Feuerbach and the End of German Classical Philosophy, From Classical Idealism to Dialectical Materialism, The Peasant War in Germany, The Revolution in Science, Utopian Socialism and Scientific Socialism*, and *The Development of Socialism from Utopia to Science*. There is a full-page photograph of Engels at the beginning of this volume.

71 (1935): 17–38

PEASANTS' AGITATION IN KHERSON PROVINCE IN 1905. Introduction by I. Kuznetsov.

This article contains an extensive report on the reasons for the peasants' unrest and on the methods of combating it written by Adjutant General Count A. P. Ignatiev to Nicholas II, July 18, 1905. It also includes Gendarmerie reports from Odessa and landowners' telegrams describing the agitation.

For references to additional material in *Krasnyi Arkhiv*, see the notes to "S. Y. Witte's Struggle with the Agrarian Revolution," 31 (1928): 81–102.

71 (1935): 39–59

MATERIALS RELATING TO THE HISTORY OF THE REVOLUTIONARY MOVEMENT IN THE ARMY IN 1905–1906 (Uprising of the Seventh Reserve Cavalry Regiment in Tambov). Introduction by P. M. Zinevich.

Major General Tiulin's report to the minister of war on the origins, incidents, and suppression of an uprising in the Seventh Reserve Cavalry Regiment in Tambov in June, 1906, is printed here.

For additional material in *Krasyni Arkhiv*, see: "S. Y. Witte's Struggle with the Agrarian Revolution," 31 (1928): 81–102; "[Comments of] Nicholas Romanov concerning the Revolutionary Movement in the Army in 1905–1906," 41–42 (1930): 215–220; "Materials Relating to the History of the Revolutionary Movement in the Army on the Eve of 1905," 43 (1930): 168–173; "Materials Relating to the History of the 'Ideological' Struggle of the Autocracy with the Army," 44 (1931): 165–170; "The Purge of the Commanding Staff of the Tsarist Army in 1906," 50–51 (1932): 211–225; "Life of Soldiers in the Tsarist Army," 98 (1940): 145–176.

71 (1935): 60–115

Moscow Military-Revolutionary Committee. Introduction by E. Rozhen.

Published here are the extensively annotated minutes of fifty-one meetings of the Moscow Military-Revolutionary Committee held from October 30 to November 14, 1917. Rozhen describes the street fighting in Moscow during this period and outlines the first steps taken by the Soviets to establish and strengthen their power in Moscow.

For minutes of other sessions of this committee in *Krasnyi Arkhiv*, see: 23 (1927): 64–198; 54–55 (1932): 80–161; 65–66 (1934): 164–192.

71 (1935): 116–136

Potash Factories in the Smolensk District in the Seventeenth Century. Introduction by A. Speransky.

The documents printed here, dated from August 31, 1669, to September 12, 1673, are the reports to Tsar Alexis Mikhailovich from I. A. Khovansky, governor of Smolensk district, and from Prince M. A. Golitsyn and other officials concerning the construction of potash factories and trade with Riga merchants.

71 (1935): 137–169

Materials Relating to the History of the Mastery of the Northern Sea Route (Bering's Expedition 1732–1743). Introduction by P. Gorin.

This article contains a report from Captain Vitus Bering, and other members of his expedition, to Empress Anna Ivanovna dated Petropavlovsk Harbor, April 18, 1741. Twenty-five instructions from the Senate to Bering, March 16, 1733, and Bering's detailed report on the execution of each of the orders also appear.

Publication of these documents is continued in 72 (1935): 160–181; 73 (1935): 191–203; 74 (1936): 142–161.

FROM AN ARCHIVIST'S NOTEBOOK

71 (1935): 170–172

THE POLICE AND A. P. CHEKHOV'S FUNERAL. Introduction by N. Belchikov.

Police Department documents concerning preparations for Chekhov's burial, as well as reports from police stationed along the route of the funeral procession on the size, conduct, and composition of the procession, are given here.

For additional material in *Krasnyi Arkhiv* on Chekhov, see: "A. P. Chekhov's Unpublished Story *Should I Speak or Keep Silent?*" 8 (1925): 237–239; "From the Archives of A. P. Chekhov," 37 (1929): 175–214; "A. P. Chekhov—Manuscripts, Letters, Materials," 97 (1939): 177–182.

71 (1935): 172–176

CHURCH FRAUD DISCLOSED AT THE OPENING OF THE RELICS OF PITIRIM TAMBOVSKY. By B. Kandidov.

Pitirim Tambovsky (1645–1698), a monk who became bishop of Tambov, was canonized by the Russian Orthodox Church in 1913. Upon order of the Tambov Soviet government, his relics were uncovered and investigated in February, 1919. Kandidov summarizes the findings.

For references to additional material in *Krasnyi Arkhiv* on the Russian Orthodox Church, see the notes to "Life in Ecclesiastical Circles before the Revolution," 31 (1928): 204–213.

VOLUME 72, 1935

72 (1935): 3–43

THE COLLAPSE OF WRANGEL. Introduction by O. Shekun.

Reprinted here, from *Pravda*, is an interview with Stalin, July 11, 1920, on the situation at the front—particularly on the danger from counter-revolutionary forces in the south. Included are documents relating to the Soviet forces in the south under the command of M. V. Frunze, dated September 2–27, 1920. Other documents deal with the formation of the southern front and the first directives of its supreme commander and with the so-called First Period of War on the Southern Front (September 27–October 27), that is, the period of struggle in the Donbas (Donets Basin) and Mariupol areas and on the right bank of the Dnieper. The formation of the Fourth Soviet Army is also covered.

Publication of these documents is continued in 73 (1935): 19–73.

For additional material in *Krasnyi Arkhiv*, see the notes to "Materials Relating to the History of the Foreign Policy of Wrangel's Government," 32 (1929): 125–157.

72 (1935): 44–50

TEN YEARS SINCE THE DAY OF M. V. FRUNZE'S DEATH. Introduction by F. Samoilov.

The documents printed here pertain to the activities of Michael Vasilievich Frunze from 1904 to 1914; they are drawn from materials in the Archive of the Revolution. A picture of Frunze appears on the first page of this volume.

For additional material in *Krasnyi Arkhiv* on Frunze, see: "Materials Relating to M. V. Frunze's Revolutionary Activity (1905–1912)," 73 (1935): 74–90; "[The Role of] M. V. Frunze in the Organization of the Victory over [A. V.] Kolchak," 93 (1939): 3–50; "M. V. Frunze on the Turkestan Front," 100 (1940): 36–78.

72 (1935): 51–109

BOULANGISM AND TSARIST DIPLOMACY. Introduction by Ts. Friedland.

The communiqués printed here are from Russian representatives in Paris; dated 1885–1889, they trace the rise of Boulangism, the political movement headed by French Minister of War General Georges Boulanger. They discuss the apprehension over radical support given Boulanger, the internal affairs of France and their effect on Russian international relations, and Boulanger's attitude toward Germany.

For additional material in *Krasnyi Arkhiv*, see "Alexander III and General Boulanger," 14 (1926): 260–262.

72 (1935): 110–119

THE STRIKE OF THE IVANOVO VOZNESENSK FACTORY WEAVERS IN 1895. Introduction by V. Sokolov.

Nine telegrams from factory inspectors Goncharov and A. Astafiev and from Governor Terenin of Vladimir province dated October 4–10, 1895, are presented here. There is also a lengthy report by Astafiev, dated November 6, 1895, to the Department of Trade and Industry describing the extent of the strike.

For additional material in *Krasnyi Arkhiv*, see: "The Execution of the Ivanovo Voznesensk Workers in 1915," 68 (1935): 97–118; "Materials Re-

A Digest of the Krasnyi Arkhiv 113

lating to the Thirtieth Anniversary of the Ivanovo Voznesensk General Strike," 69–70 (1935): 127–137.

72 (1935): 120–159

FROM LEO TIKHOMIROV's DIARY (The Stolypin Era). Introduction by V. Maksakov.

Tikhomirov's personal contact with the leading men in Russian politics makes this section of his diary, dated from October 24, 1907, to August 29, 1908, valuable for a study of the background and atmosphere of the Stolypin era.

For other sections of Tikhomirov's diary in *Krasnyi Arkhiv*, see: 38 (1930): 20–69; 39 (1930): 47–75; 40 (1930): 59–96; 41–42 (1930): 103–147; 61 (1933): 82–128; 73 (1935): 170–190; 74 (1936): 162–191; 75 (1936): 171–184. For additional material, see: "From the Archive of L. Tikhomirov," 6 (1924): 124–194; "Unpublished Memoirs of L. Tikhomirov," 29 (1928): 139–174.

72 (1935): 160–181

MATERIALS RELATING TO THE HISTORY OF THE MASTERY OF THE NORTHERN SEA ROUTE

Twenty instructions from the Russian Admiralty to Captain Vitus Bering, February 28, 1733, and Bering's report on the execution of each order appear here.

Publication of these documents was begun in *Krasnyi Arkhiv*, 71 (1935): 137–169 and is continued in 73 (1935): 191–203 and 74 (1936): 142–161.

FROM AN ARCHIVIST'S NOTEBOOK

72 (1935): 182–190

THE CHURCH AND THE REFORMS OF 1861. Introduction by Z. Gurskaia.

Dated from November 24, 1860, to April 22, 1861, the eight letters presented in these pages discuss ways by which clergymen could maintain peace and quiet among the peasants by accurately interpreting the Emancipation Manifesto of February 18, 1861. The correspondence is between Minister of Justice V. N. Panin and Chief Procurator of the Holy Synod A. P. Tolstoy and between Tolstoy and Metropolitan Filaret of Moscow.

For additional material in *Krasnyi Arkhiv*, see: "Materials Relating to the History of the Peasant Uprising against Liberation in 1861," 36 (1929): 201–204; "The Reform of 1861 and the Peasant Movement," 75 (1936):

62–82. For additional material on the church, see the notes to "Life in Ecclesiastical Circles before the Revolution," 31 (1928): 204–213.

72 (1935): 190–199

DENIKINITES CONCERNING CONDITIONS IN THE REAR OF THEIR ARMY. Introduction by Kandidov.

The report printed here, dated March 28, 1920, is from Lieutenant General Makarenko to Baron P. N. Wrangel and describes conditions in the rear of the White army under General A. I. Denikin, the evacuation of Odessa, and the work of Generals Mai-Maevsky, Sannikov, Dobrovolsky, Shilling, Borovsky, Subbotin, and Pokrovsky.

72 (1935): 200

A. A. SERGEEV

The material here is an obituary of Alexander Aleksandrovich Sergeev, secretary of the editorial board of *Krasnyi Arkhiv*, who died of a heart attack in Kislovodsk, September 19, 1935.

VOLUME 73, 1935

73 (1935): 3–18

POLICE SURVEILLANCE OF ANNA ILINICHNA ULIANOVA-ELIZAROVA (A Few Dates in the Life and Activities of Anna Ilinichna Ulianova-Elizarova). Introduction by N. Meshcheriakov.

The Police Department documents published here give a detailed account of the revolutionary activities of Lenin's sister from 1886 to 1916. There are photostatic reproductions of police data sheets and pictures of Ulianova-Elizarova.

73 (1935): 19–73

THE COLLAPSE OF WRANGEL

Publication of the documents on the collapse of Wrangel was begun in 72 (1935): 3–43.

The documents presented here are military dispatches and orders of Soviet leaders M. V. Frunze, S. M. Budenny, K. E. Voroshilov, Bliukher, [G. L.?] Piatakov, and others dated from October 28 to November 17,

1920. They deal with the general offensive of the southern army against Baron P. N. Wrangel (the operation in North Tavri, October 28—November 5) and with the campaign for the seizure of the Crimean Peninsula and the liquidation of the southern front (November 6–17). Attached is a map showing the positions of White and Soviet forces before the Soviet offensive of October 27, 1920.

For references to additional material in *Krasnyi Arkhiv*, see the notes to "Materials Relating to the History of the Foreign Policy of Wrangel's Government," 32 (1929): 125–157.

73 (1935): 74–90

MATERIALS RELATING TO M. V. FRUNZE's REVOLUTIONARY ACTIVITY (1905–1912). Introduction by O. Varentsova.

These Police Department documents outline Frunze's activities from October 30, 1905, to October 15, 1910, giving a general picture of events in Ivanovo Voznesensk. There are photostatic reproductions of police data on Frunze, as well as photographs of him.

For additional material in *Krasnyi Arkhiv*, see: "Ten Years since the Day of M. V. Frunze's Death," 72 (1935): 44–50; "[The Role of] M. V. Frunze in the Organization of the Victory over [A. V.] Kolchak," 93 (1939): 3–50.

73 (1935): 91–125

DECEMBER DAYS IN THE DONETS BASIN IN 1905. Introduction by A. Pankratova.

The documents presented here are Russian Social Democratic proclamations to the people of Ekaterinoslav province and provincial officials' reports on the unrest in that province from September to December, 1905.

For references to additional material in *Krasnyi Arkhiv*, see the notes to "S. Y. Witte's Struggle with the Agrarian Revolution," 31 (1928): 81–102.

73 (1935): 126–169

THE PEASANT MOVEMENT IN THE CENTRAL PART OF RUSSIA IN 1905 (From Materials of the Kursk, Orlov, Voronezh, and Chernigov Provinces). Introduction by M. Lurie.

Two documents are published here. The first is a report by Privy Counselor I. A. Zvegintsev to the minister of internal affairs, dated March 14, 1905, describing the peasant movement in these Central Asian provinces of Russia. The second is a report of July 12, 1905, by Litvinov, assistant director of the Land Department of the Ministry of Internal Affairs, to the minister of internal affairs on the unrest in February and March, 1905.

For references to additional material in *Krasnyi Arkhiv*, see the notes to "S. Y. Witte's Struggle with the Agrarian Revolution," 31 (1928): 81–102.

FROM LEO TIKHOMIROV's DIARY (The Stolypin Era, 1908)

Dated from August 31 to December 31, 1908, the entries from Tikhomirov's diary printed here continue the analysis of the Russian political scene and discuss the financial condition of the Russian government and the cholera epidemic in St. Petersburg in 1908. There is additional biographical material on P. A. Stolypin.

For other sections of Tikhomirov's diary published in *Krasnyi Arkhiv*, see: 38 (1930): 20–69; 39 (1930): 47–75; 40 (1930): 59–96; 41–42 (1930): 103–147; 61 (1933): 82–128; 72 (1935): 120–159; 74 (1936): 162–191; 75 (1936): 171–184.

For additional material in *Krasnyi Arkhiv* on Tikhomirov, see: "From the Archive of L. Tikhomirov," 6 (1924): 124–194; "Unpublished Memoirs of L. Tikhomirov," 29 (1928): 139–174.

MATERIALS RELATING TO THE HISTORY OF THE MASTERY OF THE NORTHERN SEA ROUTE

Printed here is the text of twelve instructions from the Russian Admiralty to Captain [M. P.] Spanberg, February 28, 1733, and a report by Captain Vitus Bering and other officers on the execution of these instructions.

Publication of these documents was begun in *Krasnyi Arkhiv*, 71 (1935): 137–169 and 72 (1935): 160–181 and is continued in 74 (1936): 142–161.

FROM AN ARCHIVIST'S NOTEBOOK

PRESNIA IN DECEMBER 1905. Introduction by M. Syromiatnikov.

The armed uprising in Presnia, a suburb of Moscow, in December, 1905, is here described in the diary of I. Y. Rusanov, who was sixteen years old at the time.

73 (1935): 209-220

MOSCOW STUDENTS AND L. N. TOLSTOY'S DEATH. Introduction by I. Luppol.

The thirty-five telegrams, circulars, and reports presented here are dated November 7–18, 1910, and describe the measures undertaken by the government to prevent mass demonstrations at the time of Tolstoy's funeral. Furnished also are police reports containing a description of student demonstrations in Moscow.

For references to additional material in *Krasnyi Arkhiv*, see the notes to "L. N. Tolstoy under the Blows of the Censor," 35 (1929): 215–235.

VOLUME 74, 1936

74 (1936): 4

N. A. DOBROLIUBOV

A portrait of Nicholas Alexandrovich Dobroliubov (1836–1861) is here reproduced, on the one-hundredth anniversary of his birth.

For additional material in *Krasnyi Arkhiv*, see: "Dobroliubov's Unpublished Articles," 15 (1926): 234–240; "New Documents concerning N. A. Dobroliubov," 75 (1936): 145–170.

74 (1936): 5–36

SEVENTY-FIVE YEARS AGO. Introduction by I. Kuznetsov.

Lenin's article on the Emancipation Manifesto of February 19, 1861, is reprinted here from the Russian edition of his *Collected Works*. Also included are excerpts from private correspondence indicating the prevailing frame of mind in provinces and villages after the reforms of 1861. These excerpts are divided into four parts: (1) "The reception of the manifesto in the villages"; (2) "The Bezdna affair"; (3) "The peasant unrest in Penza province"; (4) "The conciliators."

For references to additional material in *Krasnyi Arkhiv* on events in Bezdna, see the notes to "The Uprising in Bezdna," 35 (1929): 176–208. See also "Kandeevka Uprising in 1861," 92 (1939): 91–132.

For additional material on peasant reaction to liberation, see: "Materials Relating to the History of the Peasant Uprising against Liberation in 1861," 36 (1929): 201–204; "The Church and Reforms of 1861," 72 (1935): 182–190; "The Reform of 1861 and the Peasant Movement," 75 (1936): 62–82; "Peasant Agitation in Kharkov Province (1861–1862)," 106 (1941): 58–78.

74 (1936): 37–65

TSARISM IN THE STRUGGLE WITH THE LABOR MOVEMENT IN THE YEARS OF ITS ASCENT. Introduction by M. Lurie.

Of the various documents presented here, the first is a letter of June 30, 1913, written by N. A. Maklakov, minister of internal affairs, to S. I. Timashev, minister of trade and commerce, concerning the growth of strikes in St. Petersburg and the measures taken to end them. Timashev's reply, also given here, is dated July 26.

In addition, two secret journals of meetings of the Council of Ministers held August 8 and October 24, 1913, discuss means of combating workers' strikes.

The remainder of the material printed here is composed of three dispatches from Maklakov to the Council of Ministers and to provincial officials and one note on the measures approved, which included provisions for arbitration in labor-management disputes and provisions for the establishment of legal norms for dealing with agitators and strikers.

74 (1936): 66–91

MATERIALS RELATING TO THE HISTORY OF THE URAL FACTORIES (According to a Gendarmerie Survey). Introduction by E. Goldich.

Printed here is a report of December 4, 1910, from Colonel M. S. Komissarov, chief of the Perm Gendarmerie, to the Police Department analyzing, on the basis of Komissarov's investigations, the reasons for the unrest in the Urals. Included is a chart showing the area of factory land, the name and location of each factory, the number of workshops and of administrators, the population of the area, the size of the labor force, the percentage of unemployed and the ways in which they occupy themselves, the length of the working day and the number of shifts, and the attitude of the people toward land allotment.

74 (1936): 92–141

THE AGRARIAN MOVEMENT IN SMOLENSK PROVINCE 1905–1906. Introduction by I. Kuznetsov.

Kuznetsov states that the materials published here differ from others on the agrarian movement in that they trace the activities of the lowest, not the highest, government officials active in the movement. Given here are police, Gendarmerie, and provincial officials' reports citing uprisings and instances of violence on estates and in districts in the Smolensk province, and measures taken to quiet them. The documents also discuss reaction to the Manifesto of October 17, 1905, and peasant demands for reforms.

For references to additional material in *Krasnyi Arkhiv*, see the notes to "S. Y. Witte's Struggle with the Agrarian Revolution," 31 (1928): 81–102.

74 (1936): 142–161

MATERIALS RELATING TO THE HISTORY OF THE MASTERY OF THE NORTHERN SEA ROUTE

This is a list of thirteen instructions from Captain Vitus Bering to Captain [M. P.] Spanberg, February 23, 1733, and extracts from a report on the preparations for and accomplishments of the Kamchatka and Okhotsk expeditions. A reproduction of a physical map, drawn about 1750, of Bering's journeys and of northeastern Siberia and Kamchatka is included.

Publication of these documents was begun in *Krasnyi Arkhiv*, 71 (1935): 137–169 and continued in 72 (1935): 160–181 and 73 (1935): 191–203.

74 (1936): 162–191

FROM LEO TIKHOMIROV'S DIARY (The Stolypin Era, 1909)

Among the materials in these entries, dated from January 1, 1909, to September 8, 1911, are Tikhomirov's opinions of G. E. Rasputin, P. A. Stolypin, and L. N. Tolstoy.

For other sections of Tikhomirov's diary published in *Krasnyi Arkhiv*, see: 38 (1930): 20–69; 39 (1930): 47–75; 40 (1930): 59–96; 41–42 (1930): 103–147; 61 (1933): 82–128; 72 (1935): 120–159; 73 (1935): 170–190; 75 (1936): 171–184. For additional material, see: "From the Archive of L. Tikhomirov," 6 (1924): 124–194; "Unpublished Memoirs of L. Tikhomirov," 29 (1928): 139–174.

FROM AN ARCHIVIST'S NOTEBOOK

74 (1936): 192–195

BISMARCK CONCERNING THE SITUATION IN EUROPE IN 1868. Introduction by A. E.

Printed here is a dispatch from P. Oubri, Russian ambassador in Berlin, to Prince A. M. Gorchakov, minister of foreign affairs, November 21/December 3, 1868, which summarizes the views of Count Otto von Bismarck, expressed in a conversation with Oubri, on the political situation in France, Austria, England, Spain, Rumania, and southern Germany.

74 (1936): 195–204

Moscow University in the October Days of 1905. Introduction by A. Syromiatnikov.

The documents presented here, dated September 7 to October 22, 1905, are from Police Department archives, and trace the student movement during this period, with emphasis on the demonstrations in Moscow.

74 (1936): 204–209

N. G. Chernyshevsky in Viliuisk. Introduction by N. A.

Chernyshevsky was exiled to Viliuisk from 1872 to 1883. The documents given here, dated from 1879 to 1882, include seven communiqués between the governor of Yakutsk province and the Viliuisk police and two reports by E. Brodnikov, who attended Chernyshevsky in Viliuisk.

For references to additional material in *Krasnyi Arkhiv*, see the notes to "Materials Relating to the History of the Release of N. G. Chernyshevsky," 31 (1928): 214–219.

74 (1936): 210–212

A Journey from Petersburg to Moscow—A. N. Radishchev and Tsarist Censorship. Introduction by V. Dalago.

The letter and government report given here deal with the efforts, in 1859, of Paul A. Radishchev, the son of A. N. Radishchev, to secure permission from Alexander II to publish his father's work *A Journey from Petersburg to Moscow*, previously suppressed by the censors.

VOLUME 75, 1936

75 (1936): 3–4

On the Front of Historical Science—In the Sovnarkom of the USSR and the Central Committee of the All-Union (Bolshevik) Communist Party

The document presented here is a decision by the Council of People's Commissars (*Sovnarkom*) to revise and improve history texts.

75 (1936): 4

DECREE OF THE CENTRAL COMMITTEE OF THE ALL-UNION (BOLSHEVIK) COMMUNIST PARTY AND THE COUNCIL OF PEOPLE'S COMMISSARS OF THE USSR

A decree issued January 26, 1936, ordering the revision of textbooks appears here.

75 (1936): 5–6

REMARKS IN CONNECTION WITH THE SYNOPSIS OF THE TEXTBOOK *History of the USSR*

Presented here is the criticism, dated August 9, 1934, expressed by Stalin, A. A. Zhdanov, and S. M. Kirov of *History of the USSR*, a textbook written by the Vanag group of historians.

75 (1936): 6–7

REMARKS CONCERNING THE SYNOPSIS OF THE TEXTBOOK *Modern History*

The criticism by Stalin, S. M. Kirov, and A. A. Zhdanov of *Modern History* was published August 9, 1934; it is reprinted here.

75 (1936): 8–9

MATERIALS CONCERNING THE ORGANIZATION OF THE COMPETITION FOR THE BEST TEXTBOOK FOR BEGINNING SCHOOLS ON THE ELEMENTARY COURSE IN THE HISTORY OF THE USSR WITH A SHORT INSTRUCTION IN GENERAL HISTORY

The document presented here outlines the requirements for the book, establishes the reviewing committee, and announces the awards to be granted.

75 (1936): 10–61

MATERIALS RELATING TO THE HISTORY OF THE PEACE OF PARIS 1856. Introduction by S. P.

These twenty documents, dated from December 4/16, 1855, to April 22/May 4, 1856, are an exchange of communiqués between Russian Chancellor Count K. V. Nesselrode and Russia's representatives at the Congress of Paris, Count A. F. Orlov and Baron Philip Brunnow, on negotiations at the congress. Included among them is a dispatch from the Austrian Foreign Minister Count Karl Buol to his ambassador in St. Petersburg, Count V. Esterhazy, and a dispatch from Russian Minister of Foreign Affairs Prince A. M. Gorchakov to Orlov. In addition, there is an unsigned analysis of the political situation in Russia after the Peace of Paris.

For additional material in *Krasnyi Arkhiv*, see: "Materials Relating to the History of the Franco-Russian Agreement of 1859," 88 (1938): 182–255; "Russo-American Relations at the Time of the Civil War in the United States," 94 (1939): 97–153.

75 (1936): 62–82

THE REFORM OF 1861 AND THE PEASANT MOVEMENT. Introduction by M. Lurie.

The account printed here, entitled "From a Survey by the Land Department of the Ministry of Internal Affairs from January 1, 1861, to February 19, 1863," describes the unrest in Kazan, Tambov, Chernigov, Podolia, Smolensk, Vitebsk, Vilno, Kovno, Grodno, Vladimir, Novgorod, Tula, Penza, Viatka, Saratov, Kiev, Orenburg, Kherson, and Mogilev provinces.

For additional material in *Krasnyi Arkhiv*, see: "Materials Relating to the History of the Peasant Uprising against Liberation in 1861," 36 (1929): 201–204; "The Church and the Reforms of 1861," 72 (1935): 182–190.

75 (1936): 83–112

STUDENT MOVEMENT IN 1901. Introduction by V. Orlov.

The documents presented here are divided according to the following topics: (1) the draft of Kiev students into the army (November, 1900–January, 1901); (2) demonstrations of protest in St. Petersburg, Kharkov, and Moscow (February, 1901); (3) demonstrations at the Kazan *sobor* ("cathedral") in St. Petersburg (March 4, 1901); and (4) labor demonstrations in Kiev (March 11, 1901). Orlov writes that this is not only the first publication of these documents but also the most detailed publication of material on the student agitation in 1901.

75 (1936): 113–144

THE SEARCH FOR PRECIOUS METALS IN THE NORTH IN THE SEVENTEENTH AND EIGHTEENTH CENTURIES. Introduction by A. Birze.

Birze summarizes the history of the search for precious metals from the tenth century. The documents published here are reports on the work of prospectors from 1671 to 1681, especially on their search for silver and gold in the Archangel area and the northern regions of European Russia.

Publication of this material is continued in *Krasnyi Arkhiv*, 76 (1936): 192–220.

75 (1936): 145–170

NEW DOCUMENTS CONCERNING N. A. DOBROLIUBOV. Introduction by E. Ch.

Dated from 1853 to 1910, these documents are divided into the following groups:

1. "Dobroliubov in the Pedagogical Institute in Petersburg (1853–1857)." This material deals with Dobroliubov's admission to the Institute, his grades, and the effect on him of his parents' death.

2. "Dobroliubov and Tsarist Censorship (1872–1896)." The censors here review *Sochinenii N. A. Dobroliubova* ("The Works of N. A. Dobroliubov"), *Chego Ne Nado Delat* ("What Is to Be Done"), and *Materialy dlia Biografii N. A. Dobroliubova, Sobrannye N. G. Chernyshevskim* ("Materials for a Biography of N. A. Dobroliubov, Collected by N. G. Chernyshevsky").

3. "Demonstration at Volkovo Cemetery on the Twenty-fifth Anniversary of N. A. Dobroliubov's Death (November 17, 1886)." The documents here describe the popular demonstration at Dobroliubov's grave and the attempts of the police to disperse the crowd.

4. "The Fortieth Anniversary of N. A. Dobroliubov's Death (1901)."

For additional material in *Krasnyi Arkhiv*, see "Dobroliubov's Unpublished Articles," 15 (1926): 234–240; "N. A. Dobroliubov," 74 (1936): 4.

75 (1936): 171–184

FROM LEO TIKHOMIROV'S DIARY

These entries from Tikhomirov's diary are dated October 8, 1911, to December 30, 1912. Tikhomirov writes primarily of his financial situation, of revolutionary feeling in Russia, and of Rasputin's influence in the government.

For other sections of the diary published in *Krasnyi Arkhiv*, see: 38 (1930): 20–69; 39 (1930): 47–75; 40 (1930): 59–96; 41–42 (1930): 103–147; 61 (1933): 82–128; 72 (1935): 120–159; 73 (1935): 170–190; 74 (1936): 162–191.

For additional material on Tikhomirov, see: "From the Archive of L. Tikhomirov," 6 (1924): 124–194; "Unpublished Memoirs of L. Tikhomirov," 29 (1928): 139–174.

A Digest of the Krasnyi Arkhiv

FROM AN ARCHIVIST'S NOTEBOOK

75 (1936): 185–188

THE TOILING COSSACKS OF THE DON REGION CONCERNING THE BREST PEACE AND DEFENSE OF THE SOVIET LAND. Introduction by G. Kostomarov.

Excerpts from the stenographic report of the First Congress of Soviets of the Don Republic, April 9, 1918, and a resolution adopted by the congress favoring acceptance of the peace terms offered by the Germans at Brest Litovsk are presented here.

For additional material in *Krasnyi Arkhiv*, see "The Revolutionary Cossacks of the Don in the Struggle with Counterrevolution," 76 (1936): 24–30.

75 (1936): 188–191

A GOVERNOR IN THE ROLE OF PROPAGATOR OF THE KORAN. Introduction by P. Rusin.

Lieutenant General A. Gippius, military governor of the Ferghana region, reports here to the minister of internal affairs on his attempts in July, 1916, to convince the Uzbeks that conscription for auxiliary army work does not conflict with the teachings of the Koran.

For references to additional material in *Krasnyi Arkhiv* on conditions in Central Asia, see the notes to "The Uprising in Central Asia in 1916," 34 (1929): 39–94 and the notes to "Materials Relating to the History of the Tsarist National Minority Policy," 35 (1929): 107–127.

For additional material on affairs in Ferghana, see "Andizhan Uprising of 1898," 88 (1938): 123–181.

75 (1936): 192–196

FROM THE HISTORY OF THE SHOSTKA GUN-POWDER WORKS. Introduction by M. Syromiatnikova.

In her introduction, Syromiatnikova briefly sketches the history of the factory from its establishment in 1739 in the village of Shostka in the Ukraine. Printed here is a factory worker's letter of May 13, 1902, describing working conditions.

VOLUME 76, 1936

76 (1936): 3–23

AGITATION IN KHARKOV PROVINCE IN THE YEARS OF THE IMPERIALISTIC WAR. Introduction by P. Bilyk.

Presented here are eighteen documents, dated from July, 1914, to July, 1916, which include Social Democratic proclamations and government reports on the agitation in Kharkov villages, particularly in Nizhnaia Syrovatka and Boroml.

76 (1936): 24–30

THE REVOLUTIONARY COSSACKS OF THE DON IN THE STRUGGLE WITH COUNTERREVOLUTION. Introduction by G. Kostomarov.

Dated from December, 1917, to March, 1918, the twelve documents printed here are resolutions of the revolutionary section of the Don Cossacks, in which they recognized Soviet power, pledged allegiance to the Soviet regime, and promised to fight the White armies.

For additional material in *Krasnyi Arkhiv*, see "The Toiling Cossacks of the Don Region concerning the Brest Peace and Defense of the Soviet Land," 75 (1936): 185–188.

76 (1936): 31–48

DOCUMENTS CONCERNING THE KHODYNKA CATASTROPHE OF 1896. Introduction by A. Kobiako.

The Khodynka catastrophe occurred at the coronation ceremonies on May 18, 1896. These documents present the program for distribution of gifts at Khodynka field, a sketch of the field, the number killed and injured in the crush, the interrogation of witnesses, and two pictures of the injured and dead.

76 (1936): 49–66

WORKERS' MOVEMENT IN THE PETERSBURG FACTORIES IN MAY, 1901. Introduction by M. Syromiatnikova.

The material presented here comprises a Police Department circular warning officials to prepare for demonstrations on May 1, 1901, and a report of the Ministry of Internal Affairs on unrest in St. Petersburg in the Obukhovsk steel foundry, the Nevsky shipbuilding yards, the Nikolsk factory, the Alexandrovsk mechanical division of the Nikolaevsk railroad, and the Baltic shipyard.

76 (1936): 67–82

MATERIALS RELATING TO THE HISTORY OF THE "YAKUT UNION." Introduction by M. Konstantinov.

Dated from January to April, 1906, these twenty-two communications to the Police Department stress the role of the nationalist group "Union of Yakuts" in the unrest in Yakutia during 1906. The program and the demands of the organization are emphasized.

76 (1936): 83–155

FIRST RAILROADS IN RUSSIA. Introduction by M. Krutikov.

The eighteen annotated documents published here are dated from 1835 to 1842 and deal with proposals for the first railroads in Russia. They are reports from the Department of Transportation and from the following persons: Secretary of State Baron M. A. Korf; Minister of Finance Count E. Kankrin; a member of the Council of State, M. Speransky; Prince D. V. Golitsyn; Novgorod Governor Nicholas N. Muraviëv; Chief of the Secret Police Count A. K. Benckendorff; Nicholas I; and Professor Franz Anton von Gerstner, of the Vienna Polytechnic Institute. Von Gerstner was given the first concession, for the railroad from St. Petersburg to Tsarskoe Selo.

76 (1936): 156–191

MATERIALS RELATING TO THE HISTORY OF THE BURIATS IN THE SEVENTEENTH CENTURY. Introduction by S. Okun.

Dated from 1629 to 1705, the ten documents published here are eyewitness accounts of life among the Buriat-Mongols and the effects of Russian penetration on that life.

For additional material in *Krasnyi Arkhiv*, see "The Church and the Buriat-Mongol Russification in Tsarist Russia," 53 (1932): 100–126.

76 (1936): 192–220

THE SEARCH FOR PRECIOUS METALS IN THE NORTH IN THE SEVENTEENTH AND EIGHTEENTH CENTURIES (Conclusion)

Publication of the documents on this subject was begun in *Krasnyi Arkhiv*, 75 (1936): 113–144.

Further reports on prospecting in the northern regions of European Russia from 1680 to 1769 are given here.

FROM AN ARCHIVIST'S NOTEBOOK

76 (1936): 221–225

N. G. CHERNYSHEVSKY's [SHORTHAND] CODE. By N. Alexeiev.

A description and analysis of Chernyshevsky's shorthand, as decoded after his arrest July 7, 1862, appears here. There are illustrations of some of his symbols and a list of the word abbreviations he used.

For references to additional material in *Krasnyi Arkhiv* on Chernyshevsky, see the notes to "Materials Relating to the History of the Release of N. G. Chernyshevsky," 31 (1928): 214–219.

76 (1936): 226–230

THE SUPPRESSION BY TSARISM OF THE HONORING OF T. SHEVCHENKO's MEMORY. Introduction by N. Belchikov.

The documents given here are reports of the demonstrations which took place in 1914 on the one-hundredth anniversary of T. G. Shevchenko's birth.

For additional material in *Krasnyi Arkhiv*, see: "The Struggle of the Tsarist Government and Censorship with T. G. Shevchenko's 'Kobzar,'" 91 (1938): 255–270; "At a Great Grave," 105 (1941): 99–114.

76 (1936): 230–232

MATERIALS RELATING TO THE BIOGRAPHY OF P. G. ZAICHNEVSKY. Introduction by A. Spirova.

Printed here is an excerpt from Zaichnevsky's letter to his friend P. M. Argiropulo written in Orel on July 1, 1861, in which he outlines plans for a peasant uprising under the direction of the intelligentsia.

For additional material in *Krasnyi Arkhiv*, see "P. G. Zaichnevsky," 1 (1922): 273–279.

VOLUME 77, 1936

77 (1936): 1

PORTRAIT OF GORKY

An announcement of Maxim Gorky's death on June 18, 1936, made by the Central Committee and the Soviet of People's Commissars is printed here.

For references to additional material in *Krasnyi Arkhiv* on Gorky, see the notes to "An Article of M. Gorky Forbidden by the Censor," 45 (1931): 81–85.

77 (1936): 3–18

THE CONSTITUTION OF THE USSR

Published here is the decision of June 11, 1936, of the presidium of the Central Executive Committee of the USSR to adopt a constitution and to call an All-Union Congress of Soviets. The complete text of the proposed constitution is included.

77 (1936): 19–60

WORKERS' LETTERS TO *Zvezda* AND *Pravda*. Introduction by M. Savelev.

Dated from 1912 to 1914, these letters to the newspapers *Zvezda* ("Star") and *Pravda* are grouped under three headings: (1) "The struggle for a labor press"; (2) "The Lena execution and the rise of the labor movement"; (3) "The Bolshevik faction of the [Fourth State] Duma and the toiling masses."

77 (1936): 61–90

ILLEGAL WORK OF THE BOLSHEVIK FACTION OF THE FOURTH STATE DUMA (According to Documents of the Police Department). Introduction by M. L. Lurie.

These twenty-one Secret Police reports, dated from January, 1913, to December, 1914, reveal the agitation of the Bolshevik faction of the Fourth State Duma for strikes for an eight-hour working day. They also provide information on Bolshevik leaders A. E. Badaev, M. K. Muranov, G. I. Petrovsky, F. N. Samoilov, and N. R. Shagov.

For references to additional material in *Krasnyi Arkhiv*, see the notes to "First State Duma in Vyborg," 57 (1931): 85–99. See also "Arrest of the Duma 'Quintet' in 1914," 64 (1934): 31–51.

77 (1936): 91–116

THE KRONSTADT REBELLION OF 1906. Introduction by F. Petrov.

Printed here are eighteen reports on the armed rebellion among the Kronstadt sailors on July 19/August 1, 1906.

A Digest of the Krasnyi Arkhiv

For additional material in *Krasnyi Arkhiv*, see "The Execution of the Participants in the Kronstadt Rebellion of 1906," 43 (1930): 166–167.

77 (1936): 117–150

THE SERF PEASANTRY OF THE VILLAGE OF BARASHEV-USAD IN THE FIRST HALF OF THE NINETEENTH CENTURY. Introduction by I. Kuznetsov.

The thirty-seven letters printed here are dated from 1832 to 1853 and picture life on the estate of Countess Sophia Prokofievna Bobrinskaia in Barashev-Usad village, Simbirsk province. The letters were exchanged between the village elders and the managers of Countess Bobrinskaia's estate.

77 (1936): 151–157

AGITATIONS OF THE SERF PEASANTS OF THE VILLAGE OF KRASNYI KUT. Introduction by A. Shapiro.

The peasants of Krasnyi Kut village, Ekaterinoslav province, rebelled in July and October, 1853. The two reports given here describe their grievances.

77 (1936): 159–180

CONSTRUCTION OF A DNIEPER DOCKYARD IN THE EIGHTEENTH CENTURY. Introduction by P. M.

The documents printed here include the proposals for construction of a dockyard on the Dnieper at Kichkas, Catherine II's ukase ordering the beginning of the work in 1796, a list of workers and wages, and instructions to the director of the project.

77 (1936): 181–190

UNPUBLISHED LETTERS OF A. S. PUSHKIN. Introduction by M. Svetlova.

Presented here, together with a picture of the N. A. Goncharov home in Yaropolets, Moscow province, are photostats of the originals of two letters written by Pushkin in 1835 to his mother-in-law, Natalia Ivanovna Goncharova.

For references to additional material in *Krasnyi Arkhiv* on Pushkin, see the notes to "New Manuscripts and Materials on Pushkin," 31 (1928): 155–159.

FROM AN ARCHIVIST'S NOTEBOOK

77 (1936): 191–199

THE PROLETARIAN RED CROSS IN PETROGRAD (October, 1917—June, 1918). Introduction by M. L.

A report on the organization of the Red Cross and on its work at the beginning of the October Revolution and the Civil War is given here.

77 (1936): 200–211

ALEXANDER NEVSKY MONASTERY ON THE EVE OF THE OVERTHROW OF THE AUTOCRACY. Introduction by E. Cherniavsky.

The twelve documents presented here are excerpts from the interrogation, in 1917, of synodical officials concerning the financial situation of the Alexander Nevsky monastery and the relationship between Metropolitan Pitirim and Rasputin.

77 (1936): 211–214

MATERIALS RELATING TO THE QUESTION OF THE PROPERTY STATUS OF THE DECEMBRIST, PRINCE S. G. VOLKONSKY. Introduction by A. Kozachenko.

This is Volkonsky's note on his financial affairs, estates, and proposed expenditures for the year 1826. It includes a list showing the settlement of various accounts.

VOLUME 78, 1936

78 (1936): 2–3

TO COMRADE GREGORY KONSTANTINOVICH ORDZHONIKIDZE

In the letter published here the Central Archive Department of the USSR and the editors of *Krasnyi Arkhiv* congratulate G. K. Ordzhonikidze on his fiftieth birthday. A photograph of him is included.

For additional material in *Krasnyi Arkhiv*, see: "Materials Relating to the Activities of G. K. Ordzhonikidze in the Years of the Civil War," 78 (1936): 5–14; "A Few Dates in the Underground Party Work of G. K. Ordzhonikidze 1903–1912," 78 (1936): 15–22; "Government Bulletin on the Death of Gregory K. Ordzhonikidze," 80 (1937): 1; "Materials Relating to the Revolutionary Activities of G. K. Ordzhonikidze," 86 (1938): 169–183.

78 (1936): 5–14

MATERIALS RELATING TO THE ACTIVITIES OF G. K. ORDZHONIKIDZE IN THE YEARS OF THE CIVIL WAR (From Documents of the Central Archive of the October Revolution and the Central Archive of the Red Army)

The first of these documents is Lenin's letter of April 11, 1918, appointing Ordzhonikidze head of the Provisional Commissariat of South Russia, with responsibility for organizing the Crimea, Don, and Black Sea regions and the Northern Caucasus. The remaining documents, dated from April, 1918, to May, 1921, are Ordzhonikidze's dispatches to troops and his reports to Lenin and Stalin. There is also a photograph of Ordzhonikidze at the southern front in 1919.

For references to additional material in *Krasnyi Arkhiv*, see the notes to "To Comrade Gregory Konstantinovich Ordzhonikidze," 78 (1936): 2–3.

78 (1936): 15–22

A FEW DATES IN THE UNDERGROUND PARTY WORK OF G. K. ORDZHONIKIDZE 1903–1912

The documents printed here are Police Department reports on Ordzhonikidze's activities from 1903, when he joined the Russian Social Democratic Labor party, until 1912, when he was sentenced to hard labor in Siberia.

For references to additional material in *Krasnyi Arkhiv*, see the notes to "To Comrade Gregory Konstantinovich Ordzhonikidze," 78 (1936): 2–3.

78 (1936): 23–84

CHRONOLOGY OF GORKY'S LIFE AND WORKS. Introduction by E. Cherniavsky.

This is a chronological list compiled largely from Police Department records of the events in Maxim Gorky's life from his birth, in 1868, to 1917. A picture of Gorky appears on page 23.

For references to additional material in *Krasnyi Arkhiv*, see the notes to "An Article of M. Gorky Forbidden by the Censor," 45 (1931): 81–85.

78 (1936): 85–97

STRUGGLE FOR LAND IN 1917 (Kazan Province). Introduction by M. P.

Among the documents, dated from March 20 to September 28, 1917, printed here are telegrams from Kazan officials to the Provisional Government describing peasant unrest and the seizure of land and other property. In addition, a resolution of the Soviet of Peasant Deputies of Kazan dated

May 13, 1917, proposes solutions to problems related to land, timber, cattle, grain, and provisions, and a document from the government indicates concern over peasant disturbances, which were rapidly leading to anarchy.

78 (1936): 98–127

THE AGRARIAN MOVEMENT IN CHERNIGOV PROVINCE 1905–1906. Introduction by I. Kuznetsov.

The documents published here are dated from January 22, 1905, to August 1, 1906. They include reports on peasant unrest from landowners, from A. Khvostov, governor of Chernigov province, and from Colonel N. P. Rudov, chief of the Chernigov Gendarmerie. There are also communiqués between Count S. Y. Witte, chairman of the Council of Ministers, and P. N. Durnovo, acting minister of internal affairs; between Durnovo and the military commander of the Kiev military district; and between the Ministry of War and the Ministry of Internal Affairs.

For references to additional material in *Krasnyi Arkhiv*, see the notes to "S. Y. Witte's Struggle with the Agrarian Revolution," 31 (1928): 81–102.

78 (1936): 128–160

MATERIALS RELATING TO THE HISTORY OF THE AUTOCRACY'S STRUGGLE WITH THE AGRARIAN MOVEMENT IN 1905–1907. Introduction by M. L. Lurie.

The following documents are printed here:

1. A decree of April 10, 1905, by Nicholas II, outlining four points to be followed in stamping out peasant disorders.
2. A memorandum dated July 10, 1905, from A. Bulygin, minister of internal affairs, to the Council of Ministers, describing the 1902 disorders in Poltava and Kharkov provinces, and the draft of a proposed temporary law to combat them.
3. A letter of December 1, 1905, from P. Durnovo, of the Ministry of Internal Affairs, to Count D. M. Solsky, secretary of state.
4. Durnovo's proposal regarding the agrarian movement, made to the Council of Ministers on February 28, 1906.
5. A draft of a law concerning punishment of agitators and compensation for landowners whose property was destroyed in the course of uprisings.
6. An excerpt from proceedings of a special commission dealing with the agrarian movement.

For references to additional material in *Krasnyi Arkhiv*, see the notes to "S. Y. Witte's Struggle with the Agrarian Revolution," 31 (1928): 81–102.

78 (1936): 161–186

TSARIST RUSSIA AND THE HAWAIIAN ISLANDS. Introduction by S. Okun.

The following documents are published here:

1. A proclamation of May 21, 1816, signed by King Tomari of the two Sandwich Islands and acknowledging his willingness to accept a Russian protectorate.

2. A report of a seven-man council of the Russian-American Company on the necessity for strengthening trade relations with the Sandwich Islands, March 26, 1818.

3. An extract from the journal of Dr. George Sheffer, representative of the Russian-American Company, describing his exploits in Hawaii in 1815–1817.

4. A note from Sheffer to Alexander I on the political and commercial advantages of improving the Russian position in the Sandwich Islands, February, 1819.

5. Comments on each of Sheffer's points by the Department of Manufacturing and Internal Trade, February, 1819.

6. A supplement to Sheffer's note to Alexander I, March 2, 1819.

7. A note from the administrative officers of the Russian-American Company to the Department of Manufacturing and Internal Trade, March 18, 1819, concerning the addition of the Sandwich Islands to the Russian possessions.

8. A letter from Count K. V. Nesselrode, minister of foreign affairs, to O. P. Kozodavlev, minister of internal affairs, June 24, 1819, revealing Alexander I's attitude toward the work of the Russian-American Company.

78 (1936): 187–225

MATERIALS RELATING TO THE HISTORY OF RELATIONS OF THE KAZAKHS WITH TSARIST RUSSIA IN THE EIGHTEENTH CENTURY. Introduction by V. Lebedev.

Published here is a message from Empress Anna to Khan Abulkhair dated February, 1731, which proposes friendly coexistence under specific conditions. There are also instructions to M. Tevkelev, Russian representative to the Kirghiz-Kazakhs, dated February, 1731; a translation of a letter from Abulkhair to Tevkelev, in Ufa; three reports from Tevkelev to the Collegium of Foreign Affairs, 1731–1732; and excerpts from descriptions of living conditions among the Kirghiz-Kazakh people.

For additional material in *Krasnyi Arkhiv*, see "Materials Relating to the History of Kazakhstan in the Eighteenth Century," 87 (1938): 129–173.

78 (1936): 226–247

N. P. Balabin's Memoirs. Introduction unsigned.

Balabin was a landowner in Samara and Chernigov provinces in the 1860's. These memoirs provide autobiographical material, as well as information on the procedure he followed in establishing his starch factory, his experiences in securing land and materials, and the success of this venture.

FROM AN ARCHIVIST'S NOTEBOOK

78 (1936): 248–250

V. I. Lenin's Address to the Tula Workers

This address is a letter of December, 1919, appealing to the Tula workers to send four hundred freight cars of potatoes to Moscow to save the city from starvation. Included also are two Tula proclamations establishing the manner in which potatoes would be gathered and shipped.

78 (1936): 250–252

A. M. Gorky and the Publishing Business. Introduction by N. Nakoriakov.

This material is a note by Maxim Gorky dated December 19, 1918; it outlines the problems likely to be encountered in publishing eighteenth- and nineteenth-century Russian classical literature in popular editions.

For references to additional material in *Krasnyi Arkhiv* on Gorky, see the notes to "An Article of M. Gorky Forbidden by the Censor," 45 (1931): 81–85.

78 (1936): 252–254

Materials Relating to the History of N. G. Chernyshevsky's Exile. Introduction by V. Samoilov.

A draft of the resolution of the Council of Ministers in September, 1871, recommending the exile of Chernyshevsky to Siberia is presented in these pages.

For references to additional material in *Krasnyi Arkhiv*, see the notes to "Materials Relating to the History of the Release of N. G. Chernyshevsky," 31 (1928): 214–219.

A Digest of the Krasnyi Arkhiv 135

78 (1936): 254–262

FARMSTEADS AT THE BEGINNING OF THE NINETEENTH CENTURY. Introduction unsigned.

Printed here are excerpts from the notes of Vladimir Alekseevich Bakarev (1800–1872), architect on the estate of Prince [Alexis B.?] Kurakin from 1820 to 1828. The notes describe Prince Kurakin, his estate, and the life of 5,000 serfs who tilled the soil and worked in the factories there.

VOLUME 79, 1936

79 (1936): 3

DECISION OF THE EXTRAORDINARY EIGHTH CONGRESS OF SOVIETS OF THE USSR CONCERNING THE CONFIRMATION OF THE CONSTITUTION (BASIC LAW) OF THE UNION OF SOVIET SOCIALIST REPUBLICS

This decision (decree) was issued on December 5, 1936. A picture of Stalin is included with it here.

79 (1936): 4–18

THE CONSTITUTION (BASIC LAW) OF THE USSR

This is a reprint of the constitution adopted in Moscow on December 5, 1936.

79 (1936): 19–25

AUTOCRACY AND SUFFRAGE IN THE MINORITY REGIONS OF TSARIST RUSSIA. Introduction by I. Kovalov.

The correspondence presented here is dated from February 19, 1914, to April 2, 1916, and is concerned primarily with changes in the system of elections to the State Duma and with representation from national areas. It was exchanged between I. Goremykin, chairman of the Council of Ministers, and N. A. Maklakov, minister of internal affairs; officials of the Ministry of Internal Affairs, the Council of Ministers, the Ministry of War, and the viceroy of the Caucasus; and Goremykin and the office of the State Duma.

For additional material in *Krasnyi Arkhiv*, see "Tsarist Ministers concerning Universal Suffrage," 83 (1937): 224–225.

79 (1936): 26–33

AUTOCRACY AND WOMAN SUFFRAGE. Introduction unsigned.

The documents printed here, an exchange of communiqués between tsarist ministers, pertain to the decision by the Council of Ministers in April, 1912, not to grant women the right to vote in Duma elections.

For additional material in *Krasnyi Arkhiv*, see "Tsarist Ministers concerning Universal Suffrage," 83 (1937): 224–225.

79 (1936): 34–51

THE STRIKE IN TVER IN 1885. Introduction by N. Zhuravlev.

The documents presented here deal with the unrest and the strike in the Morozov textile factory in Tver in February, 1885, and with the economic situation in Russia in the 1880's. They are reports from the Tver police and the governor general and transcriptions of interrogations of workers and factory directors.

79 (1936): 52–66

THE KAZAN CLOTHIERS IN 1836. Introduction by E. Katsman.

Katsman reviews the history of the Kazan cloth factory, established in 1714. The documents presented here describing a strike that occurred in 1836 are an appeal by the workers to Nicholas I, a report to the Ministry of Internal Affairs, and the court's sentence on those who signed the appeal.

79 (1936): 67–100

AGITATION OF THE WORKERS AT THE MERCHANT NOSOV'S FACTORY AT SHUISK IN 1822–1824. Introduction by I. Sokolov.

Sokolov reviews the history of A. Nosov's linen factory, founded in 1788. Dated from March, 1823, to December, 1824, the documents given here consist of the protocols of the Shuisk district court in Vladimir province on the unrest in 1822, Nosov's statements to the court, and the testimony of workers and villagers.

79 (1936): 101–149

AGRARIAN RELATIONS IN PREREVOLUTIONARY DAGESTAN. Introduction by A. Birze.

A report from the office of the viceroy of the Caucasus dated August 10, 1910, on relations between the various nationalities in each of the regions of Dagestan appears here.

79 (1936): 150–174

AGITATION OF PEASANTS OF BELGOROD AND MITROPOL VILLAGES IN 1682. Introduction by A. Birze.

The reports and letters given here are from officials of Kursk province, describing the attitude of the clergy toward peasant disturbances in Belgorod and Mitropol.

FROM AN ARCHIVIST'S NOTEBOOK

79 (1936): 175–206

LYCEUM LETTERS OF A. M. GORCHAKOV 1814–1818. Introduction by M. Ts.

These thirty-eight letters by Prince Gorchakov, actually written between 1811 and 1817, were addressed to A. N. Peshchurov and his wife, Gorchakov's uncle and aunt. They describe life at the Tsarskoe Selo Lyceum and Gorchakov's friendship with A. S. Pushkin. There is an explanatory appendix and a portrait of Pushkin taken from an engraving by Geiman which appeared in *Prisoner of the Caucasus*, 1822.

For references to additional material in *Krasnyi Arkhiv* on Pushkin, see the notes to "New Manuscripts and Materials on Pushkin," 31 (1928): 155–159.

79 (1936): 207–209

AN UNPUBLISHED AUTOGRAPH OF A. S. PUSHKIN

This is a reproduction of the original manuscript of a poem written by Pushkin to Prince A. M. Gorchakov. The manuscript was discovered in the Gorchakov archives.

For references to additional material in *Krasnyi Arkhiv* on Pushkin, see the notes to "New Manuscripts and Materials on Pushkin," 31 (1928): 155–159.

VOLUME 80, 1937

80 (1937): 1

GOVERNMENT BULLETIN ON THE DEATH OF GREGORY K. ORDZHONIKIDZE

This bulletin announces Ordzhonikidze's death from a heart attack on February 18, 1937, in the Kremlin. His photograph is included.

138   *A Digest of the Krasnyi Arkhiv*

For references to additional material in *Krasnyi Arkhiv*, see the notes to "To Comrade Gregory Konstantinovich Ordzhonikidze," 78 (1936): 2–3.

80 (1937): 3–12

ALEXANDER SERGEEVICH PUSHKIN. By E. Cherniavsky.

This article is a eulogy of Pushkin on the one-hundredth anniversary of his death; it contains quotations from several of his poems. An oil portrait of Pushkin, done by V. Tropinin in 1827, is reproduced on page 3.

Volume 80 of *Krasnyi Arkhiv* is devoted almost entirely to materials on Pushkin. For additional material, see: "Dostoevsky on the Commemoration of Pushkin in the 1880's," 1 (1922): 367–405; "New Material on Pushkin," 28 (1928): 231–234; "New Material on Pushkin," 29 (1928): 218–223; "New Manuscripts and Materials on Pushkin," 31 (1928): 155–159; "A. S. Pushkin's Poem, 'The Monk,'" 31 (1928): 160–201 and 32 (1929): 183–190; "New Material concerning Pushkin's Duel and Death," 33 (1929): 222–235; "A. S. Pushkin under the Surveillance of the Police," 37 (1929): 237–245; "A. S. Pushkin and Count M. S. Vorontsov," 38 (1930): 173–185; "Unpublished Letters of A. S. Pushkin," 77 (1936): 181–190; "Lyceum Letters of A. M. Gorchakov," 79 (1936): 175–206; "An Unpublished Autograph of A. S. Pushkin," 79 (1936): 207–209.

80 (1937): 13–73

UNPUBLISHED AUTOGRAPHS OF A. S. PUSHKIN

Part I (pp. 13–20) is a publication of Pushkin's *Derevnia* ("The Village"). Part II (pp. 21–73) contains reproductions of manuscripts of Pushkin's lyceum poems. M. Tsiavlovsky has written an introduction to this section. The poems published here are "Poslanie k Natali" ("Message to Natalie"), "K Drugu Stikhotvortsu" ("To a Friend of the Poet"), "K Batiushkovu" ("To Papa"), "K Litsiniiu" ("To Litsiniia"), and "K Molodoi Vdove" ("To a Young Widow"). There is a colored portrait of Pushkin during his last years as a lyceum student.

80 (1937): 75–206

LYCEUM LECTURES (From A. M. Gorchakov's Notes). Introduction by B. Meilakh.

These are Prince Gorchakov's undated notes on lyceum lectures in law, political science, political economy, literary history, lyric poetry, and an introduction to esthetics. Included is a picture of the lyceum at Tsarskoe Selo.

80 (1937): 207–216

Pushkin's Youth (An Unpublished Article by V. Briusov)

This article by Briusov on Pushkin's early life and work was probably begun in 1924, but it was not completed, or published, before its appearance in this volume.

80 (1937): 217–239

Pushkin's Works and Tsarist Censorship (From Archive Materials). Introduction by L. Polianskaia.

Published here are five reports of the censors on works about or by Pushkin. The first report, dated October 24, 1897, deals with F. F. Pavlenkov's publication of *Illiustrirovannoi Pushkinskoi Biblioteke* ("Illustrated Pushkin Library"), Volumes 1–40. The second is dated May 24, 1899, and concerns A. I. Tsomakion's biographical sketch, *A. S. Pushkin*, published in Odessa in 1899. The third, of March 31, 1900, deals with the complete works of Pushkin published by I. D. Sytin in Moscow in 1899. The fourth, dated September 15, 1900, discusses *A. S. Pushkin: Zhizneopisanie i Sbornik Stikhotvorenii* ("A. S. Pushkin: Biography and Collection of Poems"), published in Kharkov in 1899. The fifth report, dated May 18, 1902, is about *Sochineniia A. S. Pushkina* ("Works of A. S. Pushkin"), published in St. Petersburg in 1899.

80 (1937): 240–247

Effect on Tsarist Troops of A. S. Pushkin's Ode "Freedom." Introduction by N. Belchikov.

Pushkin wrote "Freedom" in 1817 or 1819. The documents presented here are reports of army officers, dated 1827 to 1830, indicating the extent of the ode's circulation in the army and its effect on the soldiers. All copies of the ode found in the possession of soldiers were confiscated.

FROM AN ARCHIVIST'S NOTEBOOK

80 (1937): 248–250

P. A. Viazemsky and the Death of A. S. Pushkin. By N. Belchikov.

The sources for this article are the papers of Prince P. A. Viazemsky, which reflect the reaction to Pushkin's death and note preparations for an investigation of the circumstances surrounding the duel in which he was killed. There is also a picture of the house in which Pushkin died.

VOLUME 81, 1937

81 (1937): 1

PORTRAIT OF J. V. STALIN

This is a reproduction of the portrait painted by N. Kazbek. The year in which it was painted is not indicated.

81 (1937): 3–21

CONCERNING THE SHORTCOMINGS OF THE PARTY WORK AND MEASURES FOR LIQUIDATING THE TROTSKYITES AND OTHER DOUBLE-DEALERS

Printed here is the report of J. V. Stalin to the plenum of the Central Committee of the All-Union (Bolshevik) Communist Party, March 3, 1937. It treats political indifference, capitalist encirclement, contemporary Trotskyism, and the danger of complacency resulting from continued economic success; it also discusses various problems related to these matters and the solutions proposed.

81 (1937): 22–33

CONCLUDING REMARKS OF COMRADE STALIN AT THE PLENUM OF THE CENTRAL COMMITTEE OF THE ALL-UNION (BOLSHEVIK) COMMUNIST PARTY, MARCH 5, 1937

Stalin outlines here the following seven points on party organizational and political practices: (1) ways to direct the attention of workers to party politics; (2) deviationists and spies; (3) selection and placement of workers; (4) control and examination of workers and fulfillment of their tasks; (5) recognition of mistakes and learning from them; (6) ways to teach the people and to learn from them; (7) factors relating to party membership and expulsion.

81(1937): 34–104

Zvezda AND *Pravda* AND TSARIST CENSORSHIP. Introduction unsigned.

The documents printed here are Police Department, censorship committee, and court reports, dated from 1910 to 1914, on the following Russian newspapers: *Pravda, Zvezda* ("Star"), *Nevskaia Zvezda* ("Nevsky Star"), *Rabochaia Pravda* ("Labor Truth"), *Severnaia Pravda* ("Northern Truth"), *Pravda Truda* ("Truth of Labor"), *Za Pravdu* ("For Truth"),

A Digest of the Krasnyi Arkhiv

Proletarskaia Pravda ("Proletarian Truth"), *Put Pravdy* ("The Way of Truth"), *Rabochii* ("Labor"), and *Trudovaia Pravda* ("Labor Truth").

81 (1937): 105-120

IN THE TSARIST ARMY ON THE EVE OF THE FEBRUARY BOURGEOIS-DEMOCRATIC REVOLUTION (Agitation in the Two Hundred Twenty-third Odoevsky Regiment of the Thirty-fourth Army Corps). Introduction by P. Bilyk.

Published here are six reports of commanders of the Thirty-fourth Army Corps on disturbances of January 18-19, 1917, when soldiers refused to obey orders to fight. Also given is the decision of a military court, dated January 23, 1917, sentencing the five ringleaders to death and fourteen other soldiers to hard labor for terms of from six to fifteen years. This decision was reviewed January 26, 1917, and the report on the review is included.

81 (1937): 121-127

THE PEOPLE'S DEMAND FOR NICHOLAS ROMANOV'S IMPRISONMENT IN A FORTRESS. Introduction by K. G.

Dated from March 6 to June 20, 1917, thirteen resolutions of workers' groups and military and peasant organizations demanding that Nicholas II, the Imperial Family, and supporters of the tsarist regime be arrested and imprisoned in the Petropavlovsk fortress or placed under a guard of revolutionary sailors at the Kronstadt garrison, are printed here.

81 (1937): 128-146

THE PROVISIONS SITUATION IN MOSCOW, MARCH-JUNE, 1917. Introduction unsigned.

The thirty-six reports included here are from the commissar of the Moscow district to N. Kishkin, food commissar of the Provisional Government, and are concerned with demonstrations in Moscow caused by the food shortage. They also discuss ways to distribute bread in the city.

81 (1937): 147-152

FROM DOCUMENTS ON THE ORGANIZATION OF THE RED ARMY. Introduction by P. Anisimova.

The materials here are thirteen resolutions and reports, dated from March to October, 1918, of workers', peasants', and soldiers' groups on the subject of enlistments in the Red army. The documents praise the Red army, but call for more thorough organization.

81 (1937): 153–206

THE LENA MILITARY EXECUTION OF 1912. Introduction by M. L. L.

Presented here are reports of mine officials and a court report describing the shooting of workers at the Lena gold mines in 1912, when the miners marched to present their grievances to an official. An eyewitness account by one of the strikers is included in a report of the Special Committee of the Petrograd Soviet in 1917.

For additional material in *Krasnyi Arkhiv*, see "Concerning the Lena Execution," 83 (1937): 35–44.

81 (1937): 207–227

TSARISM IN THE STRUGGLE WITH A. I. HERZEN. Introduction by D. Zaslavsky.

Dated from 1849 to 1870, the documents printed here are reports of the Secret Police, censorship committee, Gendarmerie, post office, and the Ministry of Foreign Affairs on Herzen's activities, whereabouts, friends, and associates. Included also is criticism of articles by Herzen that appeared in *Kolokol* ("The Bell").

For references to additional material in *Krasnyi Arkhiv*, see the notes to "An Unpublished Letter of A. I. Herzen," 31 (1928): 224–226.

FROM AN ARCHIVIST'S NOTEBOOK

81 (1937): 228–231

WORKING WOMEN OF SOUTHERN OSSETIA IN THE STRUGGLE FOR SOVIETS. Introduction unsigned.

A report of the Organization for the Social and Political Development of Women to the meeting of the Southern Ossetian Bolsheviks, October 21, 1921, appears here. Sent to Lenin and to the Department of National Minorities and Eastern Peoples, the report stresses the role of women in the October Revolution and the Civil War, with emphasis on their work in the Caucasus.

VOLUME 82, 1937

82 (1937): 3–5

COMRADE STALIN'S LETTER TO COMPILERS OF THE HISTORY OF THE ALL-UNION (BOLSHEVIK) COMMUNIST PARTY

In this undated letter Stalin presents the essential requirements for the textbook and outlines twelve chapters, which divide the history of the Communist party from 1900 to 1937 into periods.

82 (1937): 6–17

INSTRUCTIONS TO THE DELEGATES OF THE SECOND ALL-RUSSIAN CONGRESS OF SOVIETS. Introduction by K. A. Sofronenko.

The Second All-Russian Congress of Soviets opened during the night of October 25/November 7, 1917. The fifteen documents published here contain instructions from local soviets to their delegates on the attitude to be taken toward peace with Germany, distribution of land, capital punishment, social structure, finances, working conditions, and the October Revolution.

For additional material in *Krasnyi Arkhiv*, see "Second All-Russian Congress of Soviets," 84 (1937): 12–134.

82 (1937): 18–39

THE ALL-RUSSIAN COMMUNIST SUBBOTNIK OF MAY 1, 1920. Introduction by P. Derkach.

Derkach states that the Ninth Party Congress in March, 1920, proposed turning the international proletarian holiday into a collective workday. May 1, 1920, was the first such *subbotnik*. The documents are grouped under the following headings: (1) "Party-government appeals to all workers, April 8–28, 1920"; (2) "Workers' resolutions, April 20–30, 1920"; (3) "Plans for the All-Russian *subbotnik*, April, 1920"; (4) "From a summary of the results of the *subbotnik*, May–July, 1920."

For additional material in *Krasnyi Arkhiv*, see "Assistance to the Red Army from Communist *Subbotniks* during the Civil War," 83 (1937): 14–34.

82 (1937): 40–89

THE PARTISAN MOVEMENT IN THE MARITIME PROVINCE. Introduction by M. I. Gubelman.

Given here are the minutes of five meetings of the first partisan conference in the Maritime province, May 22–26, 1919. In addition, there are orders and dispatches, dated January–April, 1920, of Sergius Lazo, chief of the military-revolutionary staff in the Far East; an appeal from the Nikolsk–Ussuriiski Communist party committee; and appeals from various partisan groups in the Far East calling for support in the struggle against the counterrevolutionaries and foreign interventionists. These documents are dated from March, 1919, to October, 1922.

For references to additional material in *Krasnyi Arkhiv* on the Civil War in the Far East, see the notes to "The Disintegration of Kolchak's Campaign," 31 (1928): 51–80.

82 (1937): 90–118

MATERIALS CONCERNING THE OCCUPATION OF NORTHERN SAKHALIN BY JAPANESE TROOPS, 1920–1925. Introduction by M. Gubelman.

The following groups of documents issued by the Japanese are published here:

1. Orders for maintaining peace and quiet and local organization on Sakhalin, issued in September, 1920, by Lieutenant General S. Kozima, commander of the Japanese expeditionary forces on the island.

2. Two declarations of a military-organizational nature, issued in August and October, 1920.

3. Orders governing mining operations, issued in August and September, 1920.

4. Regulations concerning lumbering, issued in September, 1920.

5. Regulations concerning hunting, bird and animal life, and fishing rights, issued between August, 1920, and March, 1921.

6. Regulations concerning the renting of buildings and the exchanging of chattels, issued between September, 1920, and February, 1921.

7. Banking regulations for the Alexandrovsk division of the Korean Bank.

8. Judicial procedure outlined by the Sakhalin commander of the Japanese expeditionary forces, August 30, 1920.

Other documents deal with the punishment of criminals, the surveillance of foreigners in the area, and the changing from Russian to Japanese of the names of streets in Alexandrovsk. There is also a proclamation concerning the observance of the birthday of the Japanese emperor.

A Digest of the Krasnyi Arkhiv   145

82 (1937): 119–135

MATERIALS RELATING TO THE HISTORY OF THE CIVIL WAR IN YAKUTSK IN 1922. Introduction by I. Martynov.

The following documents are published here:

1. The protocols of a meeting in Yakutsk province of merchants planning to guarantee an American loan, July 23, 1922.

2. The minutes of conferences of the leaders of the Siberian Volunteer Guards on November 2, 3, and 26, 1922, which were attended by Lieutenant General Pepeliaev, Major General Vishnevsky, Colonel Anders, Lieutenant Colonel Maltsev, and civilian officials P. A. Kulikovsky, D. T. Borisov, P. D. Filippov, and P. N. Protopopov.

3. Excerpts from an indictment of Lieutenant General Pepeliaev, January 16, 1924, for having organized the counterrevolutionary Siberian Volunteer Guards.

82 (1937): 136–163

THE RISE OF THE LABOR MOVEMENT BEFORE THE FIRST IMPERIALISTIC WAR. Introduction by M. Lurie.

Monthly reports from September, 1913, to July, 1914, of the Ministry of Trade and Industry on the labor movement and on factory strikes appear here.

For references to additional material in *Krasnyi Arkhiv*, see the notes to "The Struggle with Strikes on the Eve of the World War," 34 (1929): 95–125.

82 (1937): 164–192

MAY 1 IN TSARIST RUSSIA (1892–1903). Introduction by M. Syromiatnikova.

The documents presented here are descriptions of May Day demonstrations in St. Petersburg in 1892; in Moscow in 1897; in Kiev in 1899; in Kiev, Ivanovo Voznesensk, and Ekaterinoslav in 1900; in Tiflis and Kiev in 1901; in Moscow and Sormovo in 1902; in Nizhni Novgorod, Baku, and Tver in 1903; and in Yaroslav, Kostroma, and Vladimir on the eve of May 1, 1902.

For additional material in *Krasnyi Arkhiv*, see: "Localizing the Celebration of May First in Factories and Mills," 16 (1926): 205–209; "Speeches Made in Odessa on the First of May, 1895," 19 (1926): 203–207; "Materials Relating to the History of the Struggle with the Revolution in 1905," 32 (1929): 216–232; "May 1 Postage Stamps of the Latvian Bolsheviks in

1914," 57 (1933): 3–9; "Workers' Movement in the Petersburg Factories in May, 1901," 76 (1936): 49–66; "The Strike in Kharkov on May 1, 1900," 93 (1939): 190–208.

VOLUME 83, 1937

83 (1937): 2

A DECREE OF THE CENTRAL EXECUTIVE COMMITTEE OF THE USSR AT THE FOURTH SESSION OF ITS SEVENTH CONVOCATION

Dated July 9, 1937, this decree announces the Central Executive Committee's ratification of the regulations concerning elections to the Supreme Soviet.

83 (1937): 3–13

REGULATIONS CONCERNING ELECTIONS TO THE SUPREME SOVIET OF THE USSR

The text of the regulations adopted by the Central Executive Committee on July 9, 1937, appears here.

83 (1937): 14–34

ASSISTANCE TO THE RED ARMY FROM COMMUNIST SUBBOTNIKS DURING THE CIVIL WAR. Introduction by P. Derkach.

The documents printed here are dated from December 21, 1919, to December 10, 1920. They are party appeals to the workers for *subbotniks* (collective workdays) and workers' resolutions to assist the Red Army, to promote the progress of the war on the Polish and southern fronts, and to aid the sick, the wounded, and the families of Red army soldiers. There are also reports on the results of the aid given during the workers' leisure time.

For additional material in *Krasnyi Arkhiv*, see "The All-Russian Communist *Subbotnik* of May 1, 1920," 82 (1937): 18–39.

83 (1937): 35–44

CONCERNING THE LENA EXECUTION (The Inquiry of the Social Democratic Faction in the Fourth State Duma). Introduction by M. Lurie.

Many workers were shot during the strike in the Lena gold mines in April, 1912. The documents printed here are the inquiries made by the

A Digest of the Krasnyi Arkhiv 147

Social Democratic members of the Fourth State Duma, March 1, 1913. Bolshevik deputy M. K. Muranov's address to the Duma, March 19, 1914, on the government's explanation of the shooting is also published here.

For additional material in *Krasnyi Arkhiv*, see "Lena Military Execution of 1912," 81 (1937): 153–206.

83 (1937): 45–106

WORKING CONDITIONS DURING CONSTRUCTION OF THE PETERSBURG–MOSCOW RAILROAD (1843–1851). Introduction by M. Krutikov.

The construction of the Petersburg–Moscow railroad was ordered by Nicholas I in February, 1842. The reports of the government officials in charge of the construction which are published here provide information on the labor supply, the workers' contracts, the construction crews, the role of the police, illness among the workers, general working conditions, camp churches, hospitals, wineshops, workers' protests against difficult conditions, and the government's accounts with the workers.

For additional material in *Krasnyi Arkhiv*, see "Beginning of Railroad Construction in Russia," 99 (1940): 127–179.

83 (1937): 107–120

A RUSSIAN VOLUNTEER IN THE RANKS OF THE SPANISH INSURGENTS IN 1830. Introduction by E. Katsman.

The documents given here concern Michael Andreev Kologrivov, son of a former general in the Russian cavalry who was on trial in 1831 for having entered the service of the Spanish insurgents. Included are the order for his trial, trial arrangements made by the Senate, the court's decision, Kologrivov's letters, and the notes of Adjutant General [A. K.] Benckendorff and the governor of St. Petersburg.

83 (1937): 121–159

Moscow IN 1812 (From Memoirs of Adam Glushkovsky). Introduction unsigned.

A section of three notebooks of reminiscences by the famous ballet master Adam Glushkovsky is published here for the first time. This portion of the memoirs is a detailed account of life in Moscow immediately before and during the city's occupation by Napoleon's forces.

For the complete text of Glushkovsky's notebooks, see A. P. Glushkovsky, *Vospominaniia Baletmeistera* ("Memoirs of a Ballet Master"), published in 1940 in Moscow and Leningrad by Gosizdat "Isskusstvo" (State Publishing House—"AIT").

83 (1937): 160–183

M. E. SALTYKOV-SHCHEDRIN AS INSPECTOR GENERAL. Introduction by N. Zhuravlev.

The satirist Saltykov-Shchedrin (1826–1889) was appointed vice governor of Tver on April 3, 1860. Notes made during his inspection tours of the province in 1860 and 1861, with special emphasis on conditions in the cities of Kaliazin, Kashin, and Korchevo, are presented here.

For additional material in *Krasnyi Arkhiv* on Saltykov-Shchedrin, see: "An Unpublished Fairy Tale of M. E. Saltykov-Shchedrin: *Valiant Knight*," 2 (1922): 226–228; "M. E. Saltykov-Shchedrin and the Censorship," 2 (1922): 229–233; "M. E. Saltykov-Shchedrin's Unpublished Magazine, 'Russkaya Pravda,'" 4 (1923): 393–398; "New Materials on M. E. Saltykov-Shchedrin," 105 (1941): 156–167.

83 (1937): 184–218

ATTEMPTS AT MASTERY OF THE NATURAL RESOURCES OF OSSETIA IN THE EIGHTEENTH CENTURY. Introduction by A. M. Birze.

The documents printed here, dated 1766–1769, describe Russian penetration into the Northern Caucasus, the construction of fortresses, the establishment of settlements, and relations with the Ossetian people. With the exception of two notes to the Ossetian elders, a senate order, and a memorandum of the collegium of foreign affairs, the documents are reports of the Russian military and civilian officials in the area. There is a relief map of the Northern Caucasus, drawn in 1768.

Publication of these documents is continued in *Krasnyi Arkhiv*, 85 (1937): 148–167 and 88 (1938): 256–275.

83 (1937): 219–223

DECREE OF THE MEMBERS OF THE GOVERNMENT COMMISSION ON THE COMPETITION FOR THE BEST TEXTBOOK FOR THIRD AND FOURTH CLASSES OF SECONDARY SCHOOLS ON THE HISTORY OF THE USSR

This decree includes the judges' analysis of the textbooks submitted in the competition and the announcement that, although no first prize was awarded, the second prize went to Professor A. V. Shestakov, who edited *Kratkii Kurs Istorii SSSR* ("A Short Course in the History of the USSR"). Awards to the authors of six other textbooks are also announced. No date is given for this material.

A Digest of the Krasnyi Arkhiv 149

FROM AN ARCHIVIST'S NOTEBOOK

83 (1937): 224–225

TSARIST MINISTERS CONCERNING UNIVERSAL SUFFRAGE. Introduction by I. Kovalev.

The material printed here is a copy of a proposal for universal suffrage introduced by thirty-four deputies of the Fourth State Duma on January 30, 1913, and comments on the bill by I. Dmitriukov, secretary of the Duma, and N. A. Maklakov, minister of internal affairs.

For additional material in *Krasnyi Arkhiv*, see: "Autocracy and Suffrage in the Minority Regions of Tsarist Russia," 79 (1936): 19–25; "Autocracy and Woman Suffrage," 79 (1936): 26–33.

83 (1937): 225–227

PERSONAL EXPENSES OF MANUFACTURER M. A. MOROZOV. Introduction by N. Zhuravlev.

The personal expenses for the year 1901 of M. A. Morozov (1871–1903), one of the outstanding Russian industrialists of the nineteenth century, are listed here.

VOLUME 84, 1937

84 (1937): 3

[DECREE SETTING] THE DATE OF ELECTIONS TO THE SUPREME SOVIET OF THE USSR

The Central Executive Committee of the USSR decreed on October 11, 1937, that elections to the Supreme Soviet would be held on December 12, 1937. This decree is reproduced here, preceded by full-page portraits of Lenin and Stalin in 1917.

84 (1937): 3–4

CONCERNING THE ANNOUNCEMENT OF THE COMPOSITION OF THE CENTRAL ELECTION COMMISSION FOR ELECTIONS TO THE SUPREME SOVIET OF THE USSR

An announcement by the Central Executive Committee of the USSR dated October 11, 1937, of the appointment of fifteen members to the Central Election Commission appears here.

84 (1937): 5–11

AN APPEAL OF THE CENTRAL COMMITTEE OF THE ALL-UNION (BOLSHEVIK) COMMUNIST PARTY

This is an appeal to workers, peasants, Red army soldiers, and the Soviet intelligentsia, calling them to the polls to support the Soviet regime. It is dated December 6, 1937.

84 (1937): 12–134

SECOND ALL-RUSSIAN CONGRESS OF SOVIETS (Questionnaire Filled Out by Bolshevik Delegates to the Second Congress of Soviets). Introduction by P. Anisimova.

The introduction includes a photostatic copy of the proclamation of the Military-Revolutionary Committee of the Petrograd Soviet of Workers' and Soldiers' Deputies (formerly, the Petrograd Soviet of Workers' Deputies) dated October 25, 1917, announcing the fall of the Provisional Government. The questionnaire submitted to delegates to secure information on local soviets, conditions in their communities, politics and commerce, the press, transportation and communication, and counterrevolutionary agitation is also reproduced. The documents presented are the answers submitted by 134 of the 343 Bolshevik delegates to the Second All-Russian Congress of Soviets, which opened October 25/November 7, 1917, with 675 delegates present. Appended is a list of regions represented by the survey.

For additional material in *Krasnyi Arkhiv*, see "Instructions to the Delegates of the Second All-Russian Congress of Soviets," 82 (1937): 6–17.

84 (1937): 135–187

PREPARATION BY THE ARMY AND ITS LEADERSHIP OF THE GREAT OCTOBER SOCIALIST REVOLUTION. Introduction by O. Chaadaeva.

The documents given here, dated from March to December, 1917, reflect the concern of the Provisional Government over unrest in the army. Letters from soldiers and officers on all fronts and in numerous military units indicate the extent to which dissatisfaction had spread.

84 (1937): 188–198

ORDERS AND DECREES OF THE PETROGRAD MILITARY-REVOLUTIONARY COMMITTEE ON QUESTIONS OF THE PRESS IN THE DAYS OF THE OCTOBER REVOLUTION. Introduction by G. Kostomarov.

These documents, dated from October 25 to December 18, 1917, show how the Petrograd Military-Revolutionary Committee used the press in its

A Digest of the Krasnyi Arkhiv 151

struggle for power, how it established a "proletarian" press, and how it requisitioned "bourgeois" presses.

For additional material in *Krasnyi Arkhiv,* see "Materials Relating to the History of the October Days in Petrograd," 53 (1932): 38–62.

84 (1937): 199–260

MATERIALS RELATING TO THE PREREVOLUTIONARY PAST OF MOSCOW. Introduction by E. Cherniavsky.

The documents printed here are grouped as follows:

1. "The election of delegates to the City Duma and deputies to the State Duma." This material covers the period from 1907 to 1914.

2. "Culture and public welfare (social needs)." These documents, dated from 1907 to 1915, deal with education, the care of children, the deaf and blind, and sports.

3. "Efficiency and city management." Gas, electricity, streets, and city finances from 1909 to 1916 are discussed in this section.

4. "An unsuccessful attempt to honor Leo Tolstoy." These documents, dated from 1908 to 1914, deal with attempts to celebrate Tolstoy's eightieth birthday in 1908.

5. "Strikes in city enterprises." This material furnishes a discussion of the transportation strikes of 1913 and 1915 and includes a blacklist of strikers; also treated is the strike at the Central Electric Station in 1915.

6. "Letters to the City Duma and *Uprava.*" These are excerpts from five letters written in 1915 by Moscow residents to the City Duma and the court (*Uprava*) about the street-car strikes.

VOLUME 85, 1937

85 (1937): 3–6

COMRADE J. V. STALIN'S SPEECH

This is a reprint of Stalin's speech at a pre-election meeting of voters held at the Bolshoi Theater in the Stalin electoral district in Moscow on December 11, 1937, on the eve of elections to the Supreme Soviet. The speech was published in *Pravda* on December 12, 1937.

85 (1937): 7–28

MATERIALS RELATING TO THE TWENTIETH ANNIVERSARY OF THE THIRD ALL-RUSSIAN CONGRESS OF SOVIETS. Introduction by G. Kostomarov.

The Third All-Russian Congress of Soviets was held in January, 1918. The first group of documents presented here consists of resolutions by the deputies of the Third All-Russian Congress of Soviets on the following matters: (1) the rights of "toiling and exploited peoples"; (2) the work of the Central Executive Committee; (3) the federation of Soviet republics; and (4) the policies of the Soviet of People's Commissars on nationality problems. There is also an appeal to the working classes abroad to revolt and a similar appeal to the Cossacks.

The second group of documents indicates the attitude of the people toward the Constituent Assembly.

The third group contains instructions to delegates from their constituents.

85 (1937): 29–58

DELEGATES OF THE PETROGRAD GARRISON AT THE FRONT. Introduction by O. Chaadaeva.

Published here are instructions of the Propaganda Department of the All-Russian Central Executive Committee to delegates of the Petrograd garrison going to the front in November, 1917, on standard answers to be given to questions on the progress of the Revolution and the Soviet government's plans for the people. There are also reports from delegates on conditions in the army, political organization, and the progress of their work on the northern, western, southwestern, and Rumanian fronts.

85 (1937): 59–92

MATERIALS RELATING TO THE HISTORY OF THE REVOLUTIONARY STRUGGLE OF THE KOLOMNA WORKERS IN 1917. Introduction by K. Gulevich and G. Belkin.

The documents printed here sketch the revolutionary struggle of workers in the Kolomna machine-building factory from March 22, 1917, to February 26, 1918. They include the report of the director of the factory, protocols of workers' meetings, workers' proclamations, reports of the Soviet of Workers', Soldiers', and Peasants' Deputies of Kolomna, and a review of factory agitation by the minister of trade and industry.

85 (1937): 93–101

THE FIRST STEPS IN BUILDING SOVIET POWER IN THE VILLAGE (From Resolutions of Meetings of Peasants and Informative Résumés of the People's Commissariat of Agriculture, December, 1917—February, 1918). Introduction by G. Kostomarov.

The three resolutions of peasants' meetings in Orlov and Mogilev provinces and the two reports by the People's Commissariat of Agriculture that are given here reveal the peasants' attitude toward the Soviet regime in the provinces of Chernigov, Vitebsk, Kaluga, Moscow, Nizhni Novgorod, Tver, Novgorod, Kherson, and Yaroslav.

85 (1937): 102–137

TASEEV PARTISAN DISTRICT IN 1919. Introduction by M. Bondarenko.

Bondarenko states that Taseev is a district in the northern Kansk region of the former Yenisei province. The village of Taseevo became the center of partisan activity against A. V. Kolchak's forces in the Kansk region. The documents presented here are divided into the following groups:

1. "The development of insurrection in Taseev district, January–May, 1919."
2. "Creation of the northern Kansk partisan front against the Whites, April–August, 1919."
3. "At Ust-Kaitym, August, 1919."
4. "Taseev region under the Whites, June–September, 1919."
5. "Partisan advance on Taseevo, September, 1919."
6. "Creation of ruling organs in the Taseev Soviet region, November, 1919."
7. "The defeat of Kolchak and the establishment of Soviet power, October–December, 1919."

There is also a map of the Yenisei region.

85 (1937): 138–147

EIGHTEENTH-CENTURY PROJECT FOR CONNECTING THE MOSCOW RIVER WITH THE VOLGA. Introduction unsigned.

A letter to Lieutenant General W. de Hennin dated October 17, 1746, from Empress Elizabeth's cabinet, and his answer of October 18, 1746, regarding plans for connecting the Moscow and Volga rivers appear here.

De Hennin had been ordered by Peter the Great in 1722 to draw up these plans, and a copy of his letter of July 3, 1722, to Peter the Great containing a detailed outline of his proposals for linking the two rivers is also included. Attached is a map of de Hennin's project, as well as one of the present Volga–Moscow canal.

85 (1937): 148–167

ATTEMPTS AT MASTERY OF THE NATURAL RESOURCES OF OSSETIA IN THE EIGHTEENTH CENTURY (Continuation)

Publication of the documents on Russian penetration into the Caucasus was begun in *Krasnyi Arkhiv*, 83 (1937): 184–218 and is concluded in 88 (1938): 256–275.

The material here, dated 1768–1771, is made up of reports by Russian military and civilian officials in the Ossetian province of the northern Caucasus describing the search for minerals in that area and recording the discovery of traces of silver and lead.

VOLUME 86, 1938

86 (1938): 3–7

COMRADE IVANOV'S LETTER AND COMRADE STALIN'S ANSWER

Given here is a letter from Ivan Filipovich Ivanov, a Communist party propagandist in Manturovo region, to Stalin on January 18, 1938, about the problems involved in strengthening socialism. Stalin's reply of February 12, 1938, also presented, discusses socialism in Russia and in the world and the problem of capitalist encirclement.

86 (1938): 8–21

MATERIALS [TO BE USED IN COMMEMORATING] THE TWENTIETH ANNIVERSARY OF THE WORKERS' AND PEASANTS' RED ARMY AND NAVY (Topics for Propagandists)

These documents, dated 1938, from the Communist party's department of propaganda and agitation elaborate on the following topics: (1) "Creation of the Red army and its victories in the Civil War"; (2) "Why the Red army succeeded in destroying the White Guardists and interventionists"; (3) "The Red army, enriched by new techniques, stands confidently on guard over our country."

86 (1938): 22

THREE TELEGRAMS OF V. I. LENIN

The first telegram is addressed to workers at the Izhev factory, January 27, 1919; the second, to the Revolutionary Military Soviet of the eastern front on the occasion of the capture of Perm and Kungur, June 1, 1919; the third, to M. V. Frunze, June 16, 1919. Included also are photographs of Lenin and Stalin.

86 (1938): 23–25

J. STALIN CONCERNING THREE CHARACTERISTICS OF THE RED ARMY

A reprint of Stalin's speech at the plenum of the Moscow Soviet on the tenth anniversary of the founding of the Red army appears here. Stalin

A Digest of the Krasnyi Arkhiv 155

discusses the Red army as the army of freed workers and peasants, the army of the October Revolution, and the army of the dictatorship of the proletariat; as the army of the brotherhood of Soviet nationalities; and as the army of international brotherhood. The speech first appeared in *Pravda*, February 28, 1928.

86 (1938): 26–28

COMRADE VOROSHILOV'S ADDRESS AT THE JUBILEE SESSION OF THE PLENUM OF THE MOSCOW SOVIET, DEDICATED TO THE TENTH ANNIVERSARY OF THE RED ARMY, FEBRUARY 25, 1928

Voroshilov, chairman of the Revolutionary Military Soviet, speaks in this address of the expansion of the army and contrasts the Red army with armies in capitalist countries. A portrait of him is included.

For additional material in *Krasnyi Arkhiv* on Voroshilov, see "To Comrade Kliment Efremovich Voroshilov," 104 (1941): 1–2.

86 (1938): 29–55

MATERIALS RELATING TO THE TWENTIETH ANNIVERSARY OF THE WORKERS' AND PEASANTS' RED ARMY (From Documents on the History of the Organization of the Red Army). Introduction by Kostomarov.

The first document presented here is a directive of the Soviet of People's Commissars, January 15, 1918, announcing the basis for organization of the Red army. There are sixteen other directives, resolutions, and appeals concerning enlistments, conscription, and instruction in military science.

86 (1938): 56–92

THE WORKING CLASS AND TRADE UNIONS IN THE CREATION OF THE RED ARMY. Introduction by K. Gulevich and E. Mikhailova.

Given here are forty-eight documents, dated from February, 1918, to January, 1920. They include workers' resolutions to organize partisan detachments to be sent to the front; documents concerning the struggles against interventionists; and material depicting the struggle of the Petrograd workers against General Nicholas Yudenich. A photograph of the send-off given the first workers leaving for the front also appears.

For additional material in *Krasnyi Arkhiv*, see "Petrograd Workers in the Struggle with Yudenich," 94 (1939): 3–31.

86 (1938): 93–168

AGITATIONAL TRIPS OF M. I. KALININ IN THE CIVIL WAR YEARS. Introduction by B. Sergeev.

The documents printed here describe seven of M. I. Kalinin's trips to the front in an attempt to strengthen the ties between the central government and the people and to effect a complete mobilization of the country. The trips were as follows: (1) April 29—May 18, 1919, to the area under the command of Admiral A. V. Kolchak; (2) June 6–28, 1919, to the western front; (3) July 12—August 5, 1919, to the southern front, under General A. I. Denikin; (4) August 31—September 27, 1919, to the Turkestan front and the area under Admiral Kolchak; (5) October 24—November 19, 1919, to the southern front; (6) December, 1919, to the front under General Nicholas Yudenich and to Petrograd and Kronstadt; and (7) October 8–30, 1920, to the southern front, then under the command of Baron P. N. Wrangel. The documents in each group are prefaced by introductory remarks on the progress of the Civil War to that point, the purpose of the trip, and the number of stops and speeches made.

In addition, there is a portrait of Kalinin and pictures of a Red army meeting at his train in Alatyr in May, 1919, of Kalinin chatting with peasants in 1919, of Kalinin reviewing a parade of the International Battalion in Gomel in June, 1919, of Kalinin meeting Cossacks of the Red army in Balatov in July, 1919, and of Kalinin appearing at a Red army meeting in Khvalynsk in July, 1919.

86 (1938): 169–183

MATERIALS RELATING TO THE REVOLUTIONARY ACTIVITIES OF G. K. ORDZHONIKIDZE. Introduction unsigned.

Published here are twenty-two documents dealing with Ordzhonikidze's underground revolutionary work. They are dated from December 30, 1905, to January 8, 1913, and include court and Police Department records and Ordzhonikidze's private letters.

For references to additional material in *Krasnyi Arkhiv*, see the notes to "To Comrade Gregory Konstantinovich Ordzhonikidze," 78 (1936): 2–3.

86 (1938): 184–192

THE *Communist Manifesto* AND RUSSIAN CENSORSHIP. Introduction by E. Cherniavsky.

Given here are censors' reports of 1872, 1907, 1909, 1911, and 1912, ordering suppression of publications of the *Communist Manifesto*.

VOLUME 87, 1938

87 (1938): 3–18

MATERIALS RELATING TO THE HISTORY OF THE CELEBRATION OF INTERNATIONAL WOMEN'S DAY IN RUSSIA. Introduction by N. Krupskaia.

N. Krupskaia (Lenin's wife) states that International Women's Day, proposed by Clara Zetkin at the Copenhagen congress in 1910, was first celebrated in Russia on February 10, 1913. Dated from January 16, 1913, to February 23, 1917, the documents presented here report on government surveillance over Social Democratic activities, particularly over the celebration of International Women's Day. Also included are two intercepted letters that had been written by Krupskaia, as well as letters from abroad to *Pravda*, *Za Pravdu* ("For Truth"), and *Put Pravdy* ("The Way of Truth").

87 (1938): 19–63

GERMANY'S SEIZURE OF KIAOCHOW IN 1897. Introduction by F. P.

According to the introduction, the forty-five documents published here, dated from August 19/31, 1895, to February 25/March 9, 1898, differ somewhat from similar ones published in *Die Grosse Politik*. The documents are exchanges of diplomatic communiqués between German officials, between Russian officials, and between German and Russian officials; footnotes compare these documents with those in *Die Grosse Politik*.

For additional material in *Krasnyi Arkhiv* on the Pan-Germanic Union, see "Materials Relating to the History of the Pan-Germanic Union," 92 (1939): 215–223.

87 (1938): 64–88

ITALY'S AGGRESSIVE PLANS IN CONNECTION WITH NEGOTIATIONS CONCERNING THE RENEWAL OF THE TRIPLE ALLIANCE. Introduction by E. A.

The Italian and Russian documents presented here are dated from March, 1888, to May, 1902. The Italian documents include instructions from the chief of the Italian General Staff to Colonel Guaran, chief of the military transport division of the Italian General Staff, for carrying on secret negotiations in Vienna and Berlin in March and April, 1888; there are also six reports from Guaran on his mission. The Russian documents include dispatches from A. I. Nelidov in Rome and instructions to him from Minister of Foreign Affairs Count V. N. Lamsdorff.

87 (1938): 89–128

AGITATION OF THE CHUVASH PEASANTRY IN 1842. Introduction unsigned.

Given here is a report from Colonel Maslov of the Simbirsk Gendarmerie to Count A. K. Benckendorff, August 11, 1831, on conditions among the Chuvash peasants in Kazan province. Twenty-two police and Gendarmerie reports, dated from March 21, 1842, to January, 1843, also appear, as well as a map of Kazan province.

87 (1938): 129–173

MATERIALS RELATING TO THE HISTORY OF KAZAKHSTAN IN THE EIGHTEENTH CENTURY. Introduction by A. B.

A document entitled "Concerning the Kirghiz-Kazakh People" is reprinted here from the *Book of the Asiatic Department*, Number 21. Written in 1756, this document traces the history of Kazakhstan from 1730 to 1756.

For additional material in *Krasnyi Arkhiv*, see "Materials Relating to the History of Relations of the Kazakhs with Tsarist Russia in the Eighteenth Century," 78 (1936): 187–225.

FROM AN ARCHIVIST'S NOTEBOOK

87 (1938): 174–182

MATERIALS RELATING TO THE FIFTIETH ANNIVERSARY OF V. M. GARSHIN'S DEATH (From Materials of the Censorship Committee). Introduction by I. Novich.

Fifteen reports of the censors, dated from April 30, 1886, to October 23, 1909, are presented here. They deal with the following works by Vsevolod Mikhailovich Garshin (1855–1888): *Skazanie o Gordom Aggee* ("Legend of Proud Aggéy"), *Chetyre Dnia na Pole Srazheniia* ("Four Days on the Battlefield"), *Gordaia Palma* ("The Proud Palm"), *To, Chevo Ne Bylo* ("That Which Was Not"), *Liapushka Puteshestvennitsa* ("The Frog Traveler"), *Aiaslarskoe Delo* ("The Aiaslarsky Affair"), *Trus* ("Coward"), *Iz Zapisok Riadovogo Ivanova* ("From the Notes of Private Ivanov"), *Medvedi* ("Bears"), *Plennitsa* ("Prisoner"), *Attalea Princeps*, and *Krasnyi Tsvetok* ("The Red Flower").

For additional material in *Krasnyi Arkhiv* on Garshin, see "An Unpublished Letter of V. M. Garshin," 64 (1934): 143–144.

87 (1938): 182–187

THE STRUGGLE OF TSARIST CENSORSHIP WITH A. S. SERAFIMOVICH'S WORKS. Introduction by N. Belchikov.

The eight reports of the censors presented here, dated from 1903 to 1915, deal with the following works by Serafimovich: *Strelochnik* ("Signalman"), *Boi Petukhov* ("Battle of the Cocks"), *Stsepshchik* ("The Coupler"), *U Obryva* ("Near the Precipice"), *Pokhoronnyi Marsh* ("Funeral March"), and *Sredi Nochi* ("In the Dead of Night").

87 (1938): 187–190

BYRON IN GREECE (On the One-Hundred-and-Fiftieth Anniversary of His Birth). Introduction by A. Yurev.

Printed here are excerpts from dispatches of M. Minciaky, Russian chargé d'affaires in Constantinople, to Count K. V. Nesselrode, minister of foreign affairs, February 14/26 to June 19/July 1, 1824, concerning Byron's activities in the Greek revolt against Turkish rule.

VOLUME 88, 1938

88 (1938): 3–4

COMRADE STALIN'S SPEECH AT THE KREMLIN RECEPTION FOR WORKERS IN HIGHER SCHOOLS, MAY 17, 1938

This is a copy of Stalin's speech to educators on the subject of scientific progress.

88 (1938): 5–15

CONCERNING SCHOOLS OF HIGHER EDUCATION (Comrade V. M. Molotov's Speech at the First All-Union Conference of Workers in Higher Schools, May 15, 1938)

Presented here is a speech by Molotov on the development of higher education in the USSR, the decisive task of schools of higher education, and the significance of ideological-political education.

88 (1938): 16–75

THE TSARIST GOVERNMENT AND G. Y. SEDOV'S POLAR EXPEDITION. Introduction by S. Nagornyi.

The documents of the Ministry of Naval Affairs concerning Sedov's expedition, the first Russian expedition to the North Pole, 1912–1914, are presented here. They are divided according to the following topics:

1. Organization of the expedition. These documents outline Sedov's plans, include supplementary material from the Ministry of Naval Affairs, and establish the financing of the expedition.

2. Organization of the rescue expedition. These documents deal with the raising of additional funds, plans for sending supplies to Sedov, and reports from the expedition sent to his aid.

3. Dissolution of G. Y. Sedov's expedition. These documents record Sedov's death on Franz Joseph Land, the request by his sailors for additional aid from Nicholas II, and the return to Archangel of the remnants of the expedition. There is a map indicating the route of the expedition and a request from Sedov's father for personal financial assistance.

88 (1938): 76–122

MATERIALS RELATING TO THE HISTORY OF THE GENERAL STRIKE IN SOUTH RUSSIA IN 1903. Introduction by O. Chadaeva.

These materials contain a Police Department report to the Ministry of Internal Affairs on the labor unrest in July and August in Baku, Tiflis, Batum, Odessa, Kiev, Nikolaev, Elizavetgrad, Ekaterinoslav, and Kerch, and on the Zakavkaz railroad. Social Democratic party proclamations from committees in the Don, Odessa, Kharkov, St. Petersburg, Moscow, Tver, Tula, Nizhni Novgorod, Perm, Samara, and Borisoglebsk from July to September, 1903, also appear.

In addition, excerpts are included from four of the Police Department's weekly reports to Nicholas II, dated from July to September, 1903, and an excerpt from a telegram to the Police Department reporting on the construction of railroads in the Tsaritsyn area. A report of the prosecutor of the Nizhni Novgorod district court to the minister of justice, August 24, 1903, is also given.

88 (1938): 123–181

ANDIZHAN UPRISING OF 1898. Introduction by E. Steinberg.

On the night of May 17–18, 1898, about 1,500 natives marched on soldiers' quarters in the town of Andizhan in the Ferghana region of Turkestan. The suppression of this demonstration and the adoption of measures for preventing further agitation are discussed in the reports, printed here, of Turkestan officials to Minister of War A. N. Kuropatkin, May to September, 1898.

For references to additional material in *Krasnyi Arkhiv* on conditions in Central Asia, see the notes to "The Uprising in Central Asia in 1916," 34 (1929): 39–94 and the notes to "Materials Relating to the History of the Tsarist Minority Policy," 35 (1929): 107–127.

For additional material in *Krasnyi Arkhiv* on affairs in Ferghana, see "A Governor in the Role of Propagator of the Koran," 75 (1936): 188–191.

88 (1938): 182–255

MATERIALS RELATING TO THE HISTORY OF THE FRANCO-RUSSIAN AGREEMENT OF 1859. Introduction by F. Rothstein.

These documents include drafts of Russian and French proposals for a secret treaty and correspondence between Russian Minister of Foreign Affairs Prince A. M. Gorchakov and Prince Napoleon (Napoleon III's cousin, the son of Jerome Bonaparte), as well as between Alexander II and Napoleon III. Gorchakov's reports to Alexander II and instructions to Russian representatives in Paris and Berlin are also given.

For additional material in *Krasnyi Arkhiv* on the Congress of Paris, see "Materials Relating to the History of the Peace of Paris 1856," 75 (1936): 10–61.

88 (1938): 256–275

ATTEMPTS AT MASTERY OF THE NATURAL RESOURCES OF OSSETIA IN THE EIGHTEENTH CENTURY (Conclusion)

Publication of the documents on Russian penetration into the Caucasus was begun in *Krasnyi Arkhiv*, 83 (1937): 184–218 and continued in 85 (1937): 148–167.

Attempts to exploit the natural wealth of Ossetia are revealed in the report published here, which was sent by mine surveyor S. Voniavin to the military commander in Kizliar, Colonel Parker, on December 19, 1771. Also presented are reports from Astrakhan Governor Peter Krechetnikov to Catherine II, dated December 2, 1774, and April 24, 1775. In addition, there is a petition of the Ossetian elders to Krechetnikov to improve their living conditions and a report of November 10, 1774, from Captain A. Batyrev to the military commander in Kizliar, Colonel Shtender, on the frame of mind of the Ossetians.

VOLUMES 89–90, 1938

89–90 (1938): i–xiii

POWERFUL WEAPON OF BOLSHEVISM

These pages contain a review, written in 1938, of the textbook *Istorii Vsesoiuznoi Kommunisticheskoi Partii (Bolshevikov)* ("History of the All-Union Communist Party [Bolshevik]").

89–90 (1938): 3–29

IN MEMORY OF TWENTY-SIX BAKU COMMISSARS

Articles written by J. V. Stalin in memory of twenty-six leading Bolsheviks and their families who left Baku by boat in September, 1918, and were arrested and executed by the British are reprinted here. The articles were originally published in the issues of *Pravda* for September 20, 1933 and 1938.

89–90 (1938): 30–102

MATERIALS RELATING TO THE HISTORY OF THE CARRYING INTO EFFECT OF LENIN'S DECREE CONCERNING LAND. Introduction by A. Bolgov.

A photostat of the decree adopted by the Second All-Russian Congress of Soviets on October 26, 1917, is reproduced here. Also given are Lenin's instructions to local officials on the agrarian question; an explanation of changes resulting from the October Revolution and the land reform; a *Sovnarkom* appropriation of 10 million rubles for organizing agricultural communes; and excerpts taken from the "Information Bulletin" ("Informatsionnyi Listok") of the People's Commissariat of Agriculture, a publication devoted to materials on land reform.

For references to additional material in *Krasnyi Arkhiv*, see "Materials Relating to the History of the Struggle of Supply Detachments of Workers for Bread and the Strengthening of Soviet Power (1918–1920)," 89–90 (1938): 103–154; "Socialistic Forms of Agriculture 1918–1919," 96 (1939): 3–54; "Struggle for Bread in 1918–1919," 97 (1939): 8–43; "Materials Relating to the History of the Rise of Agricultural Communes and Artels in the USSR (1918)," 101 (1940): 122–148.

89–90 (1938): 103–154

MATERIALS RELATING TO THE HISTORY OF THE STRUGGLE OF SUPPLY DETACHMENTS OF WORKERS FOR BREAD AND THE STRENGTHENING OF SOVIET POWER (1918–1920). Introduction by K. Gulevich and R. Gassanova.

The food shortage became acute in Russia in the spring of 1918. These documents, indicating the methods by which the situation was met, are grouped under the following headings: (1) "Organization of supply detachments of workers"; (2) "Concerning activities of supply detachments in the Central Regions (1918–1921)"; (3) "From activities of supply detachments in the Ukraine (1919–1920)"; and (4) "From activities of supply detachments in the Urals and in Western Siberia (1920–1921)."

For references to additional material in *Krasnyi Arkhiv*, see notes to "Materials Relating to the History of the Carrying into Effect of Lenin's Decree concerning Land," 89–90 (1938): 30–102.

89–90 (1938): 155–207

AUSTRIAN REVOLUTION OF 1848 AND NICHOLAS I. Introduction by P. Averbukh.

Presented here are the following dispatches concerned with the Austrian Revolution: from Austrian Chancellor Count Metternich to Russian Minister of Foreign Affairs Count K. V. Nesselrode and to Nicholas I; from [F. P.?] Fonton, Russian chargé d'affaires in Vienna, to Nesselrode; from Nesselrode to Baron [P. K.] Meiendorf, Russian minister in Berlin, and to Russian Ambassador [P. I.] Medem in Vienna; from Nesselrode to E. Lebtseltern, secretary of the Austrian embassy in St. Petersburg, to Fonton, to Austrian Foreign Minister Ludwig Fikelmon, to General [A. O.] Diugamel in the Danubian principalities, to N. D. Kiselev in Paris, to Nicholas I, to Titov in Constantinople, and to Ambassador P. I. Brunnow in London; from Nicholas I to Prussian King Frederick William IV, to Metternich, and to Austrian Emperor Ferdinand IV; from Medem to Nesselrode; from Emperor Ferdinand IV to Nicholas I; from Fikelmon to Leo Tun, Austrian envoy in St. Petersburg; from Polish Viceroy I. F. Paskevich to Nesselrode.

For additional material in *Krasnyi Arkhiv* pertaining to foreign relations at this time, see "Nicholas I and European Reaction 1848–1849," 47–48 (1931): 3–49.

89–90 (1938): 208–257

PEASANT MOVEMENT AT THE END OF THE NINETEENTH CENTURY (1881–1894). Introduction by P. Sofinov.

Published here in full for the first time are the records on peasant disorders from 1881 to 1888 compiled on instructions from Count D. Tolstoy, minister of the interior. In addition to the surveys, there is a table showing the number of agrarian and industrial disorders in each province from 1881 to 1890.

89–90 (1938): 258–308

STUDENT AGITATION 1901–1902. Introduction by A. Syromiatnikov.

The revolutionary proclamations, letters, and police reports presented here are divided into the following groups: (1) demonstrations in Kharkov (November 29—December 2, 1901); (2) demonstrations in Kiev (February 2–3, 1902); (3) meeting of Moscow students (February 9, 1902); (4) demonstrations in St. Petersburg (February 8 and March 3, 1902); (5) route of students exiled to Siberia and description of conditions under which they lived.

For additional material in *Krasnyi Arkhiv*, see "Student Movement in 1901," 75 (1936): 83–112.

89–90 (1938): 309–335

MATERIALS RELATING TO THE HISTORY OF THE DEVELOPMENT OF STEAM NAVIGATION ON THE VOLGA (P. P. Melnikov's Note "Voyage on the Volga"). Introduction by M. Krutikov.

This note is a report by engineer Paul Petrovich Melnikov on his trip down the Volga in 1841 to survey the possibilities for exploiting steam navigation for commercial purposes. Melnikov had studied water and railroad transportation in the United States in 1840.

For additional material in *Krasnyi Arkhiv*, see "Beginning of Railroad Construction in Russia," 99 (1940): 127–179.

VOLUME 91, 1938

91 (1938): 3–15

CONCERNING THE FORMULATION OF PARTY PROPAGANDA IN CONNECTION WITH THE PUBLICATION OF *A Short Course in the History of the All-Union (Bolshevik) Communist Party*

Published here is a decision, issued November 14, 1938, of the Central Committee of the All-Union Communist party to use this *Short Course* as an ideological weapon in propaganda activities.

91 (1938): 16–88

SUCHAN VALLEY IN THE YEARS OF THE CIVIL WAR. Introduction by M. Gubelman.

The Suchan Valley coal basin, "the Donets Basin of the Far East," is located in the southern part of the Maritime province. The documents given here concerning the October Revolution and the Civil War in that area are grouped under the following headings:

1. "The first period of Soviet power in Suchan (1917–1918)."
2. "Suchan under the Whites and interventionists (1919)."
3. "The struggle of workers and peasants of Suchan Valley with the Whites and interventionists (1919)."
4. "Suchan under the rule of the Maritime provincial zemstvo board (January–December, 1920)."
5. "Elections to the Constituent Assembly of the Far Eastern republic (1921–1922)."
6. "Struggle of the Suchan people against the White attempts to sell the mines (March, April, 1922)."
7. "Liquidation of the White Guards and interventionists (fall of 1922)."

A map of the Vladivostok district is included.

For references to additional material in *Krasnyi Arkhiv* on the Civil War in Siberia, see "The Disintegration of Kolchak's Campaign," 31 (1928): 51–80.

91 (1938): 89–105

GERMAN OCCUPATION OF POLESIE (BYELORUSSIA). Introduction by K. Sofronenko.

The first half of the documents presented here deals with the treatment of the local population and the requisition of foodstuffs during the German occupation of Byelorussia and the Ukraine during World War I. The later documents deal with the formation of peasant partisan detachments in the Ukraine.

Some of these documents, which are dated from March to December, 1918, were published in *Pravda*, December 14, 1938.

For additional material in *Krasnyi Arkhiv*, see: "German Intervention and the Don Government in 1918," 67 (1934): 93–130; "Intervention in the Caucasus and among the Mountain Tribes," 68 (1935): 125–153; "Materials Relating to the History of the Civil War in the Ukraine in 1918," 95 (1939): 73–102.

91 (1938): 106–149

FRANCO-GERMAN CRISIS OF 1875. Introduction by A. Erusalimsky.

The diplomatic correspondence presented here deals with the following subjects: Chancellor Otto von Bismarck's conference with Count Paul Petrovich Oubri, Russian ambassador in Berlin, on Germany's preparations for war; the Radowitz mission to St. Petersburg; Russo-German discussions on the East European and Far Eastern situations; Alexander II's decision to confer with the Kaiser in Berlin and the French reaction to this visit; and the role of Russia in Franco-German relations. The documents are dated from March to June, 1875.

91 (1938): 150–198

MATERIALS RELATING TO THE HISTORY OF THE LABOR MOVEMENT IN THE 1880's AND 1890's. Introduction by B. Zlatoustovsky.

These materials consist of fifty-three Police Department reports dated from 1881 to 1894 which Zlatoustovsky says present the highlights in the growth of organized strikes. The reports provide information on the workers' demands for higher wages, shorter hours, and better working conditions; they also discuss the strikes in St. Petersburg, Nizhni Novgorod, and Yaroslav provinces, at the M. A. Morozov factory in Vladimir province in January, 1885, in the provinces of Moscow, Kaluga, Kharkov, Tver, Ekaterinoslav, Tula, Riazan, and Tomsk, in the Don Cossack area, and in the Caucasus.

The distinguishing characteristic of the labor movement in this period, according to Zlatoustovsky, was that it operated independently of the Russian Social Democratic party.

For additional material in *Krasnyi Arkhiv*, see: "The History of the 'Narodnoe Pravo,'" 1 (1922): 282–288; "Materials Relating to the History of the Labor Movement at the End of the 1890's and 'The Union for the Emancipation of the Working Class,'" 93 (1939): 119–189.

91 (1938): 199–224

AGITATION AT THE GLUSHKOVSKY CLOTHING FACTORY (1797–1798). Introduction by [Professor?] K. Sivkov.

Sivkov states that the documents printed here present the first picture of the unrest existing at the end of the eighteenth century in one of Russia's largest and oldest clothing factories (the Glushkovsky factory, established in 1719, in Kursk province). Eighteen documents, dated from September, 1797, to April, 1798, and consisting of workers' petitions for the improvement of working conditions and reports to Paul I by officials of the province, are given.

91 (1938): 225–254

MATERIALS RELATING TO THE HISTORY OF THE KARA-KALPAKS OF THE EIGHTEENTH CENTURY. Introduction by A. Birze.

Birze states that little is known or has been written about the Kara-Kalpak people. In the early years of the eighteenth century the Upper Kara-Kalpaks settled on the banks of the Chirchik river, while the Lower Kara-Kalpaks settled on the eastern shores of the Aral Sea, on the banks of the Syr Darya river. These documents, dated 1720 to 1725, are translations of Turkish and Tartar letters to Tsar Peter Alekseivich and reports of the governor of Astrakahn, I. Kikin, on the life and history of the Kara-Kalpaks.

Publication of these documents is concluded in *Krasnyi Arkhiv*, 92 (1939): 177–214. See also "Materials Relating to the History of Russia's Relations with the Turkmen in the Eighteenth Century," 93 (1939): 209–255.

91 (1938): 255–270

THE STRUGGLE OF THE TSARIST GOVERNMENT AND CENSORSHIP WITH T. G. SHEVCHENKO's "KOBZAR" (On the One-Hundred-and-Twenty-Fifth Anniversary of His Birth). Introduction by I. Kovalov.

Printed here are censors' reports and decisions of the Senate and the Ministry of Internal Affairs in 1911 and 1912 dealing with confiscations of Taras Grigorevich Shevchenko's poem "Kobzar."

For additional material in *Krasnyi Arkhiv*, see "The Suppression by Tsarism of the Honoring of T. Shevchenko's Memory," 76 (1936): 226–230; "At a Great Grave," 105 (1941): 99–114.

168   A Digest of the Krasnyi Arkhiv

FROM AN ARCHIVIST'S NOTEBOOK

91 (1938): 271–275

NEW DATA CONCERNING LADO KETSKHOVELI'S MURDER. Introduction by S. Boltinov.

Ketskhoveli, an early colleague of Stalin in the Caucasus, was arrested September 2, 1902, in Baku, where he had established an illegal press. The official reports printed here describe the shooting of Ketskhoveli in the Tiflis jail after he had failed to heed the guard's warnings to stop causing disturbances.

For references to additional material in *Krasnyi Arkhiv* on unrest in the Caucasus, see the notes to "The Struggle with the Revolutionary Movement in the Caucasus in the Stolypin Era," 35 (1929): 128–150.

91 (1938): 275–281

NEW MATERIALS CONCERNING N. G. CHERNYSHEVSKY'S DISSERTATION. Introduction by N. Belchikov.

These documents include a copy of the questions asked Chernyshevsky during his written and oral examinations in 1853 and 1854 and criticisms made of his dissertation, "The Esthetic Relations of Art to Reality," submitted while he was a candidate for an advanced degree at the University of St. Petersburg.

For references to additional material in *Krasnyi Arkhiv*, see the notes to "Materials Relating to the History of the Release of N. G. Chernyshevsky," 31 (1928): 214–219.

91 (1938): 282–283

SUBJECT INDEX OF *Krasnyi Arkhiv* FOR 1938

This is an index of *Krasnyi Arkhiv*, Volumes 86–91.

VOLUME 92, 1939

92 (1939): 5–38

COMRADE STALIN'S REPORT AT THE EIGHTEENTH PARTY CONGRESS CONCERNING THE WORK OF THE CENTRAL COMMITTEE OF THE ALL-UNION (BOLSHEVIK) COMMUNIST PARTY

Stalin's report, published here, treats of the international position of the Soviet Union, internal affairs, and means of strengthening the Communist

A Digest of the Krasnyi Arkhiv 169

party. There is also a resolution of March 14, 1939, by the congress, acclaiming the report and the work of the Central Committee.

92 (1939): 39–69

V. I. LENIN IN THE YEARS OF THE IMPERIALISTIC WAR. Introduction by Em. Yaroslavsky.

Given here are thirty documents, dated from August 5, 1914, to January 7, 1917, which include dispatches from Russian secret agents in Paris and London on the activities of Russian socialists abroad. The attitude of Lenin and the socialists toward World War I is exhibited in these documents. They also contain information on the socialist conference in London, in 1915. A picture of Lenin is included.

92 (1939): 70–90

COMMEMORATION OF THE TWENTIETH ANNIVERSARY OF J. M. SVERDLOV'S DEATH. Introduction unsigned.

Jacob Mikhailovich Sverdlov, first chairman of the Central Committee of the All-Union Communist party, died on March 16, 1919. Dated from 1903 to March, 1919, the documents that appear here include materials on his revolutionary activities, reproductions of several of his letters, and telegrams from various Soviet republics at the time of his death. There is also a picture of Sverdlov.

For references to additional material in *Krasnyi Arkhiv*, see the notes to "A Few Dates in the Life and Work of J. M. Sverdlov," 63 (1934): 98–105.

92 (1939): 91–132

KANDEEVKA UPRISING IN 1861. Introduction unsigned.

Forty-two documents, dated from March to August, 1861, are presented here. The introduction notes that the sharpest expressions of peasant unrest in 1861 were the uprisings in Bezdna village, Kazan province, and in Penza and Tambov provinces, centering in the village of Kandeevka. These documents trace the Kandeevka uprising and its suppression by tsarist officials.

For additional material in *Krasnyi Arkhiv*, see: "Materials Relating to the History of the Peasant Uprising against Liberation in 1861," 36 (1929): 201–204; "Seventy-five Years Ago," 74 (1936): 5–36.

92 (1939): 133–150

MATERIALS RELATING TO THE HISTORY OF FACTORY LEGISLATION IN 1861. Introduction by N. Zhuravlev.

The document presented here is a critical review of industrial legislation that was sent to the Ministry of Internal Affairs in August, 1861, in the name of Count [Paul T.] Baranov, governor of Tver province. It states the position of the factory owners in the province in regard to proposed legislation. M. E. Saltykov-Shchedrin was vice governor of the province at the time.

92 (1939): 151–176

MATERIALS RELATING TO THE HISTORY OF THE NENETS PEOPLE IN THE 1830's AND 1840's (The Movement of Vauli Piettomin). Introduction by K. Rozanchugov.

The first document published here is a short summary of the work of the commission established in Berezov region to study disturbances among the natives (the Nenets) in Obdorsk region. The second is a brief account, compiled in the Tobolsk provincial court, of the Obdorsk disorders promoted by the fugitive native Vauli Piettomin and his followers. Piettomin led a popular movement in northwest Siberia against merchants, traders, the local gentry, Russian officials, and native elders.

92 (1939): 177–214

MATERIALS RELATING TO THE HISTORY OF THE KARA-KALPAKS OF THE EIGHTEENTH CENTURY (Conclusion)

Publication of the documents on the Kara-Kalpaks was begun in *Krasnyi Arkhiv*, 91 (1938): 225–254.

The documents printed here are dated 1743 and include reports from Ivan Nepliuev, government adviser in Central Asia, to the Collegium of Foreign Affairs and translations of letters from the Kara-Kalpak people on living conditions in the area.

For additional material in *Krasnyi Arkhiv*, see "Materials Relating to the History of Russia's Relations with the Turkmen in the Eighteenth Century," 93 (1939): 209–255.

92 (1939): 215–223

MATERIALS RELATING TO THE HISTORY OF THE PAN-GERMANIC UNION. Introduction by A. E.

These materials contain a short dispatch, dated December 22, 1900/ January 4, 1901, from Count N. D. Osten-Sacken, Russian ambassador in Berlin, to Count Vladimir Nikolaevich Lamsdorff, minister of foreign affairs, with an enclosure on the historical development and goals of the Pan-Germanic Union. This report outlines the aims of the nationalist *Allgemeine deutscher Verband*, organized by Dr. Peters in 1886.

FROM AN ARCHIVIST'S NOTEBOOK

92 (1939): 224–231

MATERIALS RELATING TO P. A. MOISEENKO'S EXILE IN ARCHANGEL. Introduction by A. Uglovi.

Peter Anisimovich Moiseenko was one of the leaders of a strike at the Morozov factory in January, 1885. A member of the organization Northern Union of Russian Workers, Moiseenko was exiled to Archangel province for three years after the strike. The nineteen documents published here, dated from 1886 to 1889, are records of his interrogation, police instructions to the Archangel governor, and reports on Moiseenko's activities during his exile.

VOLUME 93, 1939

93 (1939): 3–50

[THE ROLE OF] M. V. FRUNZE IN THE ORGANIZATION OF THE VICTORY OVER [A. V.] KOLCHAK. Introduction by Colonel E. Boltin.

The documents presented here are grouped under the following headings:

1. "M. V. Frunze's arrival on the eastern front and the formation of the southern group (January 31—March 5, 1919)."

2. "The general advance of A. V. Kolchak's army (March 13—April 5, 1919)."

3. "Preparations for a counterattack against Kolchak (April 10–16, 1919)."

4. "Preparation for and execution of the Buguruslan operation (April 19—May 12, 1919)."

5. "The Belebeevsk operation (May 12–19, 1919)."

6. "Preparation for and execution of the Ufa operation (May 19—July 11, 1919)."

7. "Pursuing the enemy after Ufa (July 19—August 11, 1919)."

8. "Defeat of Kolchak's southern army on the way to Turkestan (August 13—October 7, 1919)."

For references to additional material in *Krasnyi Arkhiv* on Frunze and on Kolchak, see the notes to "The Disintegration of Kolchak's Campaign," 31 (1928): 51–80, and "Ten Years since the Day of M. V. Frunze's Death," 72 (1935): 44–50.

93 (1939): 51–118

RUSSIA AND PRUSSIA IN THE SCHLESWIG-HOLSTEIN QUESTION. Introduction by S. Lesnik.

Published here are dispatches from Russian and Danish officials dated from January, 1864, to September, 1865, which illustrate Russia's role in the Schleswig-Holstein conflict.

93 (1939): 119–189

MATERIALS RELATING TO THE HISTORY OF THE LABOR MOVEMENT AT THE END OF THE 1890's AND "THE UNION FOR THE EMANCIPATION OF THE WORKING CLASS." Introduction by O. Chaadaeva.

Chaadaeva writes that the importance of these documents lies in the fact that they establish the link between the Social Democrats and the labor movement. The documents, dated from December, 1895, to April, 1900, are grouped under the following headings:

1. "Reports of Minister of Internal Affairs [I.] Goremykin to Alexander III on unrest in the St. Petersburg area and on Lenin's trip abroad in the summer of 1895."

2. "Unrest in the Moscow area."

3. "Unrest in Nizhni Novgorod."

4. "The Saratov court report on the apprehension of thirty-four Social Democrats in April, 1900."

5. "The Saratov court report for 1899 on Social Democratic activities."

6. "General survey of the labor movement for 1898 and 1899."

7. "Kiev court report and labor proclamations."

8. "Kharkov court and factory inspector's reports."

9. "Ekaterinoslav Social Democratic proclamations and government reports."

A Digest of the Krasnyi Arkhiv 173

93 (1939): 190–208

THE STRIKE IN KHARKOV ON MAY 1, 1900. Introduction by Z. Dobrova.

On May 1, 1900, some 10,000 workers in Kharkov demonstrated for an eight-hour working day. The documents published here include a report by the governor of Kharkov on the growth of industry and on labor unrest in 1899, and thirteen telegrams and reports on the May Day demonstration.

For references to additional material in *Krasnyi Arkhiv* on May Day, see the notes to "May 1 in Tsarist Russia (1892–1903)," 82 (1937): 164–192.

93 (1939): 209–255

MATERIALS RELATING TO THE HISTORY OF RUSSIA'S RELATIONS WITH THE TURKMEN IN THE EIGHTEENTH CENTURY. Introduction by V. Razumovskaia.

These documents are excerpts from journals kept on expeditions to the eastern shores of the Caspian Sea in 1741 and 1745; reports by officials of the Ministry of Foreign Affairs; and an exchange of dispatches between Catherine II and officials in Astrakhan concerning the strengthening of Central Asian trade routes, the construction of fortresses, expansion into Central Asia, and life among the Turkmenian people.

FROM AN ARCHIVIST'S NOTEBOOK

93 (1939): 256–262

FROM CORRESPONDENCE OF N. I. KOSTOMAROV WITH [S. N.] SHUBINSKY, EDITOR OF *Istoricheskii Vestnik*. Introduction by G. Nikolskaia.

Dated between 1877 and 1883, the sixteen letters printed here are from N. I. Kostomarov to S. N. Shubinsky, who corresponded with many Russian historians during the second half of the nineteenth century and the beginning of the twentieth. Kostomarov collaborated with Shubinsky on *Istoricheskii Vestnik* ("The Historical Messenger") and on the journal *Ancient and Modern Russia*.

VOLUME 94, 1939

94 (1939): 3–31

PETROGRAD WORKERS IN THE STRUGGLE WITH YUDENICH. Introduction by G. Kostomarov.

Dated in October and November, 1919, the fifteen documents given here are concerned with the mobilization of Petrograd after General Nicholas Yudenich launched his October offensive. They include appeals from the Soviet government to Petrograd residents to resist Yudenich's forces and reports on production in the city's factories and on the organization of defense guards.

For additional material in *Krasnyi Arkhiv*, see "The Working Class and Trade Unions in the Creation of the Red Army," 86 (1938): 56–92.

94 (1939): 32–63

THE RAILROAD WORKERS' STRIKE IN THE TIFLIS WORKSHOPS (1900). Introduction by O. Chaadaeva.

Presented here are Social Democratic proclamations and government reports about strikes for shorter hours and higher pay in Tiflis in the summer of 1900.

For references to additional material in *Krasnyi Arkhiv* on unrest in the Caucasus, see the notes to "The Struggle with the Revolutionary Movement in the Caucasus in the Stolypin Era," 35 (1929): 128–150.

94 (1939): 64–96

CONCERNING THE PEDAGOGICAL ACTIVITY OF ILIA NIKOLAEVICH ULIANOV. Introduction by E. Medynsky.

The introduction is a biographical sketch of Lenin's father (1831–1886). The thirty-one documents given here are dated from 1872 to 1885 and are Ulianov's reports on the state of education in Simbirsk province, recommendations for improvements in library facilities, teacher-training courses, and teachers' pay and pensions, a photostat of his letter proposing the establishment of a school for girls in the city of Syzran, and his opinions on women's schools in general.

For additional material in *Krasnyi Arkhiv*, see "I. N. Ulianov's Struggle for Elementary Schools," 98 (1940): 219–239.

94 (1939): 97–153

RUSSO-AMERICAN RELATIONS AT THE TIME OF THE CIVIL WAR IN THE UNITED STATES. Introduction by M. Malkin.

Malkin traces British, French, Russian, and American relations at the time of the Civil War in the United States. The forty-three documents, published here for the first time, were selected to show Russia's official attitude toward the war. They are dated from December, 1860, to May, 1865, and are fully annotated. Most are communiqués exchanged between

Foreign Minister Prince A. M. Gorchakov and the Russian representative in Washington, Baron E. A. Stoeckel.

94 (1939): 154–188

ELECTIONS IN PARIS TO THE ESTATES GENERAL IN 1789 (From the Letters of a Contemporary). Introduction by E. Alexandrova.

These twenty-one letters were written in Paris between January 3 and May 9, 1789, by Demishel, a friend of the French revolutionary Gilbert Romm (1750–1795), who was then abroad as tutor to Baron G. A. Stroganov. Earlier, Demishel had been the Stroganov family librarian. He had secured this position through Romm, who had been the tutor of Paul A. Stroganov, Baron G. A. Stroganov's cousin.

The letters, addressed to Gabriel Dubreil, the postmaster at Riom, speak of the elections to the Estates General, the political temper in Paris late in April, and the attitude of the public toward [Jacques] Necker.

For additional material in *Krasnyi Arkhiv* on Romm, see "Great Fear in Auvergne," 94 (1939): 255–259.

94 (1939): 189–254

DESCRIPTION OF THE HISTORY OF THE KALMUCK PEOPLE. Introduction by V. Razumovskaia.

This hitherto unpublished manuscript is a description of the life of the nomadic Kalmuck people from the earliest period about which information is available. It covers the internal organization of Kalmuck society, its culture and customs, and the relations of the Kalmucks with tsarist Russia.

Written in 1761 by Vasili Bakunin, who was appointed official government translator of Kalmuck materials in 1720 and secretary for Kalmuck affairs in 1726, the account is based on materials in the Ministry of Foreign Affairs, as well as on personal experiences. It is considered particularly important because many of the seventeenth-century documents used by Bakunin have not been preserved.

Publication of this material is continued in *Krasnyi Arkhiv*, 96 (1939): 196–220.

FROM AN ARCHIVIST'S NOTEBOOK

94 (1939): 255–259

GREAT FEAR IN AUVERGNE. Introduction by K. Ratkevich.

Printed here are excerpts from letters of Gabriel Dubreil to Gilbert Romm in August, 1789, describing the great fear in Auvergne over rumors that bands of robbers were roaming through France pillaging the countryside.

For additional material in *Krasnyi Arkhiv* on Romm, see "Elections in Paris to the Estates General in 1789," 94 (1939): 154–188.

VOLUME 95, 1939

95 (1939): 3–72

MATERIALS RELATING TO THE HISTORY OF THE ELECTRIFICATION OF THE RUSSIAN SOVIET FEDERATED SOCIALIST REPUBLIC. Introduction by B. Kuznetsov.

These documents trace the development of electrification from the decree of the *Sovnarkom* ("Council of People's Commissars") of December 16, 1917, confiscating the property of the Electrical Illumination Society, to the state of progress in November, 1920. The documents consist of directives of the *Sovnarkom*, reports of the engineers in charge of construction, and minutes of the meetings of the Government Commission for the Electrification of Russia. A map showing the location of the electrical stations in operation in the RSFSR and of those to be constructed is included.

Publication of this material is continued in *Krasnyi Arkhiv*, 96 (1939): 55–72.

95 (1939): 73–102

MATERIALS RELATING TO THE HISTORY OF THE CIVIL WAR IN THE UKRAINE IN 1918. Introduction by S. Markov.

Presented here are documents concerning the Ukrainian resistance to German occupation in 1918. They are Ukrainian resolutions to fight the invaders, army officers' reports to Lenin on the progress of the fighting, and civilian officials' reports on the morale of the people. The documents are grouped under the following headings: (1) "The struggle with White bandits and the army of occupation"; (2) "The uprising in Zvenigorod and Tarashchansk districts of Kiev province"; (3) "Partisans' struggles in the 'neutral zone' (Chernigov province)"; (4) "Soviet Ukrainian troops on the offensive."

For additional material in *Krasnyi Arkhiv*, see "German Occupation of Polesie (Byelorussia)," 91 (1938): 89–105.

95 (1939): 103-136

MATERIALS RELATING TO INTERNATIONAL RELATIONS IN THE FIRST YEARS OF THE FRENCH REVOLUTION (1789-1790). Introduction by R. Averbukh.

Presented here are twenty-six documents, dated from February 16/27, 1789, to March 16/27, 1790, which are reports of and instructions to members of the Russian diplomatic corps. Averbukh states that they were selected from material gathered by the Institute of History of the Academy of Science of the USSR to appear in a four-volume publication, *Tsarism i Frantsuzskaia Burzhuaznaia Revoliutsiia XVIII Veka* ("Tsarism and the French Bourgeois Revolution of the Eighteenth Century"). They contain descriptions of the seizure of the Bastille, material on Anglo-Russian relations, and a discussion of the effect of the French Revolution on antifeudal movements in other parts of Europe, particularly in Belgium.

95 (1939): 137-155

JULY STRIKES AND DEMONSTRATIONS OF 1914. Introduction by O. Chaadaeva.

The documents printed here are proclamations of the St. Petersburg Social Democratic committee urging support of strikes and demonstrations in St. Petersburg, Moscow, Kolomna, Kharkov, Kiev, and Tver.

For additional material in *Krasnyi Arkhiv*, see: "The Struggle with Strikes on the Eve of the World War," 34 (1929): 95-125; "Tsarism in the Struggle with the Labor Movement in the Years of Its Ascent," 74 (1936): 37-65; "The Rise of the Labor Movement before the First Imperialistic War," 82 (1937): 136-163.

95 (1939): 156-163

MATERIALS RELATING TO THE HISTORY OF EVENTS IN THE UKRAINE IN 1708 (On the Two-Hundred-and-Thirtieth Anniversary of the Battle of Poltava). Introduction by N. Prokopenko.

These documents indicate the nature of Swedish and Russian relations with the Ukrainians at the time of the Battle of Poltava. They contain appeals by Peter the Great to the Ukrainians to aid the Russians, oaths of allegiance to Peter, and Swedish orders requisitioning provisions. A photostat of the signatures to one of the oaths of allegiance is reproduced.

FROM AN ARCHIVIST'S NOTEBOOK

95 (1939): 164–174

MATERIALS RELATING TO THE CENTENNIAL OF THE PULKOVO ASTRONOMICAL OBSERVATORY. Introduction by L. Polianskaia.

The Pulkovo Observatory, near St. Petersburg, was opened on August 7/19, 1839. These six documents, dated from 1833 to 1842, are reports on the acquisition of land for the observatory, the architects' plans and estimates, and a report on the instruments being made in Germany and the foreign interest in the observatory. There is also a report on the work done during the first two years that the observatory was in operation.

VOLUME 96, 1939

96 (1939): 3–54

SOCIALISTIC FORMS OF AGRICULTURE 1918–1919. Introduction by T. Shepeleva.

The initial document given here is a reprint of M. I. Kalinin's speech at the First All-Russian Congress of Agricultural Communes and Artels on December 3, 1919. The second document is a congratulatory telegram from this congress to the Seventh All-Russian Congress of Soviets, December 5, 1919.

In addition, excerpts are given from reports on agriculture presented at the agricultural congress on December 5 and 6, 1919. These reports describe conditions in Samara, Saratov, Moscow, Vladimir, Vitebsk, Vologda, Viatka, Kaluga, Nizhni Novgorod, Tula, Astrakhan, Olonets, Petrograd, Pskov, Riazan, Severo-Dvinsk, Simbirsk, Smolensk, Tambov, Tver, Cherepovets, Yaroslavl, Novgorod, Kursk, Orlov, Ivanovo Voznesensk, Kazan, and Gomel.

There are also reports of delegates to the All-Russian Conference of Agricultural Workers held in Moscow on July 21–27, 1920, which describe conditions in Petrograd, Severo-Dvinsk, Cherepovets, Pskov, Yaroslavl, Tver, Viatka, Perm, Ufa, Ekaterinburg, Gomel, Smolensk, Tambov, Kostroma, Saratov, Moscow, Vladimir, Riazan, Orlov, and Tula. Two resolutions of this conference on taxation and the establishment of handicraft industries are included.

For references to additional material in *Krasnyi Arkhiv*, see the notes to "Materials Relating to the History of the Carrying into Effect of Lenin's Decree concerning Land," 89–90 (1938): 30–102.

A Digest of the Krasnyi Arkhiv 179

96 (1939): 55–72

MATERIALS RELATING TO THE HISTORY OF THE ELECTRIFICATION OF THE RUSSIAN SOVIET FEDERATED SOCIALIST REPUBLIC (Continuation)

Publication of this material was begun in *Krasnyi Arkhiv*, 95 (1939): 3–72.

These twenty-one documents, dated from January, 1921, to November, 1922, outline plans for speeding up electrification in the RSFSR and for constructing hydroelectric stations at specified points in the republic.

96 (1939): 73–120

UNIONS IN THE STRUGGLE FOR A RISE IN THE PRODUCTIVITY OF LABOR IN THE CIVIL WAR YEARS. Introduction by R. G. and P. D.

The first group of documents presented here consists of a letter of August 13, 1918, from V. M. Molotov to workers in the Putilov factory near Petrograd and of five resolutions and appeals of union conferences in 1918 and 1920 urging a rapid transition from war to peace economy and a speed-up in production.

The second group consists of appeals to workers to expand their technical skills, to increase production, and to promote better organization. Included are charts on production. There are fourteen documents concerned with railroad workers, 1918–1920; seventeen concerning metalworkers, 1918–1920; four concerning miners, 1918–1920; and three concerning tanners, 1918–1920.

For additional material in *Krasnyi Arkhiv*, see "Materials on the History of Labor's Control over Production, 1917–1918," 103 (1940): 106–129.

96 (1939): 121–147

EPISODES FROM THE WAR ACTIVITY OF RUSSIAN AIRCRAFT 1914–1917. Introduction by Hero of the Soviet Union, Corps Commander P. Pumpur.

Commander Pumpur states that the role of the Russian air corps in World War I has not been thoroughly investigated. The thirty-five documents printed here are concerned primarily with action on the southwestern front. They are dated from August, 1914, to October, 1917, and report on the activities of specific Russian air-force units, comparing their efficiency with that of the German air force.

96 (1939): 148–171

MATERIALS RELATING TO THE QUESTION OF PATENTS FOR INVENTIONS IN RUSSIA IN THE 1830's. Introduction by A. Shapiro.

Shapiro points out that patent privileges were established by a ukase of Alexander I on June 17, 1812. The material presented here includes a report by [Jacob A.] Druzhinin, director of the Department of Industry and Internal Trade, May 25, 1826, outlining sections of the patent law which he thought needed revision. There is also a copy of a questionnaire on patent problems that was submitted to members of the Industrial Committee on November 27, 1829, and of the replies of Count A. Strogonov, I. Miatlev, V. Vsevolozhsky, E. Karneev, S. Gagarin, F. Samarin, and N. P. Polevoi. The last document is a report of Miatlev to the Industrial Committee on the methods of granting patents, the lack of capital in Russia, transportation on the Volga, and the technical skills possessed by certain Russian peasants.

96 (1939): 172–179

NOTE OF N. G. CHERNYSHEVSKY CONCERNING LIBERATION OF THE PEASANTS. Introduction by N. Alexeiev.

This note was apparently written in mid-April, 1858, and, although there is no direct indication, was probably addressed to Grand Duke Constantine Nikolaevich, member of the Main Committee on Peasant Affairs. Chernyshevsky wrote that liberation of the peasants would be disastrous unless they were given land with their freedom.

For references to additional material in *Krasnyi Arkhiv*, see the notes to "Materials Relating to the History of the Release of N. G. Chernyshevsky," 31 (1928): 214–219.

96 (1939): 180–195

TSARIST CENSORSHIP CONCERNING "POPULAR" PUBLICATIONS OF M. Y. LERMONTOV's WORKS. Introduction by Polianskaia.

Presented here are seven reports of special educational committees of the Ministry of Public Education dated from 1875 to 1903 on the following of M. Y. Lermontov's works: *Izmail Bei* ("Ismail Bey"), *Demon* ("The Demon"), *Kaznacheisha* ("The Treasurer's Wife"), *Ashik Kerib*, *Angel Smerti* ("Angel of Death"), *Pesnia pro Tsaria Vasilievicha* ("Song of the Tsar Vasilievich"), *Boiarin Orsha* ("The Boyar Orsha"), *Geroi Nashego Vremeni* ("A Hero of Our Times"), *Mtsyri* ("Novice"), *Maskarad* ("Masquerade"), and *Pesnia pro Kuptsa Kalashnikova* ("Song of the Merchant Kalashnikov").

96 (1939): 196–220

DESCRIPTION OF THE HISTORY OF THE KALMUCK PEOPLE (Continuation)

Publication of this material was begun in *Krasnyi Arkhiv*, 94 (1939): 189–254.

The description is a continuation of the history of the Kalmuck people written in 1761 by Vasili Bakunin. The period covered here is the 1730's.

96 (1939): 221–225

MATERIALS RELATING TO L. N. TOLSTOY'S BIOGRAPHY. Introduction by F. M.

Dated from November, 1891, to March, 1892, these fifteen reports by officials of Riazan province deal with Tolstoy's articles on the famine. A note from the Police Department, January 29, 1892, to the governor of Riazan province encloses a check from Alva Adams of Pueblo, Colorado, sent through the Ministry of Internal Affairs, to aid Tolstoy in his famine-relief work.

For additional material in *Krasnyi Arkhiv*, see "L. N. Tolstoy and the Relief of the Famine Victims," 6 (1924): 243–252.

96 (1939): 225–232

LETTERS OF THE ARTIST V. G. SCHWARTZ. Introduction by N. Snezhinsky.

The fifteen letters published here were written by V. G. Schwartz to his family while he was studying with [Jules] Lefebvre in Paris in 1863. They describe his professional and social life in Paris and include comments on family and international affairs. One of Schwartz's best-known paintings is "Ivan the Terrible at the Body of His Murdered Son."

VOLUME 97, 1939

97 (1939): 3–7

LEADER OF THE PEOPLE. By E. Yaroslavsky.

Yaroslavsky's article praises Stalin's role in the October Revolution and in the establishment of the Soviet regime. There is a full-page photograph of Stalin.

97 (1939): 8–43

STRUGGLE FOR BREAD IN 1918–1919. Introduction by T. Shepeleva.

Presented here are forty documents, dated from January 5, 1918, to December 23, 1919, describing the emergency measures adopted by the government to combat the famine in Russia after World War I. Part of the decree issued February 16, 1918, by the Council of People's Commissars of the USSR on the establishment of an extraordinary commission on food and transportation is translated into English in *The Bolshevik Revolution 1917–1918* by J. Bunyan and H. Fisher (Stanford, Calif.: Stanford Univ. Press, 1934), page 661. The resolution of the council on the exchange of commodities is translated in the same work, pages 665–666.

For references to additional material in *Krasnyi Arkhiv*, see the notes to "Materials Relating to the History of the Carrying into Effect of Lenin's Decree concerning Land," 89–90 (1938): 30–102.

97 (1939): 44–90

MATERIALS FOR S. M. KIROV'S BIOGRAPHY. Introduction by G. Kostomarov.

Presented here is a chronological list of S. M. Kirov's major activities (compiled from correspondence, archive materials, books, and newspapers) from August 26, 1917, to December 6, 1934, when he was buried in Red Square. A photograph of Kirov also appears.

For references to additional material in *Krasnyi Arkhiv*, see the notes to "Sergius M. Kirov, 1886–1934," 67 (1934): 3–4.

97 (1939): 91–123

MATERIALS RELATING TO THE HISTORY OF THE PRAGUE CONFERENCE. Introduction by K. Popov.

The Prague conference of the Russian Social Democratic Labor party, held in January, 1912, marked the official organization of the Bolshevik party. The documents published here outline preparations for the conference, as well as the agenda and the decisions reached. There are also government reports on the activities of the delegates.

97 (1939): 124–140

COMRADE KIROV'S ACTIVITY IN THE ORGANIZATION OF TOMSK SOCIAL DEMOCRATS. Introduction by I. Nikitinsky.

Published here are eight resolutions and proclamations of the Tomsk Social Democratic Committee and eight police and Gendarmerie reports on the activities of S. M. Kirov and his associates in Tomsk from January, 1905, to November, 1911. A photograph of Kirov is included.

A Digest of the Krasnyi Arkhiv 183

For references to additional material in *Krasnyi Arkhiv*, see the notes to "Sergius M. Kirov, 1886–1934," 67 (1934): 3–4.

97 (1939): 141–176

V. I. CHAPAEV's MILITARY CAREER. Introduction by V. Petrov and S. Orestov.

The documents printed here are excerpts from D. Furmanov's biography of V. I. Chapaev, a commander of the Red army during the Civil War. They tell of his battles against the White army in September and October, 1918; of the fall offensive of his Second Nikolaevsk Division in Uralsk; and of his appointment to the academy of the General Staff. A photograph of Chapaev also appears.

Publication of these documents is continued in *Krasnyi Arkhiv*, 98 (1940): 68–124.

97 (1939): 177–182

A. P. CHEKHOV—MANUSCRIPTS, LETTERS, MATERIALS. Introduction by A. Eiges.

A letter of March 9, 1899, from Alexander to his brother Anton P. Chekhov, details of the life of his father Paul, and a copy of the verification of the sale of the rights to Chekhov's works to the publisher A. F. Marx are presented here, along with four of Chekhov's letters— to A. S. Suvorin, S. K. Trutovsky, A. M. Yermolaev, and M. D. Belenovskaia.

For additional material in *Krasnyi Arkhiv*, see the notes to "From the Archives of A. P. Chekhov," 37 (1929): 175–214.

97 (1939): 183

CONTENTS OF THE ISSUES OF THE JOURNAL *Krasnyi Arkhiv* FOR 1939

This is a table of contents, which does not indicate the pages, of *Krasnyi Arkhiv*, Volumes 92–97.

VOLUME 98, 1940

98 (1940): 3–17

LENIN's LEGACY EMBODIED IN LIFE [A Eulogy of Lenin]

Printed here is A. S. Shcherbakov's address of January 21, 1940, delivered at a memorial meeting in the Bolshoi Theater on the sixteenth anniversary of Lenin's death.

98 (1940): 18–30

Responses to V. I. Lenin's Death

The documents presented here are messages and resolutions from organizations in Moscow, Petrograd, Archangel, Karelia, the Don area, and the Maritime province at the time of Lenin's death, in 1924. There is also a copy of the speech made by his wife, N. Krupskaia, at a meeting of the Second All-Union Congress of Soviets in 1924. The speech appeared in *Pravda* on January 30 of that year.

98 (1940): 31–67

White Finns in the Service of Anglo-French Interventionists in 1919. Introduction by G. Kostomarov.

The documents in the first section of the material presented here, dated from January 17, 1918, to June 15, 1919, contain information on the Civil War in Finland. Those in the second section, dated from January 25 to November 4, 1919, consist of correspondence between the leaders of the White army in Russia and the Allies.

For references to additional material in *Krasnyi Arkhiv*, see the notes to "The Disintegration of Kolchak's Campaign," 31 (1928): 51–80.

98 (1940): 68–124

Chapaev's Military Career

Publication of the documents on this subject was begun in *Krasnyi Arkhiv*, 97 (1939): 141–176.

The documents given here, excerpts from D. Furmanov's biography of V. I. Chapaev, provide information on the following topics: the advance of the Red army's Twenty-fifth Division on the town of Buguruslan in April and May, 1919; the activities of the same division in the Ufa operation in May and June, 1919; the division's advance to Uralsk to reinforce the Twenty-second Division in July and August, 1919; and the death of V. I. Chapaev, September 5, 1919.

98 (1940): 125–144

Materials Relating to the History of Intervention in the North. Introduction by N. Prokopenko.

The forty-eight dispatches published here, dated from March 6, 1919, to February 2, 1920, are from representatives of the counterrevolutionary governments stationed in Paris, London, Copenhagen, Belgrade, Brussels, and

Finland. British and American aid is discussed and the conditions of General C. G. Mannerheim for assisting the counterrevolutionary forces in Finland are stated.

98 (1940): 145-176

LIFE OF SOLDIERS IN THE TSARIST ARMY. Introduction by M. Semin.

Medical reports, soldiers' letters, and officers' reports on food, shelter, illness, medical supplies, and sanitation comprise the thirty-three documents, dated from 1902 to 1915, which are published here.

For references to additional material in the *Krasnyi Arkhiv*, see the notes to "[Comments of] Nicholas Romanov concerning the Revolutionary Movement in the Army in 1905-1906," 41-42 (1930): 215-220 and to "Memoirs of A. I. Kozmin," 60 (1933): 142-156.

98 (1940): 177-218

POSITION OF PEASANTS IN WESTERN BYELORUSSIA IN THE NINETEENTH CENTURY. Introduction by V. Picheta.

The official reports and peasant appeals given here describe peasant life in Byelorussia from 1828 to 1871.

98 (1940): 219-239

I. N. ULIANOV'S STRUGGLE FOR ELEMENTARY SCHOOLS. Introduction by Professor E. Medynsky.

Lenin's father, Ilia Nikolaevich Ulianov, was appointed director of elementary schools in Simbirsk in 1874. His report, "Conditions in Elementary Schools in Simbirsk Province, 1880," is printed here; it discusses the number and kinds of schools in the province, the number of teachers and students, tuition, school property, the relationship between the schools and the Ministry of Education, teacher preparation, and trade and handicraft classes.

For additional material in *Krasnyi Arkhiv*, see "Concerning the Pedagogical Activity of Ilia Nikolaevich Ulianov," 94 (1939): 64-96.

98 (1940): 240-262

HERZEN AND TSARIST CENSORSHIP (On the Seventieth Anniversary of His Death). Introduction by I. Kovalev.

Dated from 1851 to 1911, the censors' reports printed here criticize issues of A. I. Herzen's journals *Kolokol* ("The Bell"), *Poliarnaia Zvezda*

("Polar Star"), and *Pod Sud* ("On Trial"). Also included are reports on his memoirs and on *K Razvitiiu Revoliutsionnykh Idei v Rossii* ("Concerning the Development of Revolutionary Ideas in Russia"). Herzen's complete works were made available for the first time in Russia in 1917.

For references to additional material in *Krasnyi Arkhiv* on Herzen, see the notes to "An Unpublished Letter of A. I. Herzen," 31 (1928): 224–226.

FROM AN ARCHIVIST'S NOTEBOOK

98 (1940): 263–277

TSARIST CENSORSHIP CONCERNING THE UKRAINIAN WRITER I. FRANKO. Introduction by Polianskaia.

Published here are seventeen reports of the censors, dated from October, 1888, to January, 1914, on the following of Franko's works: *Na Dni* ("In the Depths"), *Lis Mikita* ("The Fox 'Mikita' "), *Kamiana Dusha* ("The Stone Heart"), *Do Svitla* ("Toward the Light"), *Perekhresni Stezhki* ("The Intersecting Roads"), *Bez Pratsi* ("Without Work"), *V Poti Chola* ("In the Sweat of One's Brow"), *Na Vichnu Pamiat Kotliarevskomu* ("To the Eternal Memory of Kotliarevsky"), *Pantalakha* ("Confusion"), *Moisei* ("Moses"), *Akordi* ("The Chords"), *Virshi na Gromadski Temi* ("Verses on Social Themes"), *13 Lit Moei Molodosti* ("Thirteen Years of My Youth").

VOLUME 99, 1940

99 (1940): 5

TO THE FAITHFUL COMPANION IN ARMS OF LENIN AND STALIN—VIACHESLAV MIKHAILOVICH MOLOTOV

Greetings from the Central Committee of the All-Union (Bolshevik) Communist party on the occasion of V. M. Molotov's fiftieth birthday, in 1940, appear here.

99 (1940): 6–7

TO THE FAITHFUL COMPANION IN ARMS OF LENIN AND STALIN, THE HEAD OF THE SOVIET GOVERNMENT—V. M. MOLOTOV

Printed here are birthday greetings from the Soviet of People's Commissars of the USSR.

99 (1940): 8-14

VIACHESLAV MIKHAILOVICH MOLOTOV (Short Biography). By G. A. Tikhomirov.

This biography of Molotov emphasizes his revolutionary activities and his faithful service to Lenin and Stalin.

99 (1940): 15-51

THE CIVIL WAR IN FINLAND (1918). Introduction by S. Markov.

The documents given here, primarily the communiqués of military and revolutionary leaders, are divided under the following headings: (1) "The preparation and provocation for the Civil War by the Finnish bourgeoisie"; (2) "The organization of the Finnish Red Guard and Workers' Guard"; (3) "Armed assistance to the proletariat of Finland"; (4) "Military action of the Red Guard and the Russian troops against the White Finns."

99 (1940): 52-71

RUSSIAN SOLDIERS' UPRISING IN FRANCE IN 1917. Introduction by Major G. Zakharov.

The thirty documents printed here shed light on the effect of revolutionary agitation on the Russian soldiers in France in 1917, their uprising during the Revolution, and the difference in habits and discipline of the French and Russian soldiers.

For references to additional material in *Krasnyi Arkhiv* on conditions in the Russian army during World War I, see the notes to "Memoirs of A. I. Kozmin," 60 (1933): 142-156.

99 (1940): 72-89

ARMED STRUGGLE OF NOVOROSSISK WORKERS IN DECEMBER, 1905. Introduction by I. Martynov.

Presented here are sixteen documents on the revolt in the city of Novorossisk which began after the Manifesto of October 17, 1905, was issued.

99 (1940): 90-126

THE PEASANT MOVEMENT IN WESTERN TRANSCAUCASIA 1902-1905. Introduction by Professor K. Sivkov.

The thirty-nine documents published here are dated from 1902 to 1905 and picture the peasant movement in Georgia and Stalin's role in it.

For references to additional material in *Krasnyi Arkhiv*, see the notes to "S. Y. Witte's Struggle with the Agrarian Revolution," 31 (1928): 81–102 and to "The Struggle with the Revolutionary Movement in the Caucasus in the Stolypin Era," 35 (1929): 128–150.

99 (1940): 127–179

BEGINNING OF RAILROAD CONSTRUCTION IN RUSSIA. Introduction by M. Krutikov.

According to Krutikov, only the first section of the report on Russian railroads dated 1871 and written by P. P. Melnikov has been located. It is given here. The paper was originally divided into the following four sections: (1) from the opening of the first railroad between Liverpool and Manchester to the beginning of work on the Nikolaevsk railroad (September, 1830—beginning of 1842); (2) from the beginning of work on the Nikolaevsk railroad to its opening (1842—November 1, 1851); (3) from the opening of the Nikolaevsk railroad to Melnikov's appointment as minister of transportation (1851–1862); and (4) Melnikov's term as minister of transportation (1862–1868).

For additional material in *Krasnyi Arkhiv* on Melnikov, see "Materials Relating to the History of the Development of Steam Navigation on the Volga," 89–90 (1938): 309–335.

VOLUME 100, 1940

100 (1940): 3–8

THE CURRENT PROBLEMS OF THE JOURNAL *Krasnyi Arkhiv*. By E. Yaroslavsky.

Yaroslavsky analyzes some of the materials published in the first one hundred issues of the journal and criticizes the work of the late M. N. Pokrovsky, historian and former editor in chief of *Krasnyi Arkhiv*. He indicates that the earlier emphasis on publication of prerevolutionary material will henceforth be shifted somewhat to Soviet historical documents in order to educate the younger generations.

100 (1940): 9–35

A SHORT REVIEW OF DOCUMENTS PUBLISHED IN *Krasnyi Arkhiv* (On the Publication of the One-Hundredth Issue of the Journal *Krasnyi Arkhiv*)

This review is the joint work of M. Feigelson, A. Popov, and N. Belchikov.

M. Feigelson analyzes the publication of documents on the history of economic thought in Russia, touching on the economic views of the Decembrists, Pushkin's lyceum lecture notes on economics, the rise of Marxism in Russia, the agrarian movement, Russia's international financial situation, foreign capital in Russia, the construction of the first Russian railroads, the Bering expeditions, the linking of the Moscow and Volga rivers, the search for precious metals in the North in the seventeenth and eighteenth centuries, the exploration of Ossetia in the eighteenth century, socialist forms of agriculture, and the history of electrification in the USSR.

A. Popov analyzes the publication of documents on the history of Russian international relations, discussing the diplomatic correspondence with Berlin in 1914, the journal of the Ministry of Foreign Affairs, the correspondence of General V. A. Sukhomlinov and N. N. Yanushkevich, the diplomatic correspondence concerning Constantinople and the Straits, the Balkan Union and the First Balkan War, the Ministry of Foreign Affairs and the *Stavka* ("General Staff"), the Czechoslovakian question, Serbia in World War I, Anglo-Russian rivalry in Persia, war finances, the Congress of Paris, Russia and the United States during the Civil War in the United States, the Alvensleben Convention with Prussia in 1863, the Paris Commune, the Congress of Berlin, Russo-German relations in 1873–1887, the Far East, the Hague Conference, and the Boxer Rebellion.

N. Belchikov discusses the publication of documents on the history of literature, mentioning material on A. S. Pushkin, A. N. Radishchev, N. V. Gogol, A. I. Herzen, T. G. Shevchenko, L. Tolstoy, I. S. Turgenev, F. M. Dostoevsky, I. A. Goncharov, Tiutchev, N. P. Ogarev, N. A. Nekrasov, M. E. Saltykov-Shchedrin, Y. P. Polonsky, N. G. Chernyshevsky, N. A. Dobroliubov, D. I. Pisarev, A. Chekhov, V. G. Korolenko, M. Gorky, J. W. Goethe, Honoré Balzac, Mitskevich, and A. France.

100 (1940): 36–78

M. V. FRUNZE ON THE TURKESTAN FRONT. Introduction by Division Commander F. Novitsky.

The documents presented here, dated from August, 1919, to September, 1920, cover the period when Frunze was commander of the Turkestan front. They are from the work *M. V. Frunze na Frontakh Turkestanskoi Voiny* ("M. V. Frunze at the Fronts of the Turkestan War"), which is reviewed in *Krasnyi Arkhiv*, 106 (1941): 173–176. There is a photograph of Frunze and one of K. E. Voroshilov with him.

For references to additional material in *Krasnyi Arkhiv* on the activities of M. V. Frunze, see the notes to "Ten Years since the Day of M. V. Frunze's Death," 72 (1935): 44–50.

100 (1940): 79–120

AGRICULTURAL EXPOSITION OF 1923. Introduction by [T?] Shepeleva.

The materials printed here describe preparations for the exhibition held in Moscow in 1923 to stimulate agricultural production in the USSR. There are reprints of speeches made by M. I. Kalinin, Clara Zetkin, and General S. M. Budenny and documents giving statistics on the exhibition, the major displays, and foreign participation. Another group of documents consists of greetings to the fair. In the last group is a report on the attitude of the foreign press toward the exposition, as well as short notes on American, Austrian, English, French, Bulgarian, Palestinian, and Persian participation.

100 (1940): 121–157

MATERIALS RELATING TO THE BIOGRAPHY OF P. F. LESGAFT. Introduction by M. Torbin.

Peter Frantsevich Lesgaft (1837–1909), a professor of anatomy at the University of Kazan, was dismissed from the faculty in 1871 for writing an article demanding greater academic freedom. Dated from 1871 to 1902, the sixty-two documents presented here are reports of the Secret Police, the Ministry of Internal Affairs, and the Kazan Gendarmerie on his activities.

100 (1940): 158–194

NEW MATERIALS CONCERNING M. V. LOMONOSOV. Introduction by I. Grabar.

These documents, dated from 1752 to 1768, deal with the establishment of the first mosaic factory in Russia. They include M. V. Lomonosov's request for government funds and his reports to the Senate on the progress of his work. Reproductions of two of Lomonosov's mosaics, a portrait of Peter the Great, and a mosaic of the Battle of Poltava appear.

100 (1940): 195–228

I. S. TURGENEV IN SPASSKOE-LUTOVINO (Reminiscences of S. G. Shchepkina). Introduction by N. Brodsky.

These are the notes of S. G. Shchepkina, one of Turgenev's neighbors, about Turgenev's visits to his estate in Spasskoe-Lutovino in Orlov province during the last years of Turgenev's life. Turgenev died in France, August 22, 1883.

For additional material in *Krasnyi Arkhiv*, see: "I. S. Turgenev's Letters to P. V. Annenkov," 32 (1929): 191–208; "From the Diary of V. P. Gaevsky (1883–1887)," 100 (1940): 229–243.

100 (1940): 229–243

FROM THE DIARY OF V. P. GAEVSKY (1883–1887). Introduction by G. Nikolskaia.

Victor Pavlovich Gaevsky (1826–1888), the friend of such literary men as I. S. Turgenev, N. A. Nekrasov, D. V. Grigorovich, and Y. P. Polonsky, was a Pushkin expert and the editor of the first collection of Turgenev's letters, published in 1884. These entries in Gaevsky's diary tell of Turgenev's funeral, the attitude of the government toward the possibility of demonstrations at the funeral, Turgenev's will, and Gaevsky's work in collecting and editing Turgenev's letters.

For additional material in *Krasnyi Arkhiv*, see: "I. S. Turgenev's Letters to P. V. Annenkov," 32 (1929): 191–208; "I. S. Turgenev in Spasskoe-Lutovino," 100 (1940): 195–228.

FROM AN ARCHIVIST'S NOTEBOOK

100 (1940): 244–254

FROM P. I. TCHAIKOVSKY'S CORRESPONDENCE. Introduction by E. Bortnikova.

Presented here are twelve letters, dated from 1869 to 1896, to S. A. Rachinsky, professor at the University of Moscow; to the rector of the Kiev Ecclesiastical Academy; to publisher A. S. Suvorin; to the Duke of Mecklemburg-Strelitz; and from composers M. A. Balakirev and N. A. Rimsky-Korsakov.

VOLUME 101, 1940

101 (1940): 3–63

MILITARY-REVOLUTIONARY COMMITTEE OF ESTONIA IN 1917 AND THE BEGINNING OF 1918 (From the Protocols of the Military-Revolutionary Committee). Introduction by I. Nikitinsky and G. Kostomarov.

In the introduction the writers state that these documents trace the activities of the Estonian Military-Revolutionary Committee during both the period of the October Revolution and the period of struggle for the establishment of Soviet power in Estonia. The committee functioned from October 23, 1917, until January 13, 1918, during which time fifty-three meetings were held. The protocols of these meetings, published here, are of particular historical value because they are the only ones which have been preserved intact. Among the matters discussed were the methods for gaining control over means of transportation and communication and over factories and newspapers. Mail censorship, arrests, and food shortages were a few of the problems acted upon.

101 (1940): 64–100

RUMANIAN ARBITRARINESS IN BESSARABIA (1918). Introduction by S. Markov.

The twenty documents printed here, dated from November, 1917, to February, 1919, describe conditions in Bessarabia during the Rumanian occupation in 1918. They consist of protests by various Bessarabian groups and orders and reports of the Rumanian occupation forces.

101 (1940): 101–121

SUPPRESSION OF THE LEFT SOCIALIST REVOLUTIONARIES' REVOLT IN MOSCOW IN 1918. Introduction by N. and K.

Published here for the first time are twenty-six documents describing the Social Revolutionary party's uprising and suppression in Moscow during July 6–13, 1918, after the defeat of its members at the Fifth All-Russian Congress of Soviets on the question of prolonging the war with Germany.

For additional material in *Krasnyi Arkhiv*, see "The Work of the Social Revolutionary Party in 1918," 20 (1927): 153–174.

101 (1940): 122–148

MATERIALS RELATING TO THE HISTORY OF THE RISE OF AGRICULTURAL COMMUNES AND ARTELS IN THE USSR (1918). Introduction by T. Zelenov.

These documents contain valuable information for the study of early Soviet agricultural problems, as well as for a study of communes as forerunners of *kolkhozes* ("collectives"). Among them is a report of the Division of Communes of the Central Commissariat of Agriculture dated March 1, 1918, a reproduction of a sample set of regulations for the organization of a commune, and a report from the board of the Moscow Agricultural Department to the People's Commissariat of Agriculture of the Russian Soviet Federated Socialist Republic, dated September 19, 1918, on communes in Moscow province. Included also are excerpts from eleven issues of *Informatsionnyi Listok* ("Information Bulletin") of the Commissariat of Agriculture, dated from July 12 to November 25, 1918, describing life on communes in the provinces of Tambov, Tver, Kostroma, Penza, Kursk, Saratov, Orlov, Yaroslav, and Riazan.

For references to additional material in *Krasnyi Arkhiv*, see the notes to "Materials Relating to the History of the Carrying into Effect of Lenin's Decree concerning Land," 89–90 (1938): 30–102.

101 (1940): 149–196

THE POLISH WAR OF 1794 IN REPORTS AND ACCOUNTS OF A. V. SUVOROV. Introduction by Professor N. Korobkov.

Most of the thirty-nine documents presented here are reports of Field Marshal Count A. V. Suvorov to Count P. A. Rumiantsev-Zadunaisky. There are, however, reports from Lieutenant General P. S. Potemkin to Suvorov and a letter from General F. Denisov to Suvorov, as well as communiqués from Lieutenant General I. E. Ferzen and Major General Count V. A. Zubov. An exchange of letters between Stanislas Augustus, king of Poland, and Suvorov also appears. The documents describe the fighting and the strategy in the war which led to the third partition of Poland.

A map of the theater of operations in Poland in 1794 is included, showing the position of Russian, Prussian, Austrian, and Polish forces. Another map shows the plan for the Battle of Maciejowice. A third map indicates strategy for the storming of Praha (Prague). There is also a portrait of Suvorov, done by the artist Bekon in Warsaw in 1795.

According to Professor Korobkov, these documents are included in the volume *Sekretnye Raporty General-Ansheffa Suvorova Zakliuchaiushchie v Sebe Vsiu Polskuiu Voinu s Maia po Konets 1794* ("The Secret Reports of General Suvorov, Covering the Entire Polish War from May to the End of 1794").

For additional material in *Krasnyi Arkhiv*, see "Letters of A. V. Suvorov," 106 (1941): 160–164.

101 (1940): 197–227

MATERIALS RELATING TO THE HISTORY OF MOSCOW (Description of Moscow after the Fire of April 10, 1629). Introduction by Professor V. Lebedev.

The first part of the material published here is a report on the damage done by the fire, while the second part contains recommendations for reconstruction of the city. The survey was made upon orders of Tsarevitch Michael Fëdorovich and Patriarch Filaret Nikitich.

FROM AN ARCHIVIST'S NOTEBOOK

101 (1940): 228–235

MATERIALS RELATING TO THE SOJOURN OF RUSSIAN TROOPS IN FRANCE IN 1917. Introduction by N. P.

This material is from a report to the Provisional Government on conditions in the Russian army in France compiled by a special commission of the Second Special Infantry Division in June, 1917. The report describes the commission's trip from Russia, military action, medical provisions, equipment, difficulties in receiving correspondence from Russia, reaction to the Revolution, and the purpose of sending Russian troops to Macedonia.

For references to additional material in *Krasnyi Arkhiv*, see the notes to "Memoirs of A. I. Kozmin," 60 (1933): 142–156.

VOLUME 102, 1940

102 (1940): 3–44

MATERIALS RELATING TO THE HISTORY OF THE STRUGGLE OF THE LITHUANIAN PEOPLE FOR SOVIET POWER IN 1918–1919. Introduction by P. Anisimova.

These forty-two documents deal primarily with the activities of the Provisional Workers' and Peasants' Government of Lithuania (headed by V. Mitskevich-Kapsukas) from December, 1918, to April, 1919. They include the Manifesto of December 16, which announced that all power was in Soviet hands; the recognition of Lithuanian independence by the Soviets; the Lithuanian government's orders concerning the army, communication, sanitation, agriculture, and finances; and the directives ordering socialization of land and the separation of church and state and of schools and church. Also included are documents of the revolutionary committee of Vilno, and other documents dealing with Lithuanian-Polish relations.

102 (1940): 45–74

MATERIALS RELATING TO THE HISTORY OF THE STRUGGLE OF THE KARELIAN PEOPLE FOR SOVIET POWER. Introduction by D. Epstein.

The thirty-nine documents given here provide data on Karelian history from April, 1920, to March, 1922, the years of the struggle to establish Soviet power in the area. Among the events discussed is the convening of the All-Karelian Soviet Congress in July, 1920.

A Digest of the Krasnyi Arkhiv 195

102 (1940): 75–113

MATERIALS RELATING TO THE HISTORY OF THE LABOR MOVEMENT IN THE UKRAINE IN 1905. Introduction by O. Chaadaeva.

The fifty-five documents presented here are dated from January, 1905, to January, 1906. At the beginning of the Revolution of 1905 the Ukraine was the most important industrial and metallurgical area in Russia. These documents sketch revolutionary events in the provinces of Odessa, Kharkov, Ekaterinoslav, Volhynia, and Podolia as reflected in Social Democratic proclamations and the reports of tsarist officials.

102 (1940): 114–156

REVOLUTIONARY EVENTS IN THE BALTIC PROVINCES IN 1905. Introduction by S. Boltinov.

The fifty-two documents printed here, dated from January, 1905, to October, 1910, trace the spread of the Revolution of 1905 in the Baltic provinces of Latvia, Estonia, and Lithuania. They include Social Democratic proclamations and the reports of tsarist agents, particularly on the events in the area of Livonia (Latvia) and of Estland (Estonia).

For references to additional material in *Krasnyi Arkhiv*, see the notes to "The Naval Punitive Battalions in the Baltic Region," 38 (1930): 165–169.

102 (1940): 157–188

MATERIALS RELATING TO THE HISTORY OF THE REVOLUTION OF 1905–1907 IN BYELORUSSIA. Introduction by A. Kobiako.

These forty-seven Social Democratic proclamations and Gendarmerie reports, dated from February 18, 1904, to August 17, 1906, describe revolutionary activities in Grodno, Minsk, Mogilev, and Vitebsk provinces and in the Brest-Litovsk district. According to Kobiako, this is their first publication.

For references to additional material in *Krasnyi Arkhiv*, see Volumes 11–12 (1925), which are devoted exclusively to publications on the Revolution of 1905.

102 (1940): 189–238

ANGLO-RUSSIAN INCIDENT WITH THE SCHOONER *Vixen* (1836–1837). Introduction by Professor S. Bushuev.

The fifty-one dispatches published here, dated from December 11/23, 1836, to June 20/July 2, 1838, during the period of Russian expansion into the Caucasus, describe Anglo-Russian tension after the Russian seizure of the British schooner *Vixen* on the eastern coast of the Black Sea in 1836. They are from the French consul in Odessa, the Russian ambassador in Constantinople, the Russian chargé d'affaires in Vienna, the French ambassador in Vienna, Vice Chancellor Count K. V. Nesselrode, the Danish attaché in Constantinople, the Russian ambassador in London, the Hanoverian ambassador in Vienna, a major in the British Dragoons, the Netherlands consul in Odessa, the Russian ambassador in Vienna, the French ambassador in Constantinople, the British ambassador in St. Petersburg, and the British ambassador in Constantinople.

VOLUME 103, 1940

103 (1940): 3–44

MATERIALS RELATING TO THE FORTIETH ANNIVERSARY OF *Iskra*. Introduction by E. Yaroslavsky.

The following documents appear here: six police reports on methods of smuggling the newspaper *Iskra* ("The Spark") into Russia during 1901 and 1902; eleven letters from Lenin's wife, Nadezhda Konstantinovna Krupskaia, written in 1902 and 1903 to Social Democrats in Odessa, Samara, Moscow, Vologda, Orel, Ekaterinburg, Tula, St. Petersburg, Astrakhan, and Ufa concerning *Iskra;* twelve letters to the editorial offices of *Iskra* written between 1901 and 1903 on conditions in schools, factories, and prisons in Kiev, St. Petersburg, Moscow, Kostroma, Yaroslavl, Odessa, and Kovrov (in Vladimir province); and four Police Department reports and one Social Democratic proclamation concerning the presses in Poltava, Kishinev, and Konotop.

103 (1940): 45–84

LEGISLATIVE ENACTMENTS OF THE SOVIET GOVERNMENT OF LATVIA (1918–1919). Introduction by A. Blumfeldt.

Blumfeldt describes the rise of the Social Democratic party of Latvia and the development of Soviet power from 1918 to 1940, when Latvia entered the Soviet Union. The documents published here are divided into two parts. The first seventeen, dated from December, 1918, to April, 1919, include the directives of the central soviet government of Latvia regarding food, taxes, nationalization of land, separation of church and state and of schools and church, and nationalization of the banks. The second group, eight documents dated from December, 1918, to July, 1919, includes local reports on the execution of the directives issued by the central government.

103 (1940): 85–105

ARMED REBELLION IN MOTOVILIKHA IN DECEMBER, 1905. Introduction by O. Chaadaeva.

A revolt in 1905 at Motovilikha, one of the oldest manufacturing centers in the Urals, was led by Jacob Kuznetsov, factory worker and member of the Perm Social Democratic committee. Printed here are sixteen police and government reports dated from September, 1905, to August, 1906, regarding the causes of the rebellion and the shooting of Kuznetsov when the police attempted to apprehend him on January 3, 1906.

103 (1940): 106–129

MATERIALS ON THE HISTORY OF LABOR'S CONTROL OVER PRODUCTION (1917–1918). Introduction by A. Persov.

The documents presented here are resolutions of factory workers throughout Russia indicating the manner in which the workers controlled production in the transition period between the October Revolution and the nationalization of industry. Workers' control over production was established by a decree of the *Sovnarkom* ("Council of People's Commissars") in November, 1917.

For additional material in *Krasnyi Arkhiv*, see "Unions in the Struggle for a Rise in the Productivity of Labor in the Civil War Years," 96 (1939): 73–120.

103 (1940): 130–159

A RUSSIAN MILITARY AGENT'S DISPATCHES ON THE ANGLO-BOER WAR. Introduction by M. Rabinovich and N. Shliapnikov.

For the most part, the twenty-four documents presented here, dated from August, 1899, to December, 1901, are the letters and reports of Colonel N. S. Yermolov, Russian military attaché in London, and Lieutenant Colonel Miller, Russian military attaché in Brussels. They discuss the military aspects of the Anglo-Boer War, public and official opinion in England, the cost of the war, and the treatment of Boer women and children. There is also a letter from E. Y. Maksimov, a Russian newspaper correspondent at the front.

For additional material in *Krasnyi Arkhiv*, see "Nicholas Romanov concerning the Anglo-Boer War," 63 (1934): 124–126.

103 (1940): 160-197

LARGA AND KAGUL (Material concerning the Military Activities of [Count P. A.] Rumiantsev-Zadunaisky). Introduction by Professor N. Korobkov.

The Russians defeated the Turks at the Battle of Kagul on the River Larga in 1770. The documents presented here are excerpts from "The Military Journal of the First Army under General-in-Chief, Count Rumiantsev," from "The White Journal of the Military Activities of Count Rumiantsev," and from orders and communiqués issued during the campaign. Included are a reproduction of a painting of Rumiantsev, a photostat of one of his letters, and a map of the Kagul battle area.

103 (1940): 198-223

D. I. PISAREV AND TSARIST CENSORSHIP. Introduction by I. Kovalev.

The censors' reports presented here are dated from 1866 to 1912. They review the following of Pisarev's writings: *Istoricheskie Idei Auguste Comte* ("Historical Ideas of Auguste Comte"), *Kartonnye Geroi* ("Cardboard Heroes"), *Vzgliady Angliiskikh Myslitelei na Umstvennyia Potrebnosti Sovremennago Obshchestva* ("Views of English Thinkers on the Intellectual Demands of Contemporary Society"), *Borba za Zhizn* ("Struggle for Life"), and *Budnichnye Storony Zhizni* ("The Trivial Sides of Life").

103 (1940): 224-230

ANCIENT RUSSIAN CHARTER OF 1368. Introduction by V. Bushuev.

This charter was written by Prince Dmitry Konstantinovich at the request of the boyars to establish the order of precedence in council ("who sits next to whom and who sits under whom").

VOLUME 104, 1941

104 (1941): 1-2

To COMRADE KLIMENT EFREMOVICH VOROSHILOV

Presented here are greetings from the Central Committee of the Bolshevik party and the Council of People's Commissars on Voroshilov's sixtieth birthday, in 1941. His photograph is included.

For additional material in *Krasnyi Arkhiv* on Voroshilov, see "Comrade Voroshilov's Address at the Jubilee Session of the Plenum of the Moscow Soviet, Dedicated to the Tenth Anniversary of the Red Army, February 25, 1928," 86 (1938): 26-28.

104 (1941): 3-53

THE CIRCULATION OF THE WORKS OF V. I. LENIN IN PREREVOLUTIONARY RUSSIA (1894-1905). Introduction by G. Kostomarov.

The documents printed here are excerpts from records of the Police Department on the books, pamphlets, and leaflets by Lenin confiscated throughout Russia. The 286 reports are arranged in chronological order.

104 (1941): 54-102

MATERIALS RELATING TO THE MILITARY ACTIVITIES OF COMRADE TIMOSHENKO DURING THE CIVIL WAR IN THE USSR. Introduction by Brigade Commander Nefterev.

The introduction is an account of Semën Konstantinovich Timoshenko's military activities as a commander of the Red army during the Civil War, and from 1939 to 1941. The documents presented here are divided into the following groups: (1) "The battle of Tsaritsyn (April-August, 1919)"; (2) "The defeat of [A. I.] Denikin (October, 1919—March, 1920)"; (3) "The battle with the White Poles (April-September, 1920)"; (4) "The defeat of [Baron P. N.] Wrangel and the liquidation of Makhno bands [followers of Makhno] in the Ukraine (October-December, 1920)." Also included are a photograph of Timoshenko, a map showing where he fought in the October Revolution and the Civil War, and a group photograph of K. E. Voroshilov, Timoshenko, S. M. Budenny, and Bakhturov and Zotov, political commissars in the army.

104 (1941): 103-142

THE REVOLUTIONARY ACTIVITY OF COMRADE V. V. KUIBYSHEV IN SAMARA (1916-1918). Introduction by A. Shefer.

The first group of documents presented here deals with Bolshevik activities in Samara from September, 1916, to February, 1917, the period during which Kuibyshev was confined in the Samara jail. The second group describes the underground activities of the Samara Bolsheviks, led by Kuibyshev. The third group covers the period of preparation, the direction of the October Revolution, and the struggle to establish Soviet power in Samara.

For additional material in *Krasnyi Arkhiv*, see: "V. V. Kuibyshev (1888–1935)," 68 (1935): 5–6; "A Few Dates in the Life and Work of V. V. Kuibyshev," 68 (1935): 119–124.

104 (1941): 143–150

STUDENT CONDITIONS IN TRADE SCHOOLS IN PREREVOLUTIONARY TVER. Introduction by N. Zhuravlev.

Dated from September to December, 1862, the twenty-two documents given here are the reports of a special commission appointed by the governor of Tver province to investigate working and living conditions in the local trade schools.

104 (1941): 151–198

USE BY THE INTERVENTIONISTS OF THE NORTHERN SEA ROUTE (1918–1919). Introduction by T. Shepeleva.

The introduction gives a historical sketch of the establishment of the Northern Sea Route and its use in tsarist and Soviet Russia. The sixty-one documents published here, dated from December 14, 1918, to October 13, 1919, outline the Allies' plans for using the Northern Sea Route to send supplies to A. V. Kolchak and to export minerals from Siberia. They include reports of Kolchak's government; instructions to Kolchak's representatives in London, Washington, Stockholm, and Paris; and a report by the director of the Ob hydrographical expedition on navigation along the Northern Sea Route in 1919.

104 (1941): 199–248

MATERIALS RELATING TO THE BELGIAN REVOLUTION OF 1830. Introduction by Professor A. Molok.

These materials, published here for the first time, present information on the Belgian Revolution of 1830 and, in addition, stress European diplomatic intrigue in the conflict between Belgium and the Netherlands. The thirty-two documents, dated from August through November, 1830, are dispatches exchanged between the ministries of foreign affairs of Russia and of the Netherlands; letters exchanged between Nicholas I and William I, King of the Netherlands; Nicholas I's notes on political events in 1830; and reports by Russia's representatives in the Netherlands and by the Netherlands' representatives in Russia.

104 (1941): 249–257

FIRST RUSSIAN SUBMARINE PROJECT. Introduction by Mikh. Gernet.

The documents presented here deal with the first Russian attempt to invent an underwater craft. Kazimir Chernovsky, a Minsk landowner, devised plans for a submarine in 1825. His plans, together with a request that the government provide funds for the submarine's construction, are published here; reports by the Department of Transportation on the feasibility of the plans also appear. Chernovsky was imprisoned in the Petropavlovsk and Schlüsselburg fortresses at this time, but no reason for his imprisonment is given.

104 (1941): 258

CONTENTS OF THE ISSUES OF THE JOURNAL *Krasnyi Arkhiv* FOR 1940

This is a table of contents for *Krasnyi Arkhiv*, Volumes 98–104.

VOLUME 105, 1941

105 (1941): 3–32

ARCHIVAL MATERIALS ON THE REVOLUTIONARY ACTIVITIES OF J. V. STALIN 1908–1913.

These documents, most of them published for the first time in this volume, cover the period of Stalin's exile in Vologoda province in 1908, his term in the Viatka prison in 1909, his return to Baku, and his exile to Tomsk in 1912. They are primarily police reports on the surveillance of Stalin in Baku, Kutais, Tiflis, Vologoda, Moscow, St. Petersburg, and Tomsk, but there is also a proclamation of the Baku Social Democratic committee, September 29, 1909, on committee activities.

105 (1941): 33–70

THE PERSIAN REVOLUTION 1905–1911 AND BOLSHEVIKS OF TRANSCAUCASIA. Introduction by E. Bor-Ramensky.

The first six of the twenty-three documents presented here are accounts of the Persian Revolution as they appeared in Georgian newspapers and as they were appraised by the Social Democratic committees in Tiflis and Baku. The next two documents present the program of the Mussulman

Social Democratic party, and two others give the program of the Persian revolutionary "bourgeois" organization *Mudzhakhid*. The final thirteen documents are tsarist officials' reports on the repercussions of Persian affairs in the Caucasus.

105 (1941): 71–98

MATERIALS RELATING TO THE HISTORY OF THE RIGHT-BANK UKRAINIAN PEASANTRY'S STRUGGLE AGAINST THE CENTRAL COUNCIL (UKRAINIAN POPULAR ASSEMBLY) AND THE PROVISIONAL GOVERNMENT IN 1917. Introduction by M. Osetrov.

The documents published here are the reports of government officials and copies of revolutionary propaganda. The first twenty-seven, dated from July 12, 1917, to March 6, 1918, provide information on the agrarian movement in Podolia and Volhynia provinces after the February Revolution of 1917. The last fifteen, dated from May 8, 1917, to February 26, 1918, deal with the agrarian movement in Kiev province.

105 (1941): 99–114

AT A GREAT GRAVE (Revolutionary Feelings among the Ukrainian Peasantry in Connection with T. G. Shevchenko's Death). Introduction by A. Yurchenko and A. Grinberg.

Taras Grigorievich Shevchenko died on February 26/March 10, 1861. The nineteen documents published here, dated from May 8 to August 8, 1861, are reports from Kiev officials on the restlessness among the peasants after Shevchenko's death and on the speeches made at his grave in the Ukraine.

For additional material in *Krasnyi Arkhiv* on Shevchenko, see: "The Suppression by Tsarism of the Honoring of T. Shevchenko's Memory," 76 (1936): 226–230; "The Struggle of the Tsarist Government and Censorship with T. G. Shevchenko's 'Kobzar,'" 91 (1938): 255–270.

105 (1941): 115–139

MATERIALS RELATING TO THE BIOGRAPHY OF SHAMIL. Introduction by S. Bushuev.

Bushuev states that since much has been written about Shamil's early career, but little about his life after he was taken by the Russians in 1859, these documents on the period from 1859 to 1871 are of great importance. Shamil succeeded in uniting the northern Caucasian tribes but was defeated by tsarist troops after the Crimean War. His capture marked the end of the Caucasian wars. After his capture he was assigned a residence at Kaluga; in 1861 he went to St. Petersburg to meet Alexander II; in 1868 he moved to Kiev; in 1869 the government granted him permission to go to Mecca; he died in Medina in 1871. The twenty-six documents published here are reports on the constant surveillance maintained over him in Kaluga, Kiev, Mecca, and Medina.

105 (1941): 140–155

TSARISM'S STRUGGLE WITH THE REVOLUTIONARY PRESS IN 1905. Introduction by I. Kovalev.

The thirteen documents printed here are dated from January, 1905, to June, 1907. Among them are three circulars of the Central Press Department to editors of noncensored periodicals and three reports by Minister of Internal Affairs A. G. Bulygin to Nicholas II on the revolutionary press. Included also are communiqués from the governor general of St. Petersburg and the governor of Vitebsk. A journal of a special meeting of the Council of Ministers and a report by Count S. Y. Witte discuss the legal aspects of propaganda. There is also a Press Department order to review all revolutionary literature in schools and libraries, as well as a Post Office and Telegraph Department order to intercept antigovernment literature.

For additional material in *Krasnyi Arkhiv*, see "Restrictions Imposed upon the Revolutionary Activities of the City and Provincial Press during 1906," 2 (1922): 280; "A Memorandum on the Labor Press of Petrograd," 10 (1925): 286–299.

105 (1941): 156–167

NEW MATERIALS ON M. E. SALTYKOV-SHCHEDRIN. Introduction by G. Zalkind.

These documents are divided into the following groups: (1) letters of M. E. Saltykov-Shchedrin to F. A. Vonliarsky in 1867, to V. V. Grigoriev in 1877, 1878, and 1879, and to A. N. Erakov in 1879 and 1885; (2) material on M. E. Saltykov-Shchedrin and on tsarist censorship, in 1876 and 1878, of the journal *Otechestvennye Zapiski* ("Notes of the Fatherland"); (3) letters written in 1857 by a contemporary, Michael Aleksandrovich Dmitriev, giving a description of M. E. Saltykov-Shchedrin. There is also a photograph of Saltykov-Shchedrin and a photostatic copy of one of his letters.

For references to additional material in *Krasnyi Arkhiv*, see the notes to "M. E. Saltykov-Shchedrin as Inspector General," 83 (1937): 160–183.

FROM AN ARCHIVIST'S NOTEBOOK

105 (1941): 168–178

MATERIALS RELATING TO THE HISTORY OF THE MOSCOW BOLSHEVIK LABOR PRESS IN THE YEARS OF REVOLUTIONARY UPHEAVAL (1913–1914). Introduction by E. Osokin.

These documents deal with confiscation of issues of the Bolshevik journals *Nash Put* ("Our Path") and *Rabochii Trud* ("Working Labor"), published in Moscow.

For additional material in *Krasnyi Arkhiv*, see: "The Socialist Press during the Imperialistic War," 2 (1922): 200–225; "The Struggle for a Labor Press on the Eve of the World War," 64 (1934): 139–143.

VOLUME 106, 1941

106 (1941): 3–39

MATERIALS RELATING TO THE THIRTY-FIFTH ANNIVERSARY OF THE FOURTH (UNIFYING) CONGRESS OF THE RSDLP. Introduction by E. Yaroslavsky.

Yaroslavsky writes that the Fourth Congress of the RSDLP (Russian Social Democratic Labor party), which opened in Stockholm on April 23, 1906, attempted to unite the Bolsheviks and Mensheviks on the issue of the role of the proletariat in the Revolution.

The documents printed here are grouped under two headings. Part I, entitled "Party Organizations in the Period of Preparations for the Congress and after the Congress," contains twenty-three documents, dated from February to September, 1906. They are pamphlets, reports of meetings, and letters from Social Democratic groups in Riga, Perm, St. Petersburg, Kharkov, Moscow, Tula, Odessa, and Kazan.

In Part II, entitled "The Police Department concerning the Fourth Congress of the Russian Social Democratic Labor Party," are thirty-one documents, dated from February to October, 1906. These are secret reports from all over Russia on the departure of delegates to the congress, as well as reports on the congress itself.

106 (1941): 40–57

AGITATION OF PEASANTS ON THE ESTATES IN GEORGIA BELONGING TO THE IMPERIAL FAMILY 1905–1906. Introduction by V. Evfimovsky.

Dated from March, 1905, to July, 1906, the letters, reports, and peasants' petitions presented here reveal agitation in Georgia on the Kakhetinsk,

Kartalinsk, and Chakhvinsk estates that were owned by the Romanov family.

For references to additional material in *Krasnyi Arkhiv*, see the notes to "S. Y. Witte's Struggle with the Agrarian Revolution," 31 (1928): 81–102 and to "The Struggle with the Revolutionary Movement in the Caucasus in the Stolypin Era," 35 (1929): 128–150.

106 (1941): 58–78

PEASANT AGITATION IN KHARKOV PROVINCE (1861–1862). Introduction by Frenkel.

The twenty-two documents published here, dated from March, 1861, to September, 1862, describe peasant unrest in Kharkov province after the Emancipation Manifesto of February 19, 1861. The documents are composed of Gendarmerie reports, petitions from peasants, and landowners' reports.

For additional material in *Krasnyi Arkhiv*, see "Materials Relating to the History of the Peasant Uprising against Liberation in 1861," 36 (1929): 201–204.

106 (1941): 79–119

MATERIALS ON THE HISTORY OF SERICULTURE IN RUSSIA. Introduction by A. Chernov.

This is a survey of 150 years of sericulture in Russia compiled by order of Nicholas I. It reviews ancient sericulture in Rome, Greece, Spain, France, Austria, and Bavaria and sericulture in Russia before the reign of Peter the Great. A more detailed account of the industry in Russia after Peter the Great is given, with statistics on production from 1798 to 1837.

106 (1941): 120–146

ENGLAND IN THE FACE OF NAPOLEON I'S INVASION (1801–1805). Introduction by A. Popov.

These documents indicate relations between England and France when England feared an invasion by Napoleon's forces. They include dispatches from S. R. Vorontsov, Russian minister in London; from Y. Smirnov, priest of the Russian church in London; and from Baron Nikolai, Russian chargé d'affaires in London. The location of the British navy, Britain's fear of French landings in northern Scotland and the Orkney Islands, and the defense measures adopted are revealed.

FROM AN ARCHIVIST'S NOTEBOOK

106 (1941): 147–156

NEW MATERIALS ON GLEB USPENSKY. Introduction by I. Gubkov.

Gubkov writes that the late-nineteenth-century Russian writer Gleb Ivanovich Uspensky was under police surveillance from 1873 until his death in 1902 in a psychiatric hospital near St. Petersburg. Part I of this material contains nineteen reports of surveillance from 1877 to 1883, while Uspensky was living in Novgorod province. Part II contains Police Department reports on his activities and whereabouts from 1882 to 1900.

106 (1941): 156–159

MATERIALS RELATING TO THE BIOGRAPHY OF KOSTA KHETAGUROV. Introduction unsigned.

Creator of Ossetian literary language and poetry, artist, and ardent nationalist, Kosta Levanovich Khetagurov was in 1899 ordered confined to quarters in Kursk province for a period of five years. (The place of confinement was later changed to Kherson.) He died on April 1, 1906, at the age of forty-seven. The government reports and personal papers of Khetagurov published here are dated from 1898 to 1916 and deal with arrangements for his exile, his move from Kursk to Kherson, and the commemoration of the tenth anniversary of his death.

106 (1941): 160–164

LETTERS OF A. V. SUVOROV. Introduction by G. Nikolskaia.

Nikolskaia states that most of these letters are published here for the first time. In 1796 Count A. V. Suvorov was appointed commander of the Russian army in Novorossiia and chose Tulchin as his general headquarters. Presented here are two of his letters to a relative, Dmitry Ivanovich Khvostov; they were written in Warsaw in March, 1795, when he was commander of Russian forces there. Also presented are nine letters written in Tulchin in 1796 and 1797 to Khvostov and one to Count V. A. Zubov, who served as a major general in the Polish War of 1794.

For additional material in *Krasnyi Arkhiv*, see "The Polish War of 1794 in Reports and Accounts of A. V. Suvorov," 101 (1940): 149–196.

CRITIQUE AND BIBLIOGRAPHY

106 (1941): 165–173

THE OFFENSIVE ON THE SOUTHWESTERN FRONT IN MAY AND JUNE, 1916

Presented here is a review by Professor N. Korobkov of a collection of documents from the Central Government Military-Historical Archive. They were published in book form in Moscow in 1940, under the title *Sbornik Dokumentov, Tsentralnyi Gosudarstvennyi Voenno-Istoricheskii Arkhiv* ("Collection of Documents, the Central Government Military-Historical Archive").

106 (1941): 173–176

A VALUABLE CONTRIBUTION TO THE HISTORY AND THEORY OF SOVIET MILITARY SCIENCE

A review by F. Yugin and N. Fironov of the book *M. V. Frunze na Frontakh Grazhdanskoi Voiny* ("M. V. Frunze at the Fronts of the Civil War") is given here. The documents appearing in the first two sections of the book were first published in *Krasnyi Arkhiv*, 93 (1939): 3–50.

APPENDIX

TITLES OF ARTICLES IN *KRASNYI ARKHIV*, VOLUMES 1–30,
AS THEY APPEAR IN PART I OF THE *DIGEST* (1947)

(The italic number in parentheses at the end of each entry
is the page number in Part I of the *Digest* [1947 ed.]. If
a new edition of Part I should appear, these numbers would
of course no longer be applicable.)

	VOLUME AND PAGE
By the Editorial Board	1 (1922): 1–2 (*1*)
Russo-German Relations	1 (1922): 3–208 (*1*)
V. A. Sukhomlinov's Correspondence with N. N. Yanushkevich	1 (1922): 209–272 (*5*)
P. G. Zaichnevsky	1 (1922): 273–279 (*7*)
The Ceremony at the Public Execution of S. G. Nechaev	1 (1922): 280–281 (*7*)
The History of the "Narodnoe Pravo"	1 (1922): 282–288 (*7*)
New Data on Zubatovism	1 (1922): 289–328 (*8*)
The History of Punitive Expeditions to Siberia (1905–1906)	1 (1922): 329–343 (*8*)
The Correspondence of Lieutenant Shmidt	1 (1922): 344–354 (*9*)
N. A. Nekrasov and the Censorship	1 (1922): 355–360 (*9*)
Report of the Censor Ratninsky on the Obituary of N. A. Nekrasov, Written for the Second Volume of "Russian Antiquities," 1878	1 (1922): 361 (*10*)
Unpublished Correspondence of N. A. Nekrasov	1 (1922): 362–366 (*10*)
Dostoevsky on the Commemoration of Pushkin in the 1880's	1 (1922): 367–405 (*10*)
The Poems of P. M. Rozengeim and A. A. Golenishchev-Kutuzov, Suppressed by the Censors	1 (1922): 406–411 (*10*)
L. N. Tolstoy and the Censorship	1 (1922): 412–416 (*11*)
Alexander III on Leo Tolstoy	1 (1922): 417 (*11*)
A Contribution to the Biography of V. G. Korolenko	1 (1922): 418–419 (*11*)
A Censor's Report on the Stories of V. G. Korolenko	1 (1922): 420–421 (*11*)
Bibliography	1 (1922): 422–438 (*11*)

	VOLUME AND PAGE
Supplement	1 (1922): 439–452 (*12*)
The Diary of A. N. Kuropatkin	2 (1922): 5–117 (*13*)
Four Letters from Prince Wilhelm of Prussia to Alexander III	2 (1922): 118–129 (*16*)
V. A. Sukhomlinov's Correspondence with N. N. Yanushkevich (Continuation)	2 (1922): 130–175 (*17*)
A Contribution to the History of the Working Class in Russia (1835–1869)	2 (1922): 176–199 (*18*)
The Socialist Press during the Imperialistic War	2 (1922): 200–225 (*19*)
An Unpublished Fairy Tale of M. E. Saltykov-Shchedrin: *The Valiant Knight*	2 (1922): 226–228 (*19*)
M. E. Saltykov-Shchedrin and the Censorship	2 (1922): 229–233 (*19*)
F. M. Dostoevsky's Letter from the Fortress	2 (1922): 234–239 (*20*)
Dostoevsky and Pobedonostsev	2 (1922): 240–255 (*20*)
I. A. Goncharov's Unpublished Letters	2 (1922): 256–262 (*20*)
I. A. Goncharov's Letters to P. A. Viazemsky	2 (1922): 263–267 (*21*)
Mickiewicz's Opinion of Polish Writers	2 (1922): 268–279 (*21*)
Restrictions Imposed upon the Revolutionary Activities of the City and Provincial Press during 1906	2 (1922): 280 (*21*)
S. V. Zubatov's Letter to A. I. Spiridovich on the Publication of "The Social-Revolutionary Party and Its Predecessors"	2 (1922): 281–283 (*21*)
General Alexeev and the Provisional Committee of the State Duma	2 (1922): 284–286 (*22*)
Correspondence regarding the Bribery of the Chinese Officials, Li-Hung-Chang and Chang Yin-Hwan	2 (1922): 287–293 (*22*)
Reports of S. D. Sazonov, Minister of Foreign Affairs, to Nicholas II, 1910–1912	3 (1923): 5–28 (*25*)
V. A. Sukhomlinov's Correspondence with N. N. Yanushkevich (Conclusion)	3 (1923): 29–74 (*25*)
The Diary of A. A. Polovtsev	3 (1923): 75–172 (*27*)
M. A. Bakunin before the Austrian Court	3 (1923): 173–198 (*27*)
M. A. Bakunin. From Reports of the Third Department	3 (1923): 199–206 (*27*)
Towards a Biography of N. O. Ogarev	3 (1923): 207–217 (*28*)
Documents concerning P. L. Lavrov	3 (1923): 218–222 (*28*)
A. I. Herzen and the Censorship of the 1890's	3 (1923): 223–228 (*28*)
N. V. Shelgunov's Proclamation "Greetings to Russian Soldiers from Their Well-Wishers"	3 (1923): 229–239 (*29*)
"The Cause of the Fires"	3 (1923): 240–242 (*29*)
S. L. Perovskaia's Unpublished Letters (1872–1873)	3 (1923): 243–250 (*29*)
Reminiscences of A. G. Dostoevskaia	3 (1923): 251–290 (*30*)
The Testament of Nicholas I to His Son	3 (1923): 291–293 (*30*)

Titles of Articles in Volumes 1–30   211

VOLUME AND PAGE

The Third Department and the Crimean War	3 (1923): 293–294 (*30*)
About the Peasant P. A. Martianov	3 (1923): 294–298 (*30*)
A Contribution to the Biographies of N. G. and O. S. Chernyshevsky	3 (1923): 298–299 (*31*)
Karakozov's Trial	3 (1923): 299–301 (*31*)
The Fate of a Certain Parody by Dostoevsky	3 (1923): 301–303 (*31*)
Balzac in Russia	3 (1923): 303–307 (*31*)
Goethe's Letters	3 (1923): 307–309 (*31*)
N. V. Gogol's Letter to V. G. Belinsky	3 (1923): 309–312 (*32*)
Reviews	3 (1923): 313–317 (*32*)
Annotations to the "Reports of S. D. Sazonov"	3 (1923): 318–319 (*32*)
Annotations to the "Diary of A. A. Polovtsev"	3 (1923): 319–326 (*32*)
Annotations to "M. A. Bakunin, from Reports of the Third Department"	3 (1923): 326–327 (*32*)
The Beginning of the War of 1914. Diary of the Ministry of Foreign Affairs	4 (1923): 5–62 (*33*)
The Diary of A. A. Polovtsev (1905)	4 (1923): 63–128 (*33*)
The Correspondence between V. N. Kokovtsov and Eduard Netzlin	4 (1923): 131–156 (*34*)
The Family Correspondence of the Romanovs	4 (1923): 157–221 (*34*)
S. G. Nechaev at the Alexeev Ravelin (1873–1882) ..	4 (1923): 222–272 (*35*)
The Polish Uprising of 1863 and Its Repercussions in Central Russia	4 (1923): 273–307 (*35*)
A Report by the Censor Matveev concerning the Destruction of Copies of a Marxist Publication ..	4 (1923): 308–316 (*36*)
K. P. Pobedonostsev's Letters to Alexander III	4 (1923): 317–337 (*36*)
Documents Relating to L. N. Tolstoy	4 (1923): 338–364 (*36*)
Two Letters from F. M. Dostoevsky to M. N. Katkov	4 (1923): 365–375 (*37*)
Two Letters from I. A. Goncharov to K. N. and P. I. Poset	4 (1923): 376–382 (*37*)
Letters of F. I. Tiutchev	4 (1923): 383–392 (*37*)
M. E. Saltykov-Shchedrin's Unpublished Magazine, "Russkaya Pravda"	4 (1923): 393–398 (*37*)
F. M. Dostoevsky's Sojourn in the City of Tver	4 (1923): 398–401 (*38*)
The Strike of the Bondaged Textile Workers	4 (1923): 401–405 (*38*)
In the 1850's	4 (1923): 405–407 (*38*)
The Funeral Oration of A. P. Shchapov over the Peasants Killed at Bezdna	4 (1923): 407–410 (*38*)
Letter of Y. V. Stefanovich to V. K. Plehve, Minister of the Interior	4 (1923): 410–411 (*39*)
The History of the Manifesto of October 17th	4 (1923): 411–417 (*39*)
The Revolutionary Movement in the Army during the World War	4 (1923): 417–424 (*39*)
The Assassination of Gregory Rasputin	4 (1923): 424–426 (*39*)
On the History of Painting in Russia	4 (1923): 426–433 (*40*)

	VOLUME AND PAGE
Appendix	4 (1923): 434–451 (*40*)
From the Editorial Board	4 (1923): 451 (*40*)
V. I. Lenin's Autographs	5 (1924): i–xv (*41*)
The Russo-German Agreement of 1905, Concluded at Björkö	5 (1924): 5–49 (*41*)
The Financial Conferences of the Allies during the World War	5 (1924): 50–81 (*43*)
The Diary of A. N. Kuropatkin (Continuation)	5 (1924): 82–101 (*44*)
The Correspondence between Nicholas II and P. A. Stolypin	5 (1924): 102–128 (*44*)
Letters Written by the Defendants in the Trial of the 193	5 (1924): 129–163 (*45*)
I. N. Myshkin's Letter to His Brother, Written in the Yakutsk Prison	5 (1924): 164–171 (*45*)
S. G. Nechaev at the Alexeev Ravelin (Continuation)	5 (1924): 172–212 (*45*)
The Supreme Command during the First Days of the Revolution	5 (1924): 213–240 (*46*)
From the Correspondence of Nicholas I in December 1825	5 (1924): 241–247 (*46*)
D. I. Pisarev's Letters from the Fortress	5 (1924): 248–257 (*47*)
Two Letters by P. E. Yakubovich	5 (1924): 258–262 (*47*)
G. V. Plekhanov and the "Amusements of the Spies"	5 (1924): 263–266 (*47*)
The Execution of Lieutenant Shmidt, Chastnik and Others	5 (1924): 266–267 (*47*)
V. Chernov and the July Days	5 (1924): 268–270 (*48*)
Rasputin as Described by the Secret Police	5 (1924): 270–288 (*48*)
Portsmouth Correspondence of S. Y. Witte and Others	6 (1924): 3–47 (*49*)
Constantinople and the Straits	6 (1924): 48–76 (*50*)
S. G. Nechaev in the Alexeev Ravelin (Conclusion)	6 (1924): 77–123 (*51*)
From the Archive of L. Tikhomirov	6 (1924): 124–194 (*52*)
The Provisional Government after the October Revolution	6 (1924): 195–221 (*52*)
Notes of Nicholas I on December 14, 1825	6 (1924): 222–234 (*54*)
Three Letters from L. N. Tolstoy to the Decembrist P. N. Svistunov	6 (1924): 235–242 (*54*)
L. N. Tolstoy and the Relief of Famine Victims	6 (1924): 243–252 (*54*)
Two Letters Written by Karl Marx	6 (1924): 253–256 (*55*)
The Suppressed Poems of Anna P. Barikova	6 (1924): 256–259 (*55*)
The Iconography of the Decembrists	6 (1924): 260 (*55*)
Workers' Address to N. V. Shelgunov (May 1, 1891)	6 (1924): 260–261 (*55*)
Portsmouth (Conclusion)	7 (1924): 3–31 (*56*)

Titles of Articles in Volumes 1–30   213

	VOLUME AND PAGE
Constantinople and the Straits (Conclusion)	7 (1924): 32–54 (*56*)
From the Diary of A. N. Kuropatkin	7 (1924): 55–69 (*59*)
An Autobiographic Note by Stepan Shiraev	7 (1924): 70–107 (*61*)
Michael Bakunin and the Expedition of the Ship "Ward Jackson"	7 (1924): 108–145 (*61*)
"Crime and Punishment"	7 (1924): 146–200 (*62*)
The Events in Omsk and Kolchak	7 (1924): 201–246 (*62*)
The Unpublished "Manifesto" of the Executive Committee of the "Narodnaia Volia"	7 (1924): 247–249 (*63*)
Unpublished Letters of L. N. Tolstoy to V. A. and K. A. Islavin Rachinsky and Others	7 (1924): 250–252 (*63*)
A Serf of 1837 and His Constitutional Aspirations ..	7 (1924): 253–254 (*64*)
Y. P. Polonsky's Poem *A Plain Story* and the Correspondence concerning his drama *Daredzhana, The Empress of Imeretinsk*	7 (1924): 254–256 (*64*)
A Glossary to Volumes 1–4 of the *Krasnyi Arkhiv* ..	7 (1924): i–xxvii (*64*)
The Diplomatic Preparations of the Balkan War, 1912	8 (1925): 3–48 (*65*)
The Notes of A. S. Ermolov	8 (1925): 49–69 (*68*)
From the Diary of A. N. Kuropatkin (Continuation)	8 (1925): 70–100 (*70*)
The Correspondence between Alexander III and Count M. T. Loris-Melikov (1880–1881)	8 (1925): 101–131 (*71*)
On the History of Loris-Melikov's "Constitution" ..	8 (1925): 132–152 (*71*)
The October Revolution and the Stavka	8 (1925): 153–175 (*73*)
The Omsk Events and Kolchak (Conclusion)	8 (1925): 176–192 (*73*)
The Ukases of E. I. Pugachev and His Staff	8 (1925): 193–206 (*74*)
The Literature of the 1860's as Reflected in the Reports of the Third Department	8 (1925): 207–232 (*74*)
F. M. Reshetnikov and the *Severnaia Pchela*	8 (1925): 233–236 (*75*)
A. P. Chekhov's Unpublished Story *Should I Speak or Keep Silent?*	8 (1925): 237–239 (*75*)
The Revolution of 1848 and French Subjects in Moscow	8 (1925): 240–241 (*75*)
During the Years of Reaction	8 (1925): 242–243 (*75*)
V. G. Korolenko's Letter to S. F. Sharapov	8 (1925): 243–244 (*76*)
Nicholas II from February 28 to March 4, 1917	8 (1925): 244–245 (*76*)
The Question of Pensions under the Provisional Government	8 (1925): 246–250 (*76*)
The Execution of Afanasy Matushenko	8 (1925): 250–254 (*76*)
Diplomatic Preparations of the Balkan War of 1912 (Conclusion)	9 (1925): 3–31 (*78*)
The Events of 1905 as Reflected Abroad	9 (1925): 32–55 (*79*)
Wilhelm II concerning the Russo-Japanese War and the Revolution of 1905	9 (1925): 56–65 (*80*)

	VOLUME AND PAGE
Peasant Unrest during 1905	9 (1925): 66–93 (*80*)
The Disturbances in the Fleet in 1915	9 (1925): 94–103 (*80*)
From the Diary of General V. I. Selivachev	9 (1925): 104–132 (*81*)
The Testimony of A. D. Protopopov	9 (1925): 133–155 (*83*)
The October Revolution and the Stavka (Conclusion)	9 (1925): 156–170 (*84*)
Around "Gatchina"	9 (1925): 171–194 (*84*)
A Paper by A. K. Boshniak	9 (1925): 195–225 (*85*)
The Marxist Periodical Press from 1896 to 1906	9 (1925): 226–268 (*86*)
"A Plan to Assassinate Wilhelm II"	9 (1925): 269–285 (*86*)
The Trisection of an Angle	9 (1925): 286–290 (*87*)
I. Balashev's Letter to P. A. Stolypin	9 (1925): 291–294 (*87*)
Gapon's Letter	9 (1925): 294–297 (*87*)
A Police Agent Writes of the Arrest of the Participants in the Attempted Assassination on March 1, 1887	9 (1925): 297–300 (*88*)
N. V. Gogol's Funeral	9 (1925): 300–303 (*88*)
Kokovtsov's Negotiations concerning the Loan of 1905–1906	10 (1925): 3–35 (*90*)
S. Y. Witte, the French Press and the Russian Loans	10 (1925): 36–40 (*91*)
Concerning the Annexation of Bosnia and Herzegovina	10 (1925): 41–53 (*92*)
The Anglo-Russian Treaty of 1907 and the Partition of Afghanistan	10 (1925): 54–66 (*93*)
Russia's Economic Status before the Revolution	10 (1925): 67–94 (*94*)
Minutes of Sessions of the Central Executive Committees of the Social Revolutionaries and the Social-Democrats of the First Assembly Held after the October Revolution	10 (1925): 95–137 (*95*)
From the Diary of General V. I. Selivachev (Conclusion)	10 (1925): 138–174 (*96*)
From the Diary of A. D. Protopopov	10 (1925): 175–183 (*97*)
M. V. Butashevich-Petrashevsky in Siberia	10 (1925): 184–216 (*98*)
From the Diary of Grand Duke Constantine Nikolaevich	10 (1925): 217–260 (*98*)
December 14, 1825 as Reflected in the Letters of Countess Maria D. Nesselrode	10 (1925): 261–285 (*99*)
A Memorandum on the Labor Press of Petrograd	10 (1925): 286–299 (*99*)
Prince E. N. Trubetskoi's Letter to Nicholas II on the Dissolution of the First State Duma	10 (1925): 300–304 (*100*)
A Sketch of C. P. Romanov by Princess D. C. Lieven	10 (1925): 305–308 (*100*)
Korff's Polemics against Herzen	10 (1925): 308–317 (*100*)
A Decembrist's Poem	10 (1925): 317–319 (*101*)
A Decembrist's Song	10 (1925): 319–321 (*101*)

Titles of Articles in Volumes 1–30

VOLUME AND PAGE

Instructions to Officials of the Alexeev Ravelin in the St. Petersburg Fortress	10 (1925): 321–327 (*101*)
Gregory Goldenberg in the Peter and Paul Fortress	10 (1925): 328–331 (*101*)
The Reptile Fund of 1914–1916	10 (1925): 332–342 (*102*)
The Dismissal of N. N. Romanov as Commander-in-Chief	10 (1925): 342–343 (*102*)
Publications of the Central Archive Department of the R.S.F.S.R.	10 (1925): 344–345 (*102*)
Material on the History of the Uprising of December 14, 1825	10 (1925): 345 (*102*)
1917 Documents and Materials	10 (1925): 345 (*103*)
Material on the History of the Labor Movement in Russia	10 (1925): 345 (*103*)
Miscellaneous Publications	10 (1925): 346 (*103*)
V. I. Lenin's Autograph	11–12 (1925): iii (*104*)
The Beginning of the Proletarian Revolution in Russia	11–12 (1925): iv–xvi (*104*)
January 9, 1905	11–12 (1925): 1–26 (*104*)
The Draft of a Manifesto concerning the Events of January 9, 1905	11–12 (1925): 26–38 (*105*)
The Manifesto of October 17	11–12 (1925): 39–106 (*106*)
From S. Y. Witte's Archive	11–12 (1925): 107–143 (*109*)
S. Y. Witte's Reports to Nicholas II	11–12 (1925): 144–158 (*110*)
Records of the Armed Struggle	11–12 (1925): 159–181 (*111*)
The Agrarian Movement of 1905, Based on Reports of Dubasov and Panteleiev	11–12 (1925): 182–192 (*111*)
The Navy during 1905	11–12 (1925): 193–262 (*113*)
The Baltic Region during 1905	11–12 (1925): 263–288 (*113*)
The Unrest in the Far Eastern Army	11–12 (1925): 289–386 (*113*)
The Attack on Presni	11–12 (1925): 387–397 (*114*)
The Punitive Expedition of Colonel Riman	11–12 (1925): 398–420 (*114*)
The Loan of 1906	11–12 (1925): 421–432 (*114*)
Nicholas II and the Revolution of 1905	11–12 (1925): 433–439 (*115*)
Letters of Nicholas II to Dubasov	11–12 (1925): 440–442 (*115*)
Concerning the Murder of N. E. Bauman	11–12 (1925): 442–443 (*116*)
The Exploits of Baron Meller-Zakomelsky	11–12 (1925): 443–444 (*116*)
Documents on the History of January 9, 1905	11–12 (1925): 444–448 (*116*)
D. F. Trepov's Papers	11–12 (1925): 448–466 (*117*)
The Suicide of N. P. Shmidt	11–12 (1925): 467–471 (*118*)
Publications of the Central Archive Department of the R.S.F.S.R.	11–12 (1925): 472–474 (*118*)
Introduction	13 (1925): iii–viii (*119*)
The Uprising of the Chernigov Regiment	13 (1925): 1–67 (*119*)
N. I. Turgenev's Memorandum	13 (1925): 68–147 (*121*)
M. F. Orlov and December 14, 1825	13 (1925): 148–173 (*121*)

	VOLUME AND PAGE
"Practical Elements of Political Economy"	13 (1925): 174–249 (*122*)
The Decembrist I. D. Yakushkin's Plan to Free the Peasants	13 (1925): 250–257 (*123*)
The Conspiracy at the Zerentuisk Mine	13 (1925): 258–279 (*124*)
"A Constitution; the State's Testament," by P. I. Pestel	13 (1925): 280–284 (*125*)
I. Y. Teleshev's Account of December 14, 1825	13 (1925): 284–288 (*125*)
An Account of December 14, 1825 by Soldiers of the Moscow Regiment	13 (1925): 288–292 (*126*)
The Execution of the Navy Decembrists	13 (1925): 292–297 (*126*)
Some Letters and Notes of V. F. Raevsky	13 (1925): 297–314 (*127*)
Concerning the Horse on Which Nicholas I Rode While Dispersing the Decembrists	13 (1925): 314 (*127*)
The Calendar of 1827	13 (1925): 314–320 (*127*)
P. I. Pestel's Will	13 (1925): 320 (*128*)
Publications of the Central Archive Department of the R.S.F.S.R.	13 (1925): 321–322 (*128*)
Documents and Research Studies on the History of the Decembrist Uprising	13 (1925): 322–323 (*128*)
Publications on the History of the Labor Movement in Russia	13 (1925): 323–324 (*128*)
Miscellaneous Publications	13 (1925): 323–324 (*128*)
The Boxer Rebellion	14 (1926): 1–49 (*129*)
M. A. Bakunin in the 1840's	14 (1926): 50–83 (*138*)
N. G. Chernyshevsky as Reported by the Agents of the Third Department (1861–1862)	14 (1926): 84–127 (*140*)
An Article by N. V. Shelgunov, Suppressed by Censors	14 (1926): 128–147 (*141*)
The Unsuccessful Provocation	14 (1926): 148–158 (*142*)
An Autobiographic Statement by A. A. Kviatkovsky	14 (1926): 159–175 (*142*)
A Letter by A. I. Barannikov	14 (1926): 176–181 (*144*)
The Agrarian Uprisings in 1917. From Documents of the Central Land Committee	14 (1926): 182–226: (*144*)
The Last Days of the Tsarist Regime (1916–1917)	14 (1926): 227–249 (*145*)
A. I. Ertel's Letter on the Murder of Sidoratsky, March 31, 1878	14 (1926): 250–252 (*146*)
Moscow during the Events of March, 1881	14 (1926): 252–257 (*147*)
The Reaction of Moscow Business Men to the Anti-Semitic Disorders of 1881	14 (1926): 258–260 (*147*)
Alexander III and General Boulanger	14 (1926) 260–262 (*149*)
On the History of the Manifesto of August 6, 1905	14 (1926): 262–270 (*151*)
The Necromancer Peren and a Russian Minister	14 (1926): 270–278 (*151*)
The First Balkan War	15 (1926): 1–29 (*153*)
March–May, 1917	15 (1926): 30–60 (*157*)
The February Revolution and European Socialists	15 (1926): 61–85 (*159*)

	VOLUME AND PAGE
Lekert's Attempt to Assassinate von Vile	15 (1926): 86–103 (*163*)
From Shcheglovitov's Archives	15 (1926): 104–117 (*164*)
Documents on the History of the Populist Movement	15 (1926): 118–149 (*165*)
New Material on S. G. Nechaev (Conclusion)	15 (1926): 150–163 (*166*)
The Financial Situation of the Decembrists	15 (1926): 164–213 (*167*)
The Government's Frame of Mind during the Epoch of the First State Duma	15 (1926): 214 (*167*)
The Agrarian Measures of 1906	15 (1926): 214–216 (*168*)
N. N. Levashov's Letters to A. N. Kuropatkin	15 (1926): 216–222 (*168*)
On the History of A. I. Ulianov's Attempt to Assassinate Alexander III	15 (1926): 222–223 (*169*)
The Visit of Viviani and Albert Thomas to Russia	15 (1926): 223–229 (*169*)
The Attempt of Nicholas II to Censor Tolstoy's Works	15 (1926): 230–234 (*170*)
Dobroliubov's Unpublished Articles	15 (1926): 234–240 (*170*)
F. E. Dzerzhinsky: From Archival Sources	16 (1926): i–xx (*171*)
The First Balkan War (Conclusion)	16 (1926): 3–24 (*171*)
The February Revolution and the European Socialists (Conclusion)	16 (1926): 25–43 (*175*)
The Romanovs and the Allies during the First Days of the Revolution	16 (1926): 44–52 (*175*)
The Uprising of the Kirghiz in 1916	16 (1926): 53–75 (*176*)
The Arrest and Trial of the Social Democratic Faction in the Second State Duma	16 (1926): 76–117 (*177*)
The Year 1861, from Notes of a Contemporary	16 (1926): 118–164 (*177*)
P. I. Pestel, from Letters of His Parents	16 (1926): 165–188 (*178*)
Reflections on the Decembrists' Uprising of 1825	16 (1926): 189–204 (*178*)
Localizing the Celebration of May First in Factories and Mills	16 (1926): 205–209 (*179*)
The Economic Prospects of a Franco-Russian Alliance after the World War	16 (1926): 210–218 (*180*)
General A. M. Stoessel's Letter to General V. G. Glazov concerning the Beginning of the Russo-Japanese War	16 (1926): 218–220 (*181*)
The Revolution of 1905–1906 as Reported by Foreign Diplomats	16 (1926): 220–224 (*182*)
A Project of F. M. Dostoevsky	16 (1926): 224–228 (*182*)
The Executions at Lisii Nos during the Years of Reaction	16 (1926): 228–237 (*183*)
Publications of the Central Archive Department of the R.S.F.S.R.	16 (1926): Appendix (*184*)
Materials and Studies on the History of the Decembrist Uprising	16 (1926): Appendix (*187*)
Materials on the History of the Labor Movement in Russia	16 (1926): Appendix (*188*)

218 *A Digest of the Krasnyi Arkhiv*

	VOLUME AND PAGE
Other Publications	16 (1926): Appendix (*188*)
The Political Situation in Russia before the February Revolution as Reported by the Gendarmery	17 (1926): 3–35 (*190*)
Revolutionary Propaganda in the Army during 1916–1917	17 (1926): 36–50 (*191*)
P. L. Bark's Report to Nicholas II on the Budget for 1917	17 (1926): 51–69 (*191*)
Bezobrazov's Circle in the Summer of 1904	17 (1926): 70–80 (*192*)
On the History of Stolypin's Agrarian Reforms	17 (1926): 81–90 (*193*)
Karakozov's Attempt of April 4, 1866	17 (1926): 91–137 (*193*)
New Material on M. A. Bakunin	17 (1926): 138–155 (*194*)
Repercussions of the Decembrist Uprising of 1825 (Conclusion)	17 (1926): 156–173 (*195*)
Nicholas I and His Chief of Staff at the Time of the Execution of the Decembrists	17 (1926): 174–181 (*196*)
The Demonstration at the Funeral of the Peasants Killed at Bezdna, Kazan Province, in 1861	17 (1926): 181–185 (*196*)
A Letter by Franz Yatsevich	17 (1926): 185–186 (*197*)
The Berlin Reports of S. S. Tatishchev to V. K. Plehve in 1904	17 (1926): 186–192 (*197*)
E. Mednikov's Letters to Spiridovich	17 (1926): 192–219 (*197*)
From the Correspondence of Nicholas II with Grand Duke V. A. Romanov	17 (1926): 219–222 (*198*)
To Shoot or to Hang?	17 (1926): 222–225 (*199*)
General Ivanov's Expedition to Petrograd	17 (1926): 225–232 (*199*)
Tsarist Diplomacy on Russia's Tasks in the East in 1900	18 (1926): 3–29 (*201*)
S. Y. Witte's Letters to D. S. Sipiagin, 1900–1901	18 (1926): 30–48 (*202*)
The Chinese Revolution of 1911	18 (1926): 49–104 (*204*)
The Jassy Conference	18 (1926): 105–118 (*205*)
Produgol (The Question of Finance Capital in Russia)	18 (1926): 119–148 (*206*)
Autobiographical Statements of M. F. Grachevsky	18 (1926): 149–162 (*207*)
The Marxist Periodical Press during 1896–1906 (Conclusion)	18 (1926): 163–194 (*207*)
A. I. Zheliabov at Alexandrovsk	18 (1926): 195–197 (*209*)
The First Shipment of the Literature of the Group "Osvobozhdenie Truda"	18 (1926): 197–201 (*210*)
V. K. Plehve's Letter to A. A. Kireev	18 (1926): 201–203 (*210*)
From Drafts of Notes by K. P. Pobedonostsev	18 (1926): 203–207 (*211*)
A Note Worthy of Attention	18 (1926): 207–214 (*211*)
The All-Russian Central Executive Committee during the July Days of 1917	18 (1926): 214–219 (*212*)
A Summary of the Lessons of 1905 Drawn up by the Police Department	18 (1926): 219–227 (*214*)

Titles of Articles in Volumes 1–30

	VOLUME AND PAGE
French Intervention in South Russia (December 1918—April 1919)	19 (1926): 3–38 (*215*)
The British in the North (1918–1919)	19 (1926): 39–52 (*218*)
England's Politics in India and Russian-Indian Relations during 1897–1905	19 (1926): 53–63 (*220*)
S. Y. Witte's Correspondence with A. N. Kuropatkin during 1904–1905	19 (1926): 64–82 (*220*)
The Diary of G. O. Raukh (1905–1906)	19 (1926): 83–109 (*220*)
F. A. Golovin's Memoirs	19 (1926): 110–149 (*221*)
A. P. Shchapov's Letter to Alexander II in 1861	19 (1926): 150–165 (*221*)
"The Land and Freedom" Party in the 1870's	19 (1926): 166–177 (*222*)
N. I. Rysakov's Testimony	19 (1926): 178–194 (*222*)
From the Correspondence of S. M. Kravchinsky	19 (1926): 195–202 (*222*)
The Report of the Destruction of the Printing Shop on Sapernyi Street	19 (1926): 202–203 (*223*)
Speeches Made in Odessa on the First of May 1895	19 (1926): 203–207 (*223*)
The Reply of the *Rabochaia Gazeta* to G. V. Plekhanov	19 (1926): 207–209 (*224*)
Two Documents Relating to the History of Zubatovism	19 (1926): 210–211 (*224*)
Twenty Years Ago	19 (1926): 212–215 (*225*)
P. A. Stolypin and Capital Punishment during 1908	19 (1926): 215–221 (*225*)
The Diplomacy of the Provisional Government in Its Struggle against the Revolution	20 (1927): 3–38 (*226*)
The Conference of the Allies in Petrograd in 1917	20 (1927): 39–55 (*226*)
From the Diary of A. N. Kuropatkin	20 (1927): 56–77 (*227*)
Bokhara during 1917	20 (1927): 78–122 (*228*)
The Diary of Nicholas Romanov	20 (1927): 123–152 (*228*)
The Work of the Social-Revolutionary Party in 1918	20 (1927): 153–174 (*230*)
F. F. Marten's Report: "Europe and China"	20 (1927): 175–185 (*230*)
The Letters of G. F. Zdanovich	20 (1927): 186–204 (*231*)
From Documents of the "People's Will" Party	20 (1927): 205–231 (*231*)
Notes of a French Agent about the Russian Government in 1802 and 1803	20 (1927): 232–237 (*232*)
The Writers' Appeal to Nicholas II in 1895	20 (1927): 237–240 (*232*)
Trepov's Draft of Nicholas II's Speech to Workers on the Events of January 9, 1905	20 (1927): 240–242 (*233*)
The Program of "The Union of Russian People" Adopted Prior to the February Revolution	20 (1927): 242–244 (*234*)
The Revolution of February 1917	21 (1927): 3–78 (*235*)
The Diary of Nicholas Romanov (Continuation)	21 (1927): 79–96 (*240*)
The Alliance of Landowners in 1917	21 (1927): 97–121 (*241*)
The Democratic Government of Georgia and the English Command	21 (1927): 122–173 (*241*)

	VOLUME AND PAGE
The Beginning of General Wrangel's Campaign ...	21 (1927): 174–181 (*243*)
Tsarist Diplomacy during the Taiping Rebellion ..	21 (1927): 182–199 (*245*)
The Society "Sviashchenaia Druzhina" (An Account for 1881–1882)	21 (1927): 200–217 (*247*)
How the Bourgeoisie Prepared for the October Revolution	21 (1927): 218–220 (*247*)
General D. G. Shcherbachev's Letter to General A. I. Denikin	21 (1927): 220–223 (*247*)
The Bribing of *Novoe Vremia* by the Tsarist Government	21 (1927): 223–226 (*248*)
The Student Union and the Execution of May 8, 1887	21 (1927): 226–231 (*248*)
L. N. Tolstoy and N. M. Romanov	21 (1927): 231–241 (*248*)
F. M. Dostoevsky as "A Member of a Secret Society"	21 (1927): 241–244 (*249*)
The Revolution of February 1917 (Conclusion) ...	22 (1927): 3–70 (*250*)
The Diary of Nicholas Romanov (Continuation) ..	22 (1927): 71–91 (*252*)
The Regional Government of the Crimea during 1918–1919	22 (1927): 92–152 (*253*)
The Correspondence of Nicholas II with Maria Fedorovna, 1905–1906	22 (1927): 152–209 (*255*)
A. N. Pipin's Plea on Behalf of N. G. Chernyshevsky	22 (1927): 210–236 (*255*)
The Escape of Yaroslav Dombrovsky	22 (1927): 236–241 (*255*)
On the History of the Nechaev Movement	22 (1927): 241–245 (*256*)
The Research of L. N. Tolstoy at the Archives of the Ministry of Justice	22 (1927): 245–250 (*256*)
The Last Romanovs on "Liberalism" and a Constitutional Regime	22 (1927): 250–251 (*256*)
Introduction by M. N. Pokrovsky	23 (1927): iii–xi (*258*)
The July Days in Petrograd	23 (1927): 1–63 (*258*)
The Moscow Military Revolutionary Committee ..	23 (1927): 64–148 (*261*)
October at the Front	23 (1927): 149–194 (*264*)
On the Eve of the Armistice	23 (1927): 195–249 (*266*)
The Diary of General V. G. Boldyrev	23 (1927): 250–273 (*266*)
July Days in Petrograd (Conclusion)	24 (1927): 3–70 (*268*)
October at the Front (Conclusion)	24 (1927): 71–107 (*269*)
Foreign Diplomats on the Revolution of 1917	24 (1927): 108–163 (*272*)
Feodor the Homeless	24 (1927): 164–200 (*274*)
Preparations for a March on Petrograd	24 (1927): 201–208 (*275*)
The Romanovs during the First Days of the Revolution	24 (1927): 208–210 (*275*)
The Financial Situation of Russia before the October Revolution	25 (1927): 3–33 (*277*)
The October Revolution in the Baltic Fleet	25 (1927): 34–95 (*277*)

Titles of Articles in Volumes 1–30 221

VOLUME AND PAGE

The Democratic Government of Georgia and the English Command	25 (1927): 96–110 (*278*)
The Anglo-Russian Agreement to Divide Spheres of Interest in China (1899)	25 (1927): 111–134 (*283*)
A Solved Problem	25 (1927): 135–181 (*288*)
The Censorship over Foreign Publications and the *Communist* of 1916	25 (1927): 183–184 (*289*)
A Historic Episode of the Balkan War	25 (1927): 184–188 (*289*)
A Soldier's Letter concerning the Events of January 9, 1905	25 (1927): 188 (*290*)
From the History of Foreign Investments in Russia	25 (1927): 189–198 (*291*)
The Struggle of the Synod against the Revolution	25 (1927): 198–201 (*292*)
Interception of Private Mail in the Beginning of the Nineteenth Century	25 (1927): 201–209 (*292*)
The Stavka and the Ministry of Foreign Affairs	26 (1928): 1–50 (*294*)
The Agrarian Policy of General Wrangel	26 (1928): 51–96 (*299*)
Letters by I. I. Vorontsov-Dashkov to Nicholas Romanov (1905–1915)	26 (1928): 97–126 (*300*)
The Diary of A. A. Bobrinsky (1910–1911)	26 (1928): 127–150 (*303*)
On the Death of N. G. Chernyshevsky	26 (1928): 151–168 (*304*)
The Conspiracy of V. M. Purishkevich's Monarchist Organization	26 (1928): 179–185 (*305*)
From the Diary of A. V. Romanov, 1916–1917	26 (1928): 185–210 (*306*)
A Statement by the "Committee for People's Salvation"	26 (1928): 210–213 (*310*)
Spiridovich and His "History of the Revolutionary Movement in Russia"	26 (1928): 213–220 (*310*)
The Stavka and the Ministry of Foreign Affairs (Continuation)	27 (1928): 2–57 (*312*)
The Moscow Duma after the October Revolution	27 (1928): 58–109 (*321*)
The Diary of Nicholas Romanov (Conclusion)	27 (1928): 110–138 (*324*)
Excerpts from Reports on the Interception of Mail by the Police Department during 1908	27 (1928): 139–159 (*327*)
Bakunin and the Dresden Uprising	27 (1928): 160–190 (*330*)
F. M. Dostoevsky's Letters	27 (1928): 191–214 (*331*)
General Skobelev's Speech in Paris in 1882	27 (1928): 215–225 (*332*)
Nicholas Romanov and Finland	27 (1928): 225–233 (*333*)
A Reverberation of the Trial of the 193	27 (1928): 233–234 (*333*)
The Stavka and the Ministry of Foreign Affairs (Continuation)	28 (1928): 3–58 (*335*)
The Moscow Duma after the October Revolution (Conclusion)	28 (1928): 59–106 (*338*)
The Provisional Government and the Constituent Assembly	28 (1928): 107–141 (*340*)
The Crimea during 1918–1919	28 (1928): 142–181 (*341*)

	VOLUME AND PAGE
The End of the Russo-Japanese War	28 (1928): 182–204 (*344*)
Excerpts from a Report on the Interception of Mail by the Police Department during 1908 (Conclusion)	28 (1928): 205–224 (*346*)
From the History of Kolchak's Campaign	28 (1928): 225–228 (*348*)
D. I. Pisarev's Poem on the Unveiling of a Monument to Nicholas I	28 (1928): 228–230 (*349*)
New Material on Pushkin	28 (1928): 231–234 (*349*)
N. G. Chernyshevsky	29 (1928): i–xvi (*351*)
The Stavka and the Ministry of Foreign Affairs (Continuation)	29 (1928): 1–54 (*351*)
The Crimea during 1918–1919	29 (1928): 55–85 (*355*)
The Provisional Government of Autonomous Siberia	29 (1928): 86–138 (*361*)
Unpublished Memoirs of L. Tikhomirov	29 (1928): 139–174 (*366*)
N. G. Chernyshevsky and the Third Department	29 (1928): 175–190 (*367*)
Julian Markhlevsky	29 (1928): 191–205 (*370*)
The French Military Mission in Siberia and the Specially Commissioned Cossack Regiments	29 (1928): 206–209 (*370*)
About Y. V. Stefanovich	29 (1928): 209–210 (*372*)
Biographic Material on D. I. Pisarev	29 (1928): 210–218 (*373*)
New Material on Pushkin	29 (1928): 218–223 (*374*)
Mikhail Nikolaevich Pokrovsky	30 (1928): 3–4 (*375*)
The Stavka and the Ministry of Foreign Affairs (Conclusion)	30 (1928): 5–45 (*375*)
From the History of the Provisional Government's Policy toward National Minorities	30 (1928): 46–79 (*380*)
P. A. Stolypin's Correspondence with Nicholas Romanov	30 (1928): 80–88 (*382*)
The Correspondence of Witte and Pobedonostsev	30 (1928): 89–116 (*383*)
The "Confession" of Gregory Goldenberg	30 (1928): 117–183 (*384*)
The Finale of the Trial of the 193	30 (1928): 184–199 (*387*)
D. P. Romanov's Letters to His Father	30 (1928): 200–210 (*388*)
The Destruction of "The Labor Alliance of Southern Russia" during 1880–1881	30 (1928): 210–217 (*391*)
Two Letters of S. I. Muravev-Apostol	30 (1928): 217–226 (*393*)

INDEX

Note.—The Library of Congress system of transliteration has been used, with some modification. Proper nouns ending in the Russian ий have been transliterated *y*, not *ii*. Adjective endings are unaltered. Words beginning with the Russian я have been transliterated *ya*, not *ia*. For example, Yasnaia Poliana, rather than Iasnaia Poliana. Words beginning with the Russian ю have been transliterated *yu*, not *iu*. For example, Yusupov, rather than Iusupov.

Russian given names have been Anglicized throughout, except where the spelling of a Russian name has been popularly accepted in English. The most literal form of transliteration has been used for patronymics. Family names have been transliterated literally unless another form is in common use in English, as in the case of Tchaikovsky.

An asterisk (*) following a name indicates the writer of an introduction to documents published in the *Krasnyi Arkhiv* or the writer of an article based on archival documents. When initials alone designate the authorship of such materials, they are, of course, indexed under the initial of the surname.

The name of the author of a book or article entered in the Index appears in parentheses after the title. If a title in English is in quotation marks, it means in most cases merely that the Russian title is also given in the *Digest*.

The present Index applies only to the *Digest* for Volumes 31–106. A list of the articles in Volumes 1–30 is given, however, in the Appendix (pp. 209–222).

A

A., E. [E. A.],* 157
A., N. [N. A.],* 120
A. S. Pushkin (A. I. Tsomakion), 139
"A. S. Pushkin: Biography and Collection of Poems," 139
A. S. Pushkin: Zhizneopisanie i Sbornik Stikhotvorenii, 139
Abulkhair, Khan, 133
Adamov, E. A.,* 20, 36, 65, 96
Adams, Alva, 181
Addis Ababa, 41
Admiralty, Russian, 113, 116. *See also* Navy, Russian.
Adrianople, 54
Adrianople, Treaty of, 36
Aehrenthal, Count A. L. von, 51
Afghanistan, 58, 106

Agadir, 20
Agrarian movement, 3, 11, 18, 24, 25, 29, 30, 34, 39, 42, 43, 56, 87, 106, 108, 109, 113, 115, 116, 117, 118, 119, 122, 125, 127, 129, 131, 132, 137, 158, 160, 161, 164, 169, 180, 187, 202, 204, 205. *See also* Revolutionary movement.
Agrarian reforms, 39, 42, 86, 117, 122, 162, 189, 192, 193
Agricultural communes and artels, 192
First All-Russian Congress of, 178
Agricultural Department, Moscow, board of, 192
Agricultural Exposition, 190
Agricultural Workers, All-Russian Conference of, 178

Agriculture, 129, 135, 178, 189, 194, 205
  Central Commissariat of, 192, 193
  People's Commissariat of, 152, 162, 192
Ahmed Riza Bey, 51
Aiaslarskoe Delo (V. M. Garshin), 158
"Aiaslarsky Affair, The" (V. M. Garshin), 158
Air force, 42, 179
Akhun, M.,* 50, 94
Akmolinsk, 65
Akordi (I. Franko), 186
Aksakov, I. S., 5
Åland Islands, 9, 10
Alaska, 50, 72
Aleutian Islands, 40
Alexander I, 64, 133, 180
Alexander II, 4, 5, 14, 16, 17, 22, 25, 30, 34, 43, 44, 57, 61, 66, 74, 120, 161, 166, 203
Alexander III, 4, 5, 7, 21, 44, 47, 58, 61, 83, 101, 172
Alexander Nevsky Monastery, 130
Alexandra Feodorovna, Empress, 56, 58, 65
Alexandra Petrovna, Grand Duchess, 59
Alexandrova, E.,* 175
Alexandrovsk, 34, 125, 144
Alexeiev, Admiral E. I., 35, 46, 47, 103
Alexeiev, General M. V., 64, 75
Alexeiev, N.,* 127, 180
Alexeiev, P. A., 53
Alexis, Tsarevitch, 2
Alexis Aleksandrovich, Grand Duke, 67
Alexis Mikhailovich, Tsar, 110
Algeciras Conference, 45, 53
Allgemeine deutscher Verband, 171
"Alliance of October 17, The," 25, 28
Allies, the, 1, 9, 15, 19, 23, 27, 31, 38, 55, 97, 101, 184, 200
All-Karelian Soviet Congress, 194
All-Russian Central Executive Committee, 152
All-Russian Communist *subbotnik,* 143
All-Russian Conference of Agricultural Workers, 178

All-Union (Bolshevik) Communist party, 90, 91, 120, 121, 140, 143, 144, 150, 154, 162, 165, 168, 186, 198
  Central Committee of, 90, 120, 121, 140, 150, 165, 168, 169, 186, 198
All-Union Conference of Workers in Higher Schools, First, 159
Alsace-Lorraine, 82
Alvenslaben Convention, 189
America, 2, 9, 27, 32, 50, 145, 174, 185, 190. See also United States.
Amur, 71
Anatra, A. A., 107
Ancient and Modern Russia, 173
Ancient Russian Charter (1368), 198
Anders, Colonel [?], 145
Andizhan, 160
Andreev, L.,* 65, 69
Andreev, Leonid, 55
"Angel of Death" (M. Y. Lermontov), 180
Angel Smerti (M. Y. Lermontov), 180
Anglo-American relations, 63, 72
Anglo-Boer War, 93, 197. See also Boer War.
Anglo-French Agreement of 1904, 45
Anglo-French relations, 45, 77
Anglo-German relations, 78
Anglo-Russian relations, 62, 73, 78, 98, 106, 177, 189, 195, 196
Anglo-Spanish conflict (1898-1899), 86
Anisimova, P.,* 141, 150, 194
Anna Ivanovna, Empress, 110, 133
Annenkov, P. V., 12
Anselme, General [?] d', 55
Anthès, Baron George Heckeren, d', 17
Antonov, P. L., 3, 4
Antony, Archbishop of Volhynia, 6
Apostolov, N.,* 26
Apraksin, Major General Count A. S., 25
Arab kingdom, 9
Aral Sea, 167
Archangel, 31, 123, 160, 171, 184
Archive Department of the USSR, Central, 130
Archive of Foreign Affairs, 48

Index

Archive of the October Revolution, Central, 131
Archive of the Red Army, Central, 131
Archive of the Revolution, 92, 112
Archive of the Revolution, Central, 104
Archive of the Revolution and Foreign Affairs, 14, 18
Argiropulo, P. M., 127
Armenia, 9, 20, 24, 62
Army, Italian, General Staff, 157
Army, Red, 65, 141, 142, 146, 150, 154, 155, 156, 183, 184, 199
  Central Archive of the, 131
  Fourth Soviet, 111
  International Battalion, 156
  Twenty-second Division, 184
  Twenty-fifth Division, 184
  Twenty-seventh Rifle Division, 65
  See also Army, Russian; Army, White.
Army, Russian, 3, 11, 18, 26, 32, 33, 34, 35, 36, 37, 46, 47, 50, 52, 53, 56, 57, 58, 60, 64, 69, 70, 75, 82, 83, 87, 88, 94, 95, 98, 103, 107, 109, 122, 139, 141, 150, 152, 185, 187, 194, 206
  Eighth, 26
  General Staff, 3, 20, 83, 96, 183, 189. See also *Stavka.*
  See also Army, Red; Army, White.
Army, White, 114, 115, 125, 153, 154, 165, 176, 183, 184. See also Army, Russian.
Arsharuni, A.,* 24
Artsybashev, [M. P.], 55
Ashik Kerib (M. Y. Lermontov), 180
Asia, 73
  Central, 18, 24, 115, 170, 173
Astafiev, A., 112
Astrakhan, 36, 161, 167, 173, 178, 196
Astrov, N. I., 6
Astrov, V.,* 25
Athens, 53
Attalea Princeps (V. M. Garshin), 158
Austria, 41, 62, 63, 75, 120, 122, 163, 190, 193, 205. See also Austria-Hungary; Hungary.
Austria-Hungary, 14, 76, 77, 96. See also Austria; Hungary.
Auvergne, 175
Aveide, Oscar, 81
Averbukh, R.,* 62, 163, 177
Avksentev, Nicholas D., 6

B

B., A. [A. B.],* 158
B., Y. [Y. B.],* 79, 92
Badaev, A.,* 95
Badaev, A. E., 95, 128
Baden-Baden, 17
Baghdad, 83, 106
Baichigirov, Alimzhan, 75
Bakarev, Vladimir Alekseevich, 135
Bakhturov, [?], 199
Baku, 145, 160, 162, 201
Bakunin, Vasili, 175, 181
Balabin, N. P., 134
Balakirev, M. A., 191
Balatov, 156
Balfour, Arthur, 2
Balkan Union, 189
Balkan War, First, 189
Balkans, 51, 62, 76, 77, 82, 106
Baltic fleet, 9, 23, 54, 59, 102
Baltic region, 33, 37, 39, 47, 195
Baltic shipyard, 125
Balzac, Honoré de, 189
Bandido Khambo-Lama, 74
Barannikov, A. I., 41
Baranov, Count [Paul T.], 170
Barashev-Usad, 129
Barmin, Vasily, 47
"Barricades in Paris," 54. See also Paris Commune.
Bastille, 177
"Battle of the Cocks" (A. S. Serafimovich), 159
Batum, 160
Batyrev, Captain A., 161
Bauman, Nicholas E., 43
Bavaria, 205
Bazarov, P. A., 20
"Bears" (V. M. Garshin), 158
Behrens, Captain [?], 97

225

Beilis, Mendel, 52, 77
Bekon, [?], 193
Belchikov, N.,* 12, 30, 56, 61, 111, 127, 139, 159, 168, 188, 189
Belebeevsk, 172
Belenovskaia, M. D., 183
Beletsky, S. P., 52
Belgium, 1, 97, 177, 200
Belgorod, 137
Belgrade, 38, 48, 54, 184
Beliavsky, N.,* 8
Belkin, G.,* 108, 152
Bell, The, 142, 185
Belousov, Andrew, 4
Benckendorff, Count Alexander Khristoforovich, 32, 33, 36, 60, 126, 147, 158
Benckendorff, Count Alexander Konstantinovich, 48, 51
Berezov, 170
Bering, Captain Vitus, 110, 113, 116, 119, 189
Bering Strait, 50
Berlin, 2, 21, 45, 51, 54, 58, 63, 78, 84, 86, 119, 157, 161, 163, 166, 171, 189
Berlin, Congress of, 85, 189
Berliner Monatshefte, 20, 68, 85
Bern, 38
Bernatsky, M. V., 10
Berzin, Y.,* 76, 90
Bessarabia, 32, 39, 192
Bez Pratsi (I. Franko), 186
Bezdna, 25, 29, 30, 117, 169
Bezradetsky, General [?], 107
Bilyk, P.,* 125, 141
Bing, Edward J., 69
Birze, A.,* 122, 136, 137, 167
Birze, A. M.,* 148
Bismarck, Prince Otto von, 8, 88, 119, 120, 166
Bitolj, 48
"Black Partition Group," 34
Black Sea, 55, 57, 90, 131, 196
Bliukher, [?], 114
"Bloody Sunday," 29, 34, 35, 39, 41, 49, 56, 103

Blumfeldt, A.,* 196
Bobrinskaia, Countess Sophia Prokofievna, 129
Bobrinsky, A. A., 5
Boer War, 108. See also Anglo-Boer War.
Boers, 108, 109, 197
Bogrov, Dmitry G., 26
Bohemia, 62. See also Czechoslovakia.
Boi Petukhov (A. S. Serafimovich), 159
Boiarin Orsha (M. Y. Lermontov), 180
Boldyrev, V. G., 6
Bolgov, A.,* 162
Bolotnikov, N.,* 75
Bolshevik Revolution, 1917–1918, The (J. Bunyan and H. Fisher), 182
Bolsheviks, 55, 79, 83, 89, 99, 100, 101, 103, 128, 142, 147, 150, 162, 182, 199, 201, 204
Bolshoi Theater, 151, 183
Boltin, Colonel E.,* 171
Boltinov, S.,* 168, 195
Bombay, 45
Bompard, Louis, 45
Bonaparte, Jerome, 161
Bonaparte, Napoleon. See Napoleon.
Bondarenko, M.,* 153
Book of the Asiatic Department, 158
Borba za Zhizn (D. I. Pisarev), 198
Borisoglebsk, 160
Borisov, D. T., 145
Boroml, 125
Borovsky, General [?], 114
Bor-Ramensky, E.,* 201
Bortnikova, E.,* 191
Bosnia, 69
Bosporus, 51, 61, 62. See also Dardanelles; Straits, the.
Boulanger, General Georges, 112
Bourgeois, Henri, 19
Boxer Rebellion, 189
"Boyar Orsha, The" (M. Y. Lermontov), 180
Brazhe, L.,* 41, 47
Brest Litovsk, 195
Brest Litovsk, Peace of, 88, 124

Index   227

Briusov, V.,* 139
Brodnikov, E., 120
Brodsky, N.,* 190
Bromlei factory, 79
Brunnow, Baron Phillip I., 36, 37, 62, 121, 163
Brussels, 13, 38, 184, 197
Bucharest, 38, 54
Buddhism, 74
Budenny, S. M., 114, 190, 199
Budkevich, S.,* 82, 103
Budnichnye Storony Zhizni (D. I. Pisarev), 198
Bülow, Prince Bernhard von, 84
Buguruslan, 172, 184
Bulatsel, [?], 54
Bulgakov, A. Y., 17
Bulgaria, 1, 51, 54, 58, 75, 82, 83, 97, 190
Bulygin, A. G., 132, 203
Bunyan, J., 182
Buol-Schauenstein, Count Karl, 122
Buriats, 74, 126
Bushuev, S.,* 195, 202
Bushuev, V.,* 198
Butashevich-Petrashevsky, M. V., 56, 57, 60
Butkevich, I. T., 40
Byelorussia, 165, 166, 185, 195
Byron, George Gordon, Lord, 159

C

Cadet party, 27, 49, 59, 63, 64, 86. *See also* Constitutional Democratic party; Popular Freedom party.
Cadet National Center
  in Ekaterinodar, 27
  in Moscow, 2
Canada, 31
Canadian-American relations (1898), 72
Capitalism and Communism (K. Marx), 78
"Cardboard Heroes" (D. I. Pisarev), 198
Carlotti, Marquis A., 1
Carnot, C. E., 75
Caspian Sea, 173
Cassini, Count [A. P.], 45, 72

Catherine II, 105, 108, 129, 161, 173
Caucasus, 20, 24, 31, 39, 52, 79, 90, 104, 105, 131, 135, 136, 142, 148, 154, 161, 166, 168, 196, 202, 203
Censorship, 11, 26, 36, 41, 55, 71, 77, 87, 101, 109, 120, 123, 139, 142, 156, 158, 159, 167, 185, 186, 192, 198, 203
Censorship of Foreign Literature, Central Committee of, 109
Central Archive of the October Revolution, 131
Central Archive of the Revolution, 104
Central Asia, 18, 24, 115, 170, 173
Central Committee of the All-Union (Bolshevik) Communist party, 90, 120, 121, 140, 150, 165, 168, 169, 186, 198
Central Election Commission, 149
Central Electric Station, 151
Central Executive Committee, All-Russian, 152
Central Executive Committee of the USSR, 128, 146, 149, 152
Ch., E. [E. Ch.],* 123
Chaadaeva, O.,* 98, 150, 152, 172, 174, 177, 195, 197
Chadaeva, O.,* 160
Chakhvinsk estate, 205
Chang, [?], 92
Chanoine, General [?], 68
Chapaev, V. I., 183, 184
Chego Ne Nado Delat (N. A. Dobroliubov), 123
Chekhov, Alexander, 183
Chekhov, Anton P., 33, 111, 183, 189
Chekhov, M. P., 33
Chekhov, Paul, 33, 183
Chemerzin, [?], 41
Cherepovets, 178
Cherkassky, Prince V. A., 5
Cherkesov, A. A., 8
Cherniavsky, E.,* 130, 131, 138, 151, 156
Chernigov, 106, 115, 122, 132, 134, 153, 176
Chërnoperedeltsy, 34

Chernov, A.,* 45, 205
Chernovsky, Kazimir, 201
Chernyshëv, Adjutant General Prince Alexander I., 38
Chernyshevsky, N. G., 7, 58, 81, 120, 123, 127, 134, 168, 180, 189
Chetyre Dnia na Pole Srazheniia (V. M. Garshin), 158
Cheville, Count Francis de, 10, 11
Chicago, Columbian Exposition in, 72
Childhood (L. Tolstoy), 26
China, 23, 31, 34, 67, 71, 76
Chinese-Eastern Railroad, 32, 38
Chinese Social and Political Science Review, 31, 67, 71, 92
Chirchik River, 167
Cholera epidemic, 36, 60, 116
"Chords, The" (I. Franko), 186
Christiana (Oslo), 38
Churchill, Winston, 2, 31, 38
Chuvash peasants, 158
Civil War, Finland, 184, 187
Civil War, Russia, 2, 10, 19, 21, 23, 27, 28, 31, 32, 38, 39, 51, 55, 63, 65, 89, 101, 111, 114, 115, 124, 125, 130, 131, 142, 144, 145, 146, 154, 155, 156, 165, 171, 172, 173, 174, 176, 179, 183, 189, 199. *See also* Intervention in Russia.
Civil War, United States, 36, 37, 72, 189
Civil War in France (1870–1871) (K. Marx), 78
Class Struggle in France 1848–1850 (K. Marx), 78
Collected Works (Lenin), 117
"Collection of Documents, the Central Government Military-Historical Archive," 207
Colorado, 181
Columbian Exposition, 72
Comintern and Profintern, appeal of Executive Committee (1924), 91
Commission of Soviet Control, 102
Communards, 54
Commune, Paris, 54, 189
Communes, Division of, 192

Communist Manifesto, The (K. Marx), 77, 78, 156
Communist party, All-Union (Bolshevik), 90, 91, 120, 121, 140, 143, 144, 150, 154, 162, 165, 168, 186, 198
Central Committee of, 90, 120, 121, 140, 150, 165, 168, 169, 186, 198
"Concerning the Development of Revolutionary Ideas in Russia" (A. I. Herzen), 186
Condition of the Working Class in England, The (F. Engels), 109
"Confusion" (I. Franko), 186
Congress of Berlin, 85, 189
Congress of Russian Social Democratic Labor party
Second, 85, 91
Third, 103
Fourth, 204
Ninth, 143
Eighteenth, 168
Congress of Soviets, All-Russian
Second, 143, 150, 162
Third, 151, 152
Fifth, 192
Seventh, 178
Congress of Soviets, All-Union
Second, 91, 184
Extraordinary Eighth, 128, 135
Congress of Soviets of the Don Republic, First, 124
Congress of Soviets of the Russian Soviet Federated Socialist Republic, Eleventh, 91
Conscription, 18, 81, 124
Conscription Bill of 1863, 81
Conservatory of Music, St. Petersburg, 52
Constantine, Grand Duke, 16, 49, 52, 56
Constantine Nikolaevich, Grand Duke, 180
Constantinople, 38, 48, 51, 54, 55, 61, 62, 106, 159, 163, 189, 196
Constituent Assembly, 152
Constitutional Democratic party, 27, 86. *See also* Cadet party; Popular Freedom party.

Constitutional reforms, 4, 128, 135
Contreras, General [?], 65
Copenhagen, 38, 157, 184
Cossacks, 124, 125, 152, 156
Council of Labor and Defense, 102
Council of Ministers, 19, 51, 69, 101, 118, 132, 134, 135, 136, 203
Council of People's Commissars of the USSR, 102, 120, 121, 176, 182, 197, 198
Council of State Defense, 3
"Coupler, The" (A. S. Serafimovich), 159
Court Department, Central Military, 94
Courts, 11, 25, 52, 95, 141, 142, 147, 151, 160, 170, 172
"Coward" (V. M. Garshin), 158
Crete, 77
Crimea, 10, 21, 42, 51, 93, 115, 131
Crimean War, 203
Curzon, G. de, 11
Czechoslovakia, 14, 18, 23, 28, 189. See also Bohemia.

D

D., F. [F. D.],* 46
D., P. [P. D.],* 179
Dagestan, 24, 136
Dalago, V.,* 96, 104, 120
Damansky, P. S., 74
Danilov, General [?], 64
Danubian principalities (1848), 163
Danzig, 8
Daragan, P. M., 30
Dardanelles, 1, 10, 72. See also Bosporus; Straits, the.
Decembrists, 31, 38, 130, 189
Degaev, Sergius, 8, 35
Delcassé, Théophile, 76
Demishel, [?], 175
Demon (M. Y. Lermontov), 180
"Demon, The" (M. Y. Lermontov), 180
Denikin, General A. I., 11, 51, 55, 63, 114, 156, 199
Denisov, General F., 193
Denmark, 97, 196
Derevnia (A. S. Pushkin), 138

Derkach, P.,* 143, 146
Desiat Zapovedei i Imushchie Klassy (A. Hoffman), 87
Development of Socialism from Utopia to Science, The (F. Engels), 109
Diachenko, V. A., 52
Diugamel, General [A. O.], 163
Dmitrash, D. G., 99
Dmitriev, Michael Aleksandrovich, 203
Dmitriukov, I., 149
Dmitry Konstantinovich, Prince, 198
Dnieper, 111, 129
Dnieper dockyard, 129
Do Svitla (I. Franko), 186
Dobroliubov, Nicholas Alexandrovich, 117, 123, 189
Dobrova, Z.,* 173
Dobrovolsky, General [?], 114
Dobrudja, 82
Dokhturov, Major F. N., 30
Dolgorukov, Prince Peter V., 22, 67
Dolgorukov, Prince V. A., 58
Dolgorukov, Vladimir, 22
Dolgorukova, Princess Catherine, 16
Dolgorukova, Princess Olga, 17
Dombrovsky, Yaroslav, 45
Don, 31, 100, 124, 125, 131, 160, 166, 184
Don Republic, First Congress of Soviets of, 124
Donbas, 111
Donets Basin, 111, 115
Dostoevsky, F. M., 56, 58, 60, 189
Dostoevsky, Michael M., 57
Drabkina, F.,* 12, 33
Dragoons, British, 196
Drenteln, Adjutant General A. R., 43, 44, 66
Drezen, A.,* 9, 23, 37, 50, 59
Druzhinin, Jacob A., 180
Dubasov, General F. V., 106
Dubensky, General Dmitry, 95
Dubreil, Gabriel, 175
Dubrovsky, S.,* 39
Dürich, [J.?], 18
Dukhovsky, [?], 71
Duma, 100, 135, 136, 151
    First State, 46, 56, 59, 64, 80, 84, 87

230 *A Digest of the Krasnyi Arkhiv*

Duma (*continued*)
 Second State, 48, 49, 69, 84, 89
 Third State, 12
 Fourth State, 15, 69, 72, 78, 82, 90, 94, 95, 104, 128, 146, 147, 149
  Military Commission of the Provisional Committee of, 46
  Military-Naval Commission of, 82, 94
 Moscow City Duma, 5, 151
Durnovo, P. N., 3, 4, 132
Dzhizak, 87

E

E., A. [A. E.],* 64, 119, 171
Ecclesiastical Academy, Kiev, 191
Education, 28, 43, 52, 53, 83, 94, 120, 121, 138, 148, 151, 159, 174, 185, 190, 194, 196, 200
 Ministry of, 36, 60, 185
 Ministry of Public, 180
Efimovich, [?], 79
Efros, N. E., 33
Egypt, 63, 72
Eiges, A.,* 183
Ekaterinburg, 178, 196
Ekaterinodar, 31, 47
 Cadet National Center in, 27
Ekaterinoslav, 115, 129, 145, 160, 166, 172, 195
Elagin, V.,* 73, 81, 101
Election Commission, Central, 149
Elections, 8, 48, 54, 56, 89, 135, 136, 146, 149, 151, 165, 175
Electric Station, Central, 151
Electrical Illumination Society, 176
Electrification of Russia, 176, 179, 189
 Government Commission for, 176
Eliot, Sir Charles, 28
Elizabeth, Empress, 153
Elizavetgrad, 160
Elpidin, M. K., 22
Emancipation Manifesto (1861), 25, 29, 30, 81, 113, 117, 205
Emelianov, I. P., 44
Emigration, 66
"Emperor of Kaffirs" (Nicholas II), 108

Engels, Friedrich, 78, 109
England, 1, 2, 9, 19, 20, 27, 28, 31, 32, 45, 51, 54, 63, 65, 67, 68, 75, 76, 78, 82, 85, 94, 97, 98, 105, 106, 109, 120, 162, 174, 184, 185, 190, 196, 197, 205
Enquist, Rear Admiral [?], 99
Entente Diplomacy and the World (B. A. Siebert) 106
Epstein, D.,* 194
Erakov, A. N., 203
Ermolov, Colonel N. S., 20
Erukhimovich, I.,* 92
Erusalimsky, A.,* 45, 82, 88, 166
Essen, M. M., 103
Estates General, 175
Esterhazy, Count V., 122
"Esthetic Relations of Art to Reality, The" (N. G. Chernyshevsky), 168
Estland, 195. *See also* Estonia.
Estonia, 2, 191, 192, 195
 Military-Revolutionary Committee of, 191
Ethiopia, 41, 42, 63
Europe (European), 11, 20, 37, 41, 48, 57, 61, 62, 63, 76, 119, 177, 200
Evfimovsky, V.,* 204
Evreinov, [?], 48
Evropeus, Emily V., 66
Exile, 17, 34, 47, 61, 91, 120, 134, 164, 171, 201, 206
Expansion, Russian, 58, 71, 142, 148, 153, 154, 161, 173, 189, 195, 196
Exploration, Russian, 110, 113, 116, 119, 122, 123, 126, 148, 153, 154, 160, 161, 189, 200

F

F., T. [T. F.],* 54
Falkenhagen, [?], 79
Famine, 72, 134, 141, 163, 181, 182, 192
Far East, 3, 35, 42, 47, 58, 63, 71, 76, 84, 85, 89, 90, 103, 107, 144, 165, 166, 189
Fashoda, 77
Faure, [François], 63, 76

Index

February Revolution, 9, 26, 46, 69, 83, 108, 141, 187, 194, 202
Fëdorov, V. A., 28
Feigelson, M.,* 188, 189
Ferdinand IV, Emperor of Austria, 163
Ferdinand of Bulgaria, 58
Ferghana, 124, 160
Ferzen, Captain Baron [?], 37
Ferzen, Lieutenant General I. E., 193
Fikelmon, Ludwig, 163
Filaret, Metropolitan of Moscow, 113
Filaret Nikitich, Patriarch, 193
Filippov, P. D., 145
Finance, Ministry of, 36, 60
Finances, Russian, 31, 35, 42, 53, 59, 78, 86, 94, 100, 130, 136, 143, 145, 151, 180, 189
Finansovoe Obozrenie, 108
Finland (the Finns), 2, 14, 15, 31, 33, 36, 52, 68, 69, 76, 184, 185, 187
  Civil War in, 184, 187
Finns. *See* Finland.
Fironov, N.,* 207
Fisher, H., 182
Flavian, Metropolitan of Kiev, 6, 77
Fonton, [F. P.?], 62, 163
"For Truth," 140, 157
Foreign Affairs, Archive of, 48
Foreign Affairs, Collegium of, 133, 170
Foreign Affairs, Ministry of, 1, 8, 9, 15, 27, 28, 31, 36, 48, 64, 65, 67, 77, 86, 90, 97, 106, 142, 173, 175, 189
"Four Days on the Battlefield" (V. M. Garshin), 158
"Fox 'Mikita,' The" (I. Franko), 186
France, Anatole, 101, 189
France, 1, 9, 10, 12, 13, 15, 18, 19, 20, 27, 28, 45, 53, 54, 55, 62, 63, 67, 72, 75, 77, 82, 83, 86, 94, 97, 100, 112, 120, 161, 166, 174, 175, 176, 184, 187, 190, 194, 196, 205
Franco-German relations, 20, 54, 166
Franco-Russian Agreement (1859), 161
Franko, Ivan, 186
Franz Joseph, Emperor, 76, 77
Franz Joseph Land, 160
Frederiks, Baron V. B., 57
"Freedom" (A. S. Pushkin), 139
Frenkel, [?],* 205
Friche, V. M., 22
Friedland, Ts.,* 112
"Frog Traveler, The" (V. M. Garshin), 158
From Classical Idealism to Dialectical Materialism (F. Engels), 109
"From the Notes of Private Ivanov" (V. M. Garshin), 158
Frunze, M. V., 111, 112, 114, 115, 154, 171, 189, 207
Fuks, S.,* 20
"Funeral March" (A. S. Serafimovich), 159
Furmanov, D., 183, 184

G

G., K. [K. G.],* 141
G., R. [R. G.],* 179
Gaevsky, V. P., 191
Gagarin, S., 180
Galicia, 77, 86
Galperin, L. E., 103
Galuzo, P.,* 18
Gapon, Father G. A., 29, 103
Garshin, V. M., 12, 97, 158
Gassanova, R.,* 163
Geiman, [?], 137
Gelfman, Geisa, 44
Gendarmerie, 32, 33, 36, 40, 43, 47, 49, 58, 60, 66, 85, 87, 109, 118, 132, 142, 158, 182, 190, 195, 205
Gendreau, [?], 19
Geneva, 22, 73
Georgia, 187, 201, 204
Gerke, A. A., 44
Germany, 1, 2, 8, 9, 15, 20, 21, 27, 45, 51, 54, 55, 58, 62, 63, 65, 67, 84, 86, 89, 95, 96, 100, 105, 112, 120, 124, 143, 157, 165, 166, 176, 178, 179, 192
Gernet, M.,* 201
Geroi Nashego Vremeni (M. Y. Lermontov), 180
Gerstner, Franz Anton von, 126
Gibraltar, 62, 86

Giers, [?], 92
Giers, A. A., 90
Giers, M., 54
Giers, N. K. de, 21, 58, 71, 83
Gippius, Lieutenant General A., 124
Girsa, Dr. [?], 28
Gitschin, 62
Gleichheit, 87
Glushkovsky, Adam, 147
Glushkovsky clothing factory, 167
Gods Are Athirst, The (A. France), 101
Goethe, J. W. von, 189
Gogol, Nicholas V., 189
Goldich, E.,* 118
Golitsyn, Prince D. V., 126
Golitsyn, Prince M. A., 110
Golitsyn, Y. N., 67
Golovin, A. V., 58
Golovin, F. A., 49, 84
Goluchowski, Count [Agenor], 76, 77
Gomel, 156, 178
Goncharov, [?], 112
Goncharov, I. A., 189
Goncharov, N. A., 129
Goncharova, Natalia Ivanovna, 129
Gorchakov, Prince A. M., 5, 16, 37, 54, 65, 88, 119, 122, 137, 161, 175
Gordaia Palma (V. M. Garshin), 158
Goremykin, Ivan, 1, 11, 135, 172
Goremykin, N. D., 49
Gorin, P.,* 110
Gorky, Maxim, 52, 55, 127, 131, 134, 189
Gorokhovskaia, E.,* 57
Grabar, I.,* 190
"Grain," 34
Grave, B.,* 59
Greece, 1, 9, 55, 82, 97, 159, 205
Grey, Sir Edward, 45
Grigoriev, V. V., 203
Grigorovich, D. V., 191
Grinberg, A.,* 202
Grishin-Almazov, General [?], 55
Grodno, 122, 195
Grosse Politik, Die, 157
Guaran, Colonel [?], 157
Gubelman, M.,* 144, 165
Gubkov, I.,* 206

Gukovsky, A.,* 10, 21, 51, 55, 63
Gulevich, K.,* 152, 155, 163
Gurskaia, Z.,* 113
Gurskaia, Z. I.,* 108
Gussev, S. I., 103
Gvozdev, K. A., 100
Gvozdevshchinism, 100, 106

H

Hague Conference, 67, 68, 76, 189
Hanotaux, [Gabriel], 63, 72
Hanover, 196
Harbin, 46
Hawaiian Islands, 72, 133
Heidelberg, 8
Helsingfors, 59
Hennin, Lieutenant General W. de, 153
"Hero of Our Times, A" (M. Y. Lermontov), 180
Herzen, A. I., 8, 12, 61, 67, 142, 185, 186, 189
Higher Schools, First All-Union Conference of Workers in, 159
Historical Ideas of Auguste Comte (D. I. Pisarev), 198
"Historical Messenger, The," 173
"Historical Revolutionary Collection" (A. I. Nevsky), 34
History of the All-Union (Bolshevik) Communist Party, 162
History of the USSR, 121
Hoffman, A., 87
Hohenlohe, [Chlodwig Karl Victor], 63
Holland, 82
Hollis, Senator [Henry F.], 10
Holy Guards, 7
Holy Synod, 40, 43, 74, 77, 113
Hungary, 1, 97. *See also* Austria; Austria-Hungary.

I

Ignatiev, Count Alexis Pavlovich, 13, 57, 107, 109
Ignatiev, N. P., 16
Ignatiev Commission, 13, 39, 42
Illiustrirovannoi Pushkinskoi Biblioteke, 139

"Illustrated Pushkin Library," 139
Imeretinsky, A. K., 94
Imperial Decree of June 3, 1907, 48
Imperial family, 9, 39, 49, 52, 59, 64, 75, 141, 204. *See also* Romanov family.
Imperial Russian Historical Society, 15, 79, 85, 101
"In the Dead of Night" (A. S. Serafimovich), 159
"In the Depths" (I. Franko), 186
"In the Sweat of One's Brow" (I. Franko), 186
India, 57, 58, 98, 106
Industrial Committee, 180
Industry, 10, 13, 15, 37, 44, 45, 72, 79, 84, 93, 99, 103, 104, 107, 108, 110, 118, 124, 134, 136, 167, 170, 173, 174, 178, 179, 180, 192, 195, 197
Industry and Internal Trade, Department of, 180
"Information Bulletin," 162, 193
Informatsionnyi Listok, 162, 193
"Inopportune" (M. Gorky), 55
Inozemtsev, M.,* 100, 104, 107
Internal Affairs, Ministry of, 36, 60, 77, 80, 116, 125, 132, 135, 136, 160, 167, 170, 181, 190
International Battalion, 156. *See also* Army, Red.
International Women's Day, 157
"Intersecting Roads, The" (I. Franko), 186
Intervention in Russia, 2, 19, 23, 27, 28, 31, 32, 42, 55, 68, 100, 101, 104, 105, 144, 155, 165, 176, 184, 185, 200. *See also* Civil War, Russia.
Ioannikii, Metropolitan of Kiev, 40
Iran, 32, 73, 78, 83, 98, 106, 189, 190
Irkutsk, 2, 19, 74, 101
Ishutin, Nicholas A., 17
Isidor, Metropolitan of St. Petersburg, 40
Iskra, 91, 196
Islam, 24, 28
"Ismail Bey" (M. Y. Lermontov), 180
Issy, Fort, 54

Istoricheskie Idei Auguste Comte (D. I. Pisarev), 198
Istoricheskii Vestnik, 173
Istorii Vsesoiuznoi Kommunisticheskoi Partii (Bolshevikov), 162
Istoriko-Revoliutsionnyi Sbornik (A. I. Nevsky), 34
Italy, 1, 9, 51, 82, 86, 94, 97, 157
"Ivan the Terrible at the Body of His Murdered Son" (V. G. Schwartz), 181
Ivanov, A.,* 104
Ivanov, Ivan, 49
Ivanov, Ivan Filipovich, 154
Ivanov, General [N. Y.], 64
Ivanov, S. L.,* 66
Ivanovo Voznesensk, 104, 107, 112, 115, 145, 178
Iz Zapisok Riadovogo Ivanova (V. M. Garshin), 158
Izhev factory, 154
Izmail Bei (M. Y. Lermontov), 180
Izvolsky, A. P., 13, 48, 54, 92

J

Jackson, J., 50
Jagdschloss Wolfsgarten, 93
January 9, 1905, 29, 34, 35, 39, 41, 49, 56, 103
Japan, 1, 2, 9, 23, 28, 32, 35, 46, 47, 52, 67, 85, 92, 97, 101, 144
Jews, 52, 69, 77, 82, 84
Joffre, General Joseph, 20
Joubert, General [P. J.], 108
Journal of Modern History, 37
Journey from Petersburg to Moscow, A (A. N. Radishchev), 120
Justice, Ministry of, 36, 60, 77, 95
Justice, St. Petersburg Chamber of, 49, 103

K

K.,* 79, 192
K Batiushkovu (A. S. Pushkin), 138
K Drugu Stikhotvortsu (A. S. Pushkin), 138
K Litsiniiu (A. S. Pushkin), 138

K Molodoi Vdove (A. S. Pushkin), 138
K Razvitiiu Revoliutsionnykh Idei v Rossii (A. I. Herzen), 186
Kagul, Battle of, 198
Kakhetinsk estate, 204
Kal, [?], 48
Kaledin, General A. M., 26
Kaliazin, 148
Kalinin, M. I., 156, 178, 190
Kalmucks, 175, 181
Kalmykov, Ataman [?], 28
Kaluga, 153, 166, 178, 203
Kamchatka, 119
Kamiana Dusha (I. Franko), 186
Kamyshansky, [?], 49
Kandeevka, 30, 169
Kandidov, [?],* 114
Kandidov, B.,* 111
Kankrin, Count E., 126
Kansk, 153
Kapital, Das (K. Marx), 77
Karaganda, 75
Kara-Kalpaks, 167, 170
Karakozov, D. M., 17, 22
Karelia, 184, 194
Kargopol, 7
Karneev, E., 180
Kartalinsk estate, 205
Kartonnye Geroi (D. I. Pisarev), 198
Kashin, 148
Katkov, M. N., 83
Katsman, E.,* 136, 147
Kazakevich, P., 80
Kazakhs, 133, 158
Kazakhstan, 158
Kazan, 22, 25, 61, 91, 122, 131, 136, 158, 169, 178, 190, 204
Kazan, University of, 190
Kazan *sobor* (St. Petersburg), 122
Kazbek, N., 140
Kaznacheisha (M. Y. Lermontov), 180
Kelin, F.,* 71
Kerch, 51, 160
Kerensky, [Alexander], 84, 88
Ketskoveli, Lado, 168
Kharkov, 14, 16, 39, 42, 44, 122, 125, 132, 139, 160, 164, 166, 172, 173, 177, 195, 204, 205
Kharkov University, 40
Kherson, 55, 109, 122, 153, 206
Khetagurov, Kosta, 206
Khlopusha, Ataman A., 105
Khodynka catastrophe (1896), 125
Kholmsen, Colonel [?], 51, 55
Khorvat, General D., 23
Khovansky, I. A., 110
Khozhdenie v Narod movement, 21
Khrapovitsky, A., 40
Khrulev, S. S., 39, 42
Khudiakov, I. I., 17
Khvalynsk, 156
Khvostov, A., 132
Khvostov, Dmitry Ivanovich, 206
Khvostov, V.,* 61, 62, 72, 85, 90
Kiaochow, 84, 157
Kichkas, 129
Kiev, 6, 8, 16, 26, 34, 40, 43, 47, 52, 77, 91, 96, 122, 132, 145, 160, 164, 172, 176, 177, 196, 202, 203
Kiev Ecclesiastical Academy, 191
Kikin, I., 167
Kirghiz-Kazakhs, 133, 158
Kirillov, G., 40, 41
Kirov, S. M., 99, 102, 121, 182
Kiselev, N. D., 163
Kishinev, 196
Kishkin, N., 141
Kislovodsk, 114
Kizliar, 161
Klevensky, M.,* 17, 34, 53
Kobiako, A.,* 125, 195
"Kobzar" (T. Shevchenko), 167
Koenig spinning and thread factory, 84
Koiander, [?], 109
Kokhmansky, [?], 48
Kokoshkin, F. F., 80
Kolchak, Admiral A. V., 2, 14, 15, 65, 68, 74, 153, 156, 171, 172, 200
Kolkhozes, 192
Kologrivov, Michael Andreev, 147
Kolokol, 142, 185
Kolomna, 152, 177

Kolomna Soviet of Workers', Soldiers', and Peasants' Deputies, 152
Komissarov, Colonel M. S., 118
Kon, Felix,* 47
Konotop, 196
Konovalov, A., 80
Konstantinov, F.,* 109
Konstantinov, M.,* 126
Koran, 124
Korchevo, 148
Korea, 47, 67
Korean Bank, 144
Korf, [?], 48, 51
Korf, Baron M. A., 126
Kornilov, General L. G., 23
Korobkov, N.,* 193, 198, 207
Korolenko, V. G., 189
Korostovets, I. Y., 98
Kostomarov, G.,* 34, 124, 125, 150, 151, 155, 173, 182, 184, 191, 199
Kostomarov, N. I., 173
Kostroma, 95, 100, 145, 178, 193, 196
Kotzebue, Count [P. E.], 8
Kovalev, A.,* 52
Kovalev, I.,* 149, 185, 198, 203
Kovalov, I.,* 135, 167
Kovno, 122
Kovrov, 196
Kozachenko, A.,* 130
Kozima, Lieutenant General S., 144
Kozmin, A. I., 88
Kozmin, B.,* 8, 14, 16, 22, 37, 44, 49, 58, 66, 73, 81
Kozodavlev, O. P., 133
Krabbe, Adjutant General N., 36
Krasikov, P. A., 103
Krasilnikov, A. A., 80
Krasnyi Kut, 129
Krasnyi Perekop, 93
Krasnyi Tsvetok (V. M. Garshin), 158
Krasovsky, A. A., 34
Kratkii Kurs Istorii SSSR (A. V. Shestakov), 148
Kravchinsky, S. M. (S. M. Stepnyak), 41, 66
Krechetnikov, Peter, 161

Kremlin, 91, 137, 159
Kritsman, [?],* 47
Krivoshein, A. V., 11
Kronstadt, 141, 156
Kronstadt Rebellion, 50, 56, 128
Kropotkin, Major General Prince Dmitry N., 44
Krupskaia, Nadezhda K., 85, 91, 103, 157, 184, 196
Krutikov, M.,* 126, 147, 164, 188
Kshesinskaia, Madame M. K., 75
Kudriavsky, [Christian E.], 65
Kuibyshev, V. V., 102, 104, 199
Kulikovsky, P. A., 145
Kungur, 154
Kuprin, [A. I.], 55
Kurakin, Prince [Alexis B.?], 135
Kuropatkin, General A. N., 18, 35, 47, 50, 56, 58, 67, 68, 76, 103, 107, 161
Kursk, 44, 115, 137, 167, 178, 193, 206
Kutais, 201
Kuzmich, Fëdor, 64
Kuznetsov, B.,* 176
Kuznetsov, I.,* 106, 109, 117, 118, 129, 132
Kuznetsov, Jacob, 197

L

L., G. [G. L.],* 76
L., M. [M. L.],* 130
L., M. L. [M. L. L.],* 142
"Labor," 141
Labor movement, 19, 75, 80, 84, 89, 92, 95, 100, 105, 107, 108, 118, 125, 128, 145, 152, 160, 166, 167, 172, 173, 174, 187, 195. *See also* Revolutionary movement; Strikes.
"Labor Truth," 140, 141
Lamsdorff, Count V. N., 45, 58, 72, 73, 92, 109, 157, 171
Land and Freedom party, 8, 37, 41
Land Department, 116
Lapin, N.,* 33, 49, 69, 72, 78, 86
Larga River, 198
Latvia, 79, 80, 195, 196
    Central Soviet Government of, 196

Lavrov, V. M., 33
Lazo, Sergius, 144
Lebedev, V.,* 133, 193
Lebtseltern, E., 163
Lefebvre, [Jules?], 181
"Legend of Proud Aggéy" (V. M. Garshin), 158
Lej Yasu, 41
Lena execution, 128, 142, 146
Lenin (Ulianov), V. I., 74, 85, 90, 91, 114, 117, 131, 134, 142, 149, 154, 157, 162, 169, 172, 174, 176, 183, 184, 185, 186, 187, 196, 199
Leningrad, 74, 99, 148. *See also* Petersburg; Petrograd; St. Petersburg.
Leninism, 75, 78
Leontiev, [?], 42
Leontiev, Colonel [?], 51, 54
Lepeshinsky, P.,* 85
Lermontov, M. Y., 180
Lesgaft, P. F., 190
Lesnik, S.,* 172
Lesovsky, Rear Admiral [S. S.], 36
Levina, M.,* 79, 84
Liapushka Puteshestvennitsa (V. M. Garshin), 158
Linevich, General N. P., 56
Linko, G.,* 84
Lipping, L. A., 21
Lis Mikita (I. Franko), 186
Lisbon, 109
Literature, 5, 6, 26, 27, 33, 34, 55, 101, 120, 123, 134, 137, 138, 139, 148, 158, 159, 167, 180, 181, 183, 189
  Central Committee of Censorship of Foreign, 109
Lithuania, 81, 194, 195
  Provisional Workers' and Peasants' Government of, 194
Lithuanian-Polish relations, 194
Litvinov, [?], 115
Liubimov, P. N., 52
Liverpool, 188
Livonia, 195. *See also* Latvia.
Lloyd George, David, 31, 38

Lobanov-Rostovsky, Prince A. B., 16, 58, 71
Lobelle, Louis de, 50
Lomonosov, M. V., 190
London, 8, 20, 31, 36, 37, 38, 45, 48, 61, 62, 68, 77, 78, 85, 106, 163, 169, 184, 196, 197, 200, 205
Lorer, N. I., 38
Loringafen, Baron Freitag von, 8
Loris-Melikov, Count M. T., 40, 44, 57, 74, 97
Ludwig Feuerbach and the End of German Classical Philosophy (F. Engels), 109
Lukomsky, General A., 26
Luppol, I.,* 117
Lurie, M.,* 115, 118, 122, 145, 146
Lurie, M. L.,* 128, 132
Luxembourg, 1, 88
Luzanov, General P. F., 50
Lvov, A. N., 40, 43

M

M., F [F. M.],* 181
M., P. [P. M.],* 129
M., V. [V. M.],* 19
M. V. Frunze na Frontakh Grazhdanskoi Voiny, 207
M. V. Frunze na Frontakh Turkestanskoi Voiny, 189
"M. V. Frunze at the Fronts of the Civil War," 207
"M. V. Frunze at the Fronts of the Turkestan War," 189
McCormick, [Robert S.], 75
Macedonia, 1, 48, 54, 194
Maciejowice, Battle of, 193
Madrid, 86
Maikov, V., 51
Mai-Maevsky, General [?], 114
Main Committee on Peasant Affairs (1858), 180
Makarenko, Lieutenant General [?], 114
Makarov, Vice Admiral S. O., 35
Makhno, 199
Maklakov, N. A., 118, 135, 149

Index 237

Maklakov, V. A., 15, 27
Maksakov, V.,* 23, 88, 89, 90, 113
Maksimov, E. Y., 197
Malkin, M.,* 174
Maltsev, Lieutenant Colonel [?], 145
Manchester, 188
Manchuria, 47
Mandelshtam, [?], 51
Mangin, General [Charles?], 10
Manifesto, Emancipation (1861). See Emancipation Manifesto.
Manifesto of 1856, parody on, 14
Manifesto of 1857, parody on, 14
Manifesto of April 17, 1905, 74
Manifesto of October 17, 1905, 25, 28, 52, 56, 74, 119, 187
Manifesto of July 8, 1907, 80
Manila, 99
Mannerheim, General C. G., 15, 185
Manturovo region, 154
Manufacturing and Internal Trade, Department of, 133
Marie Feodorovna, Empress, 26, 69
Maritime Department, 36
Maritime province, 28, 144, 165, 184
Mariupol, 111
Markov, S.,* 176, 187, 192
Marschall von Bieberstein, Baron A. H., 63
Martel, Count de, 28
Martel, René, 88, 94, 96
Martynov, I.,* 145, 187
Marx, A. F., 33, 183
Marx, Karl, 77, 78, 79
Marxism, 78, 189
"Marxist Group," 83
Masaryk, Tomáš, 14, 18
Maskarad (M. Y. Lermontov), 180
Maslov, Colonel [?], 158
"Masquerade" (M. Y. Lermontov), 180
"Materials for a Biography of N. A. Dobroliubov, Collected by N. G. Chernyshevsky," 123
Materialy dlia Biografii N. A. Dobroliubova, Sobrannye N. G. Chernyshevskim, 123

Matsudaira, [Tsuneo], 28
May Day, 79, 125, 143, 145, 173
Mecca, 203
Mecklemburg-Strelitz, Duke of, 191
Medem, [P. I.], 62, 163
Medina, 203
Mediterranean, 54
Medvedi (V. M. Garshin), 158
Medynsky, E.,* 174
Meiendorf, Baron [P. K.], 163
Meilakh, B.,* 138
Meller-Zakomelsky, General Baron A. N., 56, 72
Melnikov, Paul Petrovich, 164, 188
"Memoirs of a Ballet Master" (A. Glushkovsky), 147
Menitsky, I.,* 80, 83, 100, 106
Mensheviks, 103, 204
Meshcheriakov, N.,* 114
"Message to Natalie" (A. S. Pushkin), 138
Metallist, 96
"Metallurgist," 96
Metternich, Prince Klemens Wenzel, 163
Meyer, [George], 75
Mezentsov, Adjutant General N. V., 40, 41, 43, 44, 66
Miatlev, I., 180
Michael Fëdorovich, Tsarevitch, 193
Mikhailov, Adrian, 40, 41, 74
Mikhailov, Alexander D., 41
Mikhailova, E.,* 155
Military Commission of the Provisional Committee of the [Fourth] State Duma, 46
Military Court Department, Central, 94
Military-Historical Archives, Central Government, 207
Military-Naval Commission of the Fourth State Duma, 82, 94
Miliukov, P. N., 64, 69, 72, 76, 78, 82
Miliukov, Peter,* 103
Miller, Lieutenant Colonel [?], 197
Miller, Lieutenant General [?], 68
Minciaky, M., 159

Mining, 75, 122, 126, 142, 146, 154, 161, 165, 179, 189, 195, 200
Minority peoples, 18, 24, 28, 31, 74, 86, 87, 124, 126, 133, 135, 136, 142, 148, 158, 160, 161, 167, 170, 173, 175, 181, 194, 202, 203
Minsk, 47, 195, 201
Mints, I.,* 31, 38, 68
Mitropol, 137
Mitskevich, [?], 189
Mitskevich-Kapsukas, V., 194
Modern History, 121
Mogilev, 75, 83, 122, 152, 195
Mohammedans, 24, 48
Mohrenheim, A. P., 72
Moiseenko, Peter A., 171
Moisei (I. Franko), 186
Molok, A.,* 200
Molotov, V. M., 159, 179, 186, 187
Monastery, Alexander Nevsky, 130
Monde slave, Le, 88, 94, 96, 97
Mongolia, 31
Mongols, Buriat-, 74, 126
"Monk, The" (A. S. Pushkin), 6, 12
Monroe Doctrine, 72
Morocco, 45
Morozov, M. A., 149, 166
Morozov, P. A., 10
Morozov factory, 136, 171
Morris, Roland Sletor, 2
Mosaics, 190
Moscow, 2, 5, 14, 16, 17, 18, 25, 34, 43, 44, 46, 49, 52, 77, 79, 83, 89, 91, 98, 99, 106, 108, 110, 113, 116, 117, 120, 122, 129, 134, 135, 139, 141, 145, 147, 148, 151, 153, 160, 164, 166, 172, 177, 178, 184, 190, 192, 193, 196, 201, 204, 207
    Agricultural Department, board of, 192
    Cadet National Center in, 2
    City Duma, 5, 151
    Committee of Public Safety, 89
    Military-Revolutionary Committee, 77, 98, 110
    Soviet, 154, 155
"Moscow Journal," 83
Moscow River, 153, 189
Moscow Theological Academy, 40
Moscow University, 41, 43, 71, 83, 84, 102, 120, 191
"Moses" (I. Franko), 186
Moskovskie Vedomosti, 83
Moslem, 24, 28
Motovilikha, 197
Mtsensk, 53
Mtsyri (M. Y. Lermontov), 180
Mudzhakhid, 202
Mukden, 46
Muranov, M. K., 95, 128, 147
Muraviëv, Count M. N., 13, 63, 67, 68, 72, 76, 78, 84
Muraviëv, Nicholas N., 126
Murmansk, 68
Muromtsev, S. A., 84
Music, St. Petersburg Conservatory of, 52
Musin-Pushkin, Count Vladimir V., 90
Mussulman Social Democratic party, 201, 202
Mustoufi-al-Mamalik, 98
Mysl Truda, 96

N

N.,* 192
N., F. [F. N.],* 98
N., I. [I. N.],* 74
Na Dni (I. Franko), 186
Na Vichnu Pamiat Kotliarevskomu (I. Franko), 186
Nachalo Zhenskogo Rabochego Divizhenia v Germanii (C. Zetkin), 87
Nagornyi, S.,* 160
Nakoriakov, N.,* 134
Nakropin, Varnava, 7
Napoleon I (Napoleon Bonaparte), 147 205
Napoleon III (Louis Napoleon), 161
Napoleon, Prince (Joseph Charles Paul), 161
Napoleonic Wars, 81
Narodnaia Rasprava, 44, 49
Nash Put, 204

Natanson, Olga, 74
National Assembly, French, 54
National Minorities and Eastern Peoples, Department of, 142
Naval Affairs, Ministry of, 36, 160
Naval Congress, First All-Russian, 74
Naval Revolutionary Committee, 74
Navy, Russian, 9, 10, 23, 35, 36, 37, 46, 50, 54, 56, 57, 59, 60, 66, 72, 74, 90, 97, 99, 102, 103, 128, 141, 154
Near East, 72
"Near the Precipice" (A. S. Serafimovich), 159
Nechaev, S. G., 16, 44, 49, 50
Nechkina, M.,* 25, 30, 38
Necker, [Jacques], 175
Nefterev, Brigade Commander [?],* 199
Nekliudov, [?], 48, 51
Nekrasov, N. A., 58, 189, 191
Nelidov, [?], 48
Nelidov, A. I., 45, 53, 54, 61, 62, 109, 157
Nelidov, N.,* 14
Nenets, 170
Nepliuev, Ivan, 170
Neratov, A. A., 13, 90
Nesselrode, Count Karl V., 38, 62, 121, 133, 159, 163, 196
Netherlands, 196, 200
Nevskaia Zvezda, 140
Nevsky, A. I., 34
Nevsky, V.,* 34, 40, 85
Nevsky shipbuilding yards, 125
"Nevsky Star," 140
Nicholas I, 17, 32, 33, 36, 60, 61, 62, 126, 136, 147, 163, 200, 205
Nicholas II, 3, 9, 15, 16, 18, 26, 47, 48, 57, 58, 62, 64, 65, 66, 67, 68, 69, 71, 75, 76, 82, 93, 94, 96, 97, 101, 102, 103, 105, 107, 108, 109, 132, 141, 160, 203
Nicholas Mikhailovich, Grand Duke, 64, 75
Nicholas Nikolaevich, Grand Duke, 3, 50, 51, 59, 64, 65
Nikitinsky, I.,* 182, 191
Nikoladze, Nicholas Y., 7
Nikolaev, 55, 57, 160

Nikolaevsk railroad, 125, 188
Nikolai, Baron, 205
Nikolsk factory, 125
Nikolskaia, G.,* 94, 173, 191, 206
Nikolsk-Ussuriiski, 144
Nikolsky, Boris, 92, 105
Nizhnaia Syrovatka, 125
Nizhneudinsk, 2
Nizhni Novgorod, 99, 145, 153, 160, 166, 172, 178
North Pole, 160
Northern Sea Route, 110, 113, 116, 119, 200
"Northern Truth," 140
Northern Union of Russian Workers, 171
"Northern Workers' Paper," 96
Norway, 76, 94
Noskov, V. A., 103
Nosov, A., 136
Nostits, G. I., 20
Notes of Oscar Aveide on the Polish Uprising in 1863 (O. Aveide), 81
"Notes of the Fatherland," 203
Notovich, F.,* 69, 95, 97
Notovich, N. A., 108
"Nouveaux Documents d'histoire russe," 88, 94, 96
Novgorod, 40, 60, 122, 126, 153, 178, 206
"Novice" (M. Y. Lermontov), 180
Novich, I.,* 158
Novikov, Colonel [?], 55
Novitsky, Division Commander F.,* 189
Novonikolaevsk, 65
Novorossiia, 206
Novorossisk, 55, 187

O

Ob hydrographical expedition, 200
Obdorsk, 170
Obnorsky, [?], 54
Obukhovsk foundry, 125
Ochakov, 55, 57
October Socialist Revolution, 10, 31, 56, 73, 74, 77, 79, 89, 93, 108, 110, 130, 142, 143, 150, 152, 155, 156, 162, 165, 181, 187, 191, 197, 199

Octobrist party, 25, 28
Odessa, 8, 16, 38, 55, 107, 109, 114, 139, 160, 195, 196, 204
  Stock Exchange Committee, 107
Ogarev, N. P., 37, 67, 189
Ogarev, Natalia, 67
Okhotsk expedition (1733), 119
Okun, S.,* 126, 133
Okunev [G. N.], 54
Olminsky (Aleksandrov), M. S., 85
Olonets, 178
Omelchenko, [?], 80
Omsk, 31, 32, 65, 68, 89
"On Trial," 186
Opinions of Jerome Coignard (A. France), 101
Order Number One of Petrograd Soviet of Workers' and Soldiers' Deputies, 33
Order Number Two of Petrograd Soviet of Workers' and Soldiers' Deputies, 33
Ordzhonikidze, Gregory K., 130, 131, 137, 156
Orël, 127, 196
Orenburg, 105, 122
Orestov, S.,* 183
Organization for the Social and Political Development of Women, 142
"Origin of the Woman's Labor Movement in Germany, The" (C. Zetkin), 87
Orkney Islands, 205
Orlov, [?], 48
Orlov, Count A. F., 121, 122
Orlov, V.,* 122
Orlov province, 115, 152, 178, 190, 193
Orzheshko, D. F., 23
Osetrov, M.,* 202
Osokin, E.,* 204
Ossetia, 142, 148, 153, 154, 161, 189, 206
Osten-Sacken, Count N. D., 51, 78, 84, 171
"Otchaiannyi" (I. S. Turgenev), 12
Otechestvennye Zapiski, 203
Oubri, Paul P., 119, 120, 166

"Our Path," 204
Ovchinnikov, M. P., 29

P

P., F. [F. P.],* 157
P., M. [M. P.],* 131
P., N. [N. P.],* 194
P., S. [S. P.],* 121
Pacific Ocean, 102
Palchinsky, P. I., 79
Palestine, 190
Palitsyn, Colonel [?], 80
Palitsyn, Lieutenant General I., 3
Palladii, Metropolitan of St. Petersburg and Novgorod, 40
Pan-Germanic Union, 171
Panin, Count V. N., 113
Panitesku, [?], 80
Pankratova, A.,* 115
Pantalakha (I. Franko), 186
Paris, 10, 11, 13, 27, 31, 36, 38, 45, 48, 51, 53, 54, 63, 67, 68, 72, 86, 109, 112, 161, 163, 169, 175, 181, 184, 200
Paris, Congress of, 121, 122, 189
Paris, Peace of, 14, 121, 122
Paris Commune, 54, 189
Parker, Colonel [?], 161
Parliamentary delegation abroad, Russian, 76, 82, 94
Pashukanis, S.,* 106
Paskevich, I. F., 163
Patents, 180
Paul I, 167
Pavlenkov, F. F., 139
Pavlov, P. V., 58
Peasant Affairs, Main Committee on (1858), 180
Peasant War in Germany, The (F. Engels), 109
Pedagogical Institute in Petersburg, 123
Peiping, 31, 67, 71. *See also* Peking.
Peking, 38, 76, 92. *See also* Peiping.
Penguin Island (A. France), 101
Penza, 30, 117, 122, 169, 193
"People's Retribution, The," 44, 49
Pepeliaev, Lieutenant General [?], 145
Pepeliaev, Victor N., 2

Perekhresni Stezhki (I. Franko), 186
Perm, 2, 118, 154, 160, 178, 197, 204
Persia, 32, 73, 78, 83, 98, 106, 189, 190
Persov, A.,* 197
Pertsov, E. P., 61
Peshchurov, A. N., 137
Pesnia pro Kuptsa Kalashnikova (M. Y. Lermontov), 181
Pesnia pro Tsaria Vasilievicha (M. Y. Lermontov), 180
Peter the Great, 153, 177, 190, 205
Peter Alekseivich, Tsar, 167
Peters, Doctor [?], 171
Petersburg, 29, 91, 103, 123, 125. See also Leningrad; Petrograd; St. Petersburg.
Petersburg-Moscow railroad, 147
Petliura, Simon, 55
Petrashevsky, M. V. Butashevich-, 56, 57, 60
Petriaev, [?], 48
Petrograd, 2, 14, 15, 33, 46, 59, 73, 74, 75, 79, 81, 86, 88, 108, 130, 152, 155, 156, 173, 174, 178, 179, 184
  Soviet of Workers' and Soldiers' Deputies, 33, 150
  Military-Revolutionary Committee of, 73, 150
  Special Committee of, 142
  See also Leningrad; Petersburg; St. Petersburg.
Petropavlovsk, 110
Petropavlovsk fortress, 3, 40, 41, 141, 201
Petrov, Anton, 25, 29
Petrov, F.,* 128
Petrov, F. A.,* 99
Petrov, V.,* 183
Petrovsky, G. I., 95, 128
Philippine Islands, 72
Piatakov, [Gregory L.?], 114
Picheta, V.,* 185
Pichon, [G.?], 19
Piettomin, Vauli, 170
Piontkovsky, S.,* 89, 100, 103, 108
Pisarev, D. I., 189, 198
Pitirim, Metropolitan, 130
Planson, E. A., 46, 47

Platon, Metropolitan of Kiev, 40
Plehve, V. K. von, 35, 44, 50
Plennitsa (V. M. Garshin), 158
Pobedonostsev, K. P., 5, 40, 43
Pod Sud, 186
Podolia, 43, 122, 195, 202
Poincaré, Raymond, 45, 53, 96
Pokhoronnyi Marsh (A. S. Serafimovich), 159
Pokrovsky, General [?], 114
Pokrovsky, M. N., 27, 70, 71
Poland (the Poles), 8, 9, 22, 33, 36, 37, 38, 52, 54, 62, 63, 69, 76, 80, 81, 82, 146, 163, 193, 199
  Central National Committee of, 81
  Revolutionary Government, 81
"Polar Star," 186
Polesie, 165. See also Byelorussia.
Polevoi, N. P., 180
Poliakov, [?], 79
Polianskaia, L.,* 101, 139, 178, 180, 186
Poliansky, V.,* 93
Poliarnaia Zvezda, 185
Police Department, 24, 41, 52, 77, 79, 80, 85, 91, 92, 95, 104, 111, 114, 115, 118, 120, 125, 126, 128, 131, 140, 156, 160, 166, 181, 196, 199, 204, 206
Polish Insurrection (1830-1831), 60
Polish Insurrection (1863), 45, 81, 88
Polish War (1794), 193, 206
Politburo, 102
Polivanov, Major General A. A., 3, 56, 65
Polonsky, Y. P., 189, 191
Polovtsov, A. A., 15, 16, 59, 79, 85, 101
Polrovskoe, 30
Poltava, 132, 196
Poltava, Battle of, 177, 190
Popov, A.,* 14, 18, 31, 46, 48, 71, 73, 97, 188, 189, 205
Popov, I. I., 29
Popov, K.,* 182
Popular Freedom party, Central Committee of, 59. See also Cadet party; Constitutional Democratic party.

Port Arthur, 35, 46, 84
Portsmouth, Treaty of, 52
Portsmouth Conference, 39, 43, 46, 47
Portugal, 75
Posen, 38
Poslanie k Natali (A. S. Pushkin), 138
Post Engelsbach, 93
Post Office, 36
Post Office and Telegraph Department, 203
Potemkin, Lieutenant General P. S., 193
Pototsky, Count I. A., 39, 42
Potsdam Agreement (1911), 82
Potulov, G., 22
Poverty of Philosophy, The (K. Marx), 78
Prague (Praha), 182, 193
Pravda, 96, 111, 128, 140, 151, 155, 157, 162, 166, 184
Pravda Truda, 140
Preobrazhensky regiment, 56
Presnia, 116
Presniakov, A.,* 5
Press, 5, 11, 12, 13, 15, 16, 34, 36, 43, 54, 55, 83, 84, 87, 91, 95, 96, 97, 108, 111, 128, 140, 141, 142, 150, 151, 155, 157, 162, 166, 168, 173, 184, 185, 186, 190, 192, 196, 201, 203, 204
Press Department, Central, 203
Prince Potemkin Tavrichesky, 107
Princes Islands, 31
"Prisoner" (V. M. Garshin), 158
Prisoner of the Caucasus (A. S. Pushkin), 137
Prisons, 11, 17, 24, 45, 53, 57, 61, 196, 201
Profintern and Comintern, appeal of Executive Committee (1924), 91
Progressive bloc of Fourth State Duma, 69, 72, 78
Prokopenko, N.,* 177, 184
"Proletarian Truth," 141
Proletarskaia Pravda, 141
Propaganda, revolutionary, 11, 21, 22, 45, 53, 55, 75, 83, 94, 152, 165, 203
Propaganda Department, 152
Protopopov, [?], 54

Protopopov, P. N., 145
"Proud Palm, The" (V. M. Garshin), 158
Provisional Commissariat of South Russia, 131
Provisional Government, 9, 18, 26, 27, 38, 59, 79, 83, 84, 88, 131, 141, 150, 194, 202
Provisional Government, All-Russian, 6
Provisional Government of Autonomous Siberia, 23
Provisional Workers' and Peasants' Government of Lithuania, 194
Prussia, 172, 189, 193
Pskov, 38, 178
Public opinion, 14, 17, 20, 32, 33, 35, 51, 58, 60, 73
Pueblo, Colorado, 181
Pugachev, E. I., 105, 108
Pugachev Rebellion, 105, 108
Pulkovo Astronomical Observatory, 178
Pumpur, Corps Commander P.,* 179
Pushkin, A. S., 5, 6, 12, 17, 34, 38, 129, 137, 138, 139, 189, 191
Put Pravdy, 96, 141, 157
Putilov factory, 103, 179

R

R., F. [F. R.],* 83
Rabinovich, M.,* 197
Rabinovich, S.,* 26
Rabochaia Pravda, 140
Rabochii, 141
Rabochii Trud, 204
Rachinsky, S. A., 191
Radishchev, A. N., 120, 189
Radishchev, Paul A., 120
Radowitz, [?], 166
Rafalovich, A., 53
Railroads, 10, 50, 51, 52, 56, 71, 78, 79, 83, 106, 125, 126, 147, 160, 164, 174, 179, 188, 189
Baghdad, 83, 106
Chinese-Eastern, 32, 38
Kursk, 44
Nikolaevsk, 125, 188

Index 243

Petersburg-Moscow, 147
Siberian, 56
Siberian-Alaskan, 50
Zakavkaz, 160
Rakhmanova, T.,* 70
Rakhmetov, V.,* 14
Rankh, General [?], 56
Rasputin, Gregory E., 7, 9, 18, 65, 66, 105, 119, 123, 130
Ratkevich, K.,* 175
Razumovskaia, Countess Marie Grigorevna, 17
Razumovskaia, V.,* 173, 175
Red Army. *See* Army, Red.
"Red Canal," 93
Red Cross, 38, 42, 130
"Red Flower, The" (V. M. Garshin), 158
Red Guards, 47, 187
Red Square, 182
Rediger, General A. F., 3, 48, 56, 70, 87
Reichstag, German, 8
Religion, 5, 7, 29, 30, 52, 77, 194, 196. *See also* Russian Orthodox Church.
Rengarten, Captain I. I., 9, 23
Rennenkampf, General P. K., 56
Revolt of the Angels, The (A. France), 101
Revolution, Austrian (1848), 163
Revolution, Belgian (1830), 200
Revolution, French
  1789–1790, 177
  July, 1830, 36
Revolution, Persian (1905–1911), 201, 202
Revolution, in Russia
  Decembrist, 1825, 31, 38, 60
  of 1905, 13, 43, 46, 49, 56, 57, 70, 75, 92, 99, 103, 108, 115, 116, 120, 195
  February (1917), 9, 26, 46, 69, 83, 108, 141, 187, 194, 202
  October (1917), 31, 56, 73, 74, 77, 79, 89, 93, 108, 110, 130, 142, 143, 150, 152, 155, 156, 162, 165, 181, 187, 191, 197, 199
  See also under Archive.

Revolution, Spanish (1873–1874), 65
Revolution, Turkish (1908–1909), 48, 51, 54
Revolution in Science, The (F. Engels), 109
Revolutionary Military Soviet, 154
Revolutionary movement, 13, 14, 16, 17, 20, 24, 37, 44, 47, 50, 52, 53, 59, 75, 81, 83, 90. *See also* Agrarian movement; Labor movement; Strikes.
Riazan, 166, 178, 181, 193
Riga, 47, 110, 204
Rikhter, Captain [?], 37
Rimsky-Korsakov, N. A., 52, 191
Riom, 175
Roman Catholic Church, 64
Romanov, Xenia, 93
Romanov family, 79, 205. *See also* Imperial family.
Rome, 38, 48, 51, 75, 86, 157, 205
Romm, Gilbert, 175
Roosevelt, Theodore, 52
Rostov-on-Don, 43
Rothstein, F.,* 58, 161
Rozanchugov, K.,* 170
Rozhdestvensky, Admiral [Z. P.], 102
Rozhen, E.,* 77, 89, 98, 110
Rudov, Colonel N. P., 132
Rumania, 1, 9, 32, 54, 75, 80, 82, 120, 152, 192
Rumiantsev-Zadunaisky, Count P. A., 193, 198
Rusanov, I. Y., 116
Rusin, Admiral [?], 97
Rusin, P.,* 124
Russian-American Company, 133
"Russian History from Ancient Times" (M. N. Pokrovsky), 71
Russian Orthodox Church, 6, 7, 29, 30, 32, 40, 43, 74, 76, 103, 111, 113, 130, 137. *See also* Religion.
Russian parliamentary delegation abroad (1916), 76, 82, 94
"Russian Reading," 95
"Russian Society," 92

Russian Soviet Federated Socialist Republic, 176, 179, 192
  Eleventh Congress of Soviets of, 90
Russian Trade Committee in the United States, 10
Russkaia Istoriia s Drevneishikh Vremën (M. N. Pokrovsky), 71
Russkoe Chtenie, 95
Russkoe Sobranie, 92
Russky, General [N. V.], 64
Russo-American relations, 71, 72, 174, 189
Russo-Chinese Bank, 71
Russo-Czechoslovakian relations, 14
Russo-French relations, 72, 76
Russo-French Society of Trade, Industry, and Transport, 11
Russo-German relations, 27, 83, 166, 189
Russo-Japanese Alliance, 9
Russo-Japanese relations, 1, 58, 92
Russo-Japanese War, 35, 39, 46, 47, 49, 52, 73, 92, 103, 107
Russo-Kirghiz strike, 75
Russo-Persian relations, 73, 82
Russo-Prussian relations, 88
Russo-Turkish War, 15, 33, 57
Rykatkin, V. I., 108

S

S., A. [A. S.],* 57, 75
Sabler, V. K., 40
Sablin, M. A., 33
Sadikov, P.,* 7
St. Petersburg, 8, 17, 22, 25, 28, 34, 35, 38, 39, 40, 41, 44, 45, 46, 49, 52, 56, 60, 69, 103, 116, 118, 122, 125, 126, 139, 145, 160, 163, 164, 166, 172, 177, 178, 196, 201, 203, 204, 206
  Chamber of Justice, 49, 103
  Conservatory of Music, 52
  Theological Academy, 40
  University of, 58, 168
  See also Leningrad; Petersburg; Petrograd.
Sakhalin, 144
Salonika, 1, 48, 51, 53
Salova, N. M., 29

Saltykov-Shchedrin, M. E., 148, 170, 189, 203
Samara, 91, 134, 160, 178, 196, 199
Samarin, F., 180
Samoilov, F.,* 112
Samoilov, F. N., 95, 128
Samoilov, V.,* 134
Sandwich Islands, 133. *See also* Hawaiian Islands.
Sannikov, General [?], 114
Saratov, 122, 172, 178, 193
Savelev, M.,* 128
Savich, Colonel S. S., 3
Savitsky, Vladimir I., 10, 11
Sazonov, S. D., 1, 64, 86
Sbornik Dokumentov, Tsentralnyi Gosudarstvennyi Voenno-Istoricheskii Arkhiv, 207
Scandinavia, 82
Schilling, Baron M. F., 1, 9
Schleswig-Holstein, 88, 172
Schlüsselberg fortress, 201
"School Question, The" (C. Zetkin), 87
Schwartz, V. G., 181
Science, Academy of, 49, 52
  of the USSR, Institute of History of, 177
Scotland, 205
Second Nikolaevsk Division, 183
Second Special Infantry Division, 194
Secret Letters of the Last Tsar, The (Edward J. Bing, ed.), 69
Secret Police, 8, 32, 35, 36, 40, 43, 49, 58, 60, 66, 71, 96, 128, 142, 190
Secret Police, Rumanian, 80
"Secret Reports of General Suvorov, Covering the Entire Polish War from May to the End of 1794, The," 193
Sedov, G. Y., 160
Sekretnye Raporty General-Ansheffa Suvorova Zakliuchaiushchie v Sebe Vsiu Polskuiu Voinu s Maia po Konets 1794, 193
Seliverstov, Lieutenant General [?], 66
Sem, Polish, 36
Semennikov, V.,* 13

Semënov, Ataman Gregory, 19, 42, 101
Sementovsky-Kurilo, [?], 54
Semin, M.,* 185
Senate, 110, 167, 190
Serafimovich, A. S., 159
Serafin, Archbishop of Irkutsk, 74
Serbia, 1, 54, 97, 189
Serbo-Bulgarian relations, 54
Sereda, V. N., 14
Sergeenko, P. A., 33
Sergeev, A.,* 26, 32, 60
Sergeev, Alexander A., 114
Sergeev, B.,* 156
Sergius, Metropolitan of Moscow, 43
Sergius Aleksandrovich, Grand Duke, 39
Sergius Mikhailovich, Grand Duke, 14, 49, 75
Sericulture, 205
Serno-Solovevich, A. A., 8
Sevastopol, 10, 21, 36, 38, 57
Seventh Reserve Cavalry Regiment, 109
Severnaia Pravda, 140
Severnaia Rabochaia Gazeta, 96
Severo-Dvinsk, 178
Shagov, N. R., 95, 128
Shamil, 202, 203
Shanghai, 31
Shapiro, A.,* 129, 180
Shchegolev, P.,* 6, 38
Shchepkina, S, G., 190
Shcherbakov, A. S., 183
Shebalin, M. P., 29
Shefer, A.,* 199
Sheffer, Doctor George, 133
Shekun, O.,* 111
Shenandoah, 65
Shepeleva, T.,* 178, 182, 190
Shestakov, A.,* 87
Shestakov, A. V., 148
Shesternin, S.,* 107
Shevchenko, T. G., 127, 167, 189, 202
Shilling, General [?], 114
Shilnikov, Major General Ivan F., 101
Shilov, A.,* 29, 34
Shingarev, A. I., 94
Shipbuilding, 125, 201
Shipov, D. N., 25

Shishkin, N. P., 58, 62, 72
Shkolnyi Vopros (C. Zetkin), 87
Shliapnikov, N.,* 197
Shmidt, N. K., 44
Shmidt, Lieutenant P. P., 57
Short Course in the History of the All-Union (Bolshevik) Communist Party, A, 165
"Short Course in the History of the USSR, A" (A. V. Shestakov), 148
"Short Sketch of Recent Events in Poland, 1861–1864" (O. Aveide), 81
Shostka gun-powder works, 124
Shpitsberg, I.,* 74
Shtender, Colonel [?], 161
Shubinsky, [S. N.], 173
Shuisk, 136
Shuvalov, Count Paul Andreevich, 21, 58
Shuvalov, Count Paul Petrovich, 4, 7
Shuvalov, Count Peter Andreevich, 85
Shwimmer, Karl, 41
Siberia, 13, 19, 23, 24, 32, 34, 42, 47, 50, 56, 64, 75, 89, 91, 101, 119, 131, 134, 163, 164, 165, 170, 200
Siberian Provisional Government, 27, 28, 89
  Council on Foreign Affairs of, 23
Siberian Volunteer Guards, 145
Sickles, General D. E., 65
Sidorov, K.,* 167, 187
Siebert, Benno Aleksandrovich, 106
"Signalman" (A. S. Serafimovich), 159
Sigurantsa, 80
Simbirsk, 12, 129, 158, 174, 178, 185
Sino-Japanese War (1894–1895), 58, 67
Sivkov, K.,* 167, 187
Skazanie o Gordom Aggee (V. M. Garshin), 158
Skobelev, General M. D., 16, 35
Skobeltsyn, Major General [?], 68
Skoropadsky, General Paul, 55
Smirnov, Y., 205
Smolensk, 110, 118, 119, 122, 178
Smyrna, 51
Snezhinsky, N.,* 181
Sobolevsky, V. M., 33

Sochinenia (V. I. Lenin), 74
Sochinenii N. A. Dobroliubova, 123
Sochineniia A. S. Pushkina, 139
Social Democratic Labor party, Russian
    Second Congress of, 85, 91
    Third Congress of, 103
    Fourth Congress of, 204
    Ninth Congress of, 143
    Eighteenth Congress of, 168
Social Democratic party, 8, 21, 71, 79, 80, 83, 85, 87, 91, 92, 95, 103, 104, 115, 125, 131, 143, 146, 147, 157, 160, 166, 168, 172, 174, 177, 182, 195, 196, 197, 201, 202, 204
    in Persia, 201, 202
Social Revolutionary party, 97, 192
Socialist, 16
Society for Diffusion of Religious and Moral Education in the Spirit of the Orthodox Church, 29
Sofia, 38, 54
Sofinov, P.,* 164
Sofronenko, K. A.,* 143, 165
Soiuz Russkogo Naroda, 92
Sokolov, I.,* 136
Sokolov, V.,* 112
Sollogub, General V. I., 56
Sologub, General [?], 37
Sologub, Fëdor, 55
Soloviëv, A. K., 43
Solsky, Count D. M., 132
"Song of the Merchant Kalashnikov" (M. Y. Lermontov), 181
"Song of the Tsar Vasilievich" (M. Y. Lermontov), 180
Sormovo, 99, 145
South Africa, 108
South Russia, Provisional Commissariat of, 131
Soviet(s), 31, 49, 65, 101, 102, 110, 111, 115, 124, 125, 142, 150, 152, 153, 155, 162, 163, 165, 169, 174, 176, 181, 186, 192, 194, 196, 199, 200
    Revolutionary Military, 154
    of Peasant Deputies of Kazan, 131
    of People's Commissars, 127, 152, 155, 186. *See also* Council of People's Commissars of the USSR; *Sovnarkom.*
    of Workers', Soldiers', and Peasants' Deputies, Kolomna, 152
Soviet-Polish War, 38, 42
Sovnarkom, 120, 162, 176, 197. *See also* Council of People's Commissars of the USSR; Soviet of People's Commissars.
Spain, 65, 86, 120, 147, 205
Spanburg, Captain [M. P.], 116, 119
Spanish-American War (1898), 86
"Spark, The," 91, 196
Spasskoe-Lutovino, 190
"Special Conference on the Revision of the Standing Government Orders and Exceptional Measures for the Okhrana, The," 13. *See also* Ignatiev Commission.
Speransky, A.,* 110
Speransky, M., 126
Speyer, Alexis N., 73
Spirova, A.,* 95, 127
Spring-Rice, Sir Cecil, 45
Sredi Nochi (A. S. Serafimovich), 159
Staal, Baron [?], 78
Stalin, J. V., 78, 91, 111, 121, 131, 135, 140, 143, 149, 151, 154, 159, 162, 168, 181, 186, 187, 201
Stanislas Augustus, King of Poland, 193
"Star," 128, 140
Stasov brothers, 44
Stasova, E. D., 103
State Council, 12
Stavka, 89, 189. *See also* Army, Russian, General Staff.
Stefanik, M., 18
Steinberg, E.,* 160
Stepnyak (Kravchinsky), S. M., 41
Steppes, 24
Stock Exchange Committee, Odessa, 107
Stockholm, 38, 68, 200, 204
Stoeckel, Baron E. A., 37, 175
Stolypin, P. A., 11, 12, 13, 20, 24, 26, 28, 49, 56, 66, 113, 116, 119

"Stone Heart, The" (I. Franko), 186
Straits, the, 61, 62, 82, 90, 189. *See also* Bosporus; Dardanelles.
Strelochnik (A. S. Serafimovich), 159
Strikes, 19, 39, 43, 52, 56, 75, 79, 89, 99, 100, 103, 104, 107, 112, 118, 128, 136, 145, 146, 151, 160, 166, 171, 173, 174, 177. *See also* Labor movement; Revolutionary movement.
Stroganov, Count A., 180
Stroganov, Baron G. A., 175
Stroganov, Paul A., 175
"Struggle for Life" (D. I. Pisarev), 198
Struve, P. V., 86
Stsepshchik (A. S. Serafimovich), 159
Student und das Weib, Der (C. Zetkin), 87
Students, 11, 16, 43, 52, 83, 84, 117, 120, 122, 164
Stürmer, B. V., 9, 15
Stukantsev, Lieutenant V. T., 81
Subbotin, General [?], 114
Subbotniks, 143, 146
Suchan Valley, 165
Sudeikin, Colonel G. P., 8, 35
Suffrage, 135, 136, 149. *See also* Elections.
Sukhomlinov, General V. A., 75, 86, 189
Sukhotin, Nicholas N., 13
Sukin, I. I., 15
Summer Garden, 22
Supreme Soviet, 146, 149, 151
Suvorin, A. S., 33, 183, 191
Suvorov, Count A. V., 193, 206
Sveaborg uprising, 56, 66
Sventorzhetsky, Lieutenant E. V., 102
Sverdlov, J. M., 92, 93, 169
Svetlova, M.,* 129
Sweden, 9, 76, 82, 94, 97, 177
Swedish-Entente relations, 76
Swedish-Russian relations, 76
Syr Darya River, 167
Syroechekovsky, B.,* 31
Syromiatnikov, A.,* 164
Syromiatnikov, M.,* 116, 120
Syromiatnikova, M.,* 124, 125, 145
Sytin, I. D., 139
Syzran, 174

T

Taganrog, 64
Tager, A. S.,* 52, 77
Taiga-Mari, 65
Tambov, 57, 109, 111, 122, 169, 178, 193
Tambovsky, Pitrim, 111
Tangier, 86
Tarashchansk, 176
Tartar, 24, 28, 167
Taseev, 153
Taseevo, 153
Tashkent, 18
Tatarov, I.,* 3, 48
Tatishchev, A. A., 106
Taube, Baron M. de, 90
Tavri, 115
Tchaikovsky, N. V., 6
Tchaikovsky, P. I., 191
Tehran, 1, 73
Telesheva, L.,* 67, 76, 78, 84
"Ten Commandments and the Propertied Classes, The" (A. Hoffman), 87
Terenin, Governor [?], 112
Tevkelev, M., 133
"That Which Was Not" (V. M. Garshin), 158
Theological Academy, Moscow, 40
Theological Academy, St. Petersburg, 40
Third Department (Secret Police), 32, 40, 41, 43, 44, 49, 60, 66
13 Lit Moei Molodosti (I. Franko), 186
"Thirteen Years of My Youth" (I. Franko), 186
Thirty-Fourth Army Corps, 141
Thomas, Albert, 100
"Thought of Labor, The," 96
Tiflis, 145, 160, 168, 174, 201
Tikhomirov, G. A.,* 187
Tikhomirov, Leo, 29, 35, 39, 43, 46, 89, 113, 116, 119, 123
Tikhonov, V. A., 33

Timashev, S. I., 19, 118
Timoshenko, S. K., 199
Titov, [?], 163
Tiulin, Major General [?], 109
Tiutchev, [?], 189
"To a Friend of the Poet" (A. S. Pushkin), 138
"To a Young Widow" (A. S. Pushkin), 138
To, Chevo Ne Bylo (V. M. Garshin), 158
"To Litsiniia" (A. S. Pushkin), 138
"To Papa" (A. S. Pushkin), 138
"To the Eternal Memory of Kotliarevsky" (I. Franko), 186
"To the People" movement, 21
Tobolsk, 34, 47, 170
Tokyo, 2, 38, 92
Tolstoy, A. P., 113
Tolstoy, Count D. A., 12, 83, 164
Tolstoy, Dmitry N., 30
Tolstoy, Leo N., 26, 30, 69, 93, 117, 119, 151, 181, 189
Tomari, King of Sandwich Islands, 133
Tomsk, 19, 166, 182, 201
Tomson, [?], 75
Torbin, M.,* 190
"Toward the Light" (I. Franko), 186
Trade, 10, 11, 13, 23, 63, 76, 110, 133
Trade and Industry, Department of, 112
Trade and Industry, Ministry of, 145
Trade, Industry, Post Office, and Telegraph, French Ministry of, 11
Trade unions, 11, 155, 179
Transcaucasia, 187, 201
Transportation, Department of, 126, 201
"Treasurer's Wife, The" (M. Y. Lermontov), 180
Trial of the Twenty-one, 29, 32, 35, 41
Trial of the 193, 21
Triple Alliance, 157
Triple Entente, 20
"Trivial Sides of Life, The" (D. I. Pisarev), 198
Tropinin, V., 138
Trotsky, 102

Trotskyites, 140. *See also* Zinoviev-Trotsky bloc.
Trudovaia Pravda, 141
Trus (V. M. Garshin), 158
"Truth of Labor," 140
Trutovsky, S. K., 183
Ts., M. [M. Ts.],* 137
"Tsarism and the French Bourgeois Revolution of the Eighteenth Century," 177
Tsarism i Frantsuzskaia Burzhuaznaia Revoliutsiia XVIII Veka, 177
Tsaritsyn, 160, 199
Tsarskoe Selo, 9, 45, 126
Tsarskoe Selo Lyceum, 5, 137, 138
Tseimern, N. M., 105
Tsiavlovsky, M.,* 5, 17, 138
Tsomakion, A. I., 139
Tsushima, Battle of, 99, 102
Tula, 30, 44, 45, 47, 122, 134, 160, 166, 178, 196, 204
Tulchin, 206
Tun, Leo, 163
Turgenev, Ivan S., 12, 17, 40, 189, 190, 191
Turkestan, 18, 57, 87, 93, 156, 160, 161, 172, 189
Turkey, 9, 15, 24, 48, 51, 61, 62, 63, 72, 97, 159, 167
"Turkish Constitution, The," 48
Turkish Constitution, 1908, compared with that of 1876, 51
Turkmen, 173
Tver, 47, 136, 145, 148, 153, 160, 166, 170, 177, 178, 193, 200
Two Hundred and Twenty-third Odoevsky Regiment, 141

U

U Obryva (A. S. Serafimovich), 159
Ufa, 133, 172, 178, 184, 196
Ufa Directorate and Conference, 2, 6, 89
Uget, [?], 15
Uglovi, A.,* 171
Ukraine, 55, 69, 124, 163, 166, 176, 177, 186, 195, 199, 202
  Central Council of, 202

Index

Ulianov, Ilia Nikolaevich, 174, 185
Ulianov (Lenin), V. I., 74, 85, 90, 91, 114, 117, 131, 134, 149, 154, 157, 162, 169, 172, 174, 176, 183, 184, 185, 186, 187, 196, 199
Ulianova, M. I., 103
Ulianova-Elizarova, Anna Ilinichna, 114
"Union for the Emancipation of the Working Class," 91, 172
"Union of Russian People," 92
Union of Soviet Socialist Republics, 121, 128, 159, 168, 186, 190, 192, 196, 199
United States, 10, 23, 28, 36, 42, 56, 57, 58, 65, 71, 72, 75, 82, 94, 164, 189. *See also* America.
Untilov, [?], 25
Uprava, 151
Urals, 118, 163
Uralsk, 183, 184
Urianhaisk, 74
Urusov, [?], 51, 67
Üsküb, 48
Uspensky, Gleb, 206
Uspensky copper mine, 75
Ust-Kaitym, 153
Utopian Socialism and Scientific Socialism (F. Engels), 109
Uzbeks, 124

V

V., N. [N. V.], 13
V Poti Chola (I. Franko), 186
Valberg, Colonel [?], 50
Valk, S.,* 3, 8, 16, 29, 44, 57
Vanag, N.,* 82, 94
Vanag historical group, 121
Vannovsky, General P. S., 94
Varentsova, O.,* 115
Vasilev, Makar N., 16, 29
Vasiley, Lieutenant Colonel [?], 47
Vatican, the, 64, 77
Vavilov, Captain P. M., 102
Veber, B.,* 41
Veimar, [O. E.], 40
Verderevsky, Rear Admiral D. N., 59

Vereshchagin, G.,* 13, 50
Vereshchagin, V. V., 57, 58
Verkhoiansk, 17
Versailles, 54
"Verses on Social Themes" (I. Franko), 186
Viardot, Mme [M. (Pauline)], 12
Viatka, 37, 61, 81, 122, 178, 201
Viazemsky, Prince P. A., 17, 139
Vienna, 51, 62, 157, 163, 196
Vienna Polytechnic Institute, 126
"Views of English Thinkers on the Intellectual Demands of Contemporary Society" (D. I. Pisarev), 198
Viliuisk, 120
"Village, The" (A. S. Pushkin), 138
Vilno, 122, 194
Virshi na Gromadski Temi (I. Franko), 186
Vishnevsky, Major General [?], 145
Vistula provinces, 39
Vitebsk, 122, 153, 178, 195, 203
Vixen, 195, 196
Vladimir, 104, 105, 112, 122, 136, 145, 166, 178, 196
Vladimirova, Vera,* 83
Vladivostok, 23, 165
Volga, 24, 28, 153, 164, 180, 189
Volhynia, Archbishop Antony of, 6
Volhynia, 43, 195, 202
Volkonsky, Prince S. G., 130
Volkovo cemetery, 123
Vologda, 178, 196, 201
Vologodsky, P. V., 6, 15
Voltaire, François Marie Arouet, 6
Voniavin, S., 161
Vonliarsky, F. A., 203
Voronezh, 115
Vorontsov, Count M. S., 38
Vorontsov, S. R., 205
Vorontsov-Dashkov, Count I. I., 20, 24, 90
Voroshilov, K. E., 114, 155, 189, 198, 199
Vorozhtsov, I. P., 37
Vospominaniia Baletmeistera (A. Glushkovsky), 147
Voznesensk, 55

Vsevolozhsky, V., 180
Vuich, E. I., 103
Vyborg, 64, 80
Vyshnegradsky, Ivan A., 59
Vzgliady Angliiskikh Myslitelei na Umstvennyia Potrebnosti Sovremennago Obshchestva (D. I. Pisarev), 198

W

Wage-Labor and Capital (Karl Marx), 78
War, Ministry of, 34, 35, 36, 95, 107, 132, 135
War Industrial Committee, Central, 80, 100, 106
Warsaw, 8, 38, 81, 193, 206
Washington, D.C., 15, 37, 38, 72, 77, 175, 200
Water and Land Communications, Office of, 36
"Way of Truth, The," 96, 141, 157
West Russian Government, 2
"What Is to Be Done" (N. A. Dobroliubov), 123
White Army. *See* Army, White.
White Finns, 184, 187
White Poles, 199
White Stone, The (A. France), 101
Will of the People party, 3, 4, 7, 8, 16, 22, 29, 32, 35, 36, 44
William I, Emperor of Germany, 8
William I, King of the Netherlands, 200
William II, Kaiser, 58, 63, 68, 84, 166
William Frederick IV, King of Prussia, 163
Windisch-Graetz, Prince A. C. zu, 62
"Without Work" (I. Franko), 186
Witte, Count S. Y., 3, 25, 28, 41, 43, 46, 56, 62, 71, 89, 108, 132, 203
Women, 142, 157, 174
Workers' Guard, 187
"Working Labor," 204
"Works of A. S. Pushkin," 139
"Works of N. A. Dobroliubov, The," 123

World War I, 1, 9, 14, 18, 19, 20, 23, 32, 52, 53, 64, 69, 75, 76, 82, 83, 86, 87, 90, 94, 95, 96, 97, 98, 100, 125, 145, 166, 169, 179, 182, 187, 189, 194
Wrangel, Baron P. N., 10, 11, 21, 38, 39, 42, 63, 111, 114, 115, 156, 199

Y

Yakubovich, P. F., 29, 32, 35
"Yakut Union," 126
Yakutia, 126
Yakutsk, 120, 145
Yanushkevich, General N. N., 64, 189
Yaropolets, 129
Yaroslav, 145, 153, 166, 193
Yaroslavl, 178, 196
"Yaroslavl Factory, Large," 93
Yaroslavskaia Manufaktura, Bolshaia, 93
Yaroslavsky, E.,* 169, 181, 188, 196, 204
Yasinsky, C.,* 81
Yasnaia Poliana, 93
Yenisei province, 153
Yermolaev, A. M., 183
Yermolov, Colonel N. S., 197
Young Turk party, 48, 51
Yudenich, General N. N., 15, 155, 173, 174
Yugin, F.,* 207
Yurchenko, A.,* 202
Yurev, A.,* 159
Yusupov, Felix, 66

Z

Z.,* 93
Z., D. [D. Z.],* 101, 105
Z., P. [P. Z.],* 105
Za Pravdu, 140, 157
Zaichnevsky, P. G., 127
Zaionchkovsky, General A. M., 82
Zaitsev, V. A., 73
Zakharov, Major G.,* 187
Zalkind, G.,* 203
Zarin, Lieutenant A. S., 99
Zaslavsky, D.,* 80, 86, 90, 92, 96, 102, 108, 142
Zavadsky, P. V., 14

Zelenov, T.,* 192
Zeltser, V.,* 99
Zemliachka, P. S., 103
Zemstvo(s), 4, 5, 13, 15
Zerno, 34
Zetkin, Clara, 87, 157, 190
Zh., M. [M. Zh.],* 105
Zhdanov, A. A., 121
Zhelikhovsky, [?], 21, 22
Zhilinsky, Y. G., 20
Zhuravlev, N.,* 136, 148, 149, 170, 200
Zinevich, D.,* 50, 94

Zinevich, P. M.,* 109
Zinoviev, I., 51, 54, 102
Zinoviev, I. A., 106
Zinoviev-Trotsky bloc, 102
Ziorov, Nicholas, 40
Zlatoustovsky, B.,* 166
Zotov, [?], 199
Zubov, Major General Count V. A., 193, 206
Zvegintsev, I. A., 115
Zvenigorod, 176
Zverev, R.,* 87
Zvezda, 128, 140

www.ingramcontent.com/pod-product-compliance
Lightning Source LLC
Chambersburg PA
CBHW021138230426
43667CB00005B/160